CAMBRIDGE LIBRARY COLLECTION

*Books of enduring scholarly value*

## History

The books reissued in this series include accounts of historical events and movements by eye-witnesses and contemporaries, as well as landmark studies that assembled significant source materials or developed new historiographical methods. The series includes work in social, political and military history on a wide range of periods and regions, giving modern scholars ready access to influential publications of the past.

## Civil and Criminal Justice in the West Indies

Sir Fortunatus Dwarris (1786–1860) was an English barrister, civil servant and abolitionist. After graduating from University College, Oxford, in 1808 he was called to the bar at the Middle Temple in 1811. In 1823 Dwarris was appointed a commissioner for an Imperial Commission of Inquiry on the state of legal and slave codes of the self- governing colonies of the British West Indies. This detailed volume, first published in 1827, contains three reports summarising the Commission's findings and recommendations. Focusing on the islands of Barbados, Tobago, Dominica, and Antigua, this volume provides a detailed analysis of the various criminal and civil laws peculiar to each island, together with a description of the various courts and processes in each. The commissioners perceptively discuss and illustrate the institutionalised racism of these laws, providing valuable information for the study of slavery and emancipation and the legal history of the British West Indies.

# Civil and Criminal Justice in the West Indies

Sir Fortunatus Dwarris

Cambridge
University Press

CAMBRIDGE UNIVERSITY PRESS

Cambridge, New York, Melbourne, Madrid, Cape Town, Singapore,
São Paolo, Delhi, Dubai, Tokyo, Mexico City

Published in the United States of America by Cambridge University Press, New York

www.cambridge.org
Information on this title: www.cambridge.org/9781108024297



This edition first published 1827
This digitally printed version 2010

ISBN 978-1-108-02429-7 Paperback

# SUBSTANCE

OF

# THE THREE REPORTS

OF THE

## Commissioner of Inquiry,

INTO THE

## ADMINISTRATION

OF

## CIVIL AND CRIMINAL JUSTICE

IN THE

## WEST INDIES.

---

EXTRACTED FROM THE PARLIAMENTARY PAPERS, WITH THE GENERAL CONCLUSIONS, AND THE COMMISSIONER'S SCHEME OF IMPROVEMENT, COMPLETE AND IN FULL.

---

*LONDON:*

JOSEPH BUTTERWORTH AND SON, 43, FLEET-STREET.

1827.

J. AND T. CLARKE, PRINTERS, ST. JOHN-SQUARE, LONDON.

# FIRST REPORT,

*&c. &c. &c.*

ADDRESSED TO

THE RIGHT HONOURABLE EARL BATHURST,

&c. &c. &c.

## BARBADOS.

IN this Island, says the Reporter, his Majesty's Commissioners, Mr. Maddock and myself, in January, 1823, entered upon the performance of the duties with which we were charged; embracing, by virtue of an extension [1] of our original powers, an inquiry into the administration of justice, as well civil, as criminal, in all the islands named in our Commission.

[1] Instructions, No. 2.

Our inquiries were first directed to the state of the law of this Colony, which, so far as it is local, is to be found in the statutes of the island. In common with every person in the colony, from the judges who preside and the advocates who practise in the different courts, to the attornies, the suitors, and the public in general, we might have experienced great difficulty in procuring this information, for reasons which will be hereafter explained,

BARBADOS.

LAWS.

[2] Sir Harry Warde.

[3] Mr. Husbands.

but for the prompt and liberal assistance of the [2]governor, and the ready attention of the island [3]secretary, who is the depositary of the acts of the colonial legislature.

LAWS IN FORCE.

The Common Law of England.

Acts of Parliament.

The laws of the mother country acknowledged, and in force, here, are,

First, The common law of England:

Secondly, Such acts of Parliament as passed before the settlement of the island, and are applicable to its condition. Under the qualification contained in the last part of the rule, many entire exceptions have been admitted. Of this, the Bankrupt and Poor laws, the laws of Police, Tithes, and the [4]Mortmain Acts, furnish apt and familiar examples. A further and very striking illustration of the principle upon which particular laws have been excluded, will be found in the preamble to No. 141, Hall's Law of Barbados; "An Act to quiet "the minds of the inhabitants of this island against the "terrors and apprehensions they lie under of a spiritual "court."—"Whereas an attempt has been lately made "to erect a spiritual court in this island: And whereas "such court will *clash with the municipal laws* of this "island, *embarrass* the government, *vex* and torment the "gentry, depauperate the substantial freeholders, and "ruin the common people, now, for quieting the minds, "Be it enacted, &c. &c."

[4] The Attorney-General *v.* Stuart, 2 Merivale's Reports, 143.

Of acts, passed subsequently to its settlement, such, only, are considered to affect the colony, as have the island expressly named or virtually included in them; as is the case where laws are declared to extend, besides Barbados "to the West Indies," or "to the colonies." And all navigation acts, and acts of revenue and trade, and acts respecting shipping, are obligatory; though the colonies are not named in them.

Acts of parliament altering other acts, in force in the colonies, are considered as themselves applying there.

ACTS OF ASSEMBLY.

It is said to be a necessary qualification of acts of assembly that they shall be *reasonable* in themselves; and it is always a restriction that they shall not be *contrary* to

BARBADOS.

LAWS.

the laws of England. Acts repugnant to the laws of England, which refer to the Plantations, are absolutely void.[5]

[5] 7 & 8 W. 3. c. 22. s. 9.

Acts passed in the island, without a suspending clause, immediately that they are assented to by the governor, become and continue in force, till notice is given of their being disallowed. I am aware that a different doctrine has been advanced and ascribed to professional persons, but I could never learn, that it was seriously entertained, by any of the colonial lawyers, most competent from their familiarity with the subject, to pronounce an authoritative opinion. The question, however, was much agitated in [6]several of the colonies about the period of our arrival. Unfortunately, it was at that time mixed up with local politics, and resentments of the most perishable kind. Through these media it arrived to the Commissioners, completely disguised and distorted, so as to render it matter of *no small* difficulty to discover the simple and abstract point alone deserving their dispassionate consideration. At a future period I shall have occasion to return to the subject, and notice a representation we received; the inquiry we instituted; and the results.

[6] In Barbados and Bermuda principally.

EDITIONS OF.

There are two printed collections of the acts of the legislature of Barbados: "Hall's Laws," published in one volume folio, in 1764; and "Moore's Laws," edited in 1800, in one volume octavo; both incomplete, and the former, in a remarkable degree, inaccurate and defective. There is no later edition of their laws, and the acts passed, since the year 1800, remain in manuscript.

It is scarcely necessary to observe, that this state of the Statute Law of a country must be very inconvenient. The chief justice, a gentleman of strict integrity, and who had the manliness and candour to acknowledge in his answers to the Commissioners, that he had not been bred to the profession, and was no lawyer, made upon this subject a very just and spirited remark: "The state "of the modern Statute Law of the colony was very dis"tressing; there were sixty-seven laws in manuscript, "and in consequence they knew nothing about them;" he added, however, "that an Act passed, for printing

BARBADOS.

LAWS.

"these laws, had not been confirmed at home." On inquiry we learnt, that the act in question (for compiling and publishing a perfect edition of the laws of Barbados) was not disallowed on account of any disapprobation of the general principle. On the contrary, it is understood that his Majesty's Government were favourably disposed to promote such a publication. But it would appear that a particular clause in the act was deemed objectionable, as tending to destroy all security for the authenticity or correctness of the intended work; and it seems to have been apprehended, that, by confirming the act in the form in which it was transmitted, not only would an opportunity have been afforded for introducing material errors into the recognized edition of the Barbados Statute Book, but a precedent would have been established, of dangerous application, in the case of other colonies.

MANUSCRIPT.

Upon further inquiry, and after a painful perusal of all the statutes of the island, the Commissioners were satisfied that the manuscript acts or *laws* not in print (and of which *ignorantia neminem excusat,*) amounted not to sixty-seven acts, as the chief justice had supposed, but to 247! All these, public, acts the judges (and they no lawyers,) are *ex officio* bound to know; though not printed, or, it will afterwards appear, easily, referred to.

The acts, themselves are deposited in the colonial secretary's office, and copies are directed to be kept, in the parish churches. Persons desirous of consulting them can only do so, by applying, at the secretary's office, or to the clerk of the vestry. Upon these points, the Commissioners addressed several questions to the attorney and solicitor-general, both gentlemen of great talent and long experience in colonial affairs. The attorney-general said, "they may apply at the secretary's "office, but I do not think he is bound to let them consult the acts." The solicitor-general observed, "I doubt "whether you can insist, as a right, on seeing those "kept in the parish church." The attorney-general believed "the vestry-clerk must give a copy on payment of

BARBADOS.

LAWS.

"5*s*." Supposing the latter opinion to be correct, and that a party can procure a copy, of a specific act, from the parish church, on payment of 5*s*. still *such* copy will not be available in evidence. And, though it is quite unquestionable, as a general rule, that the bench are, judicially, bound to know every public act, which they cannot consult, still in this particular case, whether from the notoriety of the fact bearing down the presumption of law, or from the intrinsic absurdity of the supposition itself, or from loose habits and careless practice, which creep in, where the judges are not lawyers,—the course of the courts, where one of these statutes has been at all insisted on, has, always, been in direct opposition to the maxim of the books; and either the secretary is called upon to produce the original act, or an attested copy, under his hand, is received. The attorney-general states that no other evidence, than the former, would be "allowed." The chief justice and the solicitor-general say that the latter is "generally admitted." Such is the obscurity,—uncertainty,—contradiction,—confusion and error, occasioned by neglecting the ordinary and most obvious method of notifying the commands of the legislature!

Hall's Laws are "made evidence," and the exclusive right (copyright) reserved to him, under penalties recoverable, like servants' wages, before a single justice, on evidence of one witness, or confession of the parties. The same of Moore's edition[7]. Where there is occasion to give a manuscript act in evidence an examined copy should be admitted, as in England. Where the terms or *wording* of the act are the matter in dispute, the original record, I apprehend, must be produced. But the laws not collected and published by authority, with a clause in the act making the printed volume evidence, ought to be few, and those in print—and such, the judges must be generally taken to know, without the necessity of pleading or producing them.

[7] No. 67, Moore's Laws.

A fee is paid for consulting the acts at the secretary's office, and to persons requiring a transcript of the whole

BARBADOS.

LAWS.

or any part of a law, a charge is made in proportion to the folios for copying.

The first act for printing the laws (Hall's Laws, No. 100,) assigns the reasons for the measure, clearly and cogently, in the following remarkable and very *emphatic* preamble :—" Forasmuch as nothing more conduceth to " the well-being, tranquillity and benefit of any place and " people, than the preservation of their laws, and the " knowledge of them, and daily experience having ma- " nifested innumerable inconveniences that this island " hath suffered for so many years past, by not having the " laws by which they are to be regulated and governed, " their lives preserved, and their estates secured to them " and their posterity made public and open to the ready " view of all the inhabitants, for want of which many " persons of great authority in this government, not being " acquainted with all the laws that are kept in offices, or " if known not to be had on sudden occasions, for want " of which also it often happens in the multitudes of " copies which are taken from the offices, great variations " and alterations are made by heedless and unskilful " transcribers, and these copies being obtruded upon " trials, as authentic, have been the cause of unjust and " illegal determinations; and forasmuch as all our laws " on record have often been in great danger to have been " wholly lost, both by hurricane and fire; be it enacted, " &c. &c."

LAWS, HISTORY OF.

From the act No. 204, Hall's Laws, it would naturally be inferred that some steps were taken to carry into effect the revision of the laws, which was at that time felt to be necessary, and which formed part of the instructions carried out by Governor Grenville in 1752. Nothing material, however, appears to have been done, in prosecution of this object. The first thirty-six laws, in Hall's edition, (with one exception, No. 35,) were collected by Commissioners appointed by Lord Willoughby, and afterwards established by an act of the island. The explanatory return (for such it is called) of the Commissioners is contained in the words following:—" We the com-

"mittee appointed for the compiling of the laws, having "caused them to be collected and transcribed, as appears "by a writing under our hands, expressed in the page "preceding the first law entered in this book, and are "therein expressed, and be comprehended in one hun-"dred and fifty-three sheets of paper, which being now "fairly ingrossed in this book, do appear to be fifty-eight "laws, and are comprehended in the fifty-one next pre-"ceding pages. And to the end that our declaration "may be rightly understood, in regard that relateth to "the one hundred and fifty-three sheets of paper wherein "the laws were first digested, we have thought good "here to insert this present explanation. Given under "our hands the 14th day of November 1667.

BARBADOS.

LAWS, HISTORY OF.

"*Philip Bell,*
"*Constant Sylvester.*"

This document is inserted in Hall, and is certainly worth preserving for its admirable perspicuity and legal precision. Oldmixon says[8], "It is well for the inhabit-"ants of this island, that the laws are more intelligible, "than this return;" upon which their editor, Hall, with unwonted smartness, observes, "If he had read the laws, "he would not have said this."

[8] Brit. Empire in America, vol. 2, p. 28.

I have already alluded to a communication made to the Commissioners, upon the subject of their laws, enacted by the colonial legislature, and awaiting the expression of His Majesty's pleasure. The representation we received, was to the following effect:—"That great incon-"venience was felt for want of a certain rule, by which "it could be clearly known, *what* acts remain in force, "or *when* acts cease to be binding; when acts are al-"lowed at home, and when disapproved. The order in "council of 1800 (the last upon the subject) was said to "be so ambiguous, that lawyers, here, had differed from "each other, and from themselves, upon its construc-"tion."

Minutes, March 11, 1823

DURATION OF.

The facts, upon which this statement proceeded, were positively denied; the opinion it tends to countenance, I consider erroneous; the grievances, it represents, are either unfounded, or greatly exaggerated. But excusing

BARBADOS.

LAWS, HISTORY OF.

a slight taint of party feeling, and a little spleen against the lawyers, the motives which caused the communication were sufficiently respectable, and the object it had in view, of procuring a clear and precise rule, upon a subject of the greatest importance to the colonies, such, as in any light we could view it, it was impossible to disapprove.

The subject, it will be perceived, is not trivial, and deserves elucidation, on constitutional as well as legal grounds; though quite distinct from any case of complaint or crimination. As the learning it embraces is very useful, and is not generally diffused, it may be advantageous to state the information we collected, somewhat fully.

On the arrival, at the colonial department, of acts passed by the governor, council, and assembly, of any of his Majesty's colonies in the West Indies, the course pursued is as follows:

The acts of the session are referred by the secretary of state to the counsel for the colonial department, who is required to "*report his opinion upon them in point of* "*law.*" By this old and established form of expression is understood to be meant, that the counsel is to report, whether the acts, respectively, are such as, consistently with his commission and instructions, the governor was authorized to pass; whether, in the language of the statute 7 & 8 Wm. 3. c. 22. s. 9, it is repugnant to any law made in this kingdom, so far as such law may mention or refer to the plantations; and whether the act is so framed as to give full and entire effect to the purposes with which the colonial legislature may have passed it?

In pursuance of this reference, a report is made, to the secretary of state, by the counsel to his department. The acts, accompanied by this report, are then transmitted to the president of the council, with a letter from the secretary of state, desiring his lordship to lay the acts and the report before the King in council, for his Majesty's consideration.

At the first board of council, which is held after receiving this communication, the acts are referred to the lords of the committee of council for the affairs of trade and plantations, who are directed to report to the King in council, their opinion what proceedings it may be proper to take in relation to them. It is understood that the committee of trade proceed to select, from the acts thus referred to them, all such as present any point of peculiar novelty or importance, or as give rise to any question of legal difficulty. The acts thus selected, together with all private acts, are referred by their Lordships to His Majesty's attorney and solicitor-general for their opinion. When the report of the law-officers of the Crown is obtained, the lords of the committee of trade enter into the consideration of all the acts of the session, and it is understood to be a settled rule, that, in their deliberations upon this subject, they are assisted by the Secretary of State for the colonies, in his capacity of a member of the committee.

A report, from the committee of trade, is then addressed to the King in council, and in this report all the acts of the session of the colonial assembly are classed under three heads; First, if it is thought proper to *disallow* any act, the report contains a full statement of the grounds of objection, which may exist to it; secondly, if any of the acts relate to measures of general and peculiar importance and interest, it is recommended that a special order in council should pass for the *confirmation* of them; thirdly, the great majority of the acts of each year being usually little more than business of routine and continual recurrence, their Lordships are in the habit of advising, that—such acts "*should be left to their operation.*"

If this Report is adopted by the King in council, orders are drawn up, for such of the acts, as are comprised in the two first-mentioned classes. No colonial act can be disallowed, except by a regular order of the King in council.

The clerk of the council then addresses, to the secretary of state for the colonies, a letter, announcing to him the decision which has been adopted, respecting all the acts of the session, and transmitting to him all the origi-

BARBADOS.

LAWS.

nal orders in council for allowing or disallowing any particular acts.

The secretary of state communicates the result to the governor of the colony, and at the same time conveys to him the original orders in council. A list is also made out, of the acts which have neither been confirmed nor disallowed, with an intimation that *they* are to be left to their operation.

From the preceding statement, it appears, that, comparatively few, of the statutes passed in the West Indies, receive either the direct confirmation or disallowance of the King. It is clearly understood, that, so long as this prerogative is not exercised, the act continues in force, under the qualified assent, which is given by the governor in the colony itself, on behalf of the King. It is also received as a maxim, that the King may, at any time, however remote, exercise his prerogative of disallowing any colonial act, which he has not once confirmed by any order in council. This, however, may be numbered among those constitutional powers of the Crown, which have been dormant, for a long series of years, and which would not be called into action, except on some extreme and urgent occasion. It is believed, that no instance has occurred, in modern times, of the disallowance of any colonial statute, after the notification to the governor, that it " would be left to its operation."

It is deserving notice, that reference was made to an order in council of the 15th January 1800; by which it is declared, that " in all cases when his Majesty's con" firmation shall be necessary, to give validity and effect " to any act passed by the legislature of any of his Ma" jesty's colonies or plantations,—unless his Majesty's " confirmation thereof shall be obtained, within three " years, from the passing of such act, in any of the said " colonies or plantations, such act shall be considered as " disallowed." This order has been, sometimes, supposed to lay down a rule, applicable to all descriptions of colonial statutes. It is however apparent, from the words of the order itself, from the reason of the case, and from the understanding of the public offices in England, that such is not the sound construction or real effect of the order. It was made to remove a difficulty which had arisen respecting *one* particular class of colonial statutes; those, namely, which contained a clause, suspending their operation, till the pleasure of the King was known. This is the only description of statutes, respecting which it can be said, that his Majesty's confirmation is "necessary, to give them validity and effect." Without the assistance of such a general rule, it would have been impossible to know, in any particular case, whether the statute would, or would not, at some future time, be called into operation; an uncertainty, peculiarly embarrassing, in reference to private acts, which invariably contain a suspending clause.

If it were necessary or proper, in this Report, to investigate minutely, the reasons, which may have induced your Lordship and the other members of his Majesty's Government, in so large a proportion of cases, to advise the King to abstain from the exercise of his prerogative, by leaving colonial acts to their operation, instead of expressly confirming them, it might not be difficult to discover the policy and motives, which led to such results. It is indeed obvious, that there are a multitude of cases, in which it would be equally inconvenient to confirm or to disallow the acts, transmitted from the colonies. The cases are, perhaps, still more numerous, in which the act has expired, or become obsolete, or has been repealed, before the period arrives, for pronouncing the decision of his Majesty in council upon it. But it is fully sufficient, for the object I had in view, to have stated the facts and conclusions, and explained the nature and course of the proceedings.

Upon the facts which have been stated, it is not difficult, humbly, to offer an opinion.

I cannot hesitate to recommend the publication of the manuscript acts. I also feel it to be my duty to suggest, that, it is, in the highest degree, expedient, that the laws, already published, should undergo a careful examination and revision. I have every reason to believe that the colonial legislature is favourably disposed to the adoption

BARBADOS.

LAWS.

CONSOLIDATION AND AMENDMENT OF.

of such a measure. And, should a joint committee of the council and assembly of this island, be appointed, to examine and report upon the Statute Book, with a view to the consolidation and amendment of their laws, availing themselves of the research and information of the present chief justice; and could the editing a complete edition, of such amended laws, be placed under the superintendence of Mr. Hinds, or any other equally zealous, able, and distinguished lawyer, I entertain the strongest conviction that all further observations, upon this part of the subject, would be rendered quite unnecessary.

But there is one branch of the laws of peculiar interest and vital importance, and therefore demanding a separate consideration. Into this, it was the province of the Commissioners to enter, so far only as was necessary, to discover the extent, to which existing defects in the administration of justice, ought to be ascribed, not to any deficiencies in the means of execution, but to the inadequacy of the law, itself.

No 32, Hall's Laws.
[9] August 8, 1688.

It cannot fail to inflict a pang, upon the constitutional feelings, of an English reader, to be told that the first and most obnoxious of the slave-laws of this island passed in the year 1688[9], at a time when civil liberty was best understood; most ably asserted; and successfully vindicated in England! It would be most unfair to object to the Barbadians, of the present day, the opprobrious provisions of that act. It is not even fit—to allude to its enactments, without admitting, that many absurd and inhuman laws continued to disgrace the English Statute Book, at a period much later, than the date of this exceptionable law. But it is the duty of an honest inquirer, and one from which he must not shrink, after acknowledging, as he finds a sincere pleasure in doing, the vast improvements which have already taken place, and, what is more important, the growing disposition, in almost every quarter, to extend and strengthen these advantages; to point out temperately and with candor, some of the blemishes which still remain, for existing assemblies to lessen or remove.

BARBADOS.

LAWS.

The improved spirit of the age is most gratefully, as well as conspicuously, manifested, in the conferring of fresh privileges, and removal of narrow distinctions. Thus are constantly created new relations of society. Collisions ensue (such as unavoidably occur in the intercourse of life,) correcting errors; weakening prejudices; and operating most favourably upon the conditions and characters of men. Of this kind is the law of the island of 1817, which admits, *all free persons of whatever colour to be witnesses*, "provided they have been baptized "and instructed in the principles of the christian re-"ligion." MS. Law, 1817.

To the same disposition, is to be referred, the repeal of an odious law, "That if any negro, who has lived, in "the island, one year, shall run away and absent himself "from the service of his master thirty days, he shall "suffer death," as "other criminals whose offences are "made capital by No. 82," (I do not affect to state the precise words.) An act (the repealed law) recording the feelings of a remote period, when slaves, newly imported from Africa, in vast numbers, were, no doubt, often found very intractable; "and such," it says, "is their "brutish and barbarous nature, that they will not be re-"claimed by any fair means." No. 92, Hall. Repealed in 1819.

There are other instances, where improvements have been undertaken, upon too confined a plan, or without a due regard to the correspondency of parts and connection of the whole; or perhaps a measure, salutary in itself, has partly failed of its effects, because the execution was constrained and feeble, or the task intrusted to unskilful hands. An act passed in Lord Combermere's government, in 1818, repealed the fifth clause of the general slave-act, which fifth clause inflicted the punishment of slitting the nose, and burning the face with a hot iron, for a second offence, in "striking a christian" (meaning a white person); but the punishment of petit-larceny, committed by a negro, inflicted by the same general act, and left unrepealed, *(the only just ground of complaint against the present inhabitants)* is as follows: "Every "negro adjudged guilty, by confession, proof, or pro- July 29, 1818. No. 82, cl. 5.

BARBADOS.

LAWS. No. 82, cl. 13.

" bable circumstances, shall be adjudged to be publicly " and severely whipped, not exceeding forty lashes; for " the second offence, *to have his nose slit, and to be brand-* " *ed in the forehead with a hot iron, that the mark thereof* " *may remain;* and for the third, to be tried as in cases " of murder, burglary, &c., and if found guilty, suffer " death, or other punishment, as the justices think fit."

The crime in this case amounts to felony, which, in England, would have subjected the offender to severer punishment for the first offence, and he might there also, on conviction, have been branded with a hot iron; but the *slitting the nose,* I confess, does appear to me, to be a punishment, which, without danger to the colonies, might be dispensed with in petit-larcenies, as well as misdemeanors. This, I am aware, is only an oversight, but it is a great one; and it is very revolting that more consideration should not be given, to subjects of such extreme importance.

MS. Law.

1805. By a manuscript act of this date, "If any per- " son shall hereafter wilfully, maliciously, wantonly, " and without provocation, kill and murder any slave, " whether such slave be the property of the person so " killing and murdering, or of any other person, such " person so killing and murdering being duly convicted " thereof by the evidence of one or more white person " or persons, &c. shall suffer death."

This was a great improvement in the law, which before only inflicted a small fine of 25*l.* currency for the murder of a slave, and double the value to the owner, if the slave was the property of another.

Upon the wording of the act I feel it to be quite unnecessary to offer a single observation. It is obviously such, as must render a conviction, for the murder of a slave, in almost every case that can possibly occur, matter of the greatest difficulty. Yet the most extraordinary (and it seems to me) irrational provision is the rejection of all testimony, except that of *white* witnesses. Had the act admitted only *free* persons, the motive would have been intelligible, and consistent with alleged principles, and the invariable practice of the colonies. As it is, the

BARBADOS.

LAWS.

provision is not confined, to cases, in which the *accused* are also whites, but extends to prosecutions in which free negroes, or free coloured persons, are charged with the murder of a slave; so that a free person of colour, having murdered a slave, when no white man was present, not only would slaves, as in all other cases, be incompetent to give evidence, (unless No. 180, Hall's Laws is in force, which is denied)[10], but the testimony of free men, not whites, which was always admissible, in the same manner as the evidence of slaves is, FOR AND AGAINST EACH OTHER, and is now (provided they have been baptized) receivable in all cases and against all persons whomsoever, white as well as black;—would in this single instance of a most atrocious crime, requiring condign punishment, be unaccountably and indefensibly excluded!

[10] per Attorney-General.

It is clear that under the term "any persons," &c. was not intended to be included any slave. If, however, the construction put upon this expression, at any future time, should be the same in Barbados as has already obtained, in some of the other islands, the absurdity of the provision will become still more signally conspicuous.

Such HAS BEEN the crude and slovenly preparation of acts in which the life of man is deeply implicated; so perfunctory the discharge of duties,—the gravest a legislature can perform! The present legislature of Barbados contains many enlightened and valuable members; and serious will be their responsibility, if they continue to waste, in petty quarrels, the talents and capabilities of doing good, which they undoubtedly possess, and should, long since, have applied to useful and exalted purposes.

Clause 12, of No. 82 (the general Slave-Act) is very remarkable, both on account of its making "attempts to "steal" equally criminal, with stealing itself, and from the very insufficient manner in which the offence of larceny is described and guarded against. After enumerating the capital offences, in the preamble, as "murder, "burglary," &c., which be many times "committed by "negroes or other slaves, and many times maliciously "attempted by them to be committed, in which, though

Hall's Laws, No. 82. cl. 12.

BARBADOS.

LAWS.

" by divers accidents they are prevented, yet are their " crimes nevertheless heinous, and therefore deserve the " like punishment," it proceeds: "As also do many " times steal, wilfully kill, maim, or destroy one or more " horses, mares, geldings, cattle, sheep, or other quick " or dead thing of the like nature, and of the value of " 12*d.* or above; and many times by attempting to steal " from the inhabitants of this island, stock and other " goods before mentioned, of above or under the value " aforesaid, do put such inhabitants, or some of his " family, in terror, dread or jeopardy of their lives, " which several offenders, for danger of escape, are not " long to be imprisoned; and being brutish slaves, de- " serve not for the baseness of their condition to be tried " by the legal trial of twelve men of their peers or neigh- " bourhood, which neither truly can be rightly done as " the subjects of England are, nor is execution to be de- " layed towards them in case of such horrid crimes com- " mitted," &c.

Upon the construction of this clause it may be doubtful, whether, personal property, not " of the like nature " with horses, mares, geldings, cattle and sheep," if taken without " putting in terror, dread or jeopardy of their " lives, any of the inhabitants of the island," can be the subject of larceny; and the bare possibility of such a doubt, leaving much of the valuable property of the island, unprotected, must surely render some other and more explicit enactment highly desirable.

The omissions of this act, I shall find it necessary to observe upon, at a future time. At present, I shall only remark, that for *those*, for the spirit which generally pervades it; and, most particularly, for the sentiment as to the trial of slaves, expressed in the clause last above cited, this act, No. 82, is quite insufferable; and it involves, it must be admitted, no slight reproach that such a law should be allowed to *continue unrepealed*. It will be satisfactory to shew, in the progress of the Report, that slaves *are* tried in many of the other islands " by " legal trial of twelve men," that is to say, in precisely the same manner, as their owners. And it is an incon-

BARBADOS.

LAWS.

testable fact, and often very much to be regretted, that slaves are less frequently and less severely punished, for crimes, than are freemen, either in the Colonies or in England. Indeed it is a subject of vulgar clamour, with the lower description of whites, that "the black" may commit crimes, with comparative impunity. The remark is not entirely without foundation. By the civil law, and according to the criminalists, an offence committed by a slave is *crimen qualificatum;* an aggravated enormity; acquiring an intensity of guilt, from the presumption of a slave in perpetrating it. In the colonies, where no scale of punishment has been adopted, and no sanction is known of an intermediate nature, between corporal and capital punishment, a slave escapes at the utmost with a severe whipping, where, in England, for the same offence, he would be in imminent danger of being hanged.

To mitigate the severity and positive cruelty of the latter part of clause 12 of the general Slave Act, (No. 82 last above cited,) a law, No. 180, Hall's Laws, appears to have been framed. Under the former act a slave was to be immediately executed "without stay or respite; "whereby the owner or possessor of such negro or other "slave is prevented from bringing a writ of error to re-"verse the judgment or sentence, which in some in-"stances hath been thought erroneous, and many times, "by the malice or ill will of the prosecutor, as well as "by the obstinacy of the owner or possessor of the slave "complained against, the pains of death hath, in pur-"suance of the letter or construction of the said act, "been inflicted on such slave, when more proper and "effectual methods might have been used if the justices "and freeholders hath been empowered so to do, and "thereby the large sums of money that have been paid "out of the treasury, for such executed slave, might and "ought to have been saved, as well as the life of such "slave preserved. And whereas many persons in this "island having manumitted and set free several negroes, "and other slaves, without making proper provisions for "their maintenance and support, they, continuing their

BARBADOS. — LAWS.

" baseness, have, instead of supporting themselves by " honest labour and industry, through idleness and other " vices, been greatly injurious to the inhabitants, in en- " ticing and corrupting other slaves to steal and rob " their owners, presuming that as they cannot be tried " as slaves, the evidence and testimony of a slave cannot " legally be received against them, and thereby have " hitherto escaped with impunity," &c. enacts, that the justices and freeholders, who are the parties that try the charge, " or the major part of them," be " directed and " empowered to use their best endeavours to compromise " the offence between the prosecutor and owner, or pos- " sessor of such negro," &c. and where " the matter " cannot be accorded," an appeal is given. The evidence of a slave too, " where the same is supported with " very good and sufficient corroborating circumstances," is made valid " against any free negro, Indian, or mu- " latto."

Hall's Laws, No. 180, cl. 6.

By clause sixth of the same act, " whoever shall here- " after, by deed or will, or by any other ways or means " whatsoever, manumit, set free, or discharge from sla- " very, any negro or other slave or slaves, such person, " &c. shall, for the better support of such slave or slaves, " and to prevent their becoming burthensome to the pa- " rish in which he, she, or they shall live and reside, " deposit and direct to be paid into the hands of the " churchwarden, for the time being, of the said parish, " for each negro, or other slave so manumitted, &c. the " sum of 50*l.* current money, &c. And the said vestry " shall direct and appoint the sum of 4*l.* current money " for the maintenance and support of such person, so " manumitted and set free, to be annually paid to him " or her." And the churchwarden may recover the 50*l.* by action.

No. 32, Moore's Laws.

The notorious evasions of this law, and the cruel deceptions too frequently practised upon the unfortunate objects of its provision, will be more suitably considered in another place .

[11]Defect of jurisdiction, post.

This act passed in 1739, and is of a milder spirit than any of the former, and, in its tendency, a humane law.

BARBADOS.

LAWS.

But it is impossible not to observe upon the unseasonable avowal of prudential motives, ("*the large sums paid out* "*of the treasury*"), and the subordinate regard for the lives of men; ("*as well as the lives of such slaves pre-* "*served.*")

This mitigating act is also unnecessarily harsh in some of its expressions, and calculated to give great offence to a particular class, (the free negroes) against whom, exclusively, slave evidence was to be admitted. Yet as the act is drawn, such provision at that time, could never take effect, and must have been quite nugatory. The evidence of slaves is to be admitted against free negroes "in all courts of record, the same as if the slave "were free and baptized;" that is, not at all, in any court; for at that time, though free and baptized, no coloured person was admitted to give evidence. By clause eight of No. 148, passed in 1721, eighteen years before, "no person shall be admitted an evidence, in any "case whatsoever, whose original extraction shall be "proved to have been from a negro, excepting only on "the trial of negro and other slaves."

There are other parts of the act, not undeserving of attention. Such are the recital in the preamble, of the sloth and apathy, and profligate courses of the free negroes; and the extraordinary power given to the master, of compounding felonies: the former a singular fact, established, beyond contradiction, by concurrent testimonies, as existing in every age; the latter, an error of early legislation, common to all countries.

By a subsequent act, passed in 1749, "Any negro, or "other slave or slaves, may be apprehended and brought "before a justice, for any threatening, fighting, or quar- "relling one with another, or for any insolent language "or gesture to any free or white person, or for swearing, "&c. or for any misbehaviour, whereby the public may "be disturbed, or any particular person immediately ag- "grieved,"—and ordered "to be flogged, not exceeding "thirty-nine lashes, &c."

No. 196. Hall's Laws.

A law of police, calculated to repress disorderly proceedings, of the kinds here enumerated, may be highly

BARBADOS.

LAWS.

proper. But I am again bound to observe, upon the want of care and precision in framing its enactments. In every society, and particularly where slavery exists, due care *must* be taken to secure subordination. From motives of policy it is obviously impossible to admit any contemptuous behaviour towards the masters; and for the preservation of the public peace, it is absolutely necessary to punish with severity any turbulent or riotous conduct of the slaves, who, in every island, (and in this colony proportionably more than others,) compose so numerous and powerful a body. But what is the condition of any human being, who may be taken up, for what is interpreted to amount to "*an insolent gesture*;" or for "*misbehaviour, whereby any particular person is immediately aggrieved*;" no particular act, word or gesture, being designated, as constituting such inhibited behaviour? And bearing in mind, as it is necessary to do, that for these offences, thus vague, loose and undefined, a slave may be apprehended by any constable, without warrant, and convicted by any magistrate, without oath. *This* is under the municipal law, while the domestic tribunal, the competent authority of the master to coerce or punish his slave, without the interference of any person whatever, continues open, and may be resorted to.

Besides the objection to the act, from the large and general terms in which its penal provisions are expressed, the reason for passing it, assigned in the preamble, furnishes an alarming proof of the loose nature of judicial proceedings, at that period. "Whereas," it says, "though "there has been no express law for the punishment of "the said offences, yet it has been usual, from the neces-"sity and the supposed reason of the thing, to punish "the same by whipping, as directed in like cases, which "however had of late occasioned some doubts and dis-"putes to arise, &c. now to obviate these, &c."

In clause 5, No. 116, Hall's Laws, is found the following strange, and as it appears to me, impolitic, provision, which I believe has never been repealed: "Owners of "slaves, permitting negroes to go at large, and hire out "themselves, to any person or persons, or follow any

BARBADOS.

LAWS.

" trade, occupation or calling, and receive the profits " themselves, or render to the owners, or for their use, a " daily, weekly, or monthly sum of money, or any other " income or gratuity, in such case, owners suffering such " slaves to go at large and hire themselves as aforesaid, " &c. shall forfeit 10*l.*"

It would be difficult to point out a law more at variance, both with the spirit of the age, and with the manners and practice, at present prevailing in, I believe, all our colonies. It is usual with domestic slaves, (and commendably so,) to allow them to hire themselves out, to whom they please, and to retain, for their *peculium*, all the wages they are able to earn, beyond a certain fixed sum payable to the master. In other cases, a free ticket, (as it is called,) to serve other persons, is given to a deserving slave, for the express purpose of enabling him to gradually procure the sum required for the purchase of his freedom. It is very desirable that the utmost encouragement should be afforded to manumissions. They present the best, or certainly the least objectionable mode, of getting rid of slavery, safely and by imperceptible degrees; and they will be found most beneficial, both to individuals and to society, in those cases where habits of industry and the active co-operation of the slave are rendered essential to their completion.

Of the ability with which the folio volume of the laws is edited, some notion may be formed by the profound note upon No. 82, the general Slave Act; of which the vague and terrible enactments must have been read with horror: " If slaves were treated with more humanity " than they generally are, and the laws of this island, for " the well ordering and governing of them, were duly " put in execution, they might be rendered very useful " as well as valuable." It gives me great satisfaction that I can, in the faithful discharge of my official duty, conscientiously report, not that the slaves of the present day *are* generally treated with great humanity, which formed no part of our inquiries, (though I am perfectly satisfied of the *fact*, from our opportunities of observation, which were very extensive;) but, that, the laws of

BARBADOS.

SLAVE LAWS.

the island, for the "well ordering and governing of "them," are very many repealed, and the remainder disregarded!

The mild treatment, however, which slaves, in general, experience, is unquestionably owing, vastly more to the tenderness of the master, than to the security of the law; and this observation applies particularly to Barbádos and to the slave-laws in that island, which have already been reported on. Those laws no doubt are antiquated, but it does not therefore follow, that it is useless to denounce as barbarous, what is acknowledged to be disregarded. Though not for many years in force, these acts are scarcely a dead letter: they live a perpetual reproach. Repudiated, they are not removed; disavowed, they still continue; useless (it is admitted) to those for whose protection they were once deemed necessary, they present only assailable points, whose weakness invites attack,—abundantly supplied, too, with every material, that can be effectually turned against themselves.

The strongest objection to these early laws is their tendency, *effete* as they are, to perpetuate the evils and miseries of a system insensibly undergoing a beneficial change; to preserve, to no useful purpose, the sentiments and feelings, once unhappily belonging to ages and generations now no more! At the same time, it is fit to be remembered, that monuments of oppression as they are, they have been built into the social edifice; so that it is alike dangerous to prop, or suddenly remove them. Institutions of this singular nature, possessing an extensive influence over character, feelings, and habits, require to be gently let down. They fortunately are, at the present moment, and with an impulse given in the islands, (I allude particularly to the establishment of Schools for All) equably, softly, and gradually sinking! I have pointed out a few of the pernicious consequences, resulting from the barbarous provisions of the ancient laws. These deformities will doubtless be removed from every Statute Book, and improved slave-laws passed in all the colonies. The legislatures of the different islands, (Jamaica only excepted,) when free from irritation, are, by no means,

BARBADOS.

SLAVE LAWS.

unprepared, to enter upon a careful revision of their respective codes; Jamaica is already possessed of an improved body of slave statutes, and it only requires to be seen, that the administration is as satisfactory, as the laws, in the main, are excellent.

In two of the Islands, Tobago and Grenada, important changes in the law *have recently taken place.* In the former, a slave-act, conceived in the most humane and liberal spirit, securing to the slave his little property, and allowing him to sue for and recover it, in the courts of justice of the island, and containing a clause for the admission of slave testimony, in cases where other evidence is unattainable, passed two sessions ago, shortly after the Commissioners left the island. In the latter, a dignified concession of *certain* civil rights to a very deserving class of persons; a measure equally dictated by sound policy, humanity and justice; has satisfied the wishes and silenced the complaints, which are too often and very artfully represented as insatiate and unappeaseable. A consolidated and amended slave-bill is in preparation, if not in progress, in the same island. From the high reputation which Grenada has uniformly sustained, for the humanity of her laws, and which the Guardian Act alone (however imperfect) is sufficient to establish, as well as from the great liberality of sentiment, prevailing among the present inhabitants, I am sanguine in my anticipation of very decided improvement from this measure. At St. Vincent an amended slave-law, repealing the barbarous old acts, and containing some admirable regulations for the trial of slaves, at the same time and in the same manner as free persons; with this difference in their favour, that on the trial of a slave "the court are required to appoint a barrister, to act as "counsel for the prisoner;" and presenting much besides to commend, taken from the slave-laws of Jamaica, passed about the year 1819. "A free white man who has no money" said Chief Justice Wylley, "may plead his own "cause as well as he can; but the humblest of our slaves "is entitled, in such cases, to the assistance of counsel, "retained for him at the expence of the colony."—In

Examinations St. Vincent.

BARBADOS.

SLAVE LAWS.

Dominica we found improved laws, and ascertained instances of their equal administration.—The laws of Antigua are entitled to great praise; and I am happy to say the best disposition prevails in the country parts; and the improved condition of the slave, and his advancement in religious instruction upon several estates in that island, in the hands [12]of humane and zealous owners, is highly satisfactory.

[12]The Codrington estates under Colonel Osborne; Rev. W. Gilbert; J. Duncombe Taylor, Esq.

But of the Leeward Islands, (properly so called, that is to say, leeward of Guadaloupe,) it is in St. Christopher that the readiness to improve the laws, affecting slaves, is most conspicuous and creditable. The disposition I allude to has been principally manifested in the joint resolutions of the council and assembly of that island; and, however, upon consideration, or from a regard to circumstances, the letter of those resolutions may require to be modified, the spirit of them I am very sure, will never be departed from.

[13]Mr. Woodley.

The Attorney General of that colony[13], a gentleman, whom it is impossible to mention, without a testimony of respect, as a sound lawyer and most amiable man, expressed himself as follows: "The slave-laws ought to be "revised, if it were only for the purpose of expunging "many disgusting enactments, which, though generally "condemned and never put in practice, have been un-"accountably permitted to remain unrepealed. But "there is every reason to expect, from such a measure, "other and more beneficial results to the slave popula-"tion. The sentiments, which appear formerly to have "prevailed regarding that class, have in great measure "given way to the efforts of humanity, and the appeals "to religion and justice which have been made on their "behalf; and it cannot be doubted, that the improved "sense, which is now entertained, very generally, of "what is due to them, as men and fellow subjects, when "brought into practical operation, will go far to the "establishment of their just rights and the improvement "of their condition."

Indeed the principle of *amelioration*, distinct from any agitating question affecting *property*, has been every

BARBADOS.

SLAVE LAWS.

where admitted; the difficulty is found in the application and the details. Some islands, it may require to be known, are, as far as respects these improvements, *at present very considerably in advance of others.* The best laws, that can be framed upon the subject, will be, necessarily, very imperfect. An unprejudiced mind will be satisfied to discover traces of progressive advancement, and the existence of an improved moral feeling. Complete success in particular legislation (infinitely more difficult than general) is not to be expected, and is, unreasonably, as well as inconsistently, required from those, who are often represented, as incapable of any good. The futility of many regulations, contained in former meliorating acts, we found every where acknowledged; but I am not, on that account, disposed to question the sincerity of the local legislatures. The cause can be assigned—It is deeply rooted in the peculiar relation of the parties and the structure of Colonial society. If the overseer is not left entirely to himself, without scrutiny, as in Barbados, the magistrates are directed to appoint freeholders to visit plantations, as in Tobago; or guardians are appointed to superintend distributions, as in Grenada. In either case the duty is neglected or inefficiently performed. The magistrates in the one case, and the persons appointed guardians in the other, are themselves owners of estates and slaves, who would resent the intrusion of a stranger upon their own grounds, and will not therefore set an example of interference, with the property of others. It is different with *that* part of the Guardian Act which regards the receiving and investigating any complaints of slaves; an authority which *is* exercised, and is eminently useful.

The fault in these cases, it appears to me, is not in the law, or in the lawgiver; still less is there any *mala fides;* any deliberate fraud and designed evasion. What is wanting, I conceive, is A DUE ADMINISTRATION; *which can only be by indifferent persons;* and this conclusion, I apprehend, will be fully established, and the principles, upon which it depends, developed clearly, as the Report proceeds. Yet, whatever remains to be done, the con-

BARBADOS.

SLAVE LAWS

dition of the slave has, undoubtedly, of late years, very greatly improved; and I am willing, and consider it due, to ascribe some of the advantages to the meliorating acts, and think that great allowance ought to be made for their imperfections and failures. It is very different, in my view of the subject, with the perverse retention of mischievous old laws. This *wilful error* (could such a thing occur,) admits of no apology. The slave-laws of Barbados peculiarly and pre-eminently stand in need of a revision; and doubtless will receive it. The political dissentions, before alluded to, occasioned and will excuse SOME delay. At the same time I have singular pleasure in acknowledging (if I may be allowed to step aside from judicial inquiries to make the observation), the excellent establishments, for the purposes of education, to be found in this island. There are two schools, numerously attended, conducted on the principles and plan of the national schools in England: the one for poor white children; the other to which children of all colours are indiscriminately admitted; the former is ably, the latter very respectably, conducted; both, with the Divine Blessing, may be confidently expected to produce great public and private good. MUCH, HOWEVER, REQUIRES TO BE DONE TO REMOVE BLEMISHES, COEVAL ALMOST WITH THE FIRST SETTLEMENT OF THE ISLANDS, AND TO FOSTER INSTITUTIONS WISE AND LIBERAL IN THEIR NATURE, CONGENIAL WITH THE ENLIGHTENED SPIRIT OF THE AGE, AND YET ADAPTED TO THE PECULIAR CIRCUMSTANCES OF THE PEOPLE. The defects, I have pointed out, as my duty required, belong to other times, and were produced by different circumstances; the improvements I have recognized, and to which I attach the highest importance, reflect credit on the present generation; are recent, spontaneous, and their own. At some future period, with the full concurrence of the local legislatures, it may be practicable to establish a general code (*Code Noir*) proceeding upon FIXED PRINCIPLES, for all our colonies.

Quitting the subject of the laws I proceed to examine the sufficiency of the means of enforcing their execution.

In this I shall endeavour to confine myself to the notice of such matters as constitute a departure from the rules and usages of England; to which the practice of the Colonial courts is meant to be assimilated. BARBADOS. SLAVE LAWS.

## COURTS OF JUDICATURE IN BARBADOS.

COURTS, ENUMERATION OF.

The courts, established for the administration of Civil justice in the island of Barbados are—the court of chancery; the court of error, or appeal and error; the court of ordinary;—five courts of common pleas, one being held in each of five districts; the court of exchequer; the court of admiralty; and the court of escheat. Besides these general courts, there is, by a local act, a power vested in the governor, to appoint a special court of merchants and mariners; as also a court to take cognizance of cases of persons about to quit the island, in debt; which court I believe never sat. There is also what are called *warrant* actions; these are excrescences, growing out of the authority, given to a single justice, to decide claims for service, or for work and labour, by servants and labourers, and extended *very mischievously*, to those who exercise any manual labour, as shoemakers and taylors; as well as to all demands, arising from the sale of the produce of the island; and actions for cattle under the amount of 25*l.*

No. 27, Hall's Laws. No. 59, Hall's Laws, cl. 5. No. 30, Hall's Laws, cl. 11. No. 175, Hall's Laws.

The courts for the administration of Criminal justice are the court of grand session, held twice a year; the court of quarter sessions, which does not sit regularly at present; a court for the trial of slaves for capital offences, consisting of two magistrates and three freeholders, with an appeal to the governor and council; and the admiralty sessions, held *pro re natâ.*

It will be found most convenient to report upon these different courts, separately and distinctly; giving a detail of facts, and only referring to the principles of law, where it is absolutely necessary, to render the nature of proceedings or the grounds of a complaint, perfectly intelligible.

BARBADOS.

COURTS.

CHANCERY.

## COURT OF CHANCERY.

JUDGES.

"As" is similitudinary. Lord Coke, 2 Blackst.

The Court of Chancery is composed of the governor or president, with four or more members of the council. The governor in chancery, though often said to act AS CHANCELLOR, is only *PRIMUS INTER PARES.* The members of the council are appointed by a mandamus from the King, on the recommendation of the governor, who, in certain cases, has the power of suspending them, for misconduct, transmitting his reasons to England. To remove them, is said to require the concurrence of the majority of the council, in council. The members of council do not derive any emolument from the situation. Neither the governor, as chancellor, nor the president, acting as such in his absence, receives any salary or fees; which latter, I believe, is peculiar to this island. The governor, sitting as chancellor, has no assessor or professional assistance of any kind. The decision is made by a majority of votes. The votes are taken singly, beginning with the junior member of council. The votes are given publicly in open court. The attorney-general was of opinion that you could not prevent a member of council, who was not present when a cause was opened, from joining the court, just before a decree; but he had never known it done. He had known some, quit, before the determination. He thought the court should continue, composed of the same members, to the end of a suit; but not on different proceedings arising out of it, as a master's report. He remembered one instance, when the governor and five of the council sat: three were of one opinion and three of another, and, as the same members did not attend again, no decree was made, until the suit abated by the death of the parties, and the suit was not revived.

Two masters in chancery are appointed by the governor, but only one acts: the business is transacted by one They are paid by commission.

BARBADOS.

CHANCERY.

The other officers of the court are the registrar and serjeant at arms; patent offices, performed by deputies. On represesentation by the court, of misbehaviour in any of its officers, the governor can suspend the party offending, and the attornies of the patentee in the island will nominate another. But the appointment is only *pro tempore* till the principal is heard from. The nominee gives sufficient security for the profits in the interim; and the same to the principal, for any consequences that may result to HIM, from his misconduct, as deputy.

JURISDICTION.

The judges of this court are supposed to have all the authority of the Lord Chancellor of England, except in cases wholly inapplicable to the colony. They assume and exercise jurisdiction in cases of *lunacy*, without any special delegation of authority, but under the supposed general jurisdiction of the Court of Chancery. How this authority is obtained, before GRANT MADE, is not apparent; but sufficient appears to shew, that the practice is unsettled, and the law considered doubtful! Sir George Beckwith, when governor, thought, very reasonably, that he, alone, had a right to issue a commission; but determined, for security, to act with the council.—A petition is presented, in the first instance, to the governor only; he directs a hearing at the next court. The lunacy, when found, is, I believe, returned into the court; and in this way they may, possibly, but, I apprehend, mistakenly, consider themselves, as getting jurisdiction.

LUNACY.

BANKRUPTCY.

There is no system of laws, in this island, similar to the bankrupt code, in England. But the principal of the *cessio bonorum* is acknowledged, in the establishment of a court, for the relief of insolvent debtors. The remedy of course extends to persons who are not traders.

The law of descents, as regards freehold property, is the same, in this colony, as in England.

The law, governing the distribution of personal property, in cases of intestacy, in Barbados, is substantially the same, as the law, regulating the distribution, of the same species of property, in similar cases, in England.

BARBADOS.

CHANCERY.

The Court of Chancery is always open, and adjourns from time to time. It generally sits once in four weeks, and then from one day to four days; the length of the sitting, depending upon the quantity of business. Sometimes, in the hurricane season, it is adjourned for two or three months. From what the Commissioners could learn, it, sometimes, is not necessary, for the court to sit, for eight weeks and upwards. But the court must be always *open*, in case of need, to appoint a receiver to an estate, to prevent a crop being made away with.

PRACTICE.

The practice of the Court of Chancery in Barbados professes to conform to that of the Court of Chancery in England, except where it is altered by local laws, or special orders of their own.

There are above a hundred rules, prescribed by the court itself, written in a book kept by the registrar, often not at all known to persons practising in the profession. They in some instances establish a procedure different from the practice in England; as is the case particularly in regard to appraisements before sale of estates under a decree; *ne exeat insulas;* and injunctions. The early orders are often as might be expected, rude and uncouth, some very obscure and others ludicrous; the latter rules as far as they go, are generally wise and useful.

It is necessary upon the subject of mortgages,—to state just sufficient, to shew what course a mortgagee must pursue, to recover a mortgage-debt, in this island. The decree, made on a bill of foreclosure of a mortgage, is to this effect, that the money be paid into court, within a limited time, (usually a month,) and, in default of payment, a sale of the estate is directed. But to prevent a mischief, once very extensive, of estates being obtained, under these circumstances, for prices wholly inadequate, the property must be APPRAISED; and cannot be sold for less than the appraised value; without express leave from the court. The appraisement is made upon oath. The appraisers are freeholders and neighbours. They receive no fees. They are said, in general, to act conscientiously. The master cannot receive a bidding "under the appraisement." A bidder could not be held to a bidding below the estimate; but the master, it is said, reports such bidding to the court, and application is then made, for leave to sell for less than the appraised value. Upon this application, the court exercises a discretion, taking into its consideration the circumstances of the estate, and the question, whether an immediate sale is desirable? BARBADOS. CHANCERY.

The decree being, at once, for the sale of the estate, no further time is obtainable, by a defendant, for payment of the mortgage-money. But there have been recently, two cases, in which the court, with the consent of creditors, has given time, before a sale took place.

On a sale, after an appraisement, there is a deposit, which goes first to the payment of the costs of suit.

When a conveyance is made, under a sale in the master's office, though the decree is "that all proper parties "shall join in the conveyance," it was stated to be usual for the master to convey ALONE. Upon this I can only observe, that it is for a purchaser, to be advised, according to the facts, who are the *necessary parties*.

To this particular head of inquiry, may be more properly referred, certain cases brought before the Commissioners, complaining, generally, of "vexatious litigation "and ruinous expence." One was by a decayed gentleman of the name of Padmore, who stated, (I consider it best to give his own words)—"that estates in the co-"lonies are usually purchased on credit; a small por-"tion only of the purchase-money being paid down. A "mortgage, with a judgment or bond, is taken, as a se-"curity for the remainder and interest. As soon as a "bad season happens, and, owing to droughts or hurri-"canes, there is a failure of crops, interest gets in arrear, "or an instalment becomes due and cannot be paid; "when a hard creditor, of himself, or at the instigation "of a rich neighbour, who wants the estate, files his bill; "and then the ruin of the debtor is always considered "certain and complete. The law, instead of a shield to "protect him, is a two-edged sword in the hands of the "oppressor. In his (Mr. Padmore's) own case, where "the interest in arrear was 200*l.* the bill of costs came PADMORE'S CASE.

BARBADOS.

CHANCERY.

"to between 1000*l.* and 1100*l.* The estate, worth "17,000*l.* was sold for little more than 5000*l.* It was "appraised indeed, but considerably below its real "value, and not by freeholders of the immediate neigh-"bourhood, as it ought to have been." (Here there was an insinuation of connivance between a former master, and a gentleman, who, it was supposed wished to purchase the estate, but the Commissioners, though they permitted general observations, would not receive a particular charge, which, it was admitted, could not be substantiated by proof.) "The slaves he could have sold "separately (detached from the estate,) at a much higher "rate, but they came to him in a body, with most dis-"tressing cries, and threw themselves on the ground be-"fore him; when a spokesman, appointed by the rest, "fell down at his feet and implored him, in all their "names, not to separate them, both from himself and "the estate. They were ready to follow him, to the "other end of the island; but if he could not retain "them about himself; if his necessities compelled him, "to sell them; they besought him not to part friends "and relations; husbands and wives; parents and child-"ren; not to tear them from their houses and gardens, "but to let them go with the land. He could not resist "such an appeal, and he lost at least forty pounds a-head "by it. He could relate a variety of other cases, ex-"actly similar in circumstances and results, and, in com-"mon, with all other persons in the island, he had to "complain of the heavy expence of all law proceedings, "and the want of all confidence in the competency of the "judges."

## COMPLAINT OF MR. DRAKE.

DRAKE'S CASE.

This gentleman "had purchased an estate upon the "usual terms, for which he was to pay by instalments "of 1000*l.* each: of these, seven had been regularly "paid. He gave for the property 16,500*l.* and it was "sold for 8,000*l.* under a decree of the Court of Chan-

BARBADOS.

CHANCERY.

"cery. This was in 1813. There was at that time no "depreciation; on the contrary, the price of produce was "then at its highest: he had added twenty-five negroes. "If instead of being sold, the estate had been placed in "the hands of trustees, it would have cleared itself; or "if time had been given for the payment of the instal- "ment, on satisfying the interest then due, he could have "effected *that*, and would have, now, been doing well. "The estate was appraised, but it was sold for less than "the appraisement, and he had no notice, and did not "know, whether or when, the court was moved, for "leave to sell under the appraisement. The expense "of the suit were about 1000*l.* that is to say, so he un- "derstood, but no bill was ever delivered."

No proofs, oral or documentary, were produced by these gentlemen in support of their assertions.

In the registrar's return we found the following entries:—

| COMPLAINANTS. | DEFENDANTS. | TIME BILL FILED. | DATE OF FINAL DECREE. |
|---|---|---|---|
| 1811. Fawke & al. - | Padmore and al. - | 26 Sept. 1811. - | 21 Jan. 1812. |
| 1812. Went, extrix. - | Drake - | 25 Aug. 1812. - | 6 Oct. 1812. |

—by no means instances of tedious procrastination!

We were not able to trace the cases further, and had no means of ascertaining the accuracy of the *only* specific allegation; namely, that the law, as to appraisement and sale, had not been strictly complied with, in their instances, respectively. In other respects, their statements were, far, too general in their nature, and too wide in their application, to be capable of strict proof, or pointed contradiction. The only use the Commissioners could be justified in making, of relations of facts, so entirely unsupported, was, as MEDIA of information, through which they might arrive at more certain and accurate knowledge, from inquiries addressed to official persons. Accordingly, in framing the questions afterwards submitted to the attorney and solicitor-general, and others, they availed themselves largely of intelligence received through these and similar channels. In this manner, only, could they, IRREPROACHABLY, pro-

BARBADOS.

CHANCERY.

cure the information, of which they stood so greatly in need, or discharge, in any degree, however defectively, the arduous duties with which they were intrusted. When the answers were received, and could be examined with the statements, they served to remove many difficulties. The Commissioners could then discover, what was peculiar in the case, or common to it with others; what were defects in the system, or results of departure from it; what were irregularities; what were misapprehensions in the party, or what appeared wilful misrepresentations. Many charges of moment, but corroborated only by the general voice of the public, would, it is evident, be in a measure confirmed by feeble apology or prudent silence.

HUSBAND AND WIFE.

On behalf of a wife, for a separate maintenance, on account of misconduct in the husband, the remedy in Barbados, is sought by petition to this court. Relief, in such case, is never obtained by bill, but by petition.

The wife petitions by her next friend. The petition is answered by counter petition; evidence taken; and the question of misconduct entered into. Relief will be granted, although there was no agreement for a separate maintenance. The attorney-general said, "he knew "of no *law* for this, but it was an old established juris- "diction." The chief justice observed, "*Casus omissi* "in ecclesiastical matters are disposed of, in the court "of Chancery. There is no spiritual court here. No "divorce can be had, in the island. The governor has "a positive instruction against assenting to any bill "granting a divorce. Only two cases of crim. con. have "been known in the island."

REBITT'S COMPLAINT.

These statements served to explain a complaint the Commissioners received from a gentleman of the name of Rebitt, "of the jurisdiction, assumed by the court of "Chancery to entertain a petition, by a wife, for sepa- "rate maintenance, without covenant; not founded in- "deed, upon articles of agreement, between her and "her husband, but alleged ill treatment of the husband."

In England it is now the settled doctrine, according to the most recent decisions, that the court of Chancery

BARBADOS.

CHANCERY.

will not carry into execution, articles of separation between husband and wife, where no third party intervenes; the Spiritual Court having exclusive jurisdiction in granting divorce and alimony; and the court of Chancery not recognizing, in the parties, any power, to effect a partial dissolution of the marriage contract, or to vary the rights and duties arising from it. A FORTIORI, where there has been *no* agreement for the purpose, the court never decrees separation, and separate maintenance to the wife; and Lord Hardwicke distinctly said, "It is not in the power of the court to decree it."

Legard *v.* Johnson, 3 Ves. 361. Lord St. John *v.* Lady St. John, 11 Ves. 532. Wilkes *v.* Wilkes, 2 Dick. 791. Worrall *v.* Jacob, 3 Meriv. 268. Lady Head *v.* Sir Francis Head, 1 Ves. 17, S. C. 3 Atk. 547. more fully. Contra Guth *v.* Guth, 3 Bro. C. C. 614, the only instance, Lord Eldon says, (in 11 Ves. 532.) in which the court did enforce the deed.

During the Commonwealth, when there were no spiritual courts in England, the court of Chancery exercised jurisdiction, in cases of alimony, and the practice was, in all likelihood, followed by the colonies, which were much resorted to by adventurers and refugees; and were similarly circumstanced in respect to the absence of ecclesiastical courts. But upon the re-establishment of courts Christian in England, the court of Chancery no longer retained the jurisdiction, and when a bill was afterwards brought, for alimony, in that court, a demurrer was allowed. And as the court of Chancery has certainly no jurisdiction to decree a divorce, to which the power of giving alimony is consequent and incidental, the authority thus exercised in the court of Chancery, in Barbados, appears to me, at the least very questionable. But supposing it to be an encroachment, it may still be, and I am certainly inclined to think, it is, a necessary and a useful jurisdiction.

[1] 2 Shower Rep. 288. 2 Vern. 493.

Of matters, clearly within the authority of a court of equity, but local or peculiar, we observed the following:

Where the husband can sue alone, for the recovery of property belonging to him, in right of his wife, by virtue of an ASSIGNMENT from her, under a particular law of the island; there is reason to fear, the court could not, as in other cases, direct a provision to be made for her and her children: a strong objection to such a law!

A husband cannot, without an examination of the wife in the usual form, ASSIGN money due to a wife (under the same act, No. 172, Halls Laws;) but it is considered

Hall's Laws, No. 172, cl. 2.

BARBADOS

CHANCERY.

TIME.

that he may DISCHARGE it; that is, receive the money and give an effectual receipt!

Where a suit is heard on bill and answer only, and the plaintiff and defendant reside in the island, a decree is obtained, it is said, in *three* or *four* months after the filing of a bill. *Five* or *six* were afterwards mentioned to us with much greater probability. Three months and fourteen days is the shortest possible period. By order of the court the cause must be on the list A MONTH. The motion, for further time, is not a motion of course.

Where evidence is entered into, and the evidence required is obtainable in the island, though it must, in some degree, depend upon the number of witnesses, to be examined, a decree may be usually obtained in *about twelve months*. The attorney-general "has known three "or four years, but it has been much expedited of late;" the chief justice, indeed, stated that "now there is great "despatch."

1759. Ordered, "*That in future the Registrar do not receive any answer without oath, notwithstanding the consent of the parties.*"

The delay occasioned, where any of the parties to a suit, or the witnesses or documentary evidence, are out of the island, it is impossible to estimate. It appears by the MS. orders that an answer has been taken without oath, to save time and expense. Where a commission is sent out, a limited time (*six months*) is generally allowed for the return; and application afterwards made for further time. Being very expensive, a commission is rarely resorted to.

There is no examiner in this island; the registrar acts as examiner.

References by decrees are made to the master, and not to an accountant. Where a reference has been made, to take accounts, and all the accounting parties reside in the island, as far as can be ascertained, depending, as it must, on the length and intricacy of the accounts, it is said to be about *two years*, in general, before a final decree is obtained. But the chief justice said, "Being "a matter of accounting, it is sometimes very tedious; "we had lately a cause since 1751."

References are made to the master, without naming

BARBADOS.

CHANCERY. RECEIVERS.

The question whether this court ever made an order for a receiver over real or personal property; or to whom the appointment of a receiver was referred; the proceedings; security required; time of passing his accounts; &c. &c. were not brought under the consideration of the Commissioners, in this island, as they were in others,—by its becoming the subject of complaint,—either that members of council, and consequently judges of the court, were often appointed to the situation; or that no security was given for the due discharge of the trust; or that the accounts were not regularly passed before the master.

Absent defendants, and absconding debtors.

An act, (No. 201, Hall's Laws, founded on statute 5 Geo. 2. c. 25,) directs the manner in which process, in courts of equity, may be rendered effectual "against "persons who abscond, to avoid personal service, or "having estate or effects in the island reside in parts be-"yond the seas, and cannot be served with such process "or who refuse to appear." This act and the next, No. 202, to enable creditors to recover their just debts out of the effects of their absent or absconding debtors, by means of a process, in the nature of foreign attachments in London, were originally comprised in one bill, but were properly severed, under the instruction, that no two different matters should be put into one act. They are both *confirmed* acts. The former has not been found very effectual, and is little acted upon. A MS. act, framed upon the 38 Geo. 3. c. 87. applies a remedy in cases where executors, having qualified, have afterwards left the island; a law which I conceive is likely to answer the intended purpose, and prove very often useful.

MONEY PAID INTO COURT.

There appear to have been veryfew instances, where monies have been directed to be paid into court, and then in sums, not exceeding 200*l*. Monies are paid sometimes to the registrar; sometimes to the master; *either* will have a poundage. Under an order of the court of the 17th September 1810, the master gives security "for the "due and faithful discharge of the duties of his office." They have no accountant-general, or bank, or public office, where monies might be lodged and made produc-

Rules and orders, 1810

BARBADOS.

CHANCERY.

tive. The solicitor-general said, "I think there ought to "be some public office where monies might be lodged "and made productive."

Injunctions are granted by the governor, *ex parte* and alone, because, it is said, "it would not do, to await the "assembling of the members of the Court of Chancery, "as, in the mean time the mischief, sought to be pre- "vented, might be done." This is undeniable, where the case is urgent, and proceeds, upon the ground of preventing irretrievable injury; but such reason applies only to cases of "waste," or mischief in the nature of "waste;" or what may be equally pressing in commercial affairs, the negotiation of a bill or note improperly obtained; or in case of an insolvent executor getting in the assets before probate; or any other matter of urgent necessity, when there cannot be a *compensation*, to prevent irreparable mischief; and not commonly to injunctions, to stay proceedings at law, the instances, in which abuses are most probable and chiefly suspected. In such cases, in England, for the most part, injunctions are only obtained, upon the defendant's answer, or when he is in contempt, for want of an answer; unless upon special application. That, which is done, in England, in certain cases only, from absolute necessity, and for the prevention of wrongs,—the granting an injunction, immediately, before the service of the subpœna, and without notice to the opposite party, is, here, the ordinary practice in every case; with what propriety, gentlemen, familiar with the doctrines and practice of courts of equity, are most competent to decide.

1 Ves. 474. 3 Bro. C.C. 376. Kimpton and Eve, 2 Ves. and Bea. 351. 1 Fonbl. Equ. 43. *in not.*

INJUNCTIONS.

A petition is presented to the governor, signed by counsel, who however do not consider themselves answerable, for the facts, stated in the petition. A bill is filed with the registrar, and an affidavit annexed. Usually a short bill is filed first, and after the injunction is granted, a motion is made to amend the bill. The injunction is granted, as of course, and at the next court, a motion may be made to dissolve it. But a party must, first, put in his answer, before he can move to dissolve the injunction.

Injunctions, obtainable in this island, appear to be of

BARBADOS.

CHANCERY.

*Rules and Orders.*

the same nature, as those granted in England, and issuable generally for the same reasons. Much of the propriety of granting injunctions, *ex parte*, must depend upon the form of the affidavit required. By an order of this court of 1799, a party must swear "that the facts "upon which he founds his equity are true."—An excellent provision; and I believe, not practised in England, in obtaining the common injunction. But in *some* cases, I apprehend, a party ought to *do more*; to stay trial for want of an answer he ought to state his belief that the discovery, expected from the answer, will be material to the just trial of the action.

The attorney-general believed the form of the affidavit to be *too loose*, and that injunctions have been obtained with too great facility. The solicitor general thought "they might sometimes" be applied for, for purposes of delay, 'but not often:' the chief justice said, "Injunc-"tions have heretofore been sometimes kept up for seven "years. There was one lately, and it was settled in four "weeks." The injunction, in the former case, could not have been made, that "hard pillow to sleep on," which Lord Bacon recommends, "that if the plaintiff "prosecutes not with effect, he may perhaps, when he is "awake, find not only his injunction dissolved, but his "cause dismissed."

Bacon's works, vol. 4. p. 494.

Delays, by means of injunctions, were frequently complained of; but many remedies have, at different times, been applied to this vexatious evil; and, we were assured, with tolerable success. By No. 52 of rules and orders, relating to injunctions *before* judgment, it is ordered 'that they must issue seven days before the third 'court, or court for trial in the Common Pleas.'

By order nineteen, when an injunction is *granted* 'in 'any cause wherein issue is joined, it is to be expressed 'in the injunction that the plaintiff may proceed to trial, 'but not to entry of judgment.'

Rules and orders: "answered" in the copy.

By order twenty-five, explained by order seventy-three, to obtain an injunction *after* judgment, the complainant must 'deposit the money or goods recovered, with 'costs, &c. or give treble security;' "so that if he will be

Rules and orders, 25 and 73.

Lord Bacon, vol. 4.

BARBADOS.

CHANCERY.

"relieved against a judgment at common law, upon "matter of equity, he shall do it *tanquam in vinculis*, at "his peril."

These appear to me to be salutary regulations, but I speak upon such points with great diffidence.

NE EXEAT INSULA. Rules and orders.

In all petitions to the Chancellor (the course being by PETITION) for writs of *ne exeat insula*, an order of 23d Oct. 1822, (the only order appearing upon the subject,) 'vacates and sets aside all rules and orders, or any practice 'previously subsisting and prevailing contrary thereto.'

APPEALS.

An appeal lies, from a decision of this court, to his Majesty in council, if the sum sought to be recovered amounts to 500*l.* sterling. An appeal, it is said, lies only on a decree, or such interlocutory order, as amounts to a final decree. Security is given, for treble the value of the property in dispute, and for all costs and damages, occasioned by the appeal. The appeal, it is also said, suspends all proceedings, even in the master's office, as the taking accounts, &c. but the party who has obtained the decree or judgment appealed against, will not be prevented from pursuing his advantage to levy and sale, on giving security in double the sum, to make a return to the appellant if the decree should be reversed; in other words, a provisional payment takes place, with security for restitution. The appellant also gives security to prosecute the appeal within a year.

Tobago and Grenada Answers contra.

FEES and COSTS.

There was a table of fees under consideration, for this court, during the stay of the Commissioners, which was meant to be established by the authority of the court it self. The judges of the court consider themselves as having a control over fees: but the claim, it will be found, does not pass unquestioned. There are several acts in Hall, relative to fees and costs, said to be "of "dubious import," and denied to apply to the solicitors and barristers of the Court of Chancery; these, preposterous as they are, paying,

No 6, Hall's Laws.

| | |
|---|---|
| For filing a bill of complant . . | 50lbs. of sugar. |
| For filing an answer or demurrer | 40 ditto. |

No. 44, Hall's Laws.

or by a later act,

| | |
|---|---|
| For each sheet . . . . . . . | 4lbs. of sugar. |

BARBADOS. — CHANCERY.

have never been repealed, but are still existing, though not in use. These pounds of sugar may be commuted for money, at 12*s*. 6*d*. per cwt. The only act, clearly applying to compensation for *professional* services, is No. 53, Hall's Laws, which limits the allowance "UPON "ANY BILL OF COSTS" *eo nomine, and expressly*. The fees there allowed, are not the fees taken; but they are the fees which the solicitors SWEAR that they will take, "and no others." The oath will be found in Hall's Laws, No. 53, "An act to prevent the abuse of lawyers "and multiplicity of law suits." After reciting that "pleaders at law in the courts of the island have been "too much exacting in their fees, and that it often hap-"pened that many were retained, on the same side, so "that their pleadings were reiterated, and the courts "much troubled thereby," it forbids the employment of more than two, in any one cause, upon pain of "2000lbs. "of sugar;" and directs, that upon "the taxation of "costs no more shall be allowed than 100lbs. of sugar in "any plain case, and 200lbs. in any special case, for "lawyers' fees." And every attorney is still compelled to take the shocking oath "that he will increase no fees, "but be contented with, and neither directly or indirectly "take more than the set fee in this act." The fees are inadequate, and the oath improper; both, I submit, require to be altered.

No. 53. Hall's Laws.

COSTS.

Costs are, or ought to be, taxed by the registrar or the master, under order of the court. In general, when the solicitors on each side agree on the bill of costs, no taxation ever takes place. This is very improper; but no doubt the client can insist on the taxation of bills, so approved. It was a theme of universal complaint that the expences of this court were *intolerable*; and it was frequently objected that the attornies did not deliver their bills to their clients. As we were informed, with regard to the practice in the master's office, bills of costs are carried by the solicitor to the master, who taxes them, summoning the attornies, on both sides, to be present at the taxation.

BARBADOS.

CHANCERY.

It is left doubtful, from the answers we received, how far the distinction of costs between party and party, and attorney and client, would be recognized here. It does not prevail in practice, and was not familiar in name.

MR. REBITT'S COMPLAINT.

To this head belongs another complaint preferred by Mr. Rebitt. He begged to " offer, for the consideration " of the Commissioners, the bill of costs in a case Rebitt " *v.* Agard. Agard was in contempt, yet the estate (for " so it was decreed,) was to pay *his* costs. The amount " of the costs was 3,283*l.* 6*s.* 6*d.* thus,—

| | | | | | | |
|---|---|---|---|---|---|---|
| Defendant Croney, | | | | | | |
| Counsel's fees - - - | £. 447 | 6 | - | £ | *s.* | *d.* |
| Solicitor's fees - - - | 268 | 17 | 6 | | | |
| Registrar's fees - - - | 67 | 11 | 6 | | | |
| Master's fees - - - | 2 | - | - | | | |
| | | | | 785 | 15 | - |
| Defendant Agard, | | | | | | |
| Counsel's fees - - - | £. 447 | 6 | - | | | |
| Solicitor's fees - - - | 296 | 15 | - | | | |
| Registrar's fees - - - | 78 | 15 | 4 | | | |
| Master's fees - - - | 4 | 7 | 6 | | | |
| | | | | 827 | 3 | 10 |
| Defendant Prudence Serjeant, | | | | | | |
| Counsel's fees - - - | £. 223 | 13 | - | | | |
| Solicitor's fees - - - | 237 | 3 | - | | | |
| Registrar's fees - - - | 66 | 18 | 2 | | | |
| Master's fees - - - | 2 | - | - | | | |
| | | | | 529 | 14 | 2 |
| Complainant's - - - | £. 2 | - | - | | | |
| Counsel's fees - - - | 444 | 16 | - | | | |
| Solicitor's fees - - - | 291 | 18 | - | | | |
| Registrar's fees - - - | 118 | 9 | 6 | | | |
| Master's fees - - - | 283 | 10 | - | | | |
| | | | | 1,140 | 13 | 6 |
| Total amount of costs of suit - | | | | £. 3,283 | 6 | 8 |

"He (Mr. Rebitt,) possessed himself of the bill of costs, "*by stealth*. Bills are never delivered by attornies to "their clients; they agree upon them, among them-"selves, and then hand them to the master. Not only "were these enormous expences incurred, but the law-"yers having a lien, for them, upon the land, the estate "in this case, was kept for a length of time in the mas-"ter's hands, while he, (Mr. Rebitt) who had an interest "in two-thirds of it, was suffered to lie in gaol. He had "published the amount of the costs in this case: this "gave great offence, and a principal attorney told him "he would never be attended to in the courts, after-"wards; indeed he had been persecuted ever since. In "one case he had been arrested and held to bail in a "thousand pounds, in an action for words spoken. In "another, where he was prosecuting a person for per-"jury, the counsel moved the court that the prosecutor "could not give evidence in perjury, and his name was "struck off, before the indictment was sent to the grand "jury. The lower class of whites in this island were so "oppressed by the lawyers, as to be worse off than the "slaves; and *they* would look upon it as an EMANCIPA-"TION, and hail it as the first of blessings to have a "judge appointed from England. These persons (the "lower class of whites) had been prevented from coming "to the Commissioners, in numbers, by means of intimi-"dation and misrepresentation; for instance, it was in-"dustriously given out (to prevent their coming) that the "Commissioners were sent to inquire into the cases "of persons of colour only. The instant the Commis-"sioners left the country, God bless those who had been "to them! Let them appear in court if they dare! "Now, witnesses enter the box under terror; they are "sure of being abused; it is more a court of scandal "than of law; it is nothing like a court of JUSTICE at "any time, and for law, what has been law to-day, is not "law to-morrow."

Of the regularity of the proceedings in the courts of law, and the uniformity of *their* decisions, it would be

BARBADOS.

CHANCERY.

inconvenient to speak, at present, while the subject under consideration, is the conduct of the court of Chancery. But those parts of Mr. Rebitt's statement, which complain of difficulties interposed in the way of persons, desirous of attending before the Commissioners, and of hostility apprehended by others who *had* preferred complaints, render a few observations upon these particular points, not only excusable, but absolutely necessary.

The doors of the Commissioners were thrown widely open to receive complaints and representations of every kind; provided only they DID relate, more or less intimately, to the administration of justice. A notice, the most explicit, was, publicly, given of their daily attendance for that purpose. There was nothing apparent or palpable (whatever secret influence might be exercised, and that was only surmised) to prevent or impede any person inclined to visit them. The Commission, however unacceptable to a very few persons, interested in the reigning abuses, was, most generally, regarded as a signal proof of his Majesty's paternal attention to the best interests of the colony. Far from experiencing opposition, we had reason to acknowledge civilities and valuable assistance, from persons of all parties, particularly from the governor, the president, several members of council, and eminently so from Mr. Alleyne, chief justice of Hole Town, the attorney and solicitor-general, Mr. Hinds, before alluded to as an eminent barrister, Mr. Moore, another public-spirited gentleman of the bar, the speaker[2] of the House of Assembly, and Messrs. Bascome and Pile, members of the same.

[2] The Hon. Cheeseman Moe.

The direction of the judge on the prosecution for perjury, proceeded undoubtedly, upon a mistake of the law, and was acknowledged to be an error. The arrest, for unliquidated damages, in an action for words, without a special order of a judge obtained for such purpose, would be considered, in England, a great irregularity; but it is the common practice here.

The costs *do* appear shameful and oppressive. But upon this subject (of fees and costs) I shall abstain from

BARBADOS.

CHANCERY.

all remarks at present, and at a future time, when a review of all the courts in this island is concluded, observe upon them generally.

SECURITY FOR COSTS.

Security for costs is ordered in the court of Chancery, in Barbados, as in England; with this difference in the *cases*, that, here, security is always required when a party leaves the island; aud with this improvement in the MODE, that the security is not limited to 40*l.* It is not a settled sum, but such security, as the circumstances may require.

PROCEEDINGS IN COURT.

As directed by your Lordship in our instructions, we attended the first sitting of the Court of Chancery held after our arrival in the island, and heard a cause of considerable importance. The court was employed from eleven till half-past three o'clock in reading the bill, the answer, and the depositions. On inquiry we learnt, with surprise, that the judges of this court *never have before them*, and *never take home*, any papers, so that they affect to remember, accurately, a detail of important facts which required four hours and a half to read; and, in most cases, after hearing counsel, decide immediately! To satisfy ourselves of the accuracy of our conclusions upon this head, we consulted the chief justice, who is also a judge of this court. Judge Lucas observed, "to read the papers I go to the registrar's office; I "cannot have the papers *out*." Whether any of the other members of the council, were in the habit of attending the office for this purpose, was not stated. The solicitor-general, it will be seen, made a pertinent remark upon this extraordinary mode of proceeding: "he had often wondered that not in general having the "evidence and pleadings before them, and not being "professional men, they could decide, as well as they "did. If they wanted to see any papers in a case, "they must get them from the solicitor, or go to the re-"gistrar's office." At four o'clock, the court adjourned till next day, to hear the arguments. The Commissioners again attended. The speeches, were long and eloquent. At the close of every hour the counsel were

BARBADOS. — CHANCERY.

refreshed with a fee, charged "for hearing and ad- "dressing the court;" and then the cause proceeded with increased vigor and animation. The cases cited were numerous, involving nice points, and turning upon subtle distinctions; a little, it is to be feared, beyond the comprehension of the best informed country gentlemen, not qualified by previous education and habits, for the discharge of judicial duties. The governor candidly stated his regret that it was part of his duty to act as chancellor; it being the most disagreeable part of his office.

It has been seen, that the governor, acting as chancellor, has no assessor or other professional adviser of any kind, duly qualified. But, in this island, the court of Chancery is composed of the governor and council, and it remains to be stated, that none of the present members of council, except Mr. Beckles, son of the attorney-general, and to the extent afterwards mentioned, have received a regular legal education, or have been admitted to the bar. Mr. Lucas, the chief judge of the island, was a surgeon by profession. Mr. J. A. Beckles was entered at one of the inns of court in England, and resided a few years, but was not called to the bar; and on coming to Barbados, he acted as a licentiate barrister for a short time previous to his being made a judge.

Judges, unfitness of.

All the members of council, with the exception of the governor, are gentlemen owning considerable estates in the colony, and of the first respectability. Besides possessing property in their own rights, some of them are attornies of estates, on behalf of absent proprietors. One of them is a clergyman. By means of the various duties and relations, thus created; by social intercourse, by nativity, marriage, or otherwise; they are all intimately connected with the members of the colonial society in which they live. Brian Edwards says, that when a similar composition of the court of Chancery was proposed in the island of St. Christopher, "the attempt "met with decided opposition, on the ground of the in-

BARBADOS.

CHANCERY.

"conveniency of having on the chancery bench, judges, "some of whom it is probable, from their situation and "connections, may be interested in the event of every "suit, that may come before them." It would be difficult to say that the objection was not founded in reason and truth.

But there will be found upon examination, to be other defects in such a constitution of the court, and some of them intrinsic. If the judges of the other courts, are excluded from the court of Chancery, there remains little probability of a single lawyer being found upon the bench. The court is then composed of judges, honourable and well-intentioned in the highest degree, but ignorant of the law; inexperienced in dealing with facts; of necessity often connected with the parties; privately conusant of facts, localities, and secret history; anxious for a decision; impatient to return to their homes and avocations; unwilling to be summoned again; urged in short by various considerations, to an immediate judgment, upon the most difficult points and complex cases. If, on the other hand, the *judges* are admitted to be members of council, as such (besides mixing the legislative with the judicial character by which it sometimes happens that the same persons try an indictment who had before directed the prosecution,) they sit in a court of Chancery, which is often applied to for injunctions to stay proceedings in the courts of law, as well as form part of a court of Error, constituted for the express purpose of reviewing the decisions of the judges in the inferior courts. The objection is recognized, not removed, by a regulation that they shall not VOTE. They still sit in the court, and, from their presence alone, exercise the unavoidable influence, inseparably belonging to their responsible character and judicial station.

See post, Court of Error.

The body, of which the court is composed, being in its nature fluctuating,—and attendance uncertain and irregular,—the members of this court cannot always be the same; hence proceedings in the same cause may be inconveniently discussed before different judges, and judges

BARBADOS.

CHANCERY.

may decide, who have not heard the evidence or pleadings.

Not to dwell upon minor objections, the strongest repugnance is naturally felt at seeing the business of this court, (the principal tribunal for deciding cases of property,) judicially administered by persons who are not lawyers; for although the disposition to do right, and to decide conformably to law, in every member of the court, will be cheerfully acknowledged, yet the want of legal education exposes them to continual errors, occasions a want of confidence in their decisions, and is the cause of great expense, vexation, and in some instances, delay.

The chief justice said, "I am satisfied that quick and "substantial justice is afforded."

"The judges," said the attorney-general, "are not "lawyers; and it would be desirable to have a regu- "lar-bred lawyer at the head of the court of Chancery."

The solicitor-general thought "that justice was as "fairly, impartially, and expeditiously administered, *as* "*it could be under existing circumstances.*"

Mr. Hinds said, with perfect accuracy, that "when "they (the judges of this court) erred, it was for want "of information."

Corruption, it is my duty to report, (and I am highly gratified to make the representation,) was never imputed to any judge, in a single instance.

## COURT OF EXCHEQUER.

By the Chief Baron.

The court of Exchequer derives its authority from a law of the island, (No. 135, Hall's Laws) and from the governor's commission. It was formerly considered as possessing both an equity and a common-law jurisdiction. There is now no equity side of the Exchequer except on the part of the Crown; the commission is said to have been altered about forty years ago. The common-law side remains, but the right to sue in it is explained and limited by the act before cited. (No. 135). That

BARBADOS.

EXCHEQUER.

act recites, that to avoid the effect of the court-act, 28, Hall's Laws, (which required that in all actions, brought in the court of Common Pleas, the venue should be laid where the *defendant* lives) "persons have been "induced, to bring actions, in this court of Exchequer, "under pretence only of being debtors and accountants "to his sacred Majesty, against divers persons in the "island, living in different precincts; and that in conse-"quence of the unexpected adjournments of the court, "defendants have been surprised, and judgment passed "against them by default, and executions immediately "issued, to their great prejudice; and then directs that "only the governor, and certain officers there enume-"rated, and those who take the oath therein prescribed, "shall sue in this court." It is now, in effect, a court for the recovery of the King's debts only, where informations for breach of the revenue laws are filed, and little other business transacted.

This court is composed of the chief baron and four puisne barons, of whom *three* may hear and determine; and the judges are appointed by the governor, with the advice and consent of the majority of the council. They have no salary. The chief baron, and, in his absence, the senior baron, receives certain fees; the same as the chief justice of the court of Common Pleas. Any deed, affecting real property, requires to be registered, and a fee is paid on the acknowledgment. They also receive seal-money; fees for taking private examinations of married women, &c. &c. The officers of the court are the remembrancer and marshal; both patent offices, performed by deputy.

The court of Exchequer sits in the town-hall, in Bridge Town, and is appointed to be holden once every four weeks, on a Friday, throughout the year, for the trial of causes between party and party; but, for his Majesty's business, it may sit at any time. It actually sits, only as often as business requires, which is very seldom. It is not occupied more than four times a year.

By the chief baron's commission, his authority on the equity side, is limited to business between his Majesty

BARBADOS. EXCHEQUER.

and his subjects; but no instance existed, in the recollection of either the bench or bar, of any such bill having been filed. It is the same with much of the jurisdiction on the law-side of the court; no action, of which either the chief baron or the attorney-general were aware, having been brought, at any time, under the affidavit, by a Crown debtor. A few actions are occasionally brought by other privileged persons, but little business is transacted except on seizures for breach of the revenue laws; and for these the court of admiralty would in certain cases, have a concurrent jurisdiction.

7 & 8 Wm. 3. c. 22.

This court however is found to possess another—different—and very dissimilar authority. It is also a court *for the relief of insolvent debtors.* But this jurisdiction is of a nature quite distinct from its fiscal character, and is given by a law of the island. I have reason to believe that it is a wholesome power, and exercised very usefully; but it will require to be renewed, at frequent intervals; the present law only extending to persons, who had been confined, for three months before the passing of the act.

The judges of this court profess to be governed by the laws of England and the laws of the island. They did not appear to have any collection of rules or orders of the court, prescribing any peculiar modes of practice; so that where they differ from the practice of the courts in England, the variation is not recorded. Proceedings on the common-law side of this court, for the recovery of debts, are by information by the attorney-general, on behalf of the Crown, and *quo minus* by private persons. A defendant may be arrested for any sum exceeding 8*l.* whether claimed as a debt, or damages; and the latter may be unliquidated. For an alleged libel upon the attorney-general, a defendant, who was afterwards acquitted, was held to bail in 3,000*l.* For a demand, under the amount stated, (8*l.*) a bench action lies. A bench action is in the nature of the English courts of conscience, and will be considered, when I report upon the court of Common Pleas. Those freeholders, who are qualified to vote at elections, are exempted from arrest by process of this court. If bail are objected to, their sufficiency is deter-

Barbados.

Exchequer.

mined by the chief baron. If a defendant cannot procure bail, he may lie in prison an indefinite time; the plaintiff cannot be compelled to proceed with the action, and the defendant does not become supersedeable, on account of the plaintiff's neglect. The attorney-general's reply to the question of the Commissioners was in the following words: "I do not know that a plaintiff is "bound to proceed, and a defendant cannot supersede "himself: THAT IS a hardship." And yet a person thus imprisoned for debt, on mesne process, (which is only intended to compel appearance,) for a period of time of which the duration is uncertain and depends upon his adversary's pleasure, never becomes entitled to any allowance from the plaintiff, for his support. Under any circumstances, indeed, there is no allowance to debtors in prison; not to a debtor in execution. It is proper however to state that when this practice, as to the want of supersedeas, was mentioned to the chief baron, he said, "If the objection came before me, I should rule the "plaintiff to proceed, and if he did not, I should strike "out the cause." The feeling did him honour: but for the law, and the previous practice, the learning and experience of the attorney-general must be depended on.

There are no records of these courts on parchment; but copies of the proceedings are made up upon paper and kept by the proper officer.

The execution, issuing upon a judgment recovered in this court, is the same as in the court of Common Pleas; except that executions out of this court are levied all the year round, as well in vacation as term time.

The process of the court of Exchequer in England at the suit of the Crown, is supposed not to be executable in this island. Extents it was observed, are *not used here:* it should rather be said, they are used upon every occasion; such is the formidable nature of their execution. It deserves notice, that the act No. 135, regulating the course and form of proceeding on a judgment in the Exchequer, contains a saving of the rights of the Crown. But the information we were able to procure, relating to

No. 135, Hall's Laws.

BARBADOS.
EXCHEQUER.

this court, which is almost disused, and has no lawyer upon the bench, was very scanty and imperfect.

Actions, in this court, are said to be less dilatory, but more expensive, than proceedings in the other courts. Process is shorter, and a judgment more expeditiously obtained, but the fees are higher; both the fees of office and the counsel's fees.

Costs are taxed by the chief baron himself, agreeably to a docket established by him, under the authority of the governor. There is now a table of fees, which has been lately promulgated. Before that was established, the amount of fees depended entirely on CUSTOM. Of this court, it was again complained, but less specifically, that there were no regular costs, and that the fees were not the statutory ones. The same representation was made (as of the Court of Chancery), that where the attornies agree, bills of costs are never taxed. But in answer to this allegation we received a positive assurance, from the judge himself, that costs *are taxed* by the present chief baron, "always and agreeably to the docket." But the docket had been *lately* promulgated.

The attorney-general was of opinion, and no doubt rightly, that a writ of error lies from a decision of this court to the court of appeal and error in the island; the same as from the Court of Common Pleas. He never knew an appeal in revenue cases, but supposed there might be one. The chief baron was not aware of any writ of error—but only of an appeal to his Majesty in council, (which is ulterior, where the value is sufficient;) of which he remembered one instance, arising on a penal statute.

The Attorney-general thought it desirable that "a "lawyer" should preside in this court. The present chief baron is a very respectable merchant.

## COURT OF COMMON PLEAS.

There are FIVE courts of Common Pleas in Barbados; one being held in each of five districts of the island. They

BARBADOS.

COMMON PLEAS.

derive their authority from acts of the local legislature. They have the same jurisdiction as the court of Common Pleas in England, except as to fines and recoveries. The judicial establishment consists of a chief judge and four assistant judges in each court. These are appointed and removable in the same manner as the other judges, and the tenure of their offices is the same. They have no salary; the chief judge (only) receives the customary fees for proving deeds; taking examinations of married women, touching the transfer of property, &c. &c. But the amount of all the fees of the judges of the five courts, is supposed not to exceed 1,200*l.* currency per annum. "When they go out of their office," says the attorney-general, "perhaps to a lady in the country (a practice he "considers useful when persons are *in extremis*), they "receive something more, than their commission-fees." The ordinary fee is 1*l.*, but (as we were told) where a judge goes to a party's house "he expects to be paid "*liberally;* he then usually gets 5*l.*"

Substitution for Fines and Recoveries.

An act, No. 31, Hall's Laws, will serve to throw some light upon the occasion and nature of some of these acknowledgments. An old law restored by that act has the following recital: "For that the King's writs do not "run here, whereby fines and recoveries cannot be had "or levied, and yet here is as much and more use and "need of them, &c." enacts, that "a deed duly made, "&c. shall be valid to pass estates, without livery."

"But to pass an estate of freehold or inheritance, or "lease for above three years, a deed must be *acknowledg-"ed* before the governor, or one of the chief judges, and "*recorded,* at length, in the office of the secretary of the "island, within three months, &c."

There was *one* exception to the rule, requiring deeds which pass any estate of inheritance to be *enrolled.*

No. 42, Hall's Laws.

Slaves, by a law of the island, were made real property, but with a proviso, that persons, disposing of them, should not be obliged to enrol such sales "as is necessary "in the alienation of other real estates." By another act, slaves continue chattels, for the payment of debts,

BARBADOS.

COMMON PLEAS.

and may be sued for and recovered by action† personal. And *now* the act, declaring slaves real estate, is repealed, and deeds of sale, &c. of slaves, must be duly proved or acknowledged and *recorded*.

†*Detinue.*

No. 59, Moore's Laws. On a *demise of slaves to a lessee* there are usually appraisements, at the beginning and at the end of the term, and the lease contains covenants to pay for reduction in numbers and value; which has a tendency to prevent the negroes being returned diminished, or deteriorated.

No. 31, Hall's Laws. By the act first referred to, a *feme covert* "minded to "aliene her jointure, dower, &c. is to come before the "governor or any other chief judge, and be privately "asked, &c." By the same act, and from analogy no doubt to the operation and effect of a fine in England, "*five* years quiet possession is a good title to land, ex- "cepting such persons only as shall prosecute their title "to the same, within two years after the act, and mar- "ried women, &c. &c. prosecuting within one year after "the disabilities removed."

And by clause 9, it is still more expressly declared, for avoiding disputes, that it shall "be a good plea in "*bar* of such actions concerning titles to land, for the "defendant, to allege, that he, or they, whose estate he "hath, have been in quiet and peaceable possession, of "the land, in question, for and during the space of five "years." We were present upon an occasion, when such a possessory title was relied upon with complete success.

SITTINGS. The sittings of the courts are regulated by the statutes of the island. Each court sits, in its own precinct. Great complaints were at one time made of the courts being held irregularly. The attorney-general says, "they in general sit regularly *now*, as prescribed by the "acts." The solicitor-general confines this observance of the acts, to the capital, for a very sufficient reason. "The Bridge courts sit regularly, but the sittings of the "out courts are not equally exact; for they have not "always business; and it would only be oppressing ju- "rors, and other persons, to oblige them to attend, when "there is no business." The business at the out courts, "when there is any," seldom occupies more than *one*† day.

BARBADOS.

COMMON PLEAS.

†Prothonotary.

The sittings of the court appear to be sufficiently frequent, in my apprehension, if they were regular. There may, at one period, have been reason to object not to the *infrequency* but to the SHORTNESS of the sitting. It takes place monthly, from the last Monday in January, to the twenty-sixth of September, and lasts four days (in Bridge Town); but on certain statute holidays, and *on all saints days*, the courts do not sit; and, if it is a holyday, on the first court day, the court cannot, or does not, sit, on *any one of the four days;* proceeding on the notion that they must be *consecutive* days. I should, perhaps, except Bridge Town, where, upon such occasions, it does, we were informed, sit "*sometimes.*" The attorney-general said, "it is very inconvenient having so "many holidays." We endeavoured to ascertain what was the consequence of the monthly courts not sitting, and how proceedings were affected by it: The attorney-general said, "most of them go on; at least such as "can: trials of course are delayed." The third court is the court, when the defendant on bailable process, according to the practice of the island, is ruled to plead to the declaration. We asked what would be the effect of the first day of *such* court happening on a holiday: the attorney-general said, "Since you must take the rule in "court as the law now is, you cannot plead if the court "does not sit, and debtors of course delay as much as "they can." Inconvenience it is obvious, must be felt, from the suspension of proceedings. Owing to a circumstance of this kind the court did not sit from September 1822 till the end of February 1823. Certain cases however, are provided for by one of the manuscript acts.

HOLIDAYS.

As to the sufficiency of the time, (FOUR consecutive days) it is admitted, that formerly, the amount of business brought before the court at each sitting, was greatly more than they could execute with facility, in the given time. "For many months," says the attorney-general, "you could not get through." Now, it is said, they

BARBADOS.

COMMON PLEAS.

"generally get *through the paper* in the four days of the "sitting of the court," though "sometimes there will be "a hundred causes in the paper." The prothonotary has only known two instances in twelve years, of the *list* not "being gone through." There is generally however, "something left untried." Causes, in which "the par-"ties are not ready, &c." These remain on the list, and the court begins next month, where it left off.

No. 109, Hall's Laws, cl. 14.

No. 28, Hall's Laws.

Actions are commenced in these courts, by filing a declaration in the office, and serving a copy of it, together with a summons, upon the defendant personally, or at his last place of abode; except in cases of arrest. Arrests are made, by virtue of a process nnder the hand and seal of the governor, addressed to the provost-marshal or his lawful deputy. Appearance is made, on the second court day after service of the summons.

RULES AND ORDERS.

The rules of practice in these courts are said to vary a little from those of the court of Common Pleas in England. But the local regulations are not printed; and the solicitor-general, who told us they existed, had never seen them in manuscript, and believed they were not written. Being thus *traditionary*, and the knowledge of them confined to few persons, we could never discover what they were, or by whom or when established; with the exception only of one order to enforce the attendance of jurors in the precinct of Saint James; other rules sent to us being merely minutes of proceedings in court.

TIME.

A judgment may be obtained in general, on an action in this court, within a twelvemonth; a representation which the returns support. The prothonotary stated that "eighty actions, out of a hundred, were tried at the fourth (monthly) court." Yet a *continuance* is obtained, whenever a party says he has a special defence, and this more than once, without cause shewn as it ought to be, supported by affidavit. The other party claims the same indulgence, which is admitted; and thus, in some cases, the progress of a cause is impeded, and three or four months delay improperly occasioned.

ARREST.

The power of arrest is exercised in these courts, but it does not appear whence it was derived. There is no law

BARBADOS.

COMMON PLEAS.

of the island by which it is given. The only law upon the subject is the one which gives the exemptions. As we could not trace the *power*, so we found nothing in the laws which regulated the *amount*. But "for any sum "above 8*l*. by established usage, a defendant may be "arrested on mesne process." The solicitor-general said, "it seems to have arisen from *custom*;" an impossible origin, I conceive, for a power of imprisonment; but they may have brought it from England, as regulated by acts of parliament before the settlement of the island. "The practice," he added, "requires amendment and "regulation." There *is no affidavit* of the *debt*; and arrests are allowed where the claim is made in respect of *unliquidated damages*. "In an action of tort, trespass "for instance, or defamation, if damages are laid at *any* "*large amount*, the defendant may be arrested for the sum "laid in the declaration." The attorney-general said, "A man may be arrested without any affidavit, and per-"sons are often arrested, for much more than is due."

No. 59, Hall's Laws, cl. 14. No. 10, Moore's Laws.

Freeholders owning ten acres of land, and capable of *electing* or being *elected* to serve in the House of Assembly, are exempted from arrest. Not so women, or Jews, or freeholders whose deeds have not been proved. The exemption was complained of as an unjust one, and was said to have been productive of inconvenience, and this was the opinion of the solicitor-general. The attorney-general "thought the inconvenience was the other "way, from too many arrests." Certainly, imprisonment in this climate, and in such gaols as are commonly found in the West Indies, operates in every case, as the severest punishment imaginable. Besides, the island is itself "*a cage**." No person can leave it without fixing up his name in the secretary's office, to afford his creditors an opportunity of successful interference to restrain him; so that the measure of arrest is by no means one, of frequent or indispensable necessity.

*The place of confinement of run-away slaves is so called.

HABEAS CORPUS.

A *habeas corpus* is obtainable, upon application to any chief judge, by the common law, and is supposed to make a part of the governor's instructions.

The chief justice of the precinct decides as to the

BARBADOS.

COMMON PLEAS.

sufficiency of the bail, if the sum for which the defendant is arrested exceeds 200*l.*

On arrest, a bond ought to be given by the plaintiff, conditioned for the filing of the declaration in three days; engaging to prosecute his claim without greater delay. If the act is complied with, the object it had in view, is clearly, not effectuated. In a case where the defendant cannot procure bail and goes to prison, and the plaintiff does not proceed with his action, the Crown lawyers are not agreed, whether (even supposing the plaintiff's bond to be forfeited, which however they do not seem to consider it) the defendant would be entitled to his discharge.

The prothonotary told us, "If a defendant goes to "jail, as long as he lies there, proceedings do not go on, "and he does not become supersedeable on that ground. "When he is *bailed* and out of prison, he may take a "copy of the process and move for the plaintiff to be "nonprossed." Upon another occasion, it was stated, that "*when* the defendant, upon being arrested, *has* "*given bail*, the plaintiff must file his declaration, with "the prothonotary, within three days;" a construction of the act which removes a difficulty, as to the forfeiture of the plaintiff's bond, but leaves the fact of the defendant who has *not* given bail being without remedy—and entirely at the mercy of his enemy, not only unshaken, but as it appears to me completely established. The words of the act are, as follow: "And whatsoever person or persons, at whose suit, any shall be arrested, do "not within three days after serving the said arrest, file "his action, against the defendant, at the office belonging to the court, where the writ is returnable, that "then a certificate taken out from the clerk, signifying "that same, shall be a sufficient cause *to take up the* "*bail-bond*, and discharge the party or parties out of "prison." No. 59. cl. 8.

No. 59. Hall's Laws.

Whatever be the sound construction of this act, there can be no doubt that the *admitted practice* is harsh and oppressive, in the highest degree.

OYER.

The claim of OYER of any deed or writing proffered

BARBADOS.

COMMON PLEAS.

to the court (of which *profert* is made) by the adverse party, in his pleadings, is said to be commonly used as a means of delay; "*no time being fixed for giving it.*" The prothonotary has known it "*hang up causes for a* "very long time."

CONTINUANCES.

IMPARLANCES.

With a view to discover the causes, if any existed, of the imputed delay in the administration of justice, we inquired into the rules and practice relating to Oyer, Continuances, Imparlances, &c. (subjects of too technical a nature to be enlarged upon, in this Report) but learnt little more than that these matters are usually settled "*among the attornies.*" Where THEY consent, "further "time is given," or actions are "continued;" where they cannot agree, and the case is brought before the court, then—"to obtain further time to plead,"—or— "to delay trial,"—special grounds must be laid, on affidavit.

HACKETT'S CASE.

A free negro, of the name of Hackett, preferred a complaint before the Commissioners "of vexatious and "ruinous delay in the administration of justice, &c. &c. "He laid claim to ten acres of cane land in the pos- "session of Major Gaskin, who was a purchaser of the "property of which it was part, for a valuable consider- "ation, but with notice of the complainant's demand. "He, complainant, had been offered 150*l.* and five acres "of bad, rocky land, to relinquish his claim, but had re- "fused to accept it and brought his action. The defend- "ant was an assistant judge in the court in which the ac- "tion was brought. The cause was improperly called "on for trial, at a time, when there was an engagement "between the counsel, that it should not come on; and "from the great eloquence of the advocate for the de- "fendant, and the animated appeal he made to the jury, "to save the defendant from being ruined by that black "man who claimed his property, he, (complainant) lost "his cause. A writ of error was brought, and on the "candid admission of the counsel, error was confessed, "and the cause was to be entered again. But it was *not* "entered, *to that day,* he believed; and he had been "kept out of the property, six years. At first it was not

BARBADOS.

COMMON PLEAS.

"entered from the misconduct, certainly, of his own "attorney. Then Mr. Alleyne, the chief justice, was "absent, and there were not sufficient judges to try it; "as they could not make a court without the defendant "being one. But Mr. Alleyne had now been returned, "two years. The complainant then changed his attor-"ney, and provided his new attornies, Messrs. Edey and "Nusam, with the money necessary to pay the fees; but "still he did not get his cause entered. The reason "assigned by the prothonotary, was, that the defendant "would not consent to its being put upon the list. At "last, fourteen days before the court in last September, "the prothonotary took his money, to enter up the "cause upon the list. It did not come on however, "and the prothonotary told complainant he would ex-"plain '*why*' at another time; but he never did. His "own counsel returned his fee, saying, if he could not "do him any good, he would not keep his money. "Complainant then applied to another attorney, but "*he* said he was very intimate with the defendant, and "would not proceed against him, without he had 10*l*. "down. Complainant had no resource but to petition "the governor and council; defendant declaring that he "would spend 500*l*.; he would try who had the most "money; and threatening to 'throw it into chancery.' "The governor and council, in answer to the petition, "had given directions that the cause should be put upon "the list, and that Messrs. Edey and Nusam, the attor-"neys, who had taken the complainant's money to pay "the fees, should conduct the suit." Upon hearing this statement, the Commissioners desired the complainant to call at the prothonotary's office, and learn, from the officer, whether the cause was at that time upon the list. On a subsequent day, Hackett brought word that the prothonotary had answered, "*that the cause was* "*upon the list and would be tried.*" At the next court, an objection was taken to the notice of trial; which exception prevailed. It resulted, that the cause was not tried before the Commissioners left the island.

As soon as it appeared by the complaint itself, that the

BARBADOS.

COMMON PLEAS.

proceedings in this case, were judicially pending and unconcluded, the Commissioners conceived that their interference was rendered unnecessary and improper. They were bound to presume, that a proper decision would be come to and justice be duly administered, by the ordinary tribunals. It ought to be observed, that *particular expressions*, imputed to individuals, were *distinctly disavowed*, and the counsel added, "the plaintiff was mis-"taken in his claim, being" (I *think*, for the communication was oral,) "illegitimate and without title;" leaving the admitted *delay* in the trial, as it appears to me, the only subject, within the express authority of the Commissioners requiring animadversion. We did however consider ourselves justified in making an application to the chief justice of the district, in which the *defendant lived, and the action was of necessity brought*, to have the goodness *to watch the proceedings*, and see that the case was brought to trial. Mr. Alleyne obligingly promised that he would take care that the cause was tried, at the next court.

VENUE.

No. 28, Hall's Laws, cl. 13.

By the law and practice of this island, an action must be tried, where the DEFENDANT lives. A strange provision! Quite anomalous! neither consonant to the law of England, nor agreeable to the natural course of things. Where there are more defendants than one, and they live in different precincts, application is made, not to the court, but to the governor, to know in what district the plaintiff is to sue!

SPECIAL PLEADING.

The science of special pleading does not appear to be often perverted in this island to the purposes of chicane and delay. Dilatory or sham pleas are never put in. In the courts exercising a summary jurisdiction for the recovery of small debts, a copy of the account is often admitted to stand in the place of a declaration. Of this practice,—as of the mode of commencing actions by summons and service of a copy of the declaration,—I beg to observe, that I do not think any practical inconvenience has been found to result, from the relaxation of rules, intended no doubt to secure the greatest possible degree of precision and certainty.

BARBADOS.

COMMON PLEAS.

No. 28. Hall's Laws, cl. 2.

DEMURRERS, &c.

The pleadings used are intended to be, exactly the same as in the court of Common Pleas in England. "Honest" pleas in abatement, and "fair" demurrers are said to be frequent. Unfortunately there is no fixed time *for arguing them*. They are put upon the list, and "a court day set apart for them, so as not to interfere "with the jury causes or bench actions." "It is usually" says the attorney-general "a day *when there is no other* "*business*, and that may not happen *for some time*." The prothonotary said, "they are argued a *long time* "*after*." A poor woman complained to the Commis-missioners, that "having got a special verdict in her "favour, on the construction of a will in 1811, it had "never been argued yet; the defendant was dead, and "the property had passed into other hands." Being asked if she knew the reason, she said "she had no "money to pay her counsel, and none would argue it "without."

Another inconvenience was pointedly alluded to by the attorney-general. The court is "not very competent to "judge of the ground of demurrers; it gives no reasons; "it decides the *best it can*, and says, '*For* the plaintiff,' "or '*For* the defendant.'" The solicitor-general adds, "The court in giving judgment does not generally enter "into any legal argument, the judges not being profes- "sionally bred."

PLEADINGS AND PRACTICE.

The pleadings are all entered in the prothonotary's office upon one paper, and *this* serves for a *record*.

RECORD.

The jury indorse their *verdict* upon it, and it is signed by the foreman. The *venire* is not entered upon each issue, because there is only one venire upon all jury actions.

The pleadings are not opened to the court by counsel. There are no *abstracts* made for the judges. The jury is addressed by the counsel upon all the facts, and, as we ourselves heard, all the law of the case. Upon arguments on special verdicts and demurrers, &c. there are no *paper books* containing the points and authorities upon which the counsel intend to rely, made up,

BARBADOS.

COMMON PLEAS.

NISI PRIUS.

for the information of the judges; as would be very desirable.

The time of the court during the sitting of four days, is principally occupied, by the trial of jury actions.

INTERLOCUTORY BUSINESS.

The interlocutory business is insignificant. The arguments on special cases, &c. very rare. *Three* days are usually spent at nisi prius, and bench actions occupy the fourth; provided the jury actions do not engross it. The solicitor-general said, "ONE day would suffice for all the "interlocutory business and arguments;"—but it seems difficult to appropriate *one* for the purpose.

Actions at law, have at former periods, been frequently delayed for a great length of time, by means of injunctions, especially where the plaintiff resided abroad. "The payment of a just debt," said the attorney-general, "has often been delayed by these means."

DEPOSITIONS.

No. 23, Hall's Laws.

The *depositions* of witnesses unable to attend, are permitted to be used on trials, under a law of the island. "Persons going off the island, or sick or lame, or other-"wise disabled, may make depositions before the go-"vernor, or any judge-assistant, or justice, in any suit." Depositions are commonly taken before the most unfit of the persons mentioned—justices of the peace;—attornies on both sides attending. Fees are paid to the magistrate and the attornies. It is admitted that they "often "contain what is not evidence;" and we were very soon satisfied of the fact, on hearing some read.

The proof of debts, whether by specialty or simple contract, where the creditor resides and the debt accrues in England, is rendered surprisingly easy, by 5 Geo. 2. c. 7. 5 Geo. 2. c. 7.

The merchant's books are produced, and the accounts sworn to, before the lord mayor, (in London), usually by a clerk, sometimes it is said, by the merchant himself, the party in the cause. But the attorney-general observed, "We object to that (the latter) NOW, and the "court allows the objection." Yet the words of the act are, "It shall and may be lawful to and for *the plaintiff* 5 Geo. 2. c. 7.
"*or defendant*, and also to and for any witness, to ve-"rify and prove any matter or thing by affidavit or writ-

BARBADOS.

COMMON PLEAS.

"ing upon oath, or if a Quaker, by affirmation; and "every affidavit certified under the city seal, and transmitted, shall be of the same force and effect as if "sworn, *vivâ voce*, in open court." No notice is required by the act, to be given to the opposite party, to be present before the lord mayor, and no inquiry gone into. This act of parliament is loudly complained of in the islands, as a very unjust law, in its operation upon the colonial creditor. The solicitor-general said, "It is "a hard law; there is no reciprocity." But, as was observed by the attorney-general, "if it were not for "this act, the merchant must send out witnesses." We could not discover that any *injunctions* had been obtained, or bills filed for a discovery, in any of these cases; and upon the whole, though it is certainly repugnant to sound principles, to give effect to the testimony of a witness, whom the opposite party has not had opportunities of cross-examining, yet we were by no means satisfied that any practical inconvenience had been experienced in the colonies, from its enactment; while without it, we conceived the absent creditor would have great difficulties to contend with, in the recovery of his just demand in the colonial courts.

WITNESSES.

Witnesses, attending the courts of this island, do not, in general, receive their expenses.

JURIES.

An old law of the island directs that freeholders should serve on *juries* in rotation, and the provost-marshal is directed to summon them ALPHABETICALLY.

The attorney-general said, "he is so directed, but he "never does; the same persons serve over and over." A list of twenty-four jurymen is given to the judges, previous to the trial, and *they* strike out the names of twelve. Special juries are not known, in practice, in this island.

CHALLENGES. Cl. 7 and 8.

Challenges to jurors, on the ground of consanguinity and affinity, are LIMITED by No. 109, Hall's Laws, of which the preamble is remarkable:—"Whereas many "families in this island are, by frequent intermarriages, "become related to each other, by means whereof it "hath often happened, that, when a cause has been ready

BARBADOS.

COMMON PLEAS.

" for trial, it hath been put off, because two or more of " the jurors have been of kin to the plaintiff or the " defendant; for the remedy thereof, &c. be it enacted, " that, for the future, *no person shall be challenged* un- " less he be within the following degrees, &c."

When any point of law arises on the trial of a cause, and the counsel on either side, apply to the court, to have a special verdict, the judge is bound to grant and the jury to find it.

Unless reasons in arrest of judgment are filed, (which they frequently are, merely for delay,) execution issues, in fourteen days after judgment is entered up.

Arrest of judgment is moved during the sitting of the court in which the verdict is obtained; usually on the last day. The reasons are filed with the officer, and at the next court a motion is made to over-rule them, and allow the judgment to be entered; so that a month is all that can be gained by filing reasons to arrest the judgment. But if the cause is tried the last court before the vacation, (which is held in September,) the entry of judgment may be delayed by this proceeding, until the January court.

Judgments in this island are not registered; but are entered in the prothonotary's office, and where it becomes necessary, they must be searched for, THERE. Lands are bound from the judgment; which renders the circumstance material.

The writ of execution "*runs against*," or operates upon goods, lands, and body; *all at once;* somewhat resembling a statute-staple, formerly known in practice in England, but without the delay and charge of a "liberate." The lawyers are agreed, (however the practice may have been otherwise,) that the provost-marshal ought to take them, *in succession;* and now, a manuscript act directs that he shall not keep the body, if lands and goods are pointed out to him. This law was occasioned by Fitt's case, who (Fitt) was a debtor in execution, his creditor electing to take his body, in preference to having his lands at a valuation, considerably above the market price. But a new enactment could scarcely have

BARBADOS.

COMMON PLEAS.

been necessary; as the order, in which a levy should be made, was before prescribed by law, and is as follows:—1, Produce. 2, Negroes. 3, Land. 4, Body.

No. 28, Hall's Laws. LEVY AND SALE OF GOODS.

CHATTELS taken in execution, are put up to sale, and sold to the highest bidder. No notice is given, by advertisement in the public papers, of the intended sale of such goods. The course is *to put notes on the door of the marshal's office*. This mode of proceeding leads to at least a *suspicion* of abuse. The practice is also inconvenient. The attorneys are under the necessity of sending their clerks every week, to look after these notes. It is the same with all other persons interested.

SALE OF SLAVES. No. 84, Hall's Laws.

SLAVES are directed to be sold "in lots, not exceeding "the number of five negroes in one lot, unless it happens "that there be more than five of one family of negroes; "in which case it shall be lawful for the marshal to sell "a whole family in one lot;" which shews that at that early period, 1688, some attention was paid to a subject, of real interest to humanity. There is however no express direction that families *shall* be sold together; nothing that I am aware of, in any act of assembly in this island, *prohibiting the separation* of husband and wife, parents and children. The 5 Geo. 2. c. 7, declared both negroes and land, assets for the satisfaction of simple-contract debts, and liable to be sold under execution. The 57 Geo. 3. c. 119., repealed this act, so far as related to negroes, in the hope, that slaves would no longer continue liable to be severed from the estates to which they belonged. But under local acts, in almost every island, (Tobago excepted) slaves continue liable to be sold, under executions at law, or by decrees of courts of equity; that is to say, slaves in priority to the land, and land only in the event of produce and slaves not producing sufficient to satisfy the demand.

This is the case where the interests of creditors are implicated, and under forced sales. In other instances, of *voluntary* alienation, there is also no restraint upon the master's power, and no regulations for its exercise.

I am not required to offer an opinion upon doubtful questions of colonial policy. The local attachments of

BARBADOS.

COMMON PLEAS.

the slave are undoubtedly strong; but the legally attaching negroes to a barren and exhausted spot, or to a rock, from which the heavy tropical rains have washed away every particle of soil, might be often, little advantageous to the slave himself. However desirable it may appear, to prevent the prædial slave from being torn from his home and garden, it would be found very difficult, consistently with a due regard to the interests of creditors, to provide any remedy for the evil. An enactment, that slaves upon plantations should no longer be liable to be seized for the master's debts, and sold separately from the land, would be unsuitable to a state of things, in which the support of credit and the security for borrowed capital, forms the first object of attention and even of legislative care and provision. No objection of the kind occurs to a humane provision to prevent the separation of families. Such a measure is practicable and easy, and has been adopted, with the best effect, in some of the other islands. In practice, as I had opportunities of witnessing in more than one instance, it is usual for a person who thinks of purchasing a slave, to inquire first of the slave himself, Whether he likes the *place* he is going to, and the MASTER he will have to serve?

SALE OF LAND.

LANDS and houses taken under an execution, are appraised by a jury summoned by the marshal. The land is then, as it is termed, "*laid off to the creditor;*" in other words the creditor is compelled to take it at the appraised value; which is generally much more than it is really worth. This was complained of very forcibly, as an excessive hardship. It *is* commonly appraised too high, and the creditor is a loser; so that, if he does not want the land, he will not order the levy to be made; except where the defendant is in prison, in which case the levy is imperative. When appraised, lands are to be delivered to the plaintiff in eighty days, and if no redemption of them takes place within twenty more, the *marshal is to convey them* to the plaintiff and his heirs for ever.

FITT'S CASE.

No. 28, Hall's Laws, cl. 7.

BODY.

When the BODY is taken, there is no allowance to a debtor in execution, either by the plaintiff or by the public.

F 2

BARBADOS.

COMMON PLEAS.

Executions in this island are taken out and not levied, but kept as securities, having as to land, all the effect of mortgages, to be satisfied in succession. Real estate it has been noticed, is bound from the judgment; although *that* is not docketed. Executions are often lodged in the

Cl. 10.

marshal's hands, with instructions not to levy until another writ is delivered. The creditor, whose execution is executed first, gets a priority as to personal estate. An act (No. 229, Hall's Laws,) provides, that, "as execu-" tions have become the common securities of the island, "and are frequently taken out and lodged merely to "secure debts and to preserve the priority of demands, "such executions shall not be proceeded on, unless the

Cl. 11.

"creditor gives express orders, or unless some other cre-"ditor shall direct a levy to be made; and such execu-"tions may be assigned by indorsement."

Thus in satisfaction of a judgment, not only personal property, but real estate and even equities of redemption, that is equitable as well as legal interests in lands, may be taken and sold: and executions are almost regarded, in a certain qualified sense, as instruments of conveyance.

The law and the practice will be entirely new, and scarcely intelligible to an English lawyer. In this manner however, in a country where the business of estates is mostly carried on with borrowed capital, are debts easily and effectually secured; so much so, that we never received a single complaint of delay or difficulty (though we frequently did of EXPENSE) in the recovery of merchants' demands.

FEES.

The fees in these courts, have been fixed by certain acts of the legislature, but those laws,—which direct barristers and attorneys to be paid in sugar—are called obsolete, and are very naturally disregarded. We inquired if there had been any later laws, or any rules of court subsequent to those acts, by which the fees were regulated; and were informed there had NOT. We asked what was the method used in taxing costs, and by what rules taxation proceeded? we were told, "If the at-"torneys can agree, costs are never taxed at all; if they "cannot agree, costs are taxed by the chief justice; who

BARBADOS.

COMMON PLEAS.

"however, has no rule to guide him; for the allowance "of them, it is at the discretion of the attorneys first, and "then of the judge." The attorney-general observed, "The chief justice has no certain rule; but he will not "allow what is not usual; he applies to know what *is* "*usual* to the prothonotaries and the attorneys." No. 109, Hall's Laws, an act "for the better regulation of the "court of Common Pleas," says, "Some of the judges "do usually tax greater costs than others, there being "as yet no certain method for the same."

At a later period, but during the stay of the Commissioners in the island, a new table of fees for these courts, was promulgated, under the authority of the judges.

Extra costs beyond the costs allowed; what are technically called costs between attorney and client; were said not to be known in these courts.

The attorney-general was asked, "Whether it would "be an improvement, if in certain cases, a certificate of "the judge was made necessary to entitle a party to "more than 40*s.* costs?" He said, "I think it would "be an advantage, when there is *a regular judge; and it* "*is my opinion that there ought to be a chief justice from* "*England, and a consolidation of the courts.*"

The counsel in this island, receive their fees (out of court) from the client himself, and not through the medium of the attorney; and it is said can recover them by action. This was the case, when the characters of barrister and attorney were formerly blended: but I should think the doctrine doubtful at present.

CURTIS'S CASE.

James Curtis complained "of an act of partiality and "injustice in the chief judge, committed in striking off "certain fees of counsel from a bill of costs, in an action "in which he (Curtis) had obtained a verdict against "two magistrates, for false imprisonment." On inquiry, we learnt that the counsel in question, (Mr. J. Hobson) had come from another island, (St. Vincent,) to conduct the cause. The names of the counsel who sign the declaration, appear upon the record, and the judge considered it to be unusual and improper to allow the costs on taxation, of any counsel whose name was not found

BARBADOS.

COMMON PLEAS.

*there*. The rule was disputed; and the propriety of it in these islands, may be very questionable; but there appeared no ground whatever, for the imputation of corrupt or improper motives in the judge.

PHILLIPPS' CASE.

—— Phillipps brought a bill of costs in the action "Phillipps against Moe," and complained of,

"1st, Delay: that his case had been improperly kept "back two years. He could not tell *how*, except that at "one of the monthly courts, a motion had been made to "put it off, on account of the absence of a material wit-"ness. This was done without affidavit; and when the "trial at last took place the witness, represented as ma-"terial, was not called."

"2d, Improper proceedings. The judge took no notes "of the evidence, the judge did not sum up or instruct "the jury; the jury were allowed to separate before "verdict; at four o'clock in the afternoon, the court ad-"journed till next morning, and no officer was sworn to "take charge of the jury."

"3d, Expense. Where trials are so unsatisfactorily "conducted, it is a great hardship that a party can only "obtain a new trial, or prosecute an appeal, on payment "in all cases, of the costs of the former action. Here "the demand was *33l. 15s. 6d.* The costs amounted to "*64l. 16s. 4½d.* He (Mr. Phillipps) applied to a judge "to have the costs taxed, but nothing was taken off and "he had to pay the costs of taxation."

We could not procure further information as to the proceedings in the particular case, but the general practice was stated to be entirely different as to the putting off trials for absence of necessary witnesses, and allowing juries to separate before verdict. In other respects it was admitted by the answers, to agree in the main, with Mr. Phillipps's representation.

WRITS OF ERROR.

Writs of error are not often resorted to in Barbados for purposes of delay, being too expensive.

NEW TRIALS.

If a new trial is granted, it is always upon the terms, of first paying all the previous costs.

*Evidence not taken down. No summing up.*

The judges in these courts do not take down the evidence; the judges in these courts do not sum up the case;

BARBADOS.

COMMON PLEAS.

they neither state the facts, nor explain the law to the jury.

*Equitable jurisdiction.*

An equity jurisdiction, given to these courts by the laws in Hall, No. 28, clause 13, and No. 109, clause 4, never has been exercised, and is scarcely known to exist.

EVIDENCE.

A manuscript act has been before adverted to, admitting free negroes and free people of colour, who have been baptised and instructed in the principles of the Christian religion, to give evidence in any trial or suit. We inquired very solicitously, of those, who had the most favourable opportunities of hearing such witnesses examined, whether they had observed any inconvenience resulting from the admission of such evidence?

The senior justice of the peace said, "I have seen in-" credible perjury let in, by admitting free coloured per-" sons to give evidence." The solicitor-general said, "I " wish I could say that in my practice, I had observed " that attention paid by this class of people, to the so-" lemnity of an oath, which ought to be observed by " every witness."

The attorney-general said, "I believe they are often " loose in giving evidence; it has occasioned many suits, " for they are very litigious. I voted for the act, and do " not repent the support I gave it."

There does not appear to have been any conviction for perjury, of persons who had given evidence under this act.

MANUMITTED SLAVES.

All persons, who were manumitted *any where*, in the other colonies or in England, *before* the passing of this act, are entitled to give evidence. Persons manumitted *since*, to place them in a condition to enjoy this privilege, must have been enfranchized according to the law of the island. A manumission in England subsequent to the act, (a mode of emancipation by which the payment of the 50*l.* consequent on manumission,) is evaded, has the legal effect of freeing the slave, but will not enable him to give evidence.

ABSENT OR ABSCONDING DEBTORS.

No. 202, Hall's Laws, is an act to enable creditors to recover their debts, out of the effects of absent or absconding debtors. These laws resemble foreign attach-

BARBADOS. — COMMON PLEAS.

ments in London. They are a very powerful instrument in the colonies; giving the local creditor a considerable advantage over the foreign claimant; but it was complained that they were found expensive. The costs, in ordinary cases, we ascertained to be about 28*l.* 10*s.* By their means, a creditor may attach effects belonging to a defendant who has himself escaped, in whatever hands they are found. No affidavit of the debt is required by the act. A creditor not having judgment, must enter an action against such absent or absconding debtor, and serve it on the person, in whose hands or power, any effects are discovered to be, which has the effect of attaching them to the use of the plaintiff. A judgment-creditor serves a *scire facias.* The plaintiff gives security for restitution, in case the absent debtor shall appear within a year. The garnishee pleading that he has nothing in his hands of the plaintiff's to be attached, may be put to swear to the truth of his plea; but then his oath will be conclusive of the fact. The garnishee making default is without relief either in law or equity. This act was before mentioned as having been originally comprised in the same bill with No. 201, Hall's Laws. The action in *this* case is brought where the PLAINTIFF lives.

No. 202, Hall's Laws, cl. 2.

ATTACHMENT of money and goods in third persons hands.

## BENCH ACTIONS.

Actions brought for the recovery of a debt not exceeding 8*l.* are denominated bench actions; being decided without the intervention of a jury. They are tried by any one of the judges of the court of Common Pleas, on one of the court days, after the jury actions are finished. In Bridge Town always on the last of the four days. At the Out courts in general, on the same day with the jury actions; these courts usually sitting but one day, though allowed two.

No. 181. Hall's Laws.

The proceedings are regulated by an act in Hall, which gives a short form of action (or declaration), and directs, that "if the plaintiff cannot prove his demand, "the defendant shall be examined on oath, and judgment

BARBADOS.

BENCH ACTIONS.

OPPOSED TO JURY ACTIONS (NISI PRIUS.)

" be given accordingly, for what he admits to be due, but " if the defendant refuses to be sworn, then the plaintiff " shall be examined on oath and judgment for what shall " appear to be justly due," and " no such action shall " be nonsuited for any informality in law; but judgment " shall be given according to the mere right." The trial of these actions is said to take up much time. Counsel are never engaged in them, and attorneys " not always " employed." The costs are limited by law, and are very trifling.

A gentleman of the name of Murray complained loudly, but only in general terms, of the conduct of the judge in bench actions, which he said was " intemperate, " arbitrary and unjust." The attorney-general " be- " lieved that wrong *judgments had been often given, and " thought a regular judge was wanted.*"

---

PROCEEDINGS IN COURT.

During the February sittings the Commissioners attended the court of Common Pleas for Saint Michael's Precinct, held in Bridge Town. The first morning was wholly spent in hearing two undefended causes. The judges selected the jury. The pleadings were not opened by counsel. The judges had no abstract of, and never referred to, the record. Depositions were admitted in evidence, stating facts which the parties making them had—" heard and believed." The judges did not take down notes; or sum up the evidence to the jury; or make any inquiries or observations; or speak, or stir, the whole day. Though the evidence was only on one side, the jury, which was very respectable and seemed impressed with the importance of the duties they were called upon to discharge without any assistance from the bench,—left the court to deliberate. The verdict was written for them upon the record, after their return to court.

On another day, a nice and doubtful question arose upon the statute of frauds; a great number of cases were cited with appropriate observations, and these were all addressed to the *jury*. Upon the whole, though very distinguished talent was displayed at the *bar*, the pro-

BARBADOS.

BENCH ACTIONS.

ceedings were extremely irregular; there was a great loss of time and want of order; and the judges were manifestly impeded, in the execution of the duties of their trust, by the want of judicial knowledge.

The attorney-general, in reply to the question whether he could suggest any improvement in the administration of justice in this court, said: "a judge regularly "bred to the profession, would remove most incon"veniences."

## COURT OF ORDINARY.

ORDINARY.

The court of ordinary derives its authority, by commission from the Crown. The governor or president, being commander in chief of the island, is sole judge. He sits *alone*, having no legal power of calling in any assistance. The probate of wills; granting letters of administration and marriage licenses; form the subject-matters of his jurisdiction. Marriages are either by banns or license from the governor, as ordinary. They have no canonical hours in the colonies, and marry at what timé they please.

ALL wills are proved, but the probate is conclusive only as to personalty. There are no restrictions on the power of disposing of property by will in this island. The solemnities requisite to the validity of a will are nearly the same as in England; but *their* statute of frauds requires only *two* witnesses to a will of lands; and accompanied with a proviso, that "the act shall not be "construed to extend to any will, written throughout in "the hand-writing of the testator."

No. 225, Hall's Laws.

The court sits at government-house, as often as occasion requires.

Nice points it is admitted, often arise, upon the validity of contested wills.

It is doubted whether an appeal lies to the king in council, or to His Majesty, as head of the church. But the appeal from this court is direct and immediate. There is no power of enforcing the payment of costs; consesequently there is no *taxation* of them, and no table of *fees*. BARBADOS. ORDINARY.

The solitor-general thought with much reason, that if this court could have some efficient means of enforcing its decrees, it would be attended with considerable advantage. As an improvement in the administration of justice in this court, the attorney-general suggested his *usual and universal remedy, a judge;* but it is surely further necessary—to have the powers of the court enlarged and defined, and to invest the ordinary with competent authority to punish contumacy, and compel obedience to his sentence. No. 141, Hall's Laws must first be repealed; which enacts "that no ecclesiastical law "or jurisdiction shall have power to enforce, confirm or "establish any mulct or punishment, in any case what- "soever within this island." No. 141, Hall's Laws.

## COURT OF ADMIRALTY.

The court of Admiralty consists of two courts, a prize and an instance court; both held by commission issuing from the high court of Admiralty in England. Both possess the same jurisdiction as is exercised by the correspondent courts in England, as nearly as circumstances will permit. The prize court is held only in time of war. The cases in the instance court, consist of seizures by the custom-house, seamens' wages, bottomry-bonds, &c. &c.

The statute 8 and 9 W. 3. c. 22., for preventing frauds and regulating abuses in the plantation trade, is thought to give a greater power to these courts in the colonies, than is exercised by the high court of Admiralty at home; as by cl. 2., the forfeiture for trading in unqualified ships, may be sued for "*in any court* in the plantations;" which includes the court of Admiralty: but in England, only "in one of his Majesty's *courts of record.*" By cl. 6., a jurisdiction is supposed to be established in this court in all cases of unlawful importations and exporta- 8 & 9 Wm. 3. Cl. 22. Cl. 2. Cl. 6.

BARBADOS.

ADMIRALTY.

tions; and all frauds on his Majesty in his customs, and all offences against the acts of trade.

The court of Admiralty has also jurisdiction in certain cases under the abolition and registry acts.

A sole judge of both courts is appointed from home in time of war.

The court is held, as occasion requires. The officers of the court are the King's advocate; the King's proctor; the registrar; and the marshal. In time of war the judge receives a salary. The judge, in peace, is paid by fees. The King's advocate has no salary, and receives no fees for a prosecution at the Admiralty sessions. The registrar and marshal are patent officers, paid by fees. Appeals are made from the instance side, to the high court of Admiralty in England; from the prize side, to the King in council. The terms, on which the latter appeals are allowed, are regulated by the prize act. There is a great deal of business in the prize court, in time of war. The receipt of fees has sometimes exceeded the judge's salary, (which is 3,000*l.* sterling per annum;) in which case it goes on to pay the next year's stipend. There is very little business in the instance court; there have been only *five* cases within the last twelve months. Proceedings for the recovery of seamens' wages, are sometimes instituted in this court.

Burnham's case.

In an instance brought before the Commissioners, the amount of the sum in dispute, was five dollars. The judge of the Admiralty, stated, that "the usual and regular fees would have amounted to 70*l.*; but that he "had remitted half; there was no docket of fees: one "*had* been sent out by Sir William Scott, but it was "lost; he had guided himself in taking fees, by what "he could learn of the amount of those taken by his "predecessor. The fees in the court of Admiralty were "certainly high; and many instances occured of complaints made by seamen for trifling claims of wages, "some of which were afterwards compromised, in which "the expenses incurred were more considerable than in "the case before us." There was a further charge against the judge of extortion and oppression in this

BARBADOS.

ADMIRALTY.

case; but it was not substantiated, and in great measure originated in mistake and the intemperate conduct of all parties. After a long and careful investigation of the facts, the matter was explained to the entire satisfaction of the Commissioners and of the complainant, who, having from the first preferred and conducted the charge in a very candid spirit, asked and obtained leave, entirely to withdraw it.

Collectors, *passim.*

The fees of the court of Admiralty are every where excessive. Where a seizure from smugglers amounts to 100*l.* or upwards, a condemnation will not enable the captors to pay the expenses.

The Admiralty sessions are held by a separate commission, for the trial of murder, piracy, and other offences committed on the high seas. This court is composed of the judge of the Admiralty, who presides, the members of council, and all flag-officers and captains on the station. The attorney-general and King's advocate are employed. In this court no fees are taken. The sessions are held, as occasion requires.

A docket of fees sent out "by Sir Wm. Scott," and which took effect in Barbados in January, 1814, after having been accidentally lost, was discovered again during the stay of the Commissioners in the island, in January 1823. Costs are always taxed by the judge, and it is said, by THAT docket of fees.

## COURT OF APPEAL AND ERROR.

The court of Appeal and Error is composed of the governor and council. There is no lawyer upon the bench. Some of the judges are members of it, but it is provided by the governor's instructions, that they shall not vote in any case brought from the court where they have acted as judges. The governor and council decide by a majority. A writ of error, to operate as a stay of execution, must be brought within fourteen days after judgment. It only lies where the principal sum in dispute amounts to 300*l.* calculated in sterling money, and costs

BARBADOS.

COURT OF APPEAL AND ERROR.

Governor's instructions. No. 143, Hall's Laws. No. 22, Hall's Laws. No. 90, Hall's Laws.

not included. An ulterior appeal to the King in council is allowed where the value is 500*l*.

It is said that no appeal will lie for costs, *eo nomine et per se*.

The security to be given is regulated by the governor's instructions and the acts of the island.—Appeals are not frequent.

## ESCHEAT COURT.

This court sits under a commission. The cases in which it has jurisdiction are commonly; forfeitures to the Crown for want of heirs. An escheator-general is appointed by the governor. The expenses are very trifling. The observations of the solicitor-general, though they apply rather to the law upon the subject, than to the constitution or practice of the court, will probably be thought not undeserving of attention: "I think it (the forfeiture "for want of heirs) acts cruelly upon the coloured people, "who do not in general marry. Their children are il-"legitimate, and they dying without a will, their *little* "*all* becomes the property of the Crown, and their chil-"dren are left pennyless. On a petition to the governor "he may send the matter home, but in *that* there is de-"lay, and the property is often exhausted."

It would be impolitic to alter any law that may operate as an inducement to marriage. The poor coloured people no doubt, in all the islands are deplorably ignorant, and can only by degrees, become aware of the legal consequences affecting their property, from their children being born out of wedlock. As a remote consequence of certain feudal principles, of obscure northern original, the application of this doctrine to his Majesty's adopted subjects,—the unsuspecting progeny of Africa,—is extraordinary, as an historical fact,—and to a contemplative mind, and when the *leges legum* are inquired into,—furnishes much matter of curious reflection.

The grant of any allowance in such cases, depends *upon*, and must entirely proceed *from*, the grace and

BARBADOS.

ESCHEAT COURT.

favour of his Majesty; but I may be permitted to mention, that by the humanity of the Spanish law as in force in Trinidad, illegitimate children of an intestate, whose property has escheated for want of heirs, are entitled to *one sixth* of the property of their ancestor by way of *alimentary allowance.*

---

# CRIMINAL COURTS.

## COURT OF GRAND SESSIONS.

This, the principal court for the administration of criminal justice, is held under the authority of an act of the island. A commission of oyer and terminer and general gaol delivery is issued by the governor, for the trial of all capital crimes and misdemeanors, in which all those gentlemen of the island who are in the commission of the peace, are included. The person who presides is generally a member of council, or one of the chief judges; the chief justice, or the chief baron. The court is held twice a year, in June and December, and the commission is limited to *four* days. This confined period is sometimes "not sufficient for the trial of all the prisoners;" so that in cases which are not bailable, a prisoner might be detained in custody till the next grand sessions; but the present attorney-general to prevent such inconvenience, always brings forward such cases, "*as are not bailable* "*before those that are*," and he informed us there were no instances of prisoners "ever remaining over, on ac- "count of multiplicity of business."

All offences committed by free persons, coloured or otherwise, are tried at this court. The attorney-general said, "Free coloured persons have by act now, the same "privileges and liabilities, as whites. Slave evidence is "not admitted against them." The senior magistrate,

BARBADOS.

GRAND SESSIONS.

however, informed us that he had sometimes admitted slaves, "with strong corroborating circumstances, to "give evidence against free coloured people, under "Hall, 180."

This court professes in its decisions and practice, to follow the laws and rules of the criminal courts in England.

The preliminary proceedings which take place before the trial of persons accused of offences, as the complaint, warrant, apprehension, examination, and commitment, are all transacted before a justice of the peace, in the same manner as in the mother country. Depositions are taken in almost all cases, misdemeanors as well as felonies. The attorney-general said, "A deposition is not "always necessary; but as a fee is paid for them, the "justices admit them; and they may be useful if there "be equivocation of a witness." The senior justice of the peace said, "They *are* generally taken; under some "acts of the island, necessarily so; not in misdemeanors "always, but in assaults I think most usually."

All offences committed by freemen are *bailable*, except murder; all committed "by slaves, even murder." In the former case the amount is regulated by the means of the party, in the latter by the value of the slave.

Justices of the peace and coroners are by law, required to attend these courts; many do.

The magistrate binds over the party to appear and prosecute, but not always the witnesses to give evidence.

A list of commitments is made out by the gaoler, and sent to the attorney-general, who frames the indictment and conducts the prosecution; for which he receives a fee from the prosecutor, when *he* is of ability to pay it, "NOT UNDER 5*l*."

The circumstantial detail of the manner of trial of persons accused, is not a little *curious*. The presiding judge makes a complimentary speech to the governor, the council, his own friends, and the island in general; but says nothing about the proper business of the day. The duty of addressing the grand jury on the nature of

BARBADOS.

GRAND SESSIONS.

the charges presented to them, that "which" the attorney-general observed, "the court ought to do, but can- "not;" it is the practice for the attorney-general himself to execute, and it is done publicly, when he presents the bills to the grand jury, or when information is required on any points of law, in the progress of the bill before them.

No. 114, Hall's Laws.

No. 122, Hall's Laws.

In a way pointed out by certain statutes of the island, SIXTY-SIX persons are returned to serve on juries. Out of these the grand and petit juries are selected by the judge, who also nominates the foreman, called "the "judge's foreman."

Persons who have acted as grand jurors at one court, and found a bill which the defendant had traversed, may sit as petit jurors at the next court, and if not objected to, try the case. We received only an obscure hint upon the subject; I beg to refer to the answers in the examinations.

The junior counsel (when one is employed,) opens the case, or the attorney-general states the facts, and makes such observations as he thinks necessary. Counsel are always allowed to address the jury on behalf of prisoners in this court, and no inconvenience was ever found to result from such a practice.

The judge takes no notes, and delivers no opinion. The attorney-general says, "I have always thought it "my duty to sum up the evidence as impartially, as if I "were the chief justice; but I do not say any thing, as "to the weight of evidence; *that* I leave to the jury."

In capital cases (only) the judge delivers the sentence. In other cases the votes are collected, and the sense of the court being ascertained, the judgment is pronounced by the clerk of the Crown.

Prosecutors' and witnesses' costs and expenses are never allowed, in this court.

Judgment may be arrested on the same grounds as in England, but it must be determined before twelve at night on Friday.

After sentence, the governor has the power of reprieve and pardon in ordinary cases, but in treason and murder

BARBADOS.

GRAND SESSIONS.

the Crown alone can pardon; the governor suspending the execution, and sending the case home. As no notes have been taken by the judges, *no* papers or exact written information *can* be laid before the governor, to enable him to form his opinion upon the case. He can only act upon representations of the chief justice, and the attorney-general; made from recollections of the former, and notes of the latter.

No. 54, Hall's Laws.

It is the opinion of the attorney-general that there are many small offences, such as petit larcenies and assaults, brought before this court, over which the court of quarter sessions has jurisdiction, and which might be more conveniently tried *there*. Indeed, there is a law of the island, by which it is directed, that, thefts, not exceeding petit larcenies, shall be prosecuted at the next quarter sessions; but the attorney-general declares that he never knew it acted upon.

The modes of punishment of criminals convicted by due course of law in this island, are not very numerous or diversified. In cases, not thought deserving of capital punishment, they are flogging, fine, and imprisonment. Transportation has been resorted to, and in two instances convicts have been sent (though I know not under what authority) to England, to be passed to New South Wales.

A prisoner acquitted, is not always immediately set at large. The clerk of the Crown has a fee of *3l. 17s. 6d.* "claimed by custom, not established by law;" and there have been a few instances of persons having been detained, till they paid this demand. The gaoler also claims a trifling fee, but it is seldom paid; and when not of ability to pay it, prisoners are always set at large.

It was matter of very grave complaint, and the more impressive, as presenting a solitary instance of a charge of a sordid, not to say a corrupt kind, that the attorney-general of this island, was in the habit of receiving fees of various amount for entering *noli prosequis* on criminal prosecutions; and that as well, where the public was interested in the result, as where the consent of a private prosecutor could be obtained. It would be injustice on

BARBADOS.

GRAND SESSIONS.

such a charge, not to subjoin the entire answer of the accused. "It (a *noli prosequi*) *is* entered sometimes, on "payment of a fee to the attorney-general. I have never "granted one without the consent of the prosecutor, and "where it was not a gross offence. It was the course of "some former attorneys-general to do it without the con- "sent of the prosecutor; and large sums have been re- "ceived for it;"—(of this a particular and disgusting instance was then related.)

I am ready to believe that the duties of this (as it appears to me) sacred trust, have been discharged with greater disinterestedness as well as with sounder discretion, by the present attorney-general, than by any of his predecessors; but I cannot help lamenting, that the power in question, should have been exercised upon any occasion, to his own advantage. It is a faulty custom which the present attorney-general *found in his office;* it is now very much weakened and discountenanced, and I trust, it will not descend to his successor. I avail myself of the present opportunity of observing, that the answers of this gentleman to the questions of the Commissioners, display a liberality of sentiment which does him the highest honour.

The attorney-general's suggestion, for the improvement of this court, was A JUDGE.

The Commissioners were not able to attend a court of grand sessions, as there was no gaol delivery till the month of June: a circumstance which they exceedingly regretted, as they had reason to believe that *this* was a branch of the judicature of the island requiring a severe scrutiny.

The sitting of this court as we were assured, exhibits a curious spectacle. The want of an efficient judge is never so conspicuous. The accounts we constantly received, of the great want of order and decency prevailing upon these occasions, both *in* and *out* of court, we had no means of authenticating; but the acknowledged course of proceeding is sufficiently remarkable; and I fear, obnoxious to censure.

BARBADOS.

GRAND SESSIONS.

The attorney-general it was stated, will not prepare an indictment in a case which has not been before a magistrate, the magistrate receiving a fee. The grand jury will not receive a bill that is not presented by the attorney-general, the attorney-general conducting all prosecutions.

The attorney-general draws the indictment; then as has been shewn, charges the jury; expounds the law; prosecutes, and sums up; destroying of course, all distinction, between the duties of the judge and public prosecutor. This is the ordinary course. An incident, by which the proceedings are sometimes relieved in important cases, is, the attorney-general desiring his junior to exercise the right of reply, reserving himself for the summing up.

Informant a barrister.

The result of these proceedings we found, precisely what we had anticipated. The power of the attorney-general is far too extensive in the island, and as a natural consequence, his influence is regarded with extreme jealousy. The discharge of duties so incongruous, as those of prosecutor and expounder of the law, makes juries distrustful of his statements, and often occasions them to acquit improperly.

I respectfully represent to your Lordship, for the information of his Majesty, having given a faithful outline of the course of proceedings in this court, that this is an unworthy manner for Englishmen to be tried for their lives! and if the mode be as I apprehend it is, unquestionably defective, I then beg leave though less confidently, to suggest as the cause, that the judges are *not lawyers;* persons skilled in the criminal code, and duly *qualified for the regular administration* of justice.

## COURT OF QUARTER SESSIONS.

A Court of Quarter Sessions is by law established in every parish; amounting to eleven in the island. Two justices form a court; the senior taking the chair. This court, though empowered by a local act to hear and determine offences of petit larceny and misdemeanors, supposes—and acts upon the opinion, that it cannot summon a jury. This occasions the business of the sessions to be at present, confined to the appointment of constables. The meeting of the court is very irregular; occasionally, it has intermissions of its sittings of *two* or *three* years; owing sometimes to the want of two justices in a parish. The unavoidable consequence is the trial at the grand sessions, of all the petty offences which are intended and directed to be disposed of at the quarter sessions.

BARBADOS.

QUARTER SESSIONS.

Under No. 39, Moore's Laws.

This court transacting no business, is not attended by any professional persons whatsoever. The attorney-general said, he never knew any business carried on there, except the appointment of constables; "till some "time last year, when there were one or two trials for "some criminal offences, upon which the court under-"took to hear, determine and fine, without a jury."

By No. 54, Hall's Laws, (which has never been repealed,) it is directed, "as to all persons committed to "gaol for any theft, not exceeding petit larceny, that the "party complaining shall be bound to appear and pro-"secute, at the next quarter sessions."

As an advantage, the attorney-general recommended that "this court should be regulated as the quarter ses-"sions are in England." The solicitor-general, to the question Whether he could suggest any improvement in this court? answered "the *constituting a new one*."

## THE SLAVE COURT.

This court is differently constituted, according as the offence to be tried, is capital or otherwise. Murder, burglary, and other offences enumerated in the general Slave Act, are capital; as are obeah, (pretended witchcraft,) and perhaps some other offences, made so by subsequent acts. In cases of capital offences, the court is composed of two justices of the peace and three freeholders of the neighbourhood of the place, where the

MS. act.

BARBADOS.

SLAVE COURT.

offence is committed. The five compose the court; and are all judges both of the law and the fact. They are not appointed to meet at any fixed time, but only as occasion requires. On complaint, made on oath and reduced into writing, the judge if he sees cause may commit the slave to prison, unless he is bailed; which he generally is,—by his owner. Slaves are bailable in all cases, murder included. Bail is usually required to the amount of 100*l*.

If the magistrate thinks there is no foundation for the charge he dismisses the complaint; if the complainant have given a false account, he will have the expenses to pay, on acquittal of the prisoner.

If the case proceeds, the justice calls in another magistrate, and the *two* summon the freeholders. The trial takes place, as soon as the justices and freeholders can conveniently meet, generally in the course of eight or ten days. There is no limitation of time, by law.

When the court is assembled, no indictment is preferred or bill found by a grand jury: the magistrate before whom the complaint was made, is taken to have decided, that there *is sufficient ground* to put the slave upon his trial.

The same magistrate who entertained the complaint, sits upon the trial. I do not know whether the prisoner is considered as possessing any right of challenge or exception to the justices or freeholders, in a court thus constituted; as judges cannot be *recused* under any law of England, and here all are judges both of the law and the fact; or rather unite the functions of judges and jurors. At another island, (St. Christopher,) where the trial of slaves takes place before a jury of twelve men, I saw the right claimed and exercised by a prisoner, a slave, and seven jurymen successively challenged.

*Vivâ voce* evidence is always required; and may consist of the evidence of slaves, but not upon oath unless they have been baptized; in which case they are allowed to be sworn. They are "sometimes sworn on grave dirt, "according to a superstition." "A negro's wife's evi-"dence is admitted," because it is in general a nominal

BARBADOS.

SLAVE COURT.

and not a legal marriage. In the case of false evidence given by a slave, the justice or court, before which the false evidence is given, directs the offender to be flogged. This is not frequent; for unless the offence is gross the delinquent is seldom punished. The evidence of slaves was represented in *this* island, as *not* being in general correct and to be depended upon.

*Secus* at Tobago and Grenada.

An attorney very frequently attends the trial on behalf of the master, and renders professional assistance to the slave.

There is no regular record, but the magistrates who try the case keep an account of the proceedings. These are not returned to any public office, and after the lapse of a few years, it would be difficult to produce evidence to prove a former acquittal, if a slave were to be a second time apprehended for the same offence. While "neither "the slave nor the master has any remedy for the ma- "licious prosecution of the slave!"

Per Attorney-General.

If the five members of the court are agreed unanimously, a conviction takes place; otherwise the prisoner is acquitted.

Upon conviction, sentence of death must be passed in all capital cases; but an appeal may be brought by the owner of the convicted slave before the governor and council, who may affirm, reverse, or alter the sentence. In *this* case, the proceedings on the trial, are transmitted to the governor and council; without any observations, except that the justices sometimes report on the credibility of witnesses.

If there is no appeal or application for reprieve or pardon, NO copy of the trial is laid before the governor, or report madé to him or any other superior authority, before the execution takes place.

The warrant of execution is directed to the constable who attends the trial, and he executes it without delay.

There is no fixed time, or appointed or usual place, for the public execution of slave malefactors.

To counteract the natural inclination of the master to screen his slave from justice from interested motives; in the words of the act, "that the owner may not be dis-

BARBADOS. — SLAVE COURT.

"couraged to detect and discover the offences of his ne-"groes," a condemned slave is always appraised, and the value not exceeding a limited sum paid to the owner out of the public treasury. But in Barbados,* by Cl. 15,

No. 82, Hall's Laws, Cl. 15.

No. 82, Hall's Laws, "the party injured is to be first "indemnified to the extent of the injury sustained."

Cl. 16.

And by the same law, Cl. 16, "if it shall appear that "the master had not duly provided for the support of "the slave, and necessity might have compelled the said "negro to commit the offence, the whole appraised value "is to be paid to the party injured, and nothing to the "master or owner." But, unless the case were represented (as no doubt it would be,) to the governor, the execution of the slave might still proceed. The royal mercy, I venture to affirm beyond a possibility of doubt, would certainly be extended to such an offender; but that grace could only be invoked by the justices making a report of the trial; which would be a departure from their practice in common cases.

In the case of minor offences committed by slaves, complaint is made to a magistrate, but not upon oath. The magistrate summons the owner to produce the slave at the appointed time, together with such persons, as the complainant or the master wish to give evidence. The justice hears the case, and either dismisses the complaint, or orders a punishment of whipping according to the offence, from six to thirty-nine lashes. Flogging is the only punishment known in these cases; it is inflicted with the military cat (*o' nine tails*) between the shoulders. The mode of proceeding is exactly similar in cases of theft or injury by one slave against another. The owner makes the complaint. The master of the slave complained against, is summoned, and an investigation of the facts takes place before the magistrate *The information is not upon oath and there is no conviction in writing*.

The slave is not considered subject to the criminal code of England, where it is in force with free persons in this island; but is only answerable for offences, created by the slave-laws of the colony The "magistrate" says

BARBADOS.

SLAVE COURT.

the attorney-general " does not interfere, in any cases " not thus provided for."

The attorney-general of this island, was not aware of any improvement that could be made in the trial of slaves. He did not think " they would be better off, from being " tried by twelve white men." As regards the chances of escape for a valuable slave, I agree with the attorney-general, that the accused would not be a gainer by a change, calculated to ensure the conviction and punishment of the guilty without distinction. This is principally apparent from the answers of the senior justice of the peace, a gentleman who possessed extensive experience in these cases: " I think," he said, " it " would be an improvement to have a slave tried, for " capital offences, by a jury. At present, few offences " receive more than corporal punishment. There is a " great disinclination to convict capitally. Murder, " burglary, burning of houses or canes, killing of cattle, " and obeah, are capital offences; grand larceny is not. " So breaking into houses in the day time and stealing " therefrom. I have known fifty instances of slaves, who " had committed *such* offences, escaping with only a " whipping. The feeling is very strong to *acquit* slaves, " right or wrong. I have only known one instance to " the contrary in the case of Mr. Elcock's murderers."

The attention of the Commissioners was requested to a case, which had then recently occurred, of a slave who had broken open the house of his OWNER, in the night, I believe, (for we did not meet with the trial,) and stolen valuable property. The slave was tried upon the charge, but the court was of opinion that he could not be convicted of any offence, under the existing ineffectual laws.

Cl. 12, of No. 82, the act constituting the court for the trial of slaves for capital offences requires the freeholders to be " of the place nearest where the offence " was committed," which the attorney-general thought " only meant of the vicinity." It was our fortune to hear legal objections frequently taken to this construction, in other islands, and to witness great embarrassment occasioned, by the wording of similar acts, con-

BARBADOS.

SLAVE COURT.

taining nearly the same provisions. Most,—I believe ALL *of these laws*—(I am happy to say it) are, by this time repealed.

The trials under the act in this island are very unsatisfactory. We heard them pronounced "disgraceful." The judges it was said, are ignorant; the proceedings are slovenly; the charge being unwritten, so we were informed, shifts with the case; a disposition to favour where it exists, receives no check, from the want of publicity. There being no assigned place, or appointed time, for the execution of slave malefactors, the wretched convict as soon as sentence is passed, is fastened to the nearest tree; unless, which frequently happens, the owner of the soil is at hand to prevent it. In such case, the miserable culprit is dragged, from tree to tree, from estate to estate, and in one case, of then recent occurrence, the constable was at last forced to throw the exhausted sufferer off the Town Bridge, securing the rope by a lamp-post. With unfeigned respect for the opinion of the attorney-general, and admitting that there is no spell or charm in the number "*twelve*," I cannot help thinking that the poor slave, though his chances of escape might be fewer, would himself greatly prefer a trial at the grand sessions. As to trial by "white men," be the number what it may, twelve or five, by *such* persons, slaves are already tried, so that in *that* particular, their situation would not be altered, if they were tried in the same manner as freemen; as it is my unqualified opinion,—that they certainly ought to be;—and so I humbly certify.

---

RECAPITULATION AND REMARKS.

HAVING now examined in detail, the various proceedings in the different courts, established for the administration of civil and criminal justice in this island, it may be useful to shortly recapitulate the instances of DEVIATION from the usages of England, and the practical results of such departure. The same occasion will be favourable, for a brief and pointed notice of any practice or doctrines of a doubtful or exceptionable kind whether arising from local laws, or accidental circumstances; as well as to the introduction of a few miscellaneous facts and general observations. It will only remain to be considered *where* there is in this island any DEFECT OF JURISDICTION, or *whether* any *injuries* can be suffered, or *wrongs* inflicted, under the present system, without *redress*. BARBADOS. RECAPITULATION.

The principal subject of remark, because the most prominent defect in the system, is the absence of a person, informed and experienced in the principles of equity jurisprudence, to preside in the court of Chancery. Most of the complaints the Commissioners received, and a great part of the distress they found existing, certainly arise from this cause. A due administration of the powers of a court of equity would remedy many evils. As it at present exists, Chancery.

ERROR, IN MISTAKE OF JURISDICTION, was imputed to this court in cases of *lunacy*, and petitions for *separation*, and *separate maintenance*.

IMPROPER PRACTICE was objected to it, as regards *injunctions*.

IRREGULARITY, UNCERTAINTY, AND EXPENSE, were generally charged as affecting the whole of the proceedings.

The number of causes, it will be seen by the registrar's return, is very trifling. There are not, upon an average, above TEN bills filed in a year. BUSINESS.

The practice of the court of Exchequer we found exceptionable, in admitting a defendant to be arrested, in a common case, for unliquidated damages, laid at any amount the plaintiff pleased. It is still more reprehensible, in suffering a defendant to lie in prison, without remedy, if the plaintiff will not proceed in his action against him. Exchequer.

It seems doubtful whether the interests of the Crown, as regards its debtors and accountants, do not stand in need of further protection.

The island of Barbados is about thirty miles long, and sixteen miles broad; consequently smaller than any county in England; Rutland, Huntingdon and Mid-

BARBADOS.

RECAPITULATION.

dlesex only excepted. Yet this little island is rather largely endowed with five distinct —superior—independent courts of Common Pleas;—with an establishment of one chief judge, and four asssistant judges in each district. To *a consolidation of these courts, and the establishment of one court of Common Pleas for the trial of all actions, at Bridge Town*, there appears, after an attentive consideration of the subject, no sound objection. The law and the practice at present prevailing, oppose no doubt, some impediments to the measure; but such only, as are easily removeable. The act, requiring an action to be brought in the precinct where the *defendant* lives, is a provision of a singular nature, (though I will not agree to call it "discreditable,") and which it will be necessary to repeal. The custom of requiring the attendance of witnesses without payment of their necessary expenses, it will be expedient and reasonable —to alter. Both—are measures, which independently of their presenting obstacles to improvement, are objectionable ON PRINCIPLE and IN SE. The trouble and inconvenience which the change will occasion to persons residing in the country, (which, though not seriously objected, was surmised,) will be less than is usually felt by persons resorting to the circuit town, in any county in England; and ONLY THE SAME as is sustained by suitors, witnesses, and jurors, attending the *other* courts of *this* island; the court of Chancery, the court of Exchequer, and the court of Grand Sessions.

The opinion of the attorney-general it will be seen, (in more than one of his answers,) was very favourable to the measure, and he gave solid reasons for its expediency.

The party giving credit, is naturally desirous that the trial should be had, in the place where HE resides and the goods have been obtained. "When the trial is at "any of the out-courts, the expenses of counsel, who "do not commonly attend there, and have therefore "special fees, as well as of the witnesses carried from "Bridge Town to the country, fall in the end very

BARBADOS.

RECAPITULATION.

Appendix.

The president; chief justice of Hole Town; & al.

"heavily, upon the defendant." The attorney-general, it will be observed, speaks in this answer, as if the expenses of the witnesses were always allowed; but we were assured it was not generally the case. And in the minutes of proceedings, of a court holden in St. Michael's precinct, in April, 1812, I find in the case of Wood *v.* Wood, an attachment granted against a witness for not attending upon a subpœna, on proof "that the witness "was personally served," but not that "*his reasonable* "*expenses were paid or tendered to him*" The same sentiment of approval, provided the expenses of witnesses were defrayed, was expressed by many other reflecting and unprejudiced persons: but it is fair and proper to mention that the solicitor-general appears to have received, from a circumstance he stated, a somewhat different impression. Mr. Coulthurst observed, that "formerly the court did not sit regularly at the out-pre-"cincts, and credit was often refused on that account, "to persons living in such precincts; but it was not *so* "*now*." This, it will be observed, does not indicate any indisposition in the storekeeper to part with his goods, in a case in which he could recover their value in a court in town, (for which there is no rational ground,) but only manifests a reluctance, perfectly natural, to give credit to a customer whom he may be afterwards under the necessity of suing, in one of those precincts where the courts are not regularly held. And it will be remembered that the act regulating the court of Exchequer, (Hall's Laws, No. 135,) speaks of the contrivances at that time resorted to, to get rid of the *inconvenient* rule of law, that an action must be brought in the precinct where the defendant lives.

A compromise was suggested: that the court should be fixed in Bridge Town; but that there might in the course of the year, be one or more circuits of judges through the island. To this it was objected, and as we thought with great force, that "it could not conveni-"ently take place: there were no inns; the judge would "be forced to go to the houses of gentlemen in each dis-"trict. that is. to persons commonly interested in the

BARBADOS.

RECAPITULATION.

"questions to be tried in the country parts; which would "be unpleasant to the judge, and regarded with suspi- "cion by others."

Under these circumstances I beg leave to recommend a consolidation of the courts of Common Pleas, and the establishment of one court for the trial of all actions, in St. Michael's precinct in Bridge Town.

The *holidays* should be *few*, and those fixed by law.

The "law as to arrests in civil cases," the solicitor-general "thought a proper subject for consideration and "amendment."

Depositions, of persons, unable to attend the trial, containing much that is not evidence, are receivable in these courts, under a law of the island. The *vivâ voce* examination of witnesses, is of course vastly preferable, wherever it can be had; but it is said, that, from the situation and circumstances of these colonies, in which seamen and traders are, of necessity, constantly passing from island to island, the use of depositions cannot be entirely dispensed with. Still I would venture to suggest that they should be received with great caution; and care ought to be taken to have them properly framed; they should be taken before judges or commissioners; they should be comformable to the rules of evidence; and should not be permitted to be read, without satisfactory proof, that the witness is not in the island at the time of trial, and is not sent or kept out of the way by the party, to prevent his personal attendance.

A list of *twenty-four* jurymen is given to the judges previous to a trial, and they strike out the names of twelve; a practice which, considering the jealousy always felt (and still more strongly in the colonies, than in England) of the interference of judges, with the appointment of juries, certainly appears to me excessively unwise, if not improper.

Special juries are not known in practice. The persons who would be chiefly eligible to serve upon them from their condition and circumstances in life, are almost all of them upon the bench, in one or other of the different courts of the island.

BARBADOS.

RECAPITULATION.

A special verdict may be demanded by the counsel, on either side, on a point of law, arising in the course of a cause. This provision, an old edition of the statutes (Rawlins's Laws) accounts for, as being framed "with "a view to have the case sent home, the judges not being "lawyers;" from which it appears, that the inconvenience of having judges who had not received a professional education, began to be early, as it has continued to be long, severely felt. But the provision is not confined to those cases of sufficient value, in which an appeal is allowed in the last resort to His Majesty in council, (where it might be highly desirable, in order that the whole case should fully appear,) but extends to *all* cases, and must be granted upon the bare request of one party, which is likely to lead to vexation, expense and delay.

There is no advertisement in the public papers, of the sale by auction, of goods taken in execution; a note, only, is put on the door of the marshal's office. Great frauds were imputed, in consequence of this mode of proceeding, but none were proved. Sufficient INCONVENIENCE, however, was shewn, to justify the opinion, expressed by the solicitor-general, that advertisements ought to be rendered necessary.

Some provision is required to prevent the possible and cruel separation of families, when slaves are sold under executions.

The creditor, who has sued out an execution against lands and houses, is compellable to take them, at an appraisement, usually much above the real value. This is a point deserving the serious attention of the British merchant, who has taken a judgment for his security.

There is no allowance to a debtor; a prisoner in execution.

If the two attorneys can agree, costs are never taxed at all. When they are taxed, the judge has no rule to guide him, in taxation, but often applies to the attorneys themselves, to know what it is usual to allow them.* *Dec. 1822.

A table of fees was afterwards † promulgated, but without giving satisfaction, chiefly because it is contend- †Jan. 1823.

BARBADOS.

RECAPITULATION.

ed, that the regulation of fees ought to be the subject of legislative enactment.

The judges of these courts do not take down the evidence, or sum up the facts, or state the law to the jury.

Slave evidence is not admitted. The free people of colour, who have been made competent witnesses, are said to be very indifferent to the obligation of an oath; but none have yet been convicted of perjury. All persons manumitted before the act may be witnesses, not so persons manumitted since; unless the local laws have been complied with.

Bench actions. Bench actions are demands under 8*l*., decided without a jury, and by a judge ignorant of the law.

Ordinary. The governor, sitting alone, as ordinary, has no assessor, or professional assistance of any kind; and the court is without any means of enforcing its decrees.

Admiralty. The fees and costs in the court of Admiralty are exorbitantly high. Proceedings for the recovery of seamen's wages, where the subject-matter in dispute is four or five dollars, occasion an expense of 50*l*. An authority to hear and determine cases of this nature, is given in most of the other islands, to one or more justices of the peace; and I think with great advantage.

And see 59G. 3. c. 58.

Appeal and Error. The court of appeal and error, to review the decisions of the inferior courts upon writs of error, has no gentleman who has received a regular, professinal education, upon the bench. In case of a decision palpably wrong, where the sum in dispute is 200*l*. or 250*l*. (or any sum less than 300*l*.) the unsuccessful party, though injured to an extent that may be of serious consequence to *him*, perhaps to the value of his stock in trade, cannot bring his writ of error. With great deference I would observe, that the sum, for which an appeal lies from the court of first instance to the court of appeal in the island, appears to me to have been fixed too high at 300*l*.

GRAND SESSIONS. In the court of Grand Sessions, the judges or magistrates upon the bench, say and do nothing, except appoint both the grand and petit juries and their foremen; and if the judge admits an invalid excuse, for the attendance of any juror, he is liable to a fine of 50*l*. I submit

BARBADOS.

RECAPITULATION.

that a judge should not be *fined.* It is to be presumed that he will exercise a sound discretion; especially when a regular education to the profession of the law, shall be made, as it ought, a necessary qualification for the office.

The attorney-general draws the indictment; charges the grand jury; addresses the petit jury; examines the witnesses; solves any difficulties, in point of law; replies on the case; sums up the evidence; and afterwards represents the circumstances to the governor from his own notes or recollection, when execution or reprieve is under consideration. Sometimes the court is relieved from hearing a case by the entry of a *noli prosequi;* for which, instead of a FINE to the public, (the probable result of a conviction,) a FEE is paid to the attorney-general. The effect is,—a jealousy of the power of the attorney-general, and a leaning to acquit every person *he* prosecutes.

Quarter Sessions.

The court of Quarter Sessions is a nullity.

Slave Court.

The slave court is constituted very propitiously for the discharge of the criminal slave, whose master is desirous of saving him; but less favourably for the ends of public justice.

In case of conviction, the proceedings are melancholy and disgraceful. Unless an appeal is demanded, no report of the trial or representation of the case, is made to the governor, before the sentence is carried into effect; but the unfortunate convict is immediately executed, without any interval allowed him, *upon the nearest tree.*

GENERAL COMPLAINTS.

Such are the proceedings in the courts of equity and of law: and of the latter, in those appointed for the administration of civil, as well as of criminal justice. The objections we were accustomed to hear applying to all the courts, and affecting the general administration of justice, expressed in no measured terms, were as follows; "that there were no regular proceedings,"—"no settled practice,"—"great delays,"—"little uniformity in the decisions," and "the costs of suit enormous!" I shall report upon these charges succinctly and in order.

IRREGULARITY.

The first allegation is undeniable RULES in these

BARBADOS.

GENERAL COMPLAINTS.

courts are unknown, or disregarded; or only perversely and partially applied. Great irregularities are therefore constantly practised, not from bad intention, but from ignorance of law. I feel anxious to be understood, as not meaning to impute to the judges of Barbados, or to the governors who are sole chancellors in the other islands, any improper design in a single instance; but I must be permitted to say, that where they feel the greatest anxiety and use the utmost exertions to do right, not being governed by wise and fixed rules, or adhering to a settled practice the same in all cases, THEIR VERY JUSTICE IS CAPRICIOUS: and they often mistake their course and fall into fatal errors. Without dwelling invidiously on the mistakes and mischiefs of the courts as at present constituted, or repeating coarse reflections on the deficient attainments of the judges, it is sufficient to observe, that there existed a general feeling that a presiding lawyer was absolutely necessary in all the courts. A very considerable party in the colony further required "not only "that the persons to preside in their courts should have "received a regular professional education, but also that "they should be strangers to the colony; unconnected "with its inhabitants, and unaccustomed to its irregular "proceedings."

DELAY.

The charge of dilatoriness in proceedings, whether affecting the courts of law or of equity in this island at the present time, does not appear to me, to be substantiated. So great an AMOUNT OF TIME I apprehend, is not consumed, in conducting a cause or a suit to a termination in ordinary cases in Barbados, as in England. The charge, it has been seen, preferred against the judges of the court of Chancery in this island in more than one instance, was *precipitancy;* in cases however, where they acted I am bound to state for all that appeared, in perfect conformity to the law and established practice of the island. In the courts of law, delays are not frequent. Where they have occurred, they were occasioned by injunctions, or resulted from loose practice. The defect somewhere existing, is not in the established forms of procedure; which are not intricate or mischievously simple.

BARBADOS.

GENERAL COMPLAINTS.

It is not in inconvenient rules of practice, for none are prescribed or followed; it is not in want of time for transacting the business of a sitting; for much time is generally wasted, and yet every court, the paper is gone through. In my humble apprehension, the trifling delays in court (occasioned by the attorneys doing *as they please*,) and the charges of expense and uncertainty, which are more serious and better founded, all originate *in the incurable vice of the system.* The constitution of the courts themselves, is favourable to the growth of expense, and induces a suspicion of connivance at irregularities. The judge is paid by *fees*, for which he is dependent upon attorneys, whose bills it is his duty to tax. Though often estimable and excellent men in private life, the judges are very unfit for the purpose. There are twenty-five judges of the different courts of Common Pleas, and as many more must be added belonging to the other courts of the island. None of them have been prepared by previous professional education and habits, for the situation they hold. Though very far indeed from being corrupt, they are (technically speaking) ignorant, and therefore incapable of detecting corrupt practices in others. It is the same, with irregularities; they are not aware of them, having only a confused and imperfect knowledge of the rules and principles of law.

Fifty judges!

UNCERTAINTY.

In gentlemen who are not lawyers, a very accurate knowledge of adjudged cases is not to be expected. Professing to be bound by the decisions of other judges, they may not always, be acquainted with them, or they will not be so, in equal degrees.

Five—different chief judges,—presiding in independent jurisdictions; having no necessary communication; variously endowed; engaged in dissimilar occupations; having had no common studies; may, it appears to me very excusably, establish five—different—rules of law. In the court of Chancery, it is still less to be expected that the decisions should be uniform and consistent.

EXPENSE.

The next subject of animadversion, the expense of proceedings in the courts, is a topic large and difficult. Costs of proceedings in Chancery, although no stamps

BARBADOS

GENERAL COMPLAINTS.

are used, are I do believe oppressive and ruinous, and require an entire revision.

I before said, that the authority assumed by the courts to regulate fees, did not pass unquestioned. By the instructions, the governor and council are to settle "the "fees of offices." By an act of the island, a discretion is given to the chief justice, to "TAX COSTS," in his court of Common Pleas. But fees of "solicitors," it is contended, "are not included in the instructions; or any "fees, other than fees of office; that is to say, the amount "of compensation for *official services*. So, 'the local act "'gives no authority to *alter or regulate fees*. The set"'tlement of fees, it is admitted, may have become ne"'cessary, but it ought to be the subject of legislative "'enactment.'"

The views taken of such regulations in England, at different times and by the highest authorities, have not I am aware, been quite identical. I do not feel myself called upon to deliver an opinion, upon a subject so embarrassing; but I cannot abstain from expressing an anxious wish, that the point should be ascertained and established *by the authority and wisdom of Parliament*, for it occasions infinite disputes in all the colonies. In these islands, where the practice is changed and modified at pleasure, it necessarily follows that old fees are increased and new ones introduced; and this under an authority, disputed in almost every instance of its exercise. It was urged against fees being regulated by the court, that "fees were quite arbitrary," and that "under the "present system the people had no confidence in their "judges." It was not unreasonably desired that "whe"ther regulated by act or otherwise, fees should be as"certained and fixed;" that "their enormous allowance "should be resettled and reduced," and that "there "should be a taxing officer, unconnected with the prac"tising attorneys."

That there is generally a great want of confidence in their judges cannot be denied, and is very much to be lamented.

BARBADOS.

GENERAL COMPLAINTS.

A new table of fees, and an independent taxing officer, appear to be indispensably necessary.

To discover the facts necessary to form a correct opinion as to the "enormity of costs," was attended with insurmountable difficulties; and proved greatly more than the Commissioners were able to accomplish. The judges, called upon by the governor (under instructions from home,) to return the amount of their fees for the last three years, reported only as we were informed, "that "they had not yet been in office three years." The fees in the Court of Chancery, as well as in the Court of Common Pleas, were revised by the judges of the respective courts during our stay in the island; and a new table of fees of the latter promulgated, but without getting rid of the dissatisfaction existing upon the subject. The measure indeed, was not calculated to remove the objections of those, who contend that the alteration ought to be made by Act of Assembly. A table of fees, to have any chance of being observed, must afford a reasonable compensation for professional services in a climate so little favourable to health and life. In the court of Admiralty, a docket of fees "sent out by Sir William Scott, about the year 1814," after hanging a few days in the office and having its face turned to the wall, suddenly disappeared. By singular good fortune it was accidentally recovered, one or two days before the Commissioners entered upon the inquiry into proceedings in that court. From professional gentlemen it was not to be expected that bills of costs would be tendered to the Commissioners; though some were most liberally and obligingly furnished, by one very respectable solicitor, Mr. Taylor; and except in cases brought under our notice by the complaint of the parties, we did not think it proper or expedient to call for them. From the suitors themselves, we obtained a very few and these are very heavy. Remuneration in this country, for intellectual labour, ought undoubtedly, to be liberal. The intense heat of the climate renders it very painful: it is attended with constant risk of life, and total sacrifice of comfort. The expense of living, and an establishment,—house and cham-

Fees.

BARBADOS.

GENERAL COMPLAINTS.

ber-rent, &c. &c. are very considerable. But it is certainly desirable, that a suitor should be able to form some judgment of the probable expense at which he may indulge a taste for litigation.

In the court of Chancery, *ante*.

It was before stated, as the result of our inquiries upon this subject, that, where the attorneys on both sides agree, no taxation of the bills in any of the courts ever takes place. How the taxing officer can consider himself discharged from the duty he owes the suitor, from any acquiescence of his solicitor, I shall not stop to inquire. It is sufficient that it is admitted, that unless an objection be made to any of the items, the officer thinks himself relieved from the necessity of investigating the bill of costs. I submit that, in this respect, he is mistaken. All bills are supposed to be taxed; and the officer I conceive, is not exonerated from his duty, by any agreement of the solicitors. An extensive change of the practice is, I should think, in this as in many other particulars, highly desirable.

The distinction, familiar to every practising lawyer, and generally known among all persons of active occupation, of costs between party and party, and costs between attorney and client, is doubtingly recognized in this island. Yet one oppressive, and as it appeared to us, unwarrantable charge, the usual retaining fee of counsel, previous to commencing a suit in this (and every other) island, namely, 100*l.* sterling, affords a sufficient illustration, of what are necessarily considered *extra* costs or costs out of pocket, beyond the costs allowed. The distinction itself, in my view of the subject, is particularly useful and most advantageously known in practice. If the time of counsel is occupied, or extensive inquiry engaged in, at the express desire of an anxious client, the additional expense perhaps unnecessarily incurred, from the zeal and exertions of one party, cannot it appears to me, be reasonably cast upon the other.

The judges it will be observed in all the courts, receive no salary, but are remunerated by certain fees and emoluments, annexed to the performance of several of the duties of their office. "To obtain these," according

BARBADOS.

GENERAL COMPLAINTS.

to our information, "the judges are obliged to pay as-"siduous attention" out of court "to the attorneys, whose "bills they may be called upon to tax, in court." I confess this observation at first, struck me as offensive and conveying an unworthy suspicion; but such is the necessary consequence of a vicious system. It was truly stated to be "a miserable thing to see a judge dependent "upon attorneys." The name of a judge was mentioned, "who had been in the habit of going from office to office, "looking after business; to see what attorneys had deeds "to acknowledge." The emoluments of the present chief justice were supposed to be less, than some of his predecessors, "because they depended upon favour, and "he was unpopular." An answer, the Commissioners received upon this subject has been mentioned. "A "judge's fee for taking acknowledgments is 1*l*., but "where he comes to a party's house, he expects to be "paid liberally, he then usually gets 5*l*."

I feel myself justified in recommending, that the existing system be discontinued; that the receipt of fees of every kind by the judges, be entirely abolished; and that they regularly receive a stated salary. Where fees continue to be paid, as, in most cases it is proper that they should, they should form an aggregate fund, to be applied in diminution of the expenses incurred, in carrying an improved plan into execution.

In the court of Chancery, the bills of costs of this island, obtained by the Commissioners, are,—

First, a bill of costs presented by Mr. Rebitt, which, according to that gentleman's own statement, was procured "by stealth." This bill I received, with the papers, and shall duly return, but, as prompted by my own feelings, I shall abstain from remarking upon it. See Appendix

Secondly, a bill of costs presented by Mr. Taylor, a very respectable solicitor of this island, in a case of Went, executor, complainant; Ford & al. executors, defendants; which has the following minute annexed to it, rendering it, in my humble opinion, the fittest bill, that could be selected, as a specimen of the costs and ex-

BARBADOS.

GENERAL COMPLAINTS.

penses usually allowed, at the time the Commissioners reached the island:

"November 1st, 1814.—The foregoing bill of costs, "produced and submitted by the committee of the ho-"nourable the council, appointed for settling costs, &c. "when the same was approved by the said court, and it "was ordered that the same be pursued in taxing costs, "in suits, in this honourable court; as well those which, "at present, are depending, and undetermined, as others, "hereafter, to be commenced and determined, as per "minute of this date.

(Signed) *Robt. B. Clarke*, Registrar."

*Here follows the Bill of Costs.*

It will be observed that fees are always charged, for two counsel *perusing and settling every draft*, and the same for making *common motions*.

A return will also be found of "the fees receivable in the Chancery office." With the exception of a charge of 2*l.* 10*s.* for every occasion of attendance upon the chancellor, which may be thought too much, these fees seem very moderate.

In the courts of law, the costs of proceedings are less exorbitant than in the court of Chancery.

| | £ | *s.* | *d.* |
|---|---|---|---|
| Two counsel are always employed, "to peruse and settle a declaration," for which the fee is "for each" - - | 2 | 10 | 0 |
| If there be more counts than one, for each special count after the first (each) - | 1 | 5 | 0 |
| "Half that fee for the common counts, *if* "*recovered on.*" | | | |

"*Upon the action* (or declaration) after it is settled, "another fee, of the same amount, to the counsel, re-"spectively.

| | £ | *s.* | *d.* |
|---|---|---|---|
| "Upon the pleas (of the adverse party), is "allowed to each counsel, for the gene-"ral issue" - - | 1 | 5 | 0 |
| Upon a special plea - - | 2 | 10 | 0 |

and "*double matter is charged accordingly.*"

BARBADOS.

GENERAL COMPLAINTS.

| | | | |
|---|---|---|---|
| For "perusing and settling a special motion," each counsel receives - | 2 | 10 | 0 |
| For making a contested motion, each - | 1 | 5 | 0 |
| With the brief, a fee is paid to each counsel, according to the folios, of - | 5 | 0 | 0 |
| or | 2 | 10 | 0 |
| Lastly, "for attending the trial each counsel, for every hour after the first." - | 1 | 17 | 6 |

The attorney is allowed a charge in all the same cases (and of course many others) generally to the amount of half the counsel's fees.

The new docket of fees has somewhat reduced the amount of charges in the court of Common Pleas.

Salary.

I am not aware of any SALARY payable in this island in time of peace, except to the attorney-general.

PARTICULAR OFFICERS.

ATTORNEY GENERAL.

SOLICITOR GENERAL.

No. 144, Hall's Laws.

The attorney-general of Barbados receives a small salary of 200*l.* currency per annum, paid by the island. Such an allowance is a very inadequate return for all the various important and responsible duties, cast upon him by his situation. Occasionally also, the solicitor-general is called upon to perform official services in conjunction with the attorney-general; for which he receives no compensation. In one of the acts of the island, the insufficiency of the attorney-general's salary is noticed, and the act gives him *half of the penalties* created by it. In another act, the churchwardens are directed to pay a certain sum to the attorney-general, for drawing the act.

## MISCELLANEOUS.

A few brief particulars of the qualifications and duties of several other persons, more or less intimately connected with the administration of justice, will be conveniently collected in this place.

BARRISTERS.

It is now required (prospectively), that gentlemen admitted to practise as counsel in these courts shall previously, have been called to the bar, in England.

SOLICITORS.

It is necessary for gentlemen applying to act as at-

BARBADOS.

PARTICULAR OFFICERS.

torneys or solicitors in this island, to produce a certificate of having served a clerkship for five years, either in England or the West Indies; and a testimonial of good character must be signed by two barristers, which is usually done by the attorney and solicitor-general. They then receive a commission from the governor. They are formally admitted and take the prescribed oath, in every court in which they intend to practise. They do not pay any fee, and are not restricted to any precise number of clerks.

JUSTICES.

The justices of the peace in this island have cognizance of all offences against the public peace, of all indictable offences, and of all offences committed by slaves under the statutes of the island. A single magistrate tries complaints against slaves, for offences not capital. Besides felonies, the cases of misdemeanor brought before the magistrates in Bridge Town are exceedingly numerous. One gentleman, the senior justice of the peace in town, informed us, that he had "received 2,500 "complaints in fifteen months, in breaches of the peace "and misdemeanors; most of them complaints by free "coloured persons against slaves and against each other." He stated that "the police was very defective; the "white population very immoral, and the slave-laws very "ineffectual."

A due administration of executive justice in these various and important cases of felonies, capital and otherwise; misdemeanors and breaches of the peace; would obviously require a familiar acquaintance with the doctrines and practice of courts in general, as well as with the principles of criminal jurisprudence. But this, though very material, is not the only qualification required in a Barbados justice of the peace. The validity of contracts; the civil obligation implied by law, to pay for work and labour done, and goods sold and delivered; the amount of damages incurred by a party's neglect or refusal; the warranty of horses, tobacco, ginger, cotton, &c. are all determinable in a summary way by a single justice; and the course of proceeding is similar to what was before represented of bench actions.

Barbados.

Particular Officers.

No. 175, Hall's Laws.

Instead of every case so triable, being satisfactorily proved by the evidence of witnesses; "if the plaintiff "cannot prove his demand, the defendant shall be ex-"amined upon oath, and judgment given for what he "admits to be due and owing, and no more; but if the "defendant shall refuse to be sworn, then the com-"plainant shall be allowed and admitted to be sworn, "and what he shall swear to be due, shall be allowed of "and judgment entered up for."

The same execution issues after a justice's decision, as upon a judgment in the Court of Common Pleas.

The fees the magistrates receive are regulated by a late manuscript act.

It was represented to the Commissioners, and they thought, with great force of reason, that "it would be "better to have the number of magistrates limited, and "to give them salaries; requiring the magistrates of St. "Michael's to reside in Bridge Town. At present no "magistrate resides in town, which is very incovenient. "The fees received by magistrates in Bridge Town "amount to not less than 1,200*l.* a-year. These, and "the considerable sums paid to constables, thrown into "one common fund, would be sufficient to pay magis-"trates and constables, and provide for the police of the "town, now so defective."

A black girl, who stated that she had been manumitted and was free, complained "that she had been "cruelly assaulted and ill-used by a black man, a slave. "She had represented it to his master, and got no re-"dress. If she went to a magistrate, he would not "issue a warrant without her paying two dollars and a "half to an attorney; and she had not got so much "money." The Commissioners asked, *Whether she had made a trial: Had she yet preferred a complaint before a magistrate?* and were answered in the negative. They desired *that* might be done in the first instance; and they heard no more of the case.

A person called to complain of "a judgment having "passed against him by default, before a justice of the "peace, on a demand for the price of a horse, under

BARBADOS.

PARTICULAR OFFICERS.

"No. 175, Hall's Laws, when he had a good defence; "the horse having been warranted sound, but being com-"pletely foundered." On examination, he admitted that "a summons had been left at his usual place of abode, "with his brother-in-law, who lived with him;" and the Commissioners were of opinion that it was a matter in which they could not properly interfere.

I feel it necessary to observe, that a situation of which the duties are so multifarious and important, though at present no doubt filled by very respectable persons, is unfortunately from its nature and locality, not exactly suited to gentlemen of the very first rank or highest attainments in the island, and may perhaps sometimes, fall into obscure and indigent or incapable hands.

PROVOST-MARSHAL.

The duties of the PROVOST-MARSHAL are also of a comprehensive character, and by no means insignificant, though only or chiefly, ministerial. He is the executive officer of all the courts of law, and performs the duties of the Serjeant at Arms, in the court of Chancery.

Of civil matters this officer observed to us only one thing material; he had not he admitted, any *proper room or office in sufficient repair, for the care or custody of papers.*—In criminal concerns, he has the charge of the gaol and cage; and in capital cases, carries the sentence of the law into effect upon free malefactors.

The number of commitments to prison in criminal cases in each year, on an average of the last twenty years, he states to be forty-two.

The number of capital convicts executed in twenty years, has been sixteen; of whom ten were pirates.

There is no house of correction, in this island. The only place of confinement, in the island, is—one gaol—in Bridge Town. This is usually full: the persons kept in it, being debtors; all persons charged with offences; (slaves as well as others;) convicts; and, in war time, prisoners of war. It is not sufficiently large, commodious or airy. It is not by any means, secure; the wall requiring to be raised. The consequence—is, that debtors to a large amount, are not allowed to go into the yard, without giving the marshal security. The hardship of confinement to the gaol-room in such a climate, cannot be easily conceived; it must be absolutely insupportable. BARBADOS. PARTICULAR OFFICERS.

Debtors are not always separated from criminals, or men from women. Classification according to the offence or age of the accused, is out of the question; but they are divided in case of sickness.

There is no employment of prisoners in the gaol.

Criminals have an allowance of 7½*d.* a day, but no bed or gaol-dress is provided them.

Cage. The CAGE is the place of confinement for runaway slaves. It is secure—airy, clean, and the provost-marshal added, "comfortable." The owner of the slave pays a bit (7½*d.*) a day for his sustenance.

There is no *employment* of slaves, in the cage. They sit cross-legged, and do nothing. In this particular alone, (and in no other respect,) I thought the management of the cage objectionable; but the marshal observed, "I "am under a penalty not to make use of them."

CORONER. An inquest is taken on the body of a slave in this island, in the same cases and precisely in the same manner, as upon free persons. I do not find among the papers relating to this colony, any answers to the particular questions of the Commissioners; such as will be found, in reporting upon the other islands. The returns may probably have been lost or mislaid, on the unfortunate death of the secretary to the commission, which took place at Nevis, in November, 1823.

DEFECT OF JURISDICTION. It only remains to be noticed, where there is a DEFECT OF JURISDICTION, and whether any INJURIES can be SUFFERED, or WRONGS INFLICTED, under the present system, without REDRESS.

NO BANKRUPT LAWS. Whether it would be advisable to introduce a code of bankrupt laws into the jurisprudence of the colonies, the same as obtains in England; or under any modifications of that system; I am not prepared to offer an opinion. It is a question which resident merchants and lawyers, men of intelligence, are alone competent to decide. The information the Commissioners were able to procure, was hastily collected. With the greatest anxiety and the utmost exertions to be accurate, it is probable, that I

BARBADOS.

DEFECT OF JURISDICTION.

may in this Report, fall into occasional errors. This, in an inquiry so extensive, I trust will be considered, unavoidable.

No court for the trial of questions of MANUMISSION.

There is no court constituted for the express purpose, of trying questions of manumission, in these islands. In Barbados, applications are constantly made to the governor, in cases of this nature. It is impossible to discover, *how* the governor derives any authority upon the subject. He has no jurisdiction, that is apparent; and it is clear that his decisions upon a question of property, cannot be binding. Claims founded on manumission, are sometimes incidentally considered before justices of the peace; but there nowhere exists A REGULAR COURT, FOR THE TRIAL OF SUCH QUESTIONS; in which, by the benignant interpretation of the law on points respecting freedom, the condition of slavery may be gradually and imperceptibly worn away, without hazard or injustice, as was the case with villeinage in England.

A black man applied to the Commissioners, "to ask, "what course he ought to pursue under circumstances "of great hardship. The executor of his late master "(who had emancipated three house slaves, for long services and attention during his last illness) had for a "great length of time, (several years,) omitted, to make "the payment on manumission (50*l.*) to the parish, having assets, and being directed to make it by the will. "The complainant had in consequence, lost the advantage of 4*l.* per annum; which he would otherwise, "have received from the parish." The Commissioners asked: *Whether any steps had been taken to obtain legal redress?* and being answered in the negative, observed, "That they did not attend to give advice as to the recovery of rights, or to afford relief in particular cases;" —but under the peculiar circumstances, they suggested the course, which appeared to them most advisable for the party to pursue.

Two black women called, "to request assistance, for "the complete establishment of their freedom." They stated, that they had been severally emancipated in different ways; one by deed, the other by will. In both

BARBADOS.

DEFECT OF JURISDICTION.

instances, from the neglect of the owner or his representatives to pay the 50*l.* to the parish, the manumissions had become void, or were not allowed to take effect.

Several other complaints of a like nature, were preferred, during the stay of the Commissioners in the island. Sometimes, it was only surmised, that the will of a deceased master contained directions for their manumission; agreeably to a promise of the testator in his lifetime. Sometimes, the manumission was directed by the will; but no provision made for the payment to the parish. Sometimes, it was to take place after a contingency; (the estate paying off its debts). Often it was delayed and excused, for want of assets. In other instances, the enfranchisement of particular slaves was recommended to the heir, &c. &c.; cases, which a competent court might perhaps, find little difficulty in deciding. The Commissioners could only regret—that there did not exist—a fit tribunal, for judicial inquiry into these MOST PRECARIOUS RIGHTS.

A black man complained "that his manumission had "been withheld, in a case where the 50*l.* HAD been paid." On inquiry the Commissioners learnt, that, the fact of payment was disputed. No such item appeared in the churchwarden's account; (*that* officer being dead); and the parish not unreasonably, insisted upon some proof of the money having reached his hands.

No public registry of wills.

There is no public registry in this island, in which Wills, or the probates of wills proved in England; exemplifications, &c. &c. must be recorded, in order to take effect in the colony. Deeds, to pass any estate of freehold or inheritance, or any lease above three years, must it has been seen, be recorded in the office of the secretary of the island.

No legal protection to slaves.

Slaves in this island, are without LEGAL PROTECTION OR REDRESS FOR PERSONAL INJURIES. The general Slave Act No. 82, contains only one provision in their favour; securing them a scanty supply of annual clothing, less than the customary allowance from the voluntary bounty of the master. "I think," said the attorney-general, "that it is, in cases of offences committed AGAINST

BARBADOS.

DEFECT OF JURISDICTION.

"slaves, that improvements might be made." The slave court is constituted for the trial of felonies committed BY slaves; it cannot investigate offences perpetrated against them. A court, where injuries, TO slaves, may be inquired into and redressed, at present forms no part of the judicature of this island. The slave has no remedy in case of the greatest oppression by the master (or his delegate,) or the grossest injury by third persons; though the master (in case of his slave being assaulted or robbed) may have reparation in damages for the loss of service, or the injury to his property in the slave. The murder of a slave wilfully, maliciously, wantonly, and without provocation, is now a capital crime, but there is no other legislative provision, restraining the absolute power of the master over the slave, or inflicting punishment upon the owner or others, in case of cruel treatment. No other act of assembly has been framed for the protection of slaves; no tribunal is specially appointed for inquiry into their wrongs. A slave who is, or thinks himself, aggrieved, looks in vain in this island for a proper quarter, in which to prefer his complaint: it can NO WHERE be received. "Offences against slaves may be by third "persons, or by the owner. In the former case," said the attorney-general, "if a slave is injured, or if he is "even struck by a third person, the master has a remedy "by action in the courts of law; but this he must support by the evidence of free persons. If a slave is "maimed, or treated with great cruelty, by his own "master, we are all agreed here, that it is indictable at "the common law, as an offence *contra bonos mores;* "but," he adds, "I never knew an instance of such a "prosecution, and I conceive the reason to be—the difficulty of obtaining evidence."

No redress for injuries.

Except as their masters remain liable to the common-law of England.

Over slaves the justices have no jurisdiction except what is given them by the statutes of the island.

The senior justice of the peace, a gentleman who possessed extensive experience in the criminal jurisprudence affecting slaves, being asked, whether a magistrate would entertain a complaint preferred by a slave, of cruelty and ill treatment, by his master, replied, "I think there

BARBADOS.

WANT OF REMEDY.

" is no law of the island which gives a magistrate JURIS-
" DICTION over such complaints, and I think the gover-
" nor can give no such authority." In the latter part of the answer, allusion is made to the practice of the governor, in sending, (very fitly), slaves who go to him with complaints, to have their cases investigated before the magistrates. There is in BOTH a want of jurisdiction!

The provost-marshal, interrogated as to the punishment of offences committed by and against slaves, said of the latter; "The grand sessions investigate the case
" of the murder of a slave: murder is the only case in
" which the law interferes."

The Commissioners inquired anxiously—Question; Is no other injury to slaves by their owners, punishable by law, except murder?

Ans. "Short of murder, the power of the master is absolute."

Q. Cannot a slave apply to a magistrate in case of serious injury from a white, for redress or protection?

A. "Slaves *should* be able to apply to a magistrate,
" when ill treated; but it is not so."

It may be necessary to make one or two observations, upon the apparent contradiction between these statements and the opinion of the attorney-general, that such offences by a master are legally punishable by indictment. It is the more important that the point should be attentively considered, because through all the islands, we found great difficulty and uncertainty prevailing, for want of clear and precise ideas upon this subject. Indeed our labours were often lamentably increased by the total want, or unaccountable ignorance, of any *fixed principles* of colonial jurisprudence.

" The common law of England" it was sometimes said
" is not applicable to the slavery of the West Indies."
" In the absence of local laws," answered others, " slaves
" are protected by the laws of England." What is properly meant by the latter proposition I take to be *only*, the unquestionable fact—that, the common law, when unaltered by acts of parliament or acts of assembly, is the

BARBADOS.

WANT OF REMEDY.

And (*it seems*) third persons, being free subjects, *the same*.

rule of action *between free subjects* in the colonies. Not only the master then, as specified by the attorney-general, but every other person of free condition, must continue amenable to the law of England, and is properly held indictable for excessive and inordinate cruelty to slaves; even though regarded only as subjects of property, of a kind unknown in England. The same criminal law, derived from the mother country, must be in force against *third* persons, (free subjects,) as against the *master*. BOTH must be equally punishable for *scandalous* cruelty; but not I fear for whipping, beating, imprisoning, &c. without positive provision by local law.

It seems however, to have been long a prevailing opinion of the profession in other parts of the West Indies, that ALL IMMODERATE punishment and unnecessary and undue severity in a master, was punishable at common law: this notion, I apprehend, they carried somewhat too far. But it is gratifying to see men of the highest rank in their profession, corresponding as we were able to trace, many years ago, upon the means of affording protection to slaves and bringing atrocious delinquents who had been guilty of excessive cruelty, to punishment; and even disposed for such a purpose, to stretch the law (according to my view of the subject,) a little *beyond what it will bear*.

An opinion of the then attorney-general of Grenada, in answer to a letter from the attorney-general of St. Vincents, in 1798, says:—

"I have ever been of opinion, that not only murder, "but any *atrocious severity*, or even *immoderate correction* "of a slave, by his master, is indictable at common law "and punishable as a felony or misdemeanor, according "to the nature of the offence. It is true that this mode "of prosecution or punishment, may be restrained or "taken away by statute, not only expressly, but by im-"plication; as if a statute imposes another, although in-"ferior, punishment for murder or any particular species "of misdemeanor, though without any negative words, "it will be construed a virtual restraint of the common-"law punishment, &c."

BARBADOS.

WANT OF REMEDY.

Per Lord Holt, 3 Salk. 47.

An assault upon an apprentice, servant, or scholar, may be justified, "if the beating is in nature of correc-"tion only, and with a proper instrument;" and therefore *immoderate* punishment is a good reply to the justification of the action in *such* cases; or the beating, striking, scourging, &c. is laid in the indictment to have been inflicted IMMODERATELY. The authority of the master over his apprentice or scholar, being of a limited nature, he is answerable, where he exceeds it. The power of the master over his slave in Barbados, is claimed to be absolute, unless restrained by positive law; *he* then, is not confined to MODERATE CORRECTION, and is accountable to no individual, if he does not offend against the PUBLIC. Again, cases of "ATROCIOUS SEVERITY" to be indictable misdemeanors, (I do not, at present, speak of murder or mayhem), must, I should imagine, be OPEN OFFENCES, of *public* evil example, and prejudicial to the COMMUNITY, as tending to corrupt the morals of the PEOPLE. A cruel flogging of slaves in a public market-place at noon-day, openly outrages decency, and is injurious to public morals. But, however desirable it may be, to make the laws subservient to morality, I cannot see that the same offence committed out of the way of observation, and leaving no conspicuous marks upon the person, which must necessarily shock the minds and senses of others, can be proceeded against with effect, upon the same convenient principle of law. It follows, that though the laws of the island are silent upon the subject, cases of outrageous and scandalous cruelty, such as are offensive to decency—injurious to the morals of the community—and of evil example in the eye of the law, may be punishable, whether committed by the owner *or others*, without any express provision for that purpose; on the principles of the English common law. But though the sentiments of the different examinants may *thus* be easily reconciled, the doctrine when received, must be regarded as one of very confined and partial application. It can only extend (if I am right), besides murder, to mutilation and mayhem and a few extraordinary cases of excessive severity in the nature of *nuisances*, committed by white

BARBADOS.

or free persons, who are subject to the common law of England.

WANT OF REMEDY.

For the punishment of general oppression and *mal-treatment* of a slave, (as it is termed in the consolidation act of the Leeward Islands,) there is no provision by any law in Barbados. If inflicted by his master, it would be dispunishable: if perpetrated by a third person, the owner would have HIS remedy by a civil action; but the slave would still be without redress.

The common law does not apply to slaves.

Over slaves it was agreed, the magistrates have no jurisdiction, except what is given them by the statutes of the island. The common law of England has little or no relation to a state of slavery, as it exists in the British Colonies in the West Indies.

A property in slaves, has been admitted and sanctioned by acts of parliament of the mother country. From this fundamental principle (that slaves are PROPERTY) it is remarkable with how much exactness, all the peculiar maxims of this essential branch of colonial jurisprudence have been deduced. It is a perfect enthymeme! Has the master, we inquired, an absolute power over his slave? "Where the law," said the solicitor-general, "does not take away or restrain the power, the owner I "conceive, has all the authority which the English law "attaches to PROPERTY." "The power of the master "over his slave," said the attorney-general of Tobago, "depends upon his having acquired that species of PRO-"PERTY, while it could be legally acquired." A different doctrine however, it must be admitted, more humane in tendency though I think, less founded in principle, seems to have become established in the other islands.

"I look upon slaves as within the King's allegiance. "I think slaves entitled to the protection of the common "law."

*Chief Justice of Grenada.*

"I have always been of opinion, that our slaves are "entitled to the benefit both of the common and statute "law, except so far as it has been taken from them by "written laws." BARBADOS.

WANT OF REMEDY.

*Chief Justice of St. Vincent.*

"A slave in the colonies is as much within the King's "peace as any other subject, and negligence of him, cruel "usage or any species of severe and improper treatment "by his owner, or the agent of the owner, or others, "would be triable in the King's courts."

*Chief Justice of Dominica.*

The law of slavery is to be found in *a sort of common law* of the colonies, and in the acts of the local legislatures. The chief justice of Grenada calls it "a cus-"tomary law, superadded to the law of England; sup-"plemental to the common law." In this island, and I believe in all others, it was not expressly instituted or established by positive law, but obtained insensibly, and at present depends upon certain unwritten maxims and principles, (derived chiefly from the civil law) and a usage founded thereon. This, though not strictly a legal prescription, has been a uniform practice, recognized in the earliest acts of assembly; regulated at various periods of their history, and constantly admitted as legal in all their courts of justice; till it is now too late to question its authority.

Although the common law of England affords few rules or maxims, specifically applicable to the state of negro slavery in the West Indies, reference is constantly made by analogy, to the condition of villeinage, with its various properties and incidents, as it formerly existed in the mother country.

But perhaps it will be found upon inquiry, that the general principles of colonial law were, in their original, much more frequently deduced from the Roman than the Gothic code; while, at a subsequent period and in their mitigated state, they often bear a closer resemblance to the early English institution. The Roman master, if a *pater-familias*, was invested with the authority of a civil magistrate. He had a power over his slave, be-

BARBADOS.

WANT OF REMEDY.

yond imprisoning, chaining, or scourging him, extending even to life. By the fundamental principles of colonial law, of which the traces though sometimes faint, are every where discoverable, the power of the master over the slave was considered absolute. That power is now almost universally restricted and limited by law, both by provision and construction; and is therefore put upon the footing of the ancient law of villeinage, where the English lord possessed the arbitrary power of beating his slave, at his pleasure; but the villein enjoyed protection by the law, as to life and limb.

" *Vita et membra sunt sub potestate legis.*" Bracton lib. 1. c. 9. 2 Bl. Comm. p. 94.

The power of the master is delegated to inferior agents; who are like him dispunishable.

The power of the absent proprietor is necessarily delegated to his representative upon the spot. This power is liable to abuse, and the more dangerous, as the delegation descends to subordinate agents of the lowest class of whites; or to drivers, who are themselves slaves, naturally cruel, and not softened by education. The restraints upon the exercise of this power by inferior agents, I regard as extremely salutary, and do not despair of seeing them rendered operative and effectual.

Slave evidence is not admitted.

I sincerely believe the admitted defects in the execution of the criminal law against white offenders, to be properly attributable, not to any misconduct in jurymen, or to any unfitness in the institution of the trial by jury itself, for small societies of Englishmen, but to that radical error in the laws; the exclusion of slave testimony, in cases where other evidence is unattainable.

I entirely agree with the learned and liberal attorney-general, that the evil chiefly requiring an immediate and effectual remedy in this island, is the state of the criminal law, as regards *injuries inflicted upon* slaves. I believe the administration of the LAW AGAINST SLAVES to be lenient, and even lax. Though tried under a severe and barbarous code, there is good reason to believe that slaves are not often convicted on light grounds; or executed, except in very atrocious cases. The interest, and often the humanity of the master, induce him to use all the means in his power, to save the life of the slave; either by compounding the offence (which I have shewn is allowed in cases of theft and injury to private property,) or by procuring him professional advice and assistance, on his trial.

BARBADOS.

WANT OF REMEDY.

But what is to restrain a bad master, (and one such will be occasionally found, among a hundred good ones,) or a recklesss overseer, or a worthless manager, (among many who are humane and upright) in his DOMESTIC TREATMENT of slaves?

No law here regulating the quantum of punishment; hours of labour; or supply of food and clothing.

There is not in Barbados, ANY LAW, regulating the quantum and kind of punishment; the hours of labour and rest; the provision of food and (except nominally) of clothing. These are dependant on the performance of moral duties, of which good men feel the obligation, but of which the BREACH is unfortunately not cognizable before any earthly tribunal. A wicked and cruel master or delegate, so that he do not kill or maim a slave, may inflict on him ANY degree or severity of punishment. No man or set of men has legal power to call him to account, for working his slave as long as he likes; for whipping him as much as he pleases; for chaining; for starving him. A justice of the peace is indeed limited in the number of lashes HE can order a slave to receive; but a master—has uncontrolled, undefined and absolute power. Where then is the protection of the slave; and where, in case of accident, the justification of the master? The slave is without any security from injury and hopeless of redress; because no LEGAL PROTECTION is afforded him, and most of all, BECAUSE HE CAN NOT COMPLAIN. In an extreme, I grant, and rare, but still a possible case, of very grievous bodily injury inflicted upon a slave by a manager, the sufferer himself or his slave brethren who were present, cannot give evidence; though all the free persons on the premises, should have been, *designedly*, sent out of the way. In such a case a slave is not allowed to be a prosecutor. Maimed, mutilated, disfigured, dismembered, (I am putting the most *aggravated* case,) his wounds must be the only tongue, permitted to relate his wrongs. While such remains the law, all other improvements must be fruitless!

Their testimony is not admitted in courts of law.

BARBADOS.

WANT OF REMEDY.

In Grenada, I shall shew a glaring defect of justice, in an instance where some sheep, the property of a gentleman, had been stolen in open day, by free coloured persons, but in the view only of slaves who could not be witnesses. In St. Vincent, I shall refer to a very affecting case, in which the dying declaration of a black woman (a slave) murdered under very peculiar circumstances, was in consequence of this exclusion, but on sound principles of law and properly, rejected, and an acquittal rendered necessary.

But the important and delicate question, as to the admissibility of slave evidence, requires a distinct and dispassionate consideration. At present I shall only refer to the answer of the attorney-general, upon this subject. Being asked, if he thought the evidence of slaves might be properly admitted in any other and what cases, and under any and what restrictions; he replied, "I don't "see, myself, in the total absence of all white or free "coloured evidence, and where better evidence could "not be had, that any harm could result from admitting "the evidence of slaves to facts in criminal cases. The "chief difficulty would be how to swear them, so as "to make them esteem their oath binding. Most of "them HAVE an idea of God, and of a future state. I "only speak of criminal cases. I have not thought "yet of admitting their evidence in civil cases, in which "it would seldom be wanted, all contracts being only between free persons."

It is—legal protection from oppressive and cruel treatment; a power somewhere vested, in impartial magistrates, to investigate and redress the wrongs of the slave population,—that it is of infinite importance to see established.

As far as regards the owners, on the satisfactory proof of a charge of cruelty or oppression committed by *them*, the relation ought to be dissolved, and the slave, according to the offence, enfranchised or sold to a humane master. Other persons, of free condition, inflicting personal injuries upon slaves, or taking from them their little property, ought to be prosecuted CRIMINALLY;

BARBADOS.

WANT OF REMEDY.

that they ARE NOT, except in flagrant cases, can only be explained, by the greater weight of the opinion that slaves are *not* under the protection of the common law. There is said to be among the negroes of this island, (I know not with what truth) a great and rapid increase of numbers; they have access to the means of religious instruction; they are fast emerging from their state of brutal depression. Forming as they *do*, a large, fine, and healthy population, there is every reason to believe the slaves of Barbados to be generally well treated. But I consider it to be entirely owing as I before stated, *to the humane dispositions of their owners.* I see in the volume of their laws, no pledge or security for their being or continuing so, and no REDRESS where it is otherwise. I think it of public moment and a public duty to retrain, and (if it were possible without slave evidence) to punish, the few bad masters, actual or substituted, and to secure to the slave adequate protection from injuries by third persons. If, in their unimproved state and until their condition shall have been gradually altered, the negroes cannot consistently enjoy civil rights, still they ought to be protected from CRIMINAL WRONGS. Admitting even for a moment, the harsh doctrines of the Roman servile code, that slaves have not any personality, and are only to be considered *inter res*, still as subjects of PROPERTY, they should not be *misused;* and laws, to prevent and punish such maltreatment, undoubtedly ought to be passed in *this* as in other islands. Lastly, to all arguments, drawn from the EVILS of the system and strangely applied in favour of its continuance, BECAUSE slavery is a great or a *necessary* it ought not therefore to be an UNMITIGATED evil: it ought as it appears to me to be SOFTENED, precisely BECAUSE, it is contended, it cannot with safety and justice be DESTROYED.

No preference is here given to debts contracted for the support of the slave.

There is not in Barbados, as we found in many other islands, a legislative provision, that debts necessarily contracted in the cultivation and manufacture of the produce of a plantation,—as for the purchase of pro-

BARBADOS.

WANT OF REMEDY.

visions or clothing for slaves; medical attendance upon them; compensation to managers, &c. &c. 'shall form 'specific liens upon the plantation and slaves, and be 'paid and satisfied in preference to any other debt or 'encumbrance whatsoever, whether of record or spe-'cialty,' 'by the person in possession, however his pos-'session was obtained;' thus ensuring the payment of salaries, and securing their subsistence to the slaves in the first instance, out of the proceeds of their labour; a regulation, which under proper restrictions as to the amount of the debt, and the time within which it may be contracted, so as not to admit fraud or impair the value of mortgage securities, is equally just in principle and salutary in its effects. The solicitor-general said, "it had "been proposed but was very generally disapproved of." The attorney-general said, that "there was a difference "of opinion upon the subject." The chief justice; "it "opens a door to the greatest frauds. I never would "consent to it."

The slave cannot sue or prosecute if his *peculium* is invaded.

All property acquired by the slave, theoretically belongs to the master; but in practice is always enjoyed by the slave. I believe this PECULIUM to be sacred and untouched by the owner; but I am not satisfied that property in the possession of slaves, is sufficiently protected against injuries from third persons. The slave, it is notorious, cannot sue or prosecute, and can therefore only obtain redress for such wrongs, through the medium and intervention of the master. But even a kind owner will often in this climate be indisposed to exertion, and a selfish and bad one will be indifferent and unfeeling. I ought, perhaps, to add, that the Commissioners never saw or heard of a single instance, of a slave being obstructed or robbed of his little property; though thousands passed the room in which they were constantly sitting on the way to the town or market. As such goods, though in the possession of the slave, are considered in law the property of the master, the taking them away *animo furandi*, must, I suppose, amount to felony. No reason is apparent why the slave may not in

BARBADOS.

WANT OF REMEDY.

a short time, in the course of progressive improvement, be allowed to sue and prosecute in the name of his next friend his master.

No redemption from slavery.

The slave has not any means of acquiring his freedom without the consent of the master. There is no redemption from slavery, in this island by force of law; but there is from the state of manners. A manumission, is rarely, if ever, refused, where an equivalent in value can be found; and the purchase is effected, as was the case with the Romans, by regarding the *peculium* as the property of the slave for such beneficent purpose. Yet this, it seems, is not good or effectual at the common law. "No villein," according to Glanville, "could acquire "his freedom with his own money; for notwithstanding "his purchase, he might according to the law and cus-"toms of the kingdom, be brought back into villeinage; "because all the goods of a villein born belonged to his "lord, and therefore from him, he could not redeem him-"self with his own money." An extraordinary doctrine! but under these circumstances, what has so desirably obtained in practice, might if it were thought necessary be sanctioned by law.

As subjects of mortgages, entails, family settlements, &c. obstacles may occasionally arise in the way of manumissions of slaves without the consent of the mortgagee, reversioner, or party in remainder: but it is satisfactory to know that this difficulty, as it exists in all the islands, has already engaged your Lordship's attention, and that a remedy has been sought to be applied from the proper quarter.

Every negro is presumed to be a slave.

It was admitted to be a rule in Barbados, Tobago and Grenada, but repudiated as we advanced in the other islands, and is certainly by no means a universal principle of colonial law, that every negro is presumed to be a slave, unless he can legally prove the contrary. "Free "negroes constantly bring actions in our courts," said the attorney-general of St. Kitts, "and nobody ever imagined "it to be necessary for them to shew *in limine*, that they "were not slaves."

BARBADOS.

WANT OF REMEDY.

If no known owner, belongs to the Crown, and is saleable.

If a a slave have no known owner and is not claimed by any person, he is held, in this island, to belong to the Crown, and to be saleable for its benefit. On the same principle in most of the registry acts, the omission to claim a slave by duly registering him, is not made to create a presumption of liberty in his own favour, but occasions a forfeiture to His Majesty; when such slave at the discretion of the Crown, may either be enfranchised or apprenticed under the abolition act. In many colonies we found a "FREEDOM BY REPUTATION;" but this, in Grenada, is not a presumption of freedom; but the presumption of slavery being admitted, this a *proof* to repel it. In Trinidad the maxim is "*Libertas presumitur* "*nisi constat de contrario.*"

Complaints made against slaves for offences not capital, are not upon oath. I submit that the INFORMATION should be always taken UPON OATH, and I recommend that there should, in all cases, be a CONVICTION IN WRITING, which, together with all the proceedings in the case, should be returned into court, at the grand sessions.

The trial of slaves for capital offences, without the previous finding of a grand jury; without a written charge; and conducted in a very informal manner; wants the imposing solemnity of a public trial. I am of opinion that the difference in their mode of trial, has an unfavourable effect upon both the classes of inhabitants, white and black.

I shall conclude this Report of the administration of justice civil and criminal, in the island of *Barbados*, with representing to your Lordship very respectfully, that whatever other ameliorations the condition of the slave may require or receive, (into which it is not my province to enter), he ought to be protected by law, from gross personal injuries, and to have criminal justice impartially administered to him.

# TOBAGO.

TOBAGO.

HIS Majesty's Commissioners commenced their inquiry, into the administration of civil and criminal justice, in this island, on the 26th day of March, 1823. The Governor used every effort to procure them all necessary information, and was actively seconded in the endeavour by the judge, the attorney-general, the officers of the court, and the members of the bar.

There is no complete edition of the Laws of this island; no "printed code by authority;" and the want of it must be obvious. "Where information is required," said the chief justice, "recourse must be had to manu-"script laws recorded in the secretary's office, where a "person is subject to the payment of fees for every book "he looks into. If there be any dispute on the wording "of an act, it would be necessary, there being no autho-"ritative edition of the acts, to have the original record "produced in court; it is a great grievance that there "is no such edition" In this sentiment I heartily concur, and wish the revising and editing the laws of this island, were undertaken (at the request of the council and assembly,) by the learned judge, or at least placed under his intelligent care and superintendance.

TOBAGO.

LAWS.

This colony is stated to have received a constitution from England during the administration of Governor Rickets, in 1794, and is supposed to have adopted, with it, or at the period of the Cession, all the acts of parliament of Great Britain suited to its condition and circumstances.

The charter itself of the constitution is understood to be lost. The local laws now in force, are, certain acts of assembly passed before the capture of the colony in 1793, and revived in 1794, and acts passed since.

Of these the most remarkable are, *cap.* 3, *of revived laws; an act establishing a registrar's office*, which provides, "that all deeds, conveyances, &c. made in the "island, shall be recorded within two months; all "deeds executed in other places, within certain specified "times."

"Wills, whether of real or personal estate, are re- "quired to be registered, and cannot be given in evidence, "till proved and recorded."

To prevent disputes about priority—"there shall be "an indorsement on the deed of the time of the entry."

Security is given by the registrar, for the due performance of the duties of the office.

*Cap.* 25 *of c.* 3. *explaining the former act*, provides, "that no deed is to be void for want of being recorded "in due time, other than against *bonâ fide* purchasers "and creditors, who shall have recorded their securities "in due time, and without any notice of other incum- "brances."

No time, it will be seen, is limited, within which a WILL must be recorded. In this respect I think the law would admit of some improvement.

*Cap.* 31, *of former laws, revived by c.* 3. *the* COURT ACT of this island, which regulates the practice of the courts of Common Pleas, Error, King's Bench, and Grand Sessions. The proceedings in the different courts, will be necessarily considered in detail; at present I shall only observe of the court act in general terms, that though very susceptible of improvement, it was vastly superior to any thing we had yet seen.

*Cap.* 4, *of laws revived by c.* 4. "*Negroes are made* "*real estate.* Deeds of sale, conveyances, &c. of negroes "are to be proved, and recorded according to the re-"gistry act. Mules and plantation utensils are also "made real estate."

*Cap.* 8, *of laws revived by c.* 4. "*For work performed* "*and materials provided, for any sum not exceeding* 20*l.* "*artificers, labourers and servants, may complain to a sin-*"*gle justice of the peace.* So *poor settlers having cause* "*of* 10*l. or under.*"

The proceedings directed by this act, correspond with the course pursued in what are termed warrant actions at Barbados, and would be liable to the same objections. But the attorney-general in reply to the question "what "are the cases in which justices of the peace exercise a "summary jurisdiction in civil matters?" observed, "I "have never known an instance of an application to the "justices, under cap. 8, of revived laws."

*Cap.* 22, *an act to constitute a court-merchant.*

The chief justice said that he "only remembered one "instance in which the appointment of this special court "was resorted to."

"Upon affidavit and petition, the chief justice of the "Common Pleas, or if he is sick or absent from the "island, the senior assistant justice is to call a court, in "four days. The action is commenced in the usual "manner. Service of the summons having been proved "and the defendant making default, and not joining "issue, the plaintiff's evidence may be taken, and judg-"ment given for him. If the plaintiff shall neglect to "appear at any sitting of the court, he may be non-"suited. If the defendant puts in a demurrer, the plain-"tiff may amend, on payment of 15*s.* costs. Judgment "is immediately given on verdict, unless the defendant "desires a day to move in arrest of judgment, which "shall be granted by the court, so that it be not above "three days longer time, and execution shall issue "thereon, the next day after judgment, &c. Goods, "taken in execution, are to be sold at outcry, in six "days."

TOBAGO.

LAWS.

"Residents and freeholders are not required to make "the affidavit, and are empowered to arrest, and tran-"sient defendants must find bail, or remain in cus-"tody."

Debts not exceeding 10*l.* may be recovered in this court by *complaint*, without a jury; being the same mode of trial, as is known by the name of bench actions in Barbados, or of complaints in the court of Common Pleas, in this island.

The court-merchant is made a court of record.

*Cap.* 23, *of laws revived by cap.* 4. "*An act to esta-"blish a Court of Quarter Sessions in this island.*" This court is directed to be holden on the third Tuesday in January, April, July, and October. The court has 'leave to sit as long as it shall be necessary for hearing 'any business that may come before it,' and is invested 'with the same power as the court of Quarter Sessions 'in England.'

*Cap.* 32, *of former laws, revived by cap.* 4. "*An act "for the good order and government of slaves.*" Of this act the attorney-general observed, "the slave act ought "to be immediately repealed: the cruelty of some of "its clauses has rendered them almost a dead letter." The chief justice said, "there are many imperfections in "the slave-act, which ought to be remedied;" and in another place, "it is in my contemplation to alter the "act, &c."

This pledge was redeemed during the same session of the legislature; a circumstance, which supersedes the necessity of my dwelling with minuteness on the former law, now expressly abrogated. I had intended to observe upon the following provisions; "a slave com-"passing, imagining, and contriving the death of A "WHITE PERSON, shall suffer death, transportation, or "imprisonment." This it will be observed, is not confined to the case of the owner of the slave, and is enacted without requiring the proof of any overt act. I should not have noticed this objectionable provision in a repealed act, but that I still find in the improved law, "compassing the death of a white or free person," among offences that may be punished capitally.

In the enumeration in the former act, of crimes for which a slave was liable to suffer death or other discretionary punishment, two enactments were discovered in juxta-position, remarkable in different ways; one visiting the flight from slavery with undue severity; the other with great tenderness for the life of a slave, raising the value which rendered a larceny subject to capital punishment, to the unusual amount of 6*l.*—"*running off the island and stealing to the value of* 6*l.*" Upon this, however I observe the attorney-general remarks, "*it* (the slave-act) awards the punishment of death for stealing to the value of 6*l.* currency; for being, or harbouring a runaway; and for many other offences, so *trivial* in their nature, that the court appointed to try slaves for such offences always evinced the greatest reluctance to convict. Other offences of great magnitude pass unnoticed by its provisions; for instance, receiving stolen goods knowing them to be stolen, is dispunishable, and others." The learned gentleman perhaps inclines to the old opinion, that the receiver is a greater delinquent than the thief. The reason that no such provision (against receivers) was found in the former slave-act, I take to be, with submission, that such offenders generally belonged to a different class, (the free persons). Receiving stolen goods is now declared to be a *misdemeanor* by the new act.

The next clause constituted a court for the trial of slaves. This was composed in the same manner as the slave-court at Barbados, with one or two exceptions, favourable and otherwise; as for instance, the justices were *bound to report the sentence* of the court to the commander-in-chief, under a penalty; but on the other hand, there was no *appeal* from their decision. Again, difficulties often arose as to who were the "nearest magistrates," and the nearest "freeholders." Indeed there were great difficulties, according to the attorney-general, "in the way of attaining justice, from the niceties re-

TOBAGO.

LAWS.

" quired in the commitment, and the precision with " which the precept must be worded. If a magistrate " commits and sends notice to a neighbouring magistrate, " and that other magistrate refuses to attend, so that the " trial cannot be within ten days from the commitment, " no trial can be had ;, such case not being provided for " by the act."

The demerits of this act being greatly more conspicuous than any excellencies it possessed, occasioned its repeal to be decided on before the Commissioners reached the island. The chief justice said, " the constitution of " the slave-court ought to be altered. The present court " should try misdemeanors only. There should be a dif" ferent court, (the presiding judge of which ought to be " a barrister,) and in that court I think all slaves ac" cused of capital offences ought to be tried by a jury of " twelve men." The attorney-general said, " I only " speak the sentiments of the whole colony in saying, " that in capital cases, slaves should have the benefit of " trial by jury."

I refer shortly to the provisions of this act though repealed, because it was in force at the time we visited the island; and some (then) recent proceedings under it, were made the subject of a very forcible representation to the Commissioners. That communication was as follows:—" That just before the arrival of the Commis" sioners, a slave was tried on a capital charge for steal" ing a boat, running away, and enticing other slaves to " do the same; all in one charge. There were other " slaves implicated. The sitting magistrates called the " prisoners before them and desired them to *confess the* " *charge, and all they knew about it.* At the trial the ut" most irregularity prevailed; what was *said by one* " *prisoner* was allowed *to affect another;* the presiding " judge was wholly ignorant of every part of his duty; " the prisoner being convicted, was called upon for what " he had to say why sentence should not be passed against " him; and was equally surprised, with every one else " in court, when *that* sentence came to be passed, and

TOBAGO. — LAWS.

"was—sentence of death. The proceeding had disgusted every reflecting man in the colony and would "bring about a change in the law."

The slave was not executed: he was reprieved at the gallows; for slaves in this island, even under the old law, were not hanged upon trees, but put to death with becoming solemnity, in the public square. Some humane persons who felt an interest in preserving the life of the slave, proposed a legal question; "Whether he might "not be entitled to benefit of clergy, though he con-"fessedly, could not read?" The common law of England being supposed not to apply to the slave population of the island, this suggestion was considered by some, as an untenable ground in his favour; by others, as a doubtful proposition; but I notice the circumstance, because, the projected change in the law having taken place, I am gratified to see in the clause creating capital felonies, a proviso introduced,—"that all slaves shall be entitled to "the benefit of clergy, where the same is not taken "away by any act of this island, and in cases where the "same is not taken away by the statute law of England."

Within a fortnight after this transaction, two slaves apprehended on a similar charge could not be brought to trial, because no two justices could be found to act in the case, and the court in consequence, could not be summoned within the time specified by the act, namely, TEN days. The slaves were therefore released and could not be taken up again, the magistrates refusing to sign the warrant; thus causing a complete failure of justice, and dealing very unequally with different persons, accused of the same offence. The magistrates however, I beg to observe, acted from the most respectable motives, though quite mistakenly as regards their duties. The governor very properly, considered it a matter, requiring his interference; convened the magistrates in the council-chamber, and expostulated with them warmly on the dereliction of their duties. I do not know what steps were taken in the particular case; but

Clause 4, of the new act constitutes a court for the trial of capital offences, committed by slaves.

TOBAGO.

LAWS.

Clause 5, directs slaves, "to be proceeded against "before the said court, in like manner, and by such "rules, as are established and observed, for the trial of "white or free persons, in the court of King's Bench "and Grand Sessions."

By the repealed act, "*owners of plantations were re-"quired to have one acre of ground in provisions, for every "five slaves, under the penalty of 10l. for every acre want-"ing. The justices at quarter sessions, in January and "July in every year, were to direct two freeholders to in-"spect these provision grounds, and report upon oath, "upon their sufficiency or insufficiency.*"

This, as far as respects the growing a certain quantity of provisions upon every estate, was a very salutary regulation, and it is deeply to be regretted that it could not be enforced. But it was, and always would be, disregarded; the duty it imposed being of an invidious nature, and any interference with the internal management of private property, a measure at all times, most particularly obnoxious. The quarter sessions for appointing the visiting freeholders, and perhaps for that very reason, were never held. By the new Slave Act it is very insufficiently provided, that "owners or possessors of "slaves shall afford to each and every of their slaves "'SUFFICIENT FOOD' and 'GOOD AND SUFFICIENT "'CLOTHING' under fixed penalties; and neglect to "furnish food and clothing shall be deemed a misde-"meanor, and the guardians appointed by clause 25 of the "same act may direct a prosecution." These guardians "are, the president of the council, the speaker of the "House of Assembly, and the judges of the court of "Common Pleas, who are invested by the act with full "power and authority to entertain all complaints, made "to them by any slave, in respect of cruelty, ill usuage, "or violation of any of the provisions of the act, with "power to summon evidence, &c.: *it being reasonable,*" says the act, "*that slaves should have some established tri-"bunal to resort to.*"

This is an excellent provision, and does great credit to the legislature of Tobago; as do many of the other clauses of the act. The old law it should be stated, required "an allowance of clothing once a year;" "made "the willingly and wickedly killing a slave 'murder;' "and provided, that slaves might be chained and punished by a moderate whipping, or some other moderate "correction suitable to the fault, but that it should not "be lawful to torture or mutilate slaves, or punish them "with cruelty;" and the act punished parties offending therein with fine and imprisonment.

If the repealed act was not so inhuman as the laws we had hitherto seen, the new law contains improvements, we have no where else, had the happiness to meet with. By clause 22, "in cases of murder, mayhem of, or cruelty "to, slaves by white or free persons, in case no white "or free person was present, &c. *the evidence of two slaves* "*shall be admissible.*"

So, the whipping of slaves by the owner is restricted to twenty stripes, and if a punishment exceed twelve stripes, it must be inflicted in the presence of one white or free person.

"Drivers are not permitted to punish slaves but by "the express order of the owner, &c. &c. &c."

It is observable, that by the repealed act, owners concealing negroes guilty of felony lost the price allowed on conviction.

The same act restrained the owner from granting permission to slaves to hire out themselves to other masters, under the same penalty as the law of Barbados, before reprobated on account of its tendency to obstruct manumissions.

An act, passed in 1775, for "*establishing a court of* "*Chancery in this island, consisting of the governor and* "*four members of council, who should, in all cases con-* "*form to the rules, proceedings and practice of the court* "*of Chancery in England,*" and confirmed by his Majesty in council the 12th day of July 1776, is not found among the revived laws again put in force after the recovery of the island in 1793; from which time the constitution of the court appears to have been altered.

TOBAGO.

LAWS.

Cap. 49, of former laws, revived by c. 4. *To prevent clandestine departures from the island.* Ticket Act.

This act is said to be defective, as persons putting up their names at the beginning of the year, are entitled to a ticket at any time during the twelvemonth. They may contract debts subsequently to the notice, and go away without any warning. It is usual in other islands, after a stated time generally six weeks, to require the party to put up his name *de novo.* But this, is in a peculiar degree matter of internal legislation, and only of individual concern.

1808. *The first act, establishing a public chain-gang, and for the commuting the punishments of slaves, for labour on the roads and public works.*

1809. *Giving authority to employ slaves convicted of offences upon the streets of Scarborough.* The act of 1808 was amended and enlarged in 1809, and a new act passed in 1817.

Very opposite opinions are entertained by different persons, of this system of penal labour. If only slaves convicted of offences, (*servi pœnæ*, as they were called by the Romans,) are employed upon public works, to me this course appears less objectionable, than imprisonment without occupation. An incontestable abuse, is the practice, I hope no longer existing in any colony, of masters sending their slaves to the gaol or workhouse for punishment at their discretion, making what ought to be a public punishment for the sake of example, subservient to private malice or vengeance.

1812. *An Act for the more effectually securing "the "payment of certain debts, contracted for the use and be- "nefit of estates and plantations against the effect of sales "or disposal thereof, or change of property therein, on "the death of proprietors.*

"All stores, or other supplies from Europe, or else- "where, necessary for the cultivation and manufacture "of the produce of the plantations of this island and its "dependencies, and the maintenance of the slaves and "cattle employed therein, which shall be afforded, and

TOBAGO.

LAWS.

" which shall have been afforded or supplied, within " twelve months, previous to any sale, conveyance, &c. " &c. shall be a debt charged upon the new owner, and " recoverable from him in the same manner, except as to " the liability of his person; and all trusts created, &c. " shall be deemed and taken to be a change of property.

*Clause* 2. "Attorneys, medical attendants, overseers, " managers, &c. are enabled to recover a year's salary, " in the same manner; delivering an account a calendar " month before action brought.

*Clause* 3. "Debts for supplies, &c. *a lien* on the estate, " and in case of the death of the owner, to be paid in " preference to any encumbrance whatsoever be it of re- " cord or specialty, by the person in possession, however " his possession was obtained.

*Clause* 4. "Salaries, &c. recoverable in like manner.

*Clause* 5. "Form of action shall be debt." An act which has been found productive of very beneficial consequences in this island. So advantageous has it proved, that it has been recently extended. Instead of impairing credit or contributing to fraud, as was apprehended at Barbados, it has improved the one and led to dealings untainted by the other.

1815. *An Act to amend the court Act.* Slaves may be recovered by ejectment, apart and distinct from lands.

1821. *To make horned cattle, horses and asses, real estate.*

1821. "*Relating to masters and seamen.*" Of this act, the attorney-general observes: "The justices have a ju- " risdiction, but the act says nothing about process to " bring the captain before the justice; so that they think " they have not jurisdiction, when as is usual, the captain " stays on board and cannot be taken up on shore." 59 Geo. 3. c. 58.

1822. "*Amended Police Act.*" The chief justice and attorney-general it will be seen, contend that the title of this Act is a complete *misnomer*.

COURTS, ENUMERATION OF.

Pursuing the same order in the distribution of the subject, as was before found convenient in reporting upon the island of Barbados, I shall next consider the means of carrying the laws into execution. The courts of judi-

TOBAGO.

LAWS.

cature of the island will be first enumerated generally. The jurisdiction of the respective courts will then be ascertained, and their proceedings analytically considered; with this difference only from the former branch of the inquiry, that the variations in the law and practice of the colonial courts, constituted with the same or similar powers and functions in every island, will be more frequently the subjecs of remark, than the departure of *any* from the usages of England.

The courts for the administration of Civil Justice in the island of Tobago, are, the court of Chancery, the court of Exchequer, the court of Common Pleas; a Complaint court, for the recovery of debts under 10*l.* appointed by the court act; the court of Ordinary; the court of Escheat; and a special and occasional court, the court-merchant.

The courts for the administration of Criminal Justice are, the court of King's Bench and Grand Sessions; the Instance court of Admiralty (according to the chief justice's classification); and the slave Court. There is, also, a special commission, under which Admiralty sessions may be held, as occasion requires; and the governor has always the power of issuing a special commission of Oyer and Terminer.

## COURT OF CHANCERY.

What was the original constitution of this court does not clearly appear; but it is stated to have been REVIVED shortly after the capture of the colony, by an Act passed in February 1794. The governor *is now, sole* chancellor, and is supposed to possess all the authority of the lord chancellor of England.

The chancellor sits the first and third Monday in every month, and on other days, on application for a special court.

The jurisdiction in cases of lunacy is only conjectural, and the Commissioners were referred to the governor's instructions.

TOBAGO.

CHANCERY.

There are no *bankrupt* laws, or *general* Act, for the relief of *insolvent* debtors.

The practice is considered to be the same as in the court of Chancery in England. "There are a few rules," says the attorney-general, "different from those in Eng- "land, generally understood but no where collected, "making a difference as to the time of answering, "owing to our situation of colonies. If in Europe, a "defendant has *nine* months to answer a bill, if in ano- "ther colony, *three* months."

The description of business is the same as in England.

The officers of the court are the same as in the court of Chancery in Barbados, except that there is only one master, and *he* is also examiner.

The attorney-general said, "I have a bill now prepared to make an *infant* a *ward* of court." In the minutes of the court of Chancery, the Commissioners found an order of the 19th of February 1821. "*In the matter of* "*Catherine Lowry, a minor,*" whereby "she is ordered "to be made a ward of court, and that the master do "take an account of her property." We asked "whe- "ther such order was according to the practice of this "court?" The chief justice said, "I did not know till "now, that such an order had been made by the court of "Chancery, and I consider it as irregular and incon- "sistent with the practice."

In (*probably*) the same case (*but no cause or petition was stated in the registrar's book,*) we found an order, "that Rebecca Lowry and Catherine her daughter, do "give their attendance on a day mentioned, to answer "whatever the court may then and there object against "them; and that the registrar do give them notice to "that effect." We inquired "whether such order was "agreeable to the established mode of proceeding?" Chief justice, "Not when I practised in the court."

TIME.

On bill and answer only, (the plaintiff and defendant residing in the island,) the attorney-general thought a decree might be obtained in this court in *four* or *five* months after the filing of a bill. The chief justice said, he should think, in *twelve* months. Very little more time

TOBAGO.

CHANCERY.

would be taken where evidence was entered into; the evidence being obtainable in the island. A decree might still be had, the attorney-general thought, in about *seven* months.

When a reference has been made to take accounts, all the accounting parties residing in the island, *fifteen* months, according to the chief justice, might complete the suit.

If a party is absent and has no attorney in the island, "THEY CANNOT REACH HIM."

Where parties to the suit or witnesses or documentary evidence are *out* of the island, besides *nine* months to answer, *eight* months would be granted to take the evidence.

Proceedings upon bills of foreclosure of a mortgage it is said, seldom occur here. Where an estate has been decreed to be sold for the payment of creditors, the court of Chancery has always given time, with a view of making the sale productive, and to benefit both the creditors and debtor.

On sales, the master has an enormous fee of *six* per cent. on the gross amount, and he gets a fee on his report of sale or no sale. Both the chief justice and the attorney-general admitted that this was "*too* "*much*," and the former said, "*two per cent.* would be "sufficient."

There is no act of this island requiring the appraisement of an estate, previous to a sale in the master's office; but an appraisement *has* taken place by order of the court, on motion. It was *directed to three planters* to value an estate. Their service was gratuitous.

When a conveyance is made under a sale in the master's office the master alone conveys, and the attorney-general believes half the titles in the colony depend on *his* conveyance. There is however, no direction in the decree, that interested persons should join in the conveyance.

Estates in the master's office, in the same manner as lands at marshal's sale, are sold entire, subject to encumcumbrances; and are never sold in lots.

TOBAGO

CHANCERY.

Injunctions have been granted on petition, but *that* the attorney-general believes to be a mistake of the practice. "They were formerly granted on bill, with affi-"davit sworn before the master, which went to all the "allegations of the bill and that it would make a good "defence at law."

The court has the same jurisdiction as to injunctions, as the court of Chancery in England. We asked, "WHEN a defendant was at liberty to move to dissolve an "injunction?" The chief justice did not know—"the "present practice of this court; believing its proceedings "are not regulated by the rules and practice of the "courts at home." The attorney-general said, "the "practice appears to have been very irregular."

To the question, "whether the decisions of this court "were uniform and consistent, and governed by former "determinations of their own or other judges?" the reply of the chief justice, was "the decisions of this court "are complained of. I don't know by what rule they "are made. A professional chancellor is desirable." The attorney-general answered, "I cannot say, that I "think the decisions of this court uniform or consistent. "I do not think it governed by the weight of authorities. "For I have known cases wherein, though the unvary-"ing course of decisions was in favour of a point, every "authority proved unavailing. It is quite impossible to "say, whether the judgments of this court are *consistent* "*with each other* or not; as the bar can never form any "opinion of the grounds on which they rest; no *ratio* "*decidendi* ever being given."

Costs in this court are taxed by the master, according to a docket of fees which ought to be exhibited in the secretary's office, "but which," said the chief justice, "has not been for a long time there, and is said to be "lost. There is now, I believe," Mr. Pigot added, "a new docket of fees settled by the governor, in which "his own fees and others are fixed; which fees are higher, "than those in the former docket."

Fees had before been regulated from time to time by

TOBAGO.

CHANCERY.

FEES AND COSTS.

the governor and council; as latterly by the chancellor alone, without the authority being disputed.

The distinction, as to costs between party and party, and between attorney and client, is known and acted upon in this island.

Bills of costs are not delivered to the client, but the opposite attorney has a copy of the bill, with notice that it is to be taxed at a given time. "In a small bill," the attorney-general says, "it is considered better to pay "than have the bill taxed; as the master is paid *3l.* 12*s.* "per hour for taxation, besides fees for attendance to "the counsel, who have per hour half the amount of "the master's fees." And this according to the learned gentleman, supplies the *reason* which was not apparent, "why solicitors usually audit each other's bills."

The retaining fee of counsel allowed by the docket is *36l.* (currency) "*50l.* is commonly taken;"—and in important cases, it is very well known, a great deal more.

It is not usual to give a fee with the brief, the two branches of the profession being united in this island, and the advocate and attorney the same person.

The attorney-general affirmed with great seriousness, that "the fees to the officers of court, generally amount "to twice as much in a suit, as those of the counsel and "solicitor in his twofold capacity!" I am much afraid that the SUITOR will engross all the pity, bestowed on the occasion.

Mr. Sotherall, party to a suit, called to complain "that "in a cause of Sotherall and Wife *v.* Trustees of George "Morrison, a motion being made on the part of the "plaintiff, to take the bill *pro confesso* against the de-"fendant, for want of an answer, the defendant on af-"fidavit and documents produced, prayed further time "to answer; when the chancellor, instead of allowing "time to answer, at once dismissed the bill before an-"swer." The Commissioners suggested that Mr. Sotherall might petition the chancellor for a re-hearing.

Several other instances of alleged irregularities and

mistaken practice were brought under the notice of the Commissioners, but from motives of delicacy they refrained from calling upon the chief justice or attorney-general to express any opinion of their fitness, and thought it best to make such proceedings the subject of private discussion, with the chancellor. In the end, they were perfectly satisfied, not only of the powerful intellect and unshaken honour and probity of Sir Frederick Robinson, but also of his attention to business, and zeal and anxiety to do right; at the same time they could not help perceiving with regret his extreme liability to be wrong. The want of judicial habits and vague notions of equity, considered merely as informal, substantial justice, tend unavoidably to such results; till the suppletory exercise of sovereign reason, which should be equally regulated, exact and certain with the maxims of universal law, becomes desultory,—loose,—wild and of all things —the most inconstant!

To the question, "What improvements he could suggest in the administration of justice in this court?" the chief justice replied, "I do not exactly know how "the law is administered now in the court of Chancery; "but, it ought to be, according to the law of England "and the rules of practice of the court of Chancery "there. Those laws and rules of practice can best be "administered by a professional gentleman; for it cannot be expected that a person not having a professional "education, can be competent to preside in a court of "such high importance." The attorney-general said, "I agree that regularity of practice cannot be expected, "as the court is constituted at present. No person can "administer the law, who has not been educated to the "law. But if things remain as they are, I still think it "would be a great advantage, if the rules of court peculiar to ourselves, were embodied and promulgated "to the profession."

TOBAGO.

EXCHEQUER.

## COURT OF EXCHEQUER.

This court is recognized by the court act, and was therefore rather revived than established by Governor Ricketts in 1794, at which time a chief baron was appointed. No court however, is known to have been held till the year 1815, when the appointment of chief baron which had long been vacant, was again filled up, and puisne barons appointed, and the court sat several days for the first and last time, in the case of Cohens, a defaulter.

Per Attorney-General, court of Exchequer.

The authority of the court and its rules are alike unknown, as the charter of the constitution is missing, and no records of the court can be found in the island. "To "protect the Crown and make this court efficient, its "whole constitution should be new modelled, &c."

## COURT OF COMMON PLEAS.

This court derives its authority from the court act, and possesses the usual jurisdiction of the supreme civil court, in the colonies. A chief judge presides, with three assistant judges. The chief justice is appointed by the Crown; the assistant judges by the governor. All hold during pleasure. The salary of the chief justice was 3,000*l.* currency, equal to 1,200*l.* sterling. By a late act it has been reduced. The fees and perquisites of the office are, upon an average, about 150*l.* currency. The assistant judges have no salary, and do not usually transact that part of the business which is remunerated by fees.

It is not made necessary by any law, that, "even the "chief justice" should be professionally educated, though of course no other than a barrister, is likely to be appointed from England. The other judges are planters or merchants, the most intelligent and respectable gentlemen in the island, but not often addicted to studious

TOBAGO.

COMMON PLEAS.

pursuits, or qualified to administer, interpret or apply the laws. Mr. Christopher Irvine is a remarkable exception.

The court sits every month, from April to August, (both inclusive) as directed by the act. The sitting may continue TEN days, but has never lasted more than EIGHT, and seldom more than THREE days, and there has never been any arrear of business. There are no holidays, but great inconvenience arises from a vacation of seven months.

The decisions of the court are almost entirely governed by the laws, usages and practice of the courts in England. The court act prescribes certain rules for pleading, but very few; and when none are prescribed, the practice is governed by the practice in England.

The time required for obtaining a judgment in this court, when the parties and their witnesses are in the island, and no means of delay are used, and no points arise upon the pleadings, is THREE MONTHS. When every method of delay is used, judgment may still be obtained in the five "TERMS," on a process begun in the early courts; unless an injunction issues, in which case the delay cannot be ascertained.

Actions are commenced by filing a declaration. Good service of process upon absent defendants, who have no attorney upon record in the island, is by nailing up a copy of the declaration on the court-house door; and this applies equally, to defendants, who have never been in the island, as to those who have just quitted it.

Appearance is entered in a brief manner by counsel in the secretary's book, under the entry of the action. This is preferable to the practice in many of the other islands, where appearances are entered *on* the court-day.

The court act directs that special bail shall be required where the cause of action exceeds 10*l.*; except in the case of transient persons, who may be arrested for any sum. No affidavit of the debt is required by the act; but the chief justice supplies the omission, without authority for the purpose. Arrests however, are seldom resorted to, from the operation of the ticket act. UNDER-

TOBAGO.

COMMON PLEAS.

WRITING, as it is termed, (the proceeding, by which persons about to quit the island may be stopped by their creditors,) cannot be effected, without an affidavit of the debt; and it is the same in this island with ATTACHMENTS.

The judges have a discretionary power, by the court act, " of moderating or settling, for what sum bail shall " be accepted, in any action not founded on judgment, " specialty, note or bill;" but no instance of its exercise has been known; owing, it is supposed, to the infrequency of arrests.

The court act directs that no person whatever be exempted from arrest. An exemption, however, is allowed under the militia act; " for persons, horses and " mules, while on duty."

Arrests are not allowed in respect of unliquidated damages.

A habeas corpus is obtainable both by common law and by the statute.

By the 14th clause of the court act, when a defendant shall be in custody of the marshal by virtue of a warrant of arrest, and notice given to the plaintiff of his being in custody, a declaration shall be filed in two days, or the defendant shall be discharged with costs, by the judge. But a plaintiff is not obliged to declare against some of several defendants, who are in custody, till special bail is put in for the others, or their persons are surrendered; in which case a declaration must be filed in two days.

Debts due to defendants, are attachable in the hands of their debtors in this island, under the court act. Such attachments are often resorted to. An action (declaration) must be previously filed, and there must be an affidavit of debt. If an attachment is *laid* after action brought and BEFORE judgment, the expense is about 9*l.*; if AFTER judgment, about half that sum. To give the attachment effect, a summons is taken out after judgment, and interrogatories are served with it upon the garnishee, who is then examined before the judge. The judge makes an order according to circumstances, as directed by the act.

TOBAGO.

COMMON PLEAS.

No unnecessary delay it is said, attends the progress of a cause in this island by demands of oyer; by imparlances; continuances; dilatory or sham pleas; &c. &c. "I watch continuances after the first court," said the chief justice, "and will not let them get over the year." But the attendance of three judges (of whom two are not lawyers,) is required when pleas in abatement, demurrers, special verdicts, &c. are argued, and the difficulty of procuring THAT attendance is often a cause of considerable delay. Whether the special court for hearing arguments in such matters, must be held within the *ten* days appointed by the court act, is left doubtful. It *has been* held at other times; and convenience requires that it should be. But the attorney-general thinks the court would not have jurisdiction, beyond the ten days. It is matter of some importance, and the point ought to be settled.

An extraordinary and objectionable practice prevails in this island, under the operation of clause 58 of the court act. It is usual to commence an action, and obtain a judgment by consent or default IN court, in cases where the defendant, to save trouble and expense, has consented to confess a judgment, OUT of court; thus occasioning unnecessary expense to the parties and a hindrance of other business of the court.

Depositions are admitted in evidence, without affidavit of the continued absence from the island at the time of the trial, of the parties making them.

Special juries are known in practice here, and are struck in the same manner, as in England.

Special verdicts must be found when applied for. If the jury insist on finding a general verdict, it is a good ground for granting a new trial without costs. *This* course of proceeding, pointed out by the court act, was not clearly seen at Barbados; where the case had occurred a little before our arrival, and occasioned great heart-burnings.

A new trial, or arrest of judgment, is granted in the first instance in this island, and not a rule *nisi*. But the party applying for it, must give four days notice of

TOBAGO.

COMMON PLEAS.

the grounds on which he moves, and must serve the judges with copies of the notice. This practice the chief justice observed, has long obtained, and saves expense. The attorney-general complained that it rested only upon long practice, and was not established by any known rule, and when he first came to the island his clients suffered from his ignorance of a form, nowhere prescribed, and rendered accessible to the profession.

COURT ACT.

Executions bind from the delivery. The marshal is directed, by the act, to minute the time they come into his hands, and to *levy*, in the order and course in which they are received.

Goods, chattels, and slaves, *not annexed to the freehold*, are directed to be sold at Outcry. Notice of the sale is required to be given to the defendant, and to be published in the Gazette, ten days before the sale. And besides the publication in the paper, bills are sent round the town.

*Unattached* slaves are ordered to be sold, one by one; except mother and child under twelve years of age. Slaves annexed to the freehold, are sold along with the other real estate. A sale of slaves or other property mortgaged with any plantation is declared void.

The whole term and interest in leases is to be sold entire.

Of lands and tenements, the sale is to be on the fortieth day after the levy, and notice must be given in the Gazette within ten days. An appraisement takes place, but only to assist the judgment of the marshal as to the sufficiency of the levy. He *may* sell under the appraised value, and indeed *must* sell to the highest bidder.

An equity of redemption may be sold at marshal's sale.

The marshal conveys to the purchaser. The marshal's conveyance duly registered bars entails, &c.

Purchasers of lands for above 500*l.* on giving security, are allowed eight months for payment of the purchase-money. The security required is a recognizance with sureties, under forfeiture of twenty per cent. in case of failure of payment. Such indulgence is said to be

TOBAGO.

COMMON PLEAS.

necessary; (this not being, as it is termed, a *ready-money country*,) to enable purchasers to procure funds, from Great Britain. And it is considered useful, as occasioning estates to be sold for higher prices, and nearer their actual value, than could otherwise be obtained. At first this allowance, of eight months after the forty days, struck us as unnecessarily and inconveniently long; but, on reflection, we were satisfied of its expediency. Law proceedings in the colonies, in the absence of injunctions, are seldom objectionable on the score of delay. Every proceeding is calculated, and appears to have been designed, to secure despatch *to a certain point;* to accelerate the recovery of judgments, and taking out and lodging executions. AFTERWARDS great indulgence is usually shewn.

When the PERSON is taken, there is no allowance in this island to a debtor, a prisoner in execution.

Upon the clause in the court act, providing that no execution shall be levied or goods or chattels sold between the 30th day of September and the 1st day of April, the attorney-general remarks, "I think the clause,— "which could have been beneficial only in the extreme "infancy of the colony,—is now injurious both to the "creditor and the debtor."

Costs are taxed by the secretary of the court, by a docket of fees (which, however, had been "long lost" before our arrival, and when we inquired respecting it, was said "to be only of late put up,") and, as that table is very imperfect, by reference also to taxed costs in other causes. The verdict carries the costs with it in all cases, unless the costs are restricted by the court act. This the chief justice says, is "the rule of the island."

Counsel's fees are paid by the client. When execution issues, the costs with the counsel's and attorney's fees, are added to the amount, and a levy is made for the whole. A counsel as such, does not bring an action for fees, but the two branches of the profession being united, he may bring an action as an attorney for costs, counsel's fees being charged as items.

The present chief justice has presided in this court for

TOBAGO.

COMMON PLEAS.

nineteen years. During that time there has been only one APPEAL. The judgment, which had been reversed by the court of Error in the island, was AFFIRMED at home.

The attorney-general thought "the decisions of this "court while a professional chief justice had presided in "it, had been uniform and consistent with the decisions "of the courts at home. But whether the court was "governed by previous determinations of their own, he "felt a difficulty in answering; from this defect in their "method: there is no *postea* entered; no record made up; "nothing more than a short note of the judgment entered "in the court-book from the verdict on the back of the "declaration. So that when the original papers are "lost or mislaid, as is generally the case, there is nothing "known of a cause except its result." The same gentleman had before stated, that "the papers, especially "in the secretary's office, are not conveniently arranged "or easily consulted, &c. so that it would be quite in "vain, to inquire for the original proceedings in any "action or criminal prosecution, which took place *five* "years ago."

It is the opinion of the chief justice, "that the ap-"pointment of the courts to be held at other times than "they now are, would improve the administration of "justice, and the credit of the colony." "And," he adds, "I think it essential to the due administration of "justice that the chief justice at least should have been "admitted to the bar in England." The attorney-general agrees, "that it would be an advantage, if instead "of five courts together, and the last *one*, in which "*judgment cannot be obtained*, the 'terms' were al-"tered; and," the learned gentleman proceeds, "if the "criminal courts were to sit nearly *at the same time* it "would be an improvement, and save considerable ex-"pense in the summoning of juries."

## COURT OF COMPLAINTS, CALLED AT BARBADOS, BENCH ACTIONS.

COMPLAINTS.

In this court, actions are brought for sums under 10*l.* and determined without a jury.

The sitting is regulated by the court act, and takes place the day preceding the holding of the court of Common Pleas, with a limited power of adjournment.

Complaints may be tried before any judge of the Common Pleas, but the chief justice generally entertains them. One day commonly suffices for such business. The parties attend in person.

An account filed by the plaintiff, of which a copy is served on the defendant with a summons, is a sufficient allegation of the plaintiff's demand, without a declaration.

The whole costs of a complaint up to the judgment are not more than 27*s.* The judge has a fee of 5*s.* or 5*s.* 6*d.*

This summary jurisdiction is considered by the chief justice as beneficial, and he thinks it might be usefully "extended to demands to the amount of 20*l.* always "supposing a professional gentleman to preside in the "court."

## COURT OF ORDINARY.

This court is held under instructions from the Crown, before the governor alone; having cognizance of probates of wills; letters testamentary; and licenses for marriage.

All wills are proved, and the originals are left with the registrar and deposited in the office.

All marriages are by license of the governor as ordinary, on an affidavit before the secretary.

TOBAGO.

ORDINARY.

The chief justice is not aware of any means by which separate maintenance can be obtained by a wife in this island.

The chief justice does not know *what* means are used to compel payment of costs in this island. There is no process of excommunication, and he had not heard of any proceeding on a contempt.

As there is no ecclesiastical Court, Mr. Pigott considers it desirable that the powers of this court should be enlarged and defined.

## COURT OF ADMIRALTY.

This court derives its power by commission from England. It has jurisdiction in this island only as an instance court; matters of prize being decided in other colonies, where a prize court is instituted.

There was no Admiralty judge at the time the Commissioners were in the island, and the business was "at "a stand, for want of a judge." There were two cases ripe for trial, against parties under prosecution for not making a return under the registry act, which could not be brought on, there being no judge in the court. "The "governor," according to the attorney-general, assigned as a reason for not appointing to the situation,—"that "he could not find a fit person." "*In other islands*"—the attorney-general proceeded, "*the chief justice of the "Common Pleas is also, judge of this court.*" We found it to be frequently, but not invariably, the case.

Admiralty sessions may be held as occasion requires, under a commission then recently arrived from England, for the trial of piracy, murder, and other offences committed upon the high seas. But no court had at that time ever sat, under the commission.

Costs are said to be taxed in this court by the registrar, ACCORDING TO FEES ESTABLISHED BY USAGE.

The registrar of this court does not give security: as it seems very desirable that he should.

TOBAGO.

COURT OF APPEAL.

## COURT OF APPEAL AND ERROR.

This court "is established by the court act." The governor and council are the judges. Where any of these sat judicially in the court below, they only attend in the court of error "to give information."

The proceedings upon writs of error, are attended with considerable expense. It is the same with appeals to his Majesty in council; occasioned as we were told, by the cost of taking out copies of papers.

The chief justice said, "the court *should* consist of professional persons, competent to decide upon points of law determined by lawyers." I agree, in thinking, that, where the judge below is a regular barrister, an appeal to a court composed of the governor and three planters, can seldom serve any other purpose than increased expense and delay.

"The whole system of appeal requires amendment." Per Chief Justice.

"The whole constitution of the court of Error is "faulty." Per Attorney-General.

## COURT OF ESCHEAT.

There is a court of Escheat in this island; according to the chief justice.

Cases of intestacy are not so frequent as formerly, but some occur every year.

Slaves escheating are not considered as virtually freed.

The escheator reports the verdict to the chancellor in court. If there are slaves, the chancellor directs them to be sold; with the real estate, if they are annexed to it; separately, if they are unattached. The net proceeds, after deduction of heavy expenses, are brought into court, and placed at the disposal of the chancellor.

The attorney-general "fears extreme hardship has "arisen in some cases."

# CRIMINAL COURTS.

## COURT OF KING'S BENCH AND GRAND SESSIONS.

The court of Grand Sessions is established by the court act, for the trial of all offences committed by white or free coloured persons.

It sits at the court-house, but only ONCE a year, on the first Tuesday in October.

The court is composed of all members of council and justices of the peace. The commission of the chief justice does not extend to *this* court. He sits in it, with only the rank of a common justice.

The proceedings before trial, as to the warrant, apprehension, examination and commitment, are the same as in England. The practice of the magistrates in taking depositions, recognizances, &c. is believed to be very loose.

The indictment is drawn by the attorney-general; to whom a fee has been generally paid for this service, by the public.

Grand jurors are required by the court act, to be "persons of the best note." We inquired from what class they were chosen; the chief justice said, "the fact "is this: Freeholders are scarce, and could not be had "for both juries. The petit jury by the act *must* be "freeholders; but there are not enough for grand jurors "and petit jurors *both;* and therefore grand jurors are "many of them, chosen from others than freeholders; "such as managers, overseers, &c. They take *a mixture* "*for the grand jury*, owing to the small population."

If the grand jury are desirous of advice on points of law, they apply to the court.

The case, for the prosecution is opened by counsel, (the attorney-general), who is not confined to a mere statement of facts, but also makes observations. Counsel also address the jury on behalf of the prisoner.

TOBAGO.

GRAND SESSIONS.

The evidence, sometimes, *is* summed up by the judges; sometimes NOT. The judgment is supposed to be FINAL. The chief justice said, he "knew not to what court a "writ of error could be taken. There is no court of "King's Bench with a superintending power."

Prosecutors and witnesses are not allowed their costs and expenses.

Capital offences are extremely rare. Fine and imprisonment are the usual punishments. Transportation "is "not used."

"There are many cases very fit for a properly constituted court of quarter sessions, and it would be convenient such a court should sit, unless the sitting of "the grand sessions were more frequent." Per Chief Justice.

*Noli prosequis* are supposed "never to have been "granted for money in this colony." Per Attorney-General.

A defendant in a misdemeanor may traverse the indictment to the next court, "which carries the matter "over FOR A YEAR, and sometimes MORE. If an of"fence is committed in November, it will be eleven "months before it can be tried, and then if the defendant "traverses, it stands over a year longer, making twenty"three months." "This," observed the attorney-general, "is a proof, that a more frequent holding of this "court would be proper. Our gaols are so bad, and the "climate such, that confinement in gaol is a great pu"nishment."

The chief justice thought he could suggest "very great "improvements in this court. The court at least ought "to have *one presiding judge*, who has been admitted to "the bar in England. Such a judge would know the "laws, usages and practice that govern the criminal "courts in England, and which ought to govern them "here. Besides, by altering the constitution of the "court and diminishing the number of judges, many "who now compose it, would be left to serve in the im"portant character of *grand jurors* of the country. Again, "the court ought to sit *oftener* than it now does; for

TOBAGO.

GRAND SESSIONS.

"great inconvenience may occur by offenders, either "being confined for a long space of time, or put to the "necessity of finding sureties for their appearance at a "remote period; one of which circumstances amounts "to punishment before conviction, and the other in case "of a stranger, to a grievous hardship."

I have great pleasure in quoting this passage from an answer replete with valuable suggestions and useful information.

## COURT OF QUARTER SESSIONS.

The court of quarter sessions at Tobago is constituted similarly to those appointed to be held in Barbados, except that there is only *one* court established for the island. But like them it never sits; the business that should be done there, being all transacted at the grand sessions.

## THE SLAVE COURT.

The old slave court appointed by the act in force in April 1823, had the same jurisdiction, and was composed in the same manner, as the slave court in Barbados. The limits of offences however were better ascertained by the act of *this* island, and crimes more exactly defined. Punishments remained the same: that is, accordingly as the cases were capital or penal,—death or whipping.

The information in this island, was taken upon oath, and read as the charge on the trial. The only record was the justice's book, and the only officer appointed to take charge of it, the constable who attended the magistrates. Slaves were not admitted to *bail*. The evidence of slaves was admitted for and against each other, and the chief justice thought it in general correct, though sometimes confused and contradictory. This he attributed to want of intellect or cultivation. There was no *appeal;* but it was imperative by the Court Act, upon the justices to lay the proceedings before the governor within a specified time. The warrant for the execution of a slave, was directed to the provost-marshal, and *he* carried the sentence into effect. TOBAGO. SLAVE COURT.

The chief justice thought "the evidence of slaves "might be admitted under certain restrictions, in crimi-"nal cases. He had it in contemplation to alter the act, "and proposed to introduce, in certain cases and to a "certain extent, the evidence of slaves."

By the promised act, passed in September 1823, a new slave-court is constituted for the trial of slaves for capital offences in the same manner as white or free persons are tried; officers of the court are appointed; bail is directed to be taken and made receivable at any time of the year; depositions, recognizances and other papers are required to be lodged in the crown-office, four days before the court-day; and the chief justice of the Common Pleas is placed at the head of the court to preside on the trial. New Slave Act of 1823. Cl. 8. Cl. 9. Cl. 12. Cl. 15.

By the same act, slaves accused of offences not capital may be committed to gaol by a justice of the peace. The committing magistrate is then to associate to himself "one other justice of the peace, and these two shall "summon five of the most respectable freeholders to "meet them *at the public court-house* in the town of "Scarborough. And the said two justices, and one of "the justices of the court of Common Pleas, are declared "a court, with full power to examine, &c. and, on "proof of guilt, to sentence the offender or offenders "to imprisionment or corporal punishment or both; and "the said freeholders shall be a jury for the trial of all "offences within the jurisdiction of the court, and the "verdict of such jury is hereby required to be 'una-"nimous.'"

The clause contemplated by the chief justice for the admission of slave evidence, "*in certain cases and to a* "*certain extent,*" appears to have been adopted and makes

TOBAGO.

SLAVE COURT.

Cl. 22.

part of the act. It is found Cl. 22, and provides as follows: "And whereas it may happen, that in cases of "cruelty or other injury to slaves by white or free persons, no other evidence than that of slaves can be "procured, by reason whereof such cruelty cannot be "punished or redressed," &c.—"That, in all cases where "any white or free person, or any white or free person "acting under his, her or their authority, is or are charged "with wilful murder or mayhem of, or cruelty to, any "slave or slaves, it shall and may be lawful, in case no "white or free person was present, or can be produced, "to prove the facts relating to such imputed murder, "mayhem, or cruelty, to admit the evidence of TWO "slaves to prove the facts and circumstances attending "such imputed murder, mayhem, or cruelty, and that the "concurrent evidence of such two slaves to such facts "and circumstances, if unimpeached as to their credi-"bility, shall have the same effect, in point of law, as "if a white or free person had proved the same facts "and circumstances attending such murder, mayhem, "or cruelty, and the slave suffering such mayhem, or "cruelty, shall be admitted to be one of the two evi-"dences."

But though the remark of the chief justice, occurring where it did, (*in an answer in this court, as to the value of slave testimony*) has occasioned the mention of both these great, solid, and lasting improvements, in this place; the latter is a topic, more properly belonging to the court of Grand Session, in which such white or free offender must take his trial. In the slave-court slaves were before competent witnesses, although opposed to the testimony of free persons. They are now admissible in the superior court in certain cases, where other evidence is unattainable, and that is of itself, a protection to them; is of incalculable advantage to the progress of improvement; and is very creditable to Tobago, which has been the first island to adopt it.

## RECAPITULATION AND REMARKS.

RECAPITULATION.

I cannot add any thing new or material, to what I before took the liberty of remarking, upon the absolute and pressing necessity, for a person skilled in the doctrines and practice of courts of equity to preside, in relief of the governor, or governor and council as it may happen, in such courts in the colonies. But it may not be amiss to fortify the opinions I before ventured to express, by the observations of experienced lawyers in the colonies, and the tradition of according sentiments in illustrious authorities at home. The chief justice said, "There "should be a regular lawyer in the court of Chancery. "In Lord Loughborough's time it was the opinion of "the chancellor that it was wanted. At a later period "I have a letter from Mr. Percival, in answer to an ap-"plication of mine for some independent salary, that it "was the intention of Government to put the judicial "establishments in the colonies upon a better footing." We found a general persuasion in this island that such improvement in their judicature was quite essential; that it would be speedily afforded; and would begin where it was most wanted, in the court of Chancery. Great irregularities were objected to the present system; much was said of "erroneous decisions," of "bills dismissed "before answer," "demurrers overruled without argu-"ment," "sequestrations issued in the first instance," "orders in a cause without a bill filed," "sales directed "of property belonging to parties not before the court," &c. &c. In our endeavours to collect the opinions of the most intelligent persons in the colony, we met the constant requisition for "*a regular-bred lawyer to preside in "the court of Chancery.*" We inquired into their reasons and from the information we acquired I am bound to state, were BOTH fully convinced of the absolute necessity of the measure. We found no ILL DESIGN, COR-

CHANCERY.

TOBAGO.

RECAPITULATION.

RUPTION OR OPPRESSION: the motives of the judge were pure, his carriage upright; but great disorder and confusion prevailed; no man felt himself secure; and injustice was OFTEN PRACTISED, without being intended, or even dreamt of.

The rules and orders of the court should unquestionably, be collected and published to the Profession; or, at least, placed within reach of persons desirous of consulting them. The Commissioners applied for copies to the registrar (who is also secretary of the island; deputy colonial secretary; clerk of the crown; clerk of the privy and legislative council; registrar of the court of Ordinary; registrar of the court of Vice-Admiralty; deputy registrar and clerk of the courts of King's Bench and Common Pleas, &c.!) but without success.

The *master's fees*, or at least his commission or per centage (six per cent.), seem to me to require reduction.

COMMON PLEAS.

In the court of COMMON PLEAS, besides the objectionable practice of requiring all judgments to be confessed IN court during the sittings, there is little to observe upon, except their *protracted vacation*. The chief justice said upon this subject, "It is very inconvenient to have "SEVEN months, when all proceedings are stopped, and "you cannot have any benefit of process. By sham "pleading you may get through the five months, and "then you throw it over the year. If judgment is got "in July, execution cannot be had till next spring. "The Common Pleas and criminal court should be both "held *four* times a year. You might have all the jurors "collected at one and the same time. If there were two "circuits yearly of TEN days each, it would be enough "for this island. But not for the court of Chancery or "the interlocutory business of the other courts. There "must be a *resident* judge for that."

The practice as to judgments, and the suspension of all judicial proceedings from April to September inclusive, both depend upon, and are provisions of, the court act. Of this law the chief justice remarked, "The court act "might be improved. *One act I think, might be framed "very usefully, to do for all the islands.*"

TOBAGO.

RECAPITULATION.

It is a serious deficiency in the court act, that it does not require an affidavit of debt previous to an arrest. It is said that this defect is supplied *in the practice;* but it may be doubtful whether such interposition of the court is warranted by law. The chief justice remarked, evidently with a due sense of its importance, " In some islands " they ATTACH without affidavit, as well as arrest; *here* " we require affidavits in both."

Delay is frequently occasioned by the clause (in the court act) requiring *three* judges to form a court of Special Pleading. The attorney-general said, *in March,* " There is a case standing over since last July, on ac- " count of the non-attendance of three judges."

In the court of Common Pleas, a gentleman, " regu- " larly bred to the English bar," DOES preside in this island, and we did not hear any complaints of this court. We attended a court of complaints, and a sitting of the court of special pleading for the hearing of a motion for a new trial. The business was conducted in a very satisfactory manner.

There is nothing remarkable in any of the other civil courts of this island.

GRAND SESSIONS.

The court of grand sessions, the supreme criminal court in this island, is held in October. It was found very distressing to have but *one* gaol delivery, in a year. By means of a traverse, a defendant can put off a trial a twelvemonth, and the trial may, in an extreme case, take place twenty-three months and upwards, after the commission of the offence.

Though there is a judge, a very able and intelligent lawyer in the island, the chief justice does not preside in the court of grand session.

The grand jury are chosen from a very unusual and undesirable class of persons.

THE SLAVE COURT *has been re-modelled.*

TOBAGO.

GENERAL COMPLAINTS.

## GENERAL COMPLAINTS.

Irregularity.

Of irregularity and uncertainty in the practice and decisions of the court of Chancery, my duty has already painfully required me to speak, with sufficient copiousness.

Delay was never imputed to that court. On the contrary it was thought by many, that the measures in this island, were too prompt and decisive.

Expense.

Expense in law proceedings, was the subject of constant and vehement remonstrance; but we could not procure any bill of costs for business done in the court of Chancery, to which it chiefly referred. One bill for an action brought in the court of Common Pleas, in a case which had been mentioned to us, we applied for and obtained, from the party I believe.

## PARTICULAR OFFICERS.

JUDGES.

The tenure of office of all the judges was DURING PLEASURE; but by the new slave act, it is provided, that "the chief justice of the court of Common Pleas for the "time being, and two puisne justices, to be appointed "by his excellency the commander-in-chief for the time "being, whose commissions shall be *quam diu se bene* "*gesserint*, shall be a court, &c."

ATTORNEY-GENERAL.

The attorney-general of this island has no salary or stated fees, and performs various important duties requiring his anxious and unremitted attention without any compensation whatsoever. For drawing indictments and conducting prosecutions in capital cases, the fee has generally been paid by the public. The attorney-general "submits his account annually to the Legislature, who "deal with it in their discretion;" in other words, admit

TOBAGO:

PARTICULAR OFFICERS.

or reduce the amount, as the Crown-officer is regarded with favour or dislike.

Thus the law-officer of the Crown, (the only one in the island) to whom questions arising out of the state of slavery of the most delicate nature, are constantly submitted; by whom public prosecutions, often very invidious, are necessarily conducted; whose services, upon constitutional points and in every legal difficulty, the colonial government habitually exacts; is left unrequited; must make his *charge* for business done; and is even for payment of such, his *account*, entirely dependent upon the humour of the House of Assembly!

BARRISTERS.

There is said to be a rule among the manuscript rules and orders, "that every person admitted to act as counsel in the courts of this island, must have been called to the bar in England;" but such a rule if it exists, has not been acted upon. Formerly an examination of a candidate for the bar, previous to his admission, took place before the attorney-general or other Crown lawyer, and the judges afterwards admitted to the bar of their respective courts, such persons as produced testimonials of their sufficiency. Now "the governor exercises the right of admisston," said the chief justice, "as we understand, under the King's instructions. They are admitted to act only 'during pleasure;' a form it is said, directed by the instructions. I should think the propriety of such an admission very questionable, as it affects the independence of the bar. If such license is granted to act 'during pleasure,' it ought at least to be expressed during 'His Majesty's pleasure.'" Some gentlemen of the bar addressed the Commissioners to the same effect. They pressed very strongly "that counsel should not be licensed *during pleasure;* that they should be made independent and enabled to advocate their client's cause with an honest warmth."

The attorney-general it will be seen, explains and qualifies the power of admission to practice at the bar, claimed and exercised by the governor. The governor grants a license to plead during pleasure, in *his own* courts (the courts of Chancery and Ordinary,) and in the other

M

TOBAGO.

courts, "when the judges of those other courts shall "have admitted them."

ATTORNEYS.

The two branches of the Profession are united in this island, and a person may be authorised to practise BOTH, without having been regularly educated to *either*. No previous study or attendance upon courts is rendered necessary; even a clerkship for a certain number of years is not required.

JUSTICES OF PEACE.

The duties attached to the office of a justice of the peace in this island, are the same as in England, with the addition of those arising out of a state of slavery and several statutory appointments. All the jurisdiction of magistrates over slaves is derived it is said, from the slave act.

The attorney-general sees no prospect under the present law that the justices will agree to meet and hold quarter sessions; "as there is NO PENALTY ON NON-ATTENDANCE, in the act constituting them."

The police of the colony is in a wretched state, there being no fund for "its support, and no magistrates specially appointed to superintend it. The repeal of a "wholesome law has tended to the relaxation of the "system of police." Under that act, sittings in rotation of the magistrates were held twice a-week at the court-house, with a constable in attendance, and "an allowance was made to the justices and the constable at the "public expense, which was considered reasonable, as "penalties were inflicted on the justices and constable "for neglect or refusal. The penalties are 'swept away;' "it is 'OPTIONAL with the magistrates now to attend,' "the vigilance and energy of justices and constables "have ever since constantly declined!" Such is the lamentable account given by the attorney-general. The provost-marshal "is confident that eight tenths of the "complaints brought before the magistrates, for many "years past, have been for persons when in liquor quarrelling and fighting in the streets."

Provost Marshal's Return.

CORONERS.

There are two coroners in this island, appointed and removable by the governor. There is no act of the island directing inquests to be taken, either in the case of free persons or slaves. They are taken in the same cases and pursue the same method as in England, as nearly as circumstances will permit. TOBAGO.

CORONERS.

The coroner is guided in the performance of his duties by the laws of England. Information of the cases in which inquests are to be held is received from the owner or manager, or sometimes from the negroes. The senior coroner (who has been in office SIX years,) HAS received information from the negroes, not having heard from the attorney or manager. He had no reason to think that any case of death by severity had occurred, of which he had not received information. He had, in one instance only, held an inquest over a slave killed by the severity of a master or other person acting under his authority. The verdict "did not amount to murder," but the attorney-general thought proper to prosecute; "when the "bill was ignored."

PROVOST MARSHAL.

The deputy provost-marshal said there was only one *place of confinement* in this island; he could not call it a *gaol.* If a prisoner was confined in it, he must be *put in irons for security.* In *that*, such as it was, were confined debtors, criminals both the free and the slave, convicts, prisoners of war, and under an act then recently passed he believed, lunatics.

CONSTABLES.

Constables are appointed in this island by the court of King's Bench, and removed it was COMPLAINED, by the governor. The situation is one of considerable profit; from 700*l.* to 800*l.* or 1,000*l.* a year. GAOLERS are appointed and removable by the provost-marshal.

WANT OF REMEDY. Executors do not duly account.

We saw in this island great numbers of poor coloured people complaining of the conduct of *executors*, and representing that they could not get their *legacies* paid them. On inquiry, the most intelligent of these admitted that the grievance was not exclusive or peculiar to any one class or colour, but extended they believed to all legatees in the West Indies. We mentioned the ordinary remedies in the court of Chancery (bills filed for a discovery—account of assets, &c.), but they shook their heads and left us. Yet these cases, which became very numerous as we proceeded through the islands and were

TOBAGO.

WANT OF REMEDY.

often truly distressing, are no doubt principally to be ascribed to the want of a DUE ADMINISTRATION of the powers unquestionably existing in a court of equity.

Persons of colour in this island can sue and be sued in the courts of law, and are competent witnesses, but are not admitted as jurors.

No schools in this island.

There is no public school in this island for the education or spiritual improvement of young slaves and other children of colour. The chief justice said, "there are "two of the Wesleyan methodists here; they are very "good people, and have done a vast deal of good. "There is a very large attendance upon them."

Slaves required more protection.

Though in this island, the power of the master over the slave, was under the old slave law wholesomely qualified, by "*short of cruelly treating, torturing, mutilating* "*or killing him*," the chief justice observed, "I have al-"ways felt that slaves required more protection. Slave "evidence must be let in. A manager to windward sent "all the overseers, all white and free persons out of the "way. He then gave a negro 150 lashes. The negro "was brought (*in a state—of which he might have died*,) "to us, the sitting magistrates. We had *no means of* "*proving it*. I upon this proposed a bill either to ad-"mit slave evidence, or to make the accused purge him-"self on oath. The bill was not approved." The attorney-general said, "I think that in cases of cruelty to "slaves by their masters or others, where the evidence "of free persons could not be obtained, that the testi-"mony of one or more slaves should be admitted, leaving "it to the jury to judge of their credibility. I know as "a magistrate, cases of extreme cruelty that have passed "unpunished, for want of this evidence. I believe that "many slaves are more to be credited than many mu-"lattoes and free coloured people."—"It is very com-"mon when they wish to be cruel to send all the free "people out of the way. I have known many such "cases. I think it a very common cause of discontent "among the slaves, (of whom many have been before "me as a magistrate,) that when they have been ill-"treated and bring their fellow slaves as evidence, such

TOBAGO.

WANT OF REMEDY.

" witnesses cannot be received. They go away with a " feeling of injustice. I think no danger would attend " the admitting them."

Slave evidence.

Under the new act, as has been shewn, the evidence of slaves is admitted in some cases and to a certain extent.

*By clause* 19, the master's power of punishment is limited to moderate correction; and by *clause* 21, the driver's is taken away.

Guardians of slaves.

*By clause* 25, certain persons of the highest station and first consequence in the island, including the chief justice, are appointed official guardians of slaves. They meet when complaints are preferred, in order to their investigation.

Slave's property secured to him.

He may sue.

*By clause* 35, a slave may bring all actions personal and recover his own property, and his slavery shall not be pleaded in bar; the same clause having first secured to him the legal right to the latter. "Whereas the ne-" groes have always been in the habit of enjoying their " personal property without control, yet nevertheless, in " order that such right may be ascertained by legal pro-" vision, &c. be it, &c. that any slave in possession of " personal property of any description whatsoever fairly " acquired, shall be entitled to hold the same without " the let, hindrance, claim, &c., and may freely and " without control, sell, barter, grant, or bequeath the " same;" measures which seem to afford full protection to the slave, both as to person and property.

The chief justice being asked "Whether the provi-" sions of the old slave-act, requiring justices in sessions " to appoint freeholders to inspect the provision grounds, " and report upon the sufficiency or insufficiency of the " clothing of slaves, were ever put in force?" replied, " I have never known it done, and it is not necessary, as " the negroes ARE well fed, clothed and taken care of."

Sufficient food and clothing.

*Clause* 34 of the new act requires owners to afford "suf-" ficient food and clothing to their slaves," under penalties fixed in the clause. It were to be wished that the quantum of food and clothing *to be considered sufficient* were fixed by law; but it is in some measure satisfactory that it is not left to the owner, however generally humane;

TOBAGO.

WANT OF REMEDY.

the official guardians of the slaves (who are not themselves managers, like the Grenada guardians, but the president of the council, speaker, chief justice, &c.) being appointed the judges of the "sufficiency."

There are two measures of improvement, alluded to by the attorney-general, which are not included in the new act, but are probably reserved for consideration and adoption at a future period. "There may be cases in "which there would be a risk to a slave, in returning to "his master, after having preferred a charge of cruelty "against him. I think that in cases where there might "be a dread of a repetition of cruelty, whether the pro-"ceeding fail or not, the judge should have the power "of certifying, that the party or witnesses should be "sold, and the produce be paid to the owner of the "slave. I think too the slave, as under the Spanish "code, should always be allowed to buy his own freedom "on appraisement, by a person appointed on behalf of "the owner, and a person named by the guardian of the "slave, with power to them to choose an umpire. I "think also that on the application of a slave to another "person, such person ought to be at liberty to purchase "such slave, under such appraisement as before men-"tioned."

Since the passing of the new act, the same gentleman has expressed an opinion that "the power of the master "has been limited in almost every point essential to the "well-being and comfort of the slave;" with which satisfactory assurance from a quarter, in which so much solicitude for improvement and so great liberality of sentiment had been displayed, I shall most respectfully beg leave to conclude my Report upon the administration of justice in the island of Tobago.

# GRENADA.



His Majesty's Commissioners entered upon the duties of the office with which they were charged in this island, on the 28th day of April, 1823. From the Governor they received valuable assistance: the readiest information was constantly afforded them by other official persons.

Eight ordinances for the government of this island, are stated to have been issued by General Melville (the first English governor) and the general council, between the 28th of July, 1765, and the 12th of April, 1766; of which *three* related to the government of slaves; *three* to the establishment of courts of justice, (on the English model;) one to the collecting of taxes; and one regulated the election of the members of the general assembly.

There is a collection of the laws of Grenada from the year 1763 to the year 1805, edited by Mr. George Smith, formerly chief justice, and an act of March 15th, 1809, "making the printed collection of the laws of Grenada "lately published by the chief justice of this colony, le- "gal evidence in all courts within these islands." There are also two Supplements of laws, collected and printed at subsequent times, coming down to the 4th of March,

GRENADA.

LAWS.

1819; and about twenty acts remaining in manuscript. The edition of the laws by Mr. George Smith is a very judicious and creditable performance.

I shall mention very succinctly, a few of the principal acts.

*No.* 8, *Smith's laws, is an act for establishing and regulating a registrar's office.*

*No.* 14, *Amending this act* provides that deeds, &c. executed as required, may be registered at any time, and that deeds not registered in time, shall be void only "against subsequent purchasers and mortgagees for va-"luable consideration, &c."

*No.* 9, *To make slaves, cattle, horses, mules, asses, coppers, stills and plantation utensils, real estate of inheritance, and declaring widows dowable of them, as of lands and tenements.*

*Clause* 4. Deeds, conveyances, &c. of negroes to be *proved* and *recorded.* This act is explained by No. 12, which provides that executors may inventory slaves, horned cattle, &c. which shall be deemed *assets*, and subject to the payment of debts.

*Clause* 3. Tenants for life or by the curtesy sending slaves off the island when liable for the payment of debts, without the consent of the reversioner, may be sued for treble their value.

So, tenant for life—destroying, maiming or disabling slaves, &c.

*No.* 10, *constitutes a court-merchant*, with the same powers as in the other islands.

*No.* 13, "*The statute of frauds shall—by virtue of this* "*act—be adjudged and extended to and be in force here.*"

*No.* 16, *An Act for* "*preventing and punishing those* "*who shall wilfully fire, burn or destroy any canes, dwell-*"*ing-houses, or any other edifices.*"

*Clause* 7. "Where ANY PERSON OR PERSONS shall "unlawfully and maliciously burn, or cause to be burned, "or aid, advise, or consent to such burning of any man-"sion or dwelling-house, or mill-house, boiling-house, "still-house, curing-house, corn-house, store-house, "wharf-house, or ship, &c. &c. or piece of sugar-canes,

" or plantain-walk, or coffee, cocoa, cotton, or any other " trees, the act shall be adjudged felony, the offender " shall be indicted before the King's Bench and Grand " Sessions, and on conviction suffer death without benefit " of clergy."

Under the terms " any person or persons,"—considering the particular injuries to be guarded against and the persons most likely to commit them,—slaves must be meant to be included, and they are therefore triable for this offence of ARSON, before the court of King's Bench and Grand Sessions; and, I should apprehend, no where else.

*No.* 17. " *One justice of the peace is empowered, upon " complaint, to determine wages between master and servant, and to make an order for payment, and if such " order be contempted or neglected, to issue forth his warrant in nature of an execution; provided the contract " does not exceed* 50*l. currency.*"

*No.* 25. *An Act for* " *supplying the want of fines and " recoveries* in these islands, and for making any deed " or deeds duly executed and acknowledged before any " of His Majesty's justices of the court of Common " Pleas, in England or Ireland, or any of these islands, " equivalent to a fine and recovery, duly and regularly " levied and suffered, &c." Upon this act the attorney-general observes, " Under No. 25, Smith's Laws, *femes " covert* only, may give a deed the effect of a fine, by " going before a judge of the Common Pleas in England " or Ireland, or the colonies and acknowledging it. " There is no provision for Scotland. The title and preamble of the act are general, and seem to extend to " other persons desirous of levying fines or suffering recoveries."—In the body of the act, I find, that, " A " deed or deeds in due form of law made and executed " by husband and wife, of the plantations and other hereditaments of the wife, or of hereditaments whereof " the husband was solely or in his own right seised at " any time during the coverture, or whereof the husband " was seised in right of his wife, or jointly with his wife,

GRENADA.

LAWS.

"OR BY ANY TENANT IN TAIL GENERAL OR SPECIAL, "OR OTHER PARTY OR PARTIES FROM WHOM ANY IN-"TEREST PASSES, acknowledged before any justice of "the Common Pleas in England or Ireland or the co-"lonies, shall be declared as effectual as if the parties "had levied fines or suffered recoveries." So that I conceive the learned gentleman has fallen into a trifling mistake as to the operation of this statute; of no importance whatever, except for the sake of accuracy.

*No. 27.* "*An Act for establishing a court for hearing "and determining errors on writs of error to be brought "from the judgment of the court of Common Pleas or Ex-"chequer,*" &c.

And *such* court is "declared to be a court of record, "and to have the same power and authority, as far as "relates to all proceedings, in cases of error only, as "His Majesty's court of King's Bench, at Westminster, "hath with respect to the judgments of His Majesty's "court of Common Pleas in England."

This act is amended by No. 88, which provides very wholesomely, that instead of the governor and FIVE members of the council, *a number not easily collected*, the court shall consist of the governor and not less than THREE members; *who shall not be members of any court out of which the error arises.*

*No. 29,* "*An Act for rendering the process in the court "of Chancery effectual in certain cases against persons who "being out of the jurisdiction of the court refuse to appear "thereto.*"

The provisions are important; the law being in force and acted upon constantly.

No. 30. *An act for re-establishing a court of King's Bench and Grand Sessions, &c.* The style and title of this court and the number and description of persons composing it, are altered by No. 87, by which this court and the court of Common Pleas are united in one grand court, called the Supreme Court of Judicature, which has all the jurisdiction of the courts of King's Bench, Common Pleas and Exchequer in England, and consists of one chief justice (always a lawyer) and four assistant justices. A plan deserving of notice and perhaps of imitation, in a country where one lawyer to preside, is all that is obtainable; and even *that* is not made indispensably necessary, on account of the difficulty and uncertainty of procuring a barrister to fill the situation.

*Clause* 24. Persons stealing in dwelling-houses, stores, &c. to the value of 10*l.*, RECEIVERS OF STOLEN GOODS! and harbourers of felons, are to suffer death.

No. 33. *For the better security of the interest of mortgagees.* Mortgaged slaves are not to be sold, separate from the plantation with which they are mortgaged, except with the consent in writing of the mortgagee, or a certificate of neighbours of their being useless to the plantation. Any sale, without such consent or certificate, is made void. When slaves are mortgaged previous to a judgment and execution, the defendant's right and interest in the whole mortgaged premises is to be sold; and if he shews any slave so mortgaged to be levied on, he shall be deemed to have wilfully *removed* the same.

*Clause* 4. Prescribes the formalities to be observed by the marshal, when he levies on slaves belonging to a plantation, so as to give sufficient notice to a mortgagee, and enable him to lodge in the marshal's office an extract from the mortgage-deed, and affidavit of the identity of the slaves; in which case, if the execution-creditor do not proceed in ten days, the marshal is to deliver the slaves to the mortgagee; or the marshal may, if required by the execution-creditor, advertise for sale and sell at the end of seventy days computed from the day of levy, all the RIGHT, TITLE, INTEREST, AND EQUITY OF REDEMPTION of the defendant in the plantation and slaves. The execution-creditor may contest the mortgagee's prior claim and title in a mode pointed out by the same clause of the act.

No. 44. *To supply defects of former parish registers as to marriages, and to prescribe how Catholics may have baptism, marriage, and burials,* provides that all marriages of free persons shall be by banns or license, and that "baptisms or burials may take place according to

GRENADA.

LAWS.

"Romish rites, but must be registered with those of "Protestants. Persons professing the Catholic religion "may be married by their own clergy, but such marriages are declared of no force or effect as to giving a "right of dower, inheritance, or any other right derived "from a legal marriage."

No. 54. *An Act "for the more effectual trial and punishment of criminal slaves, and to authorise justices to "appoint constables, in cases of emergency."*

By this act the slave-court of this island is established, and its manner of proceeding regulated. Neither the constitution of the court itself nor its mode of acting are much to be commended; and it is gratifying to find the attorney-general's rather confident opinion, ("I am pretty "certain," he says,) "that a regulation establishing a "different mode of trial for capital offences, will be "shortly adopted by the legislature of the island."

Per Attorney General.

In Grenada there is no penalty upon a justice refusing or neglecting to act. If after taking the depositions and ascertaining that there are sufficient grounds for putting the accused upon his trial, the magistrate neglects to proceed within the ten days prescribed by the act, the slave cannot be tried; but must be released, and taken up again and tried.

"Two justices may appoint constables, in all cases of "emergency."

*Clause 3.* "Slaves personally insulting, &c. or in any "manner contemptuously treating any white or free "person, harbouring runaways, gaming, fighting, or "guilty of any crime, which by the law of England "would be deemed larceny, shall be punishable for any "such offence, at the discretion of any one justice of the "peace; not to extend to life or limb." Contemptuous behaviour, gaming, fighting, and stealing are classed together as offences, *ejusdem generis!*

No. 62 *is the court act of this island.*

No. 64, *authorising trials for murder in cases where the stroke was inflicted, or "poison administered at sea,* and the "*death only* happens within Grenada or the Grenadines, "and *vice versâ,* (the *stroke* being within the island, &c.);"

such offences are made triable, as if the offence had happened in these islands.

*Clause* 2. Persons capitally indicted, are to be admitted to make full defence, by their counsel, not exceeding two in number and assigned by the court.—This, which is the *usage* in other islands, is here an express provision by positive law. The preamble is curious: "And whereas "the denial to prisoners upon their trial upon the general issue in any capital crime, of full defence by counsel, "is grounded on a false principle, and is totally repugnant to the humane treatment of prisoners by the "English laws in other respects; Be it, &c."

No. 68 *relates, inter alia, to* what shall be sufficient evidence of *enfranchisement of slaves.*

*Clause* 1, "Acts of freedom by deed, last will, or other"wise, may be recorded at any time. The originals or "certified copies may be pleaded and given in evidence."

*Clause* 2, "Negroes and mulattoes, claiming to be free "by birth, are to prove such claim by the affidavit of two "credible freeholders, before two justices of the peace."

Justices are to grant *certificates* of such claim and proof of freedom, under their hands and seals.

Where there is neither manumission nor proof of freedom by birth, a claim of freedom *by repute* may be proved, certified and given in evidence in like manner, if the party have been so reputed for five years; *proviso*, that such proof shall not be conclusive, if opposed by the production of other testimony by the adverse party; and provided also, that the party claiming to be free, is not to be debarred from adducing further proof of his, her, or their freedom.

No. 81, *For "the punishment of slaves under sentence of "banishment or confinement to hard labour in chains who "shall escape, or attempt to escape, from their places of "confinement, &c."* is a hard and severe law.

No. 82, *The Guardian Act of Grenada* recites that "provisions should be adopted, for rendering the servi"tude and labour of slaves as limited and easy as pos"sible; and as this cannot be more effectually attained, "than by compelling the owners and masters of slaves

GRENADA.

LAWS

" sufficiently and properly to lodge, feed, clothe, and " maintain them, as well during health and their capacity " for labour as in time of sickness, old age and infirm- " ities; by prescribing reasonable bounds to the power " of masters and others having the charge of slaves; by " introducing them to the knowledge of the Christian " religion, and affording them opportunity of improving " in morality; and by constituting a proper tribunal of " guardianship for the hearing, examination and redress " of their grievances and security of their rights and " immunities hereby granted and established; Be it,"&c.

*Clause* 1. " Possessors or owners of estates are to pro- " vide for and allow to at least every head of a family " of slaves thereto attached, one good and comfortable " house, &c.; and shall also allot for every slave above " the age of fourteen, such a portion of land, as in the " estimation of the guardians, shall be deemed sufficient, " &c.; and shall allow from noon, in some one day of " every week, for the purpose of cultivating it; which " said grounds, when once allotted, shall not be ex- " changed, capriciously, without the consent of the " slave."

*Clause* 2. " Owners may give a weekly allowance of " provisions, in lieu of grounds, but there shall always " be a small allotment to each slave contiguous to the " negro-houses, for the purpose of cultivating a garden, " for their sole use and benefit."

*Clause* 3. Requires an annual allowance of (*vaguely*) decent and sufficient clothing to be approved by the guardians, under a penalty.

*Clause* 4. Proprietors shall provide comfortable lodg- ing, ample provision, and decent clothing, for slaves "*not* " attached to or resident on estates."

*Clause* 5. " Proprietors, attorneys, managers, and " overseers are restrained from other punishment than " imprisonment, in a proper and wholesome place of con- " finement; or whipping to the extent of thirty-nine " lashes at one time, and for any one offence.— " When a proprietor is resident on the estate, or has an " attorney resident thereon, the manager, overseer, &c.

GRENADA.

LAWS.

" shall not exceed twelve lashes at any one time, or for " one offence; provided, that if the fault is of such enor- " mity as to deserve a more exemplary punishment, such " offending slave shall be carried before two justices of " the peace."

*Clause* 6. " If any proprietor, attorney, or manager, " shall, upon any pretence whatsoever, inflict heavier, " greater, or other kind of corporal punishment than " those, in that respect, limited and prescribed, every " such proprietor, &c. shall be proceeded against, as if " the offence were committed against a free person; and " in very atrocious cases, accompanied with very aggra- " vated circumstances of inhumanity or mayhem, the " guardians are empowered to dispose of such slave to " some person of humane repute."

*Clause* 7. Regulates the " working hours" *but very insufficiently, as it excepts from the restriction, the* " MAK- " ING OF SUGAR."

*Clause* 10. " Upon every plantation, shall be erected " a good and sufficient hospital," in a " healthy situa- " tion." The manager is required to keep " a hospital- " book with the names of the slaves admitted; the dates " of their admission; and also of their dismission or " death; and in which shall be inserted, by the surgeon " the nature of the complaints or diseases; and by *clause* " 11 *and* 12, an account of the birth and death shall be " annually given in, and, in the latter, the surgeon " shall certify the cause of the death to the best of his " knowledge, &c."

*Clause* 13. " Female slaves, having six children liv- " ing, shall be exempted from hard labour."

*Clause* 14. " Any master, &c. mutilating or dismem- " bering a slave shall be punishable by fine, and imprison- " ment; and the justices may discharge such slave from " servitude, and direct the fine to be paid to the trea- " surer. The treasurer in consideration thereof paying " 10*l*. per annum to the discharged slave."

*Clause* 15. " The assembly shall nominate and appoint " guàrdians every year."

*Clause* 16. " Gives the oath to be taken by the

GRENADA.

LAWS.

"guardians under a penalty for neglect or refusal either "to act or be sworn into the office, or for abusing its "powers."

*Clause* 18. "It may be lawful for the guardians and "they are hereby authorised and required once in every "six months to visit the estates to hear and inquire into "the complaints, and inspect the grounds of the slaves, "and to examine the manager, overseer, surgeon, &c. "as to any suspicious circumstances relative to their "treatment, and to sue or prosecute offenders at the ex-"pense of the public treasury, &c.

*Clause* 19. "*Repealed by No.* 9. *second supplement.*"

*Clause* 23. "*Also repealed by No.* 9, *second supplement.*

The attorney-general observed of the Guardian Act, "I think *that*, a very excellent law, if it were carried "into effect." We inquired whether it was wholly in-effectual: "It is not a dead letter, because a know-"ledge of the existence of the act makes proprietors "of slaves more careful than they otherwise might be. "The misfortune is, that proper persons cannot be "found to carry it into effect. They are *those*, who "may be liable to it themselves, who are the guar-"dians. Perhaps a man may be guardian one year, and "his neighbour the next, which would prevent his acting "strictly, according to the act. They are generally at-"torneys of estates, or managers. I think the parts of "the act regulating the *amount of punishments* allowed "to be inflicted by managers and overseers *are* carried "into effect. The parts that are *not* carried into effect, "are, those, which require the guardians to visit the "negro-grounds, and see that proper food and clothing "is administered. The act does not specify what parti-"cular quantity of food and clothing, but it is left to "the guardians to say *what is* necessary food and cloth-"ing. This ought to be regulated with more certainty. "I think this might be easily improved; and the act so "amended, be rendered very beneficial." The chief justice agreed "that the existence of the act *did* render "persons more careful."

His Excellency the Governor at the request of the Commissioners, obligingly communicated the following observations:

" The guardians never act, except upon representation " from the governor, on complaint of the slaves made to " him. In such cases I think the act certainly operates as " a check, and is beneficial.

" The guardians are found willing to act, but they re- " fuse to take the oath prescribed by the act, on account " of clause 1, which requires them to appoint and look " after the provision-grounds; to be judges of the suf- " ficient quantity of meat and fish; and other duties of " that kind.

" There are no persons to be found to fill the situation " such as must have been contemplated by the act, who " are, as they ought to be, independent. They are " chiefly overseers or managers. Can *they* be expected " to say that the clothing or food, furnished by their em- " ployers, is insufficient? Or if they do, may they not " be afraid of the charge being retaliated on estates " under their management?

" Since March, 1821, there are fifty-two instances " of applications under this act; out of these, redress " was afforded in certain instances, and the charge re- " ported groundless in others. There are only two cases " in which I have seen occasion to direct a prosecution " during my administration of the government, and the " prosecution was not attended with success, in either " instance. Bills were found by the grand jury, but the " prisoners were acquitted. The first was in 1819, where " the slave had undergone two whippings, and after the " last, had the part washed with beef-pickle, and, as she " represented, with pepper in it. The guardians re- " ported this '*a case of severity, aggravated by cruel* " *treatment afterwards*.' The other case was from the " same estate, but under a different manager. An old " man and his daughter were severely flogged, as they " stated, owing to the refusal of the girl to submit to " the embraces of the manager. On their return home " after making a complaint, the manager put them in the

GRENADA.

LAWS.

"stocks. Upon this, I directed a prosecution: Mr. C. "was indicted, but on the trial general good conduct of "the manager, and the kind treatment of the slaves, ap-"pearing, he was acquitted. There was also a complaint "about clothing: I ordered an investigation by the "guardians. This was in September. The guardians "reported that only a part of that year's clothing had "been given to the negroes, at that late period of the "year. In April in the next year, there was another "complaint from the same estate. The guardians re-"ported that the slaves *had* received their full allowance, "for that year. But the complainants, who were women, "persisted in the assertion that they had only received "sufficient cloth to make them an apron each, and that "they had received no further clothing, the preceding "year, after September.

"It does not appear what is the full allowance of "clothing, the guardians allude to. It is obvious, that "it should be fixed and determinate, which by the Guar-"dian Act, it is not."

The attorney-general it will be seen, made the same representation as to the effect of the oath required of the guardians by clause 16. "Most of the guardians evade "taking the oath, as they do not like to meddle with "their neighbours." The Crown-officer likewise speaks of the failure of the prosecutions, and perhaps betrays a little soreness upon the occasion, which is perfectly natural. "I have indicted in three instances where the "guardians sent their report to the governor, and he "submitted the same to me, as proper cases for prose-"cution. On two of those indictments the parties were "acquitted, and I thought them cases for conviction. In "one case I filed an information, thinking it a case of "cruelty requiring to be early taken notice of. In all "cases between black or coloured persons and whites, "the prejudice of juries is very strong in favour of "whites. All attorneys-general have complained of the "difficulty of succeeding in these prosecutions." Upon this statement the chief justice remarked, "In the case "alluded to by the attorney-general," (he did not spe-

GRENADA.

LAWS.

cify which of the three cases, but I suppose the *last*) "I thought the verdict was right; there was a deficiency "of evidence. Indeed I think the acquittals in these "cases do not arise from any repugnance in juries to "find the accused guilty, but from want of evidence, "owing to slave testimony not being received. What "is generally tendered is hearsay evidence of slaves; "not slaves themselves; I never knew *them* tendered."

The guardians listen to the complaints of slaves and act upon their evidence, yet when proceeding upon their statements they direct a prosecution, such evidence is not receivable at the trial!

The result of our inquires, among the most intelligent and unprejudiced persons in the colony may be stated as establishing, that the Guardian Act though not quite efficient is yet very useful. "IT INSPIRES TERROR." "IT IS A VERY CONSIDERABLE CHECK." "THERE ARE "GREAT AMELIORATIONS, SINCE IT WAS ESTABLISHED," were some of the many answers we received, from gentlemen of all parties we addressed upon the subject. Mr. Maddock however, I ought to state, continued rather sceptical, upon the point of its effecting *any* good.

No. 87. *Establishing the Supreme Court.*

No. 88. *Amending the Court of Error.*

No. 89. *An Act "to ratify and confirm all such verdicts "and assessments of damages upon interlocutory judgments "by default or confession, or upon demurrer: to substantiate all proceedings had thereon, in cases where final "judgments have been omitted to be entered; to render it "unnecessary to enter judgments at large in certain cases; "and to regulate the proceedings on motions to set aside "judgments."*

The *preamble* recites that "in divers actions, verdicts "have been found, ascertaining the debt or damages respectively, or such debt or damages have been ascertained by confession, or assessed by inquiry, &c. and "writs of execution, possession, *scire facias*, and other "proceedings, have been issued, although no final judgments have been signed or entered whereon to ground

GRENADA. LAWS.

"the same, by reason whereof such proceedings are "liable to be questioned and set aside for irregularity."

*Clause* 1. "Provides that such verdicts shall not be "set aside for want of form, or not signing final judg-"ment," &c.

## FIRST SUPPLEMENT.

No. *An Act for recording all laws passed since* 1805, *and all laws to be passed and all proclamations, &c.*

No. 30. *An Act for the more effectually securing the payment of certain debts contracted for the use and benefit of estates and plantations against the effect of sales, or change of property or death of the proprietor.*

In *clause* 2, is contained a *proviso*, that a bill of particulars shall be furnished a *month* before the action brought. The attorney-general said, "No. 30, first supplement, "gives a priority, and is a very good and beneficial act." But is not its operation confined to new owners in cases of change of property?

## SECOND SUPPLEMENT.

No. 2. *An Act to make the printed collection of the laws of Grenada, lately published by the chief justice, legal evidence in all courts.* The preamble justly recites that "nothing can be more conducive to the good order of "society than that every individual may have access to "the rules by which *they* are bound to regulate their "conduct," &c.

No. 8. "*For the relief of persons manumitted by last "will and testament.*"

*Clause* 1. "Persons, acting as guardian or next friend "of any slave directed to be manumitted by will, may "institute a suit in equity, for the purpose of establish-"ing his freedom, and in case of doubts existing as to

GRENADA LAWS.

" the solvency of the testator's estate, may call for and " take an account thereof."

*Clause* 2. " If the insolvency be apparent to the court, " the judge is directed to order the slave to be appraised, " and if the slave or any person on his behalf will pay " the appraisement, then to decree his manumission, and " such decree to be valid, even should the parties be out " of the jurisdiction," &c.

No. 9. " *Repealing so much of the Guardian Act as* " *related to a fine of* 100*l. payable on manumissions.*"

*Clause* 2. " Persons manumitted or enfranchised whe- " ther by will or otherwise since the passing of the " Guardian Act, but who have not paid the sum of 100*l*. " as required by that act, are declared to be free, upon " proof of such act of manumission being duly recorded " in the registrar's office."

With this kind and liberal measure, I shall gladly, conclude my enumeration of the most important of the laws of Grenada.

## COURTS.

ENUMERATION OF.

The courts established for the administration of Civil Justice in this island are the court of Chancery; the supreme court of Judicature; the court of Ordinary; an instance court of Admiralty; a court of Error; and the court-merchant, established by No. 10, Smith's Laws, but now become obsolete.

The courts established for the administration of Criminal Justice are, the Supreme Court in its character of a court of King's Bench and Grand Sessions; the Admiralty Sessions and the slave-court. There is no Escheat Court in this island, but, in cases of escheat a commission is issued as in England.

GRENADA.

CHANCERY.

## COURT OF CHANCERY.

The court of Chancery in this island, derives its authority from the King's proclamation in 1763, and the governor's commission. The governor sits alone as chancellor, with authority similar to that of the sole chancellors in the other islands. The laws and rules are the same as in England, excepting some alterations made by a colonial act, No. 29, and a few rules, laid down at different times by the court itself, for its guidance or convenience: as 25th May, 1812, "It is ordered, "that the relief sought by the plaintiff in a bill filed in "this court, be henceforth distinctly stated in writing, "with as much brevity and suppression of technical "terms as the nature of the case will admit."

The court sits whenever there is occasion; on an average from twenty to thirty times in a year. The business brought before the court is chiefly bills of foreclosure, and questions as to priority of encumbrances; and by an act of the island, the court of Chancery here has jurisdiction in cases of manumission in certain cases, where freedom is left by will, and the executor having assets, neglects to manumit the slave.

There is only one master, who is paid by fees; he does not in this island give any security.

The master alone, appoints a receiver.

A receiver of an estate gives security in double the amount of one year's crop: of other property, in proportion to the value of it. His account ought to be passed yearly before the master, and his salary to be paid only, on accounting.

ALEFSENS'S COMPLAINT.

One of many complaints preferred by Charles Robert Alefsen before his Majesty's Commissioners, was to the following effect: "That having an interest in the Co- "rinth estate, he ought to have been admitted before

*Receiver.*

"the master, to except to the person appointed receiver

GRENADA.

CHANCERY.

" to that property. He applied to be so admitted and " was refused." Abstractedly, I should imagine that all parties interested in the plantation, had a right to go before the master, and ought to have a voice in the appointment; but it appears that by the practice of this island, the master has a discretionary power of appointing whom *he* pleases.

The master is allowed two and a half per cent. on receipt, and two and a half per cent. on payment, of moneys.

Where an estate is decreed to be sold in the master's office, no appraisement is made previous to the sale.

Injunctions.

Injunctions are known to be granted in two cases: to stay proceedings at law, and to restrain the shipment of produce; and this on bill, supported by affidavit.

Bills of costs are delivered to the client, and taxed in all cases by the master, according to a table of fees established by the chancellor.

An absent plaintiff gives security for costs, 40*l.*

A fee of ten johs or more according to the importance of the suit, is given to the counsel and solicitor, (the two characters being blended in this island,) previous to commencing a suit.

No fee is given with the brief.

A fee is given for the argument, five johs or more, according to the nature of it.

There is a fee on all motions, according to their nature.

Alefsen's second complaint.

Per Attorney-General.

It was one of Mr. Alefsen's grounds of complaint, that he was not allowed to be heard in person in the court of Chancery. " There is no rule in any court in this island prohibiting a party from being heard in person." We mentioned the subject to the chancellor, and regretted to find that Mr. Alefsen's conduct, upon a recent occasion, had been highly indecorous and offensive to the court. Mr. Alefsen admitted the impropriety of some of his expressions, but added, the word "*lie escaped me for want of an English word to say,*

GRENADA.

CHANCERY.

" '*contradiction*' or '*denial*;' *equivalent to our French* " *expressions*."

The colonial master in chancery said, " I acted as " secretary to General Maitland from June, 1808, to the " time he went to England in 1809, and again from 1810 " to 1811. I was also secretary to General Ainslie for " eight or ten months; so to General Shipley. I also " acted as secretary to President Harvey. I can take " upon me to state, that the duties of the office of chan- " cellor have been complained of by them all, as most " irksome. I have seen General Maitland with a large " table of books before him, taking great pains and get- " ting deep in difficulties, &c."

*Alefsen's third complaint.*

Charles Robert Alefsen had addressed a letter to the Chancellor at Government House, relating to a cause in which he (Alefsen) was a party; and reflecting upon the conduct of a gentleman at the bar, also a party to the suit. The chancellor carried this letter into court, and after expressing strong displeasure at being written to privately upon public business, ordered it to be placed upon the files of the court. As soon as the letter was filed, the barrister whose conduct was the subject of its animadversion, addressed the court. " The letter thus " filed having become a proceeding in the cause" (a proposition which was assented to by the chancellor without perceiving its tendency,) " he begged to move " that it should be referred to the master for scandal and " impertinence." The motion was granted; and the master reported the whole letter, from the date to the signature, to be *scandalous*. The letter was no doubt very acrimonious and intemperate in its expressions. A motion was then made, of which Mr. Alefsen complained that he had no notice, " to tax the costs of the " reference, and that Mr. Alefsen might pay them and " that the scandal might be expunged." " I attended " afterwards," continued Mr. Alefsen " at the taxation. " The master read the bill, and told me he had given " 20*l*. for damages to Mr. Sharpe (the barrister.) Before " the master, Mr. Sharpe said ' he would punish me for "a libel.' I said, '*that* is the proper course, *why* do "you not go to *a jury?*' I found afterwards in the "bill,

| | | | |
|---|---|---|---|
| "Drawing the bill of costs and taxing | £ 20 | 0 | 0 |
| "The bill was taxed at - - - | 146 | 4 | 4 |

"An attachment issued for non-payment of these costs, "upon which I was arrested and am now lying in gaol." —The Commissioners being of opinion, that the letter in question had been unadvisedly put upon the files of the court; that it was not such a proceeding in the cause as ought to have been referred to the master for scandal and impertinence; and that damages were improperly given by the master for injury to character; advised the chancellor before he left the island, (General Rial being about to leave for England,) to make an order, *for taking the letter off the files of the court, and discharging Mr. C. R. Alefsen from custody under the attachment for non-payment of costs, except costs out of pocket.*

In the view of the attorney-general "it would be very "desirable to have a professional gentleman as chancel-"lor, if he could be permanently resident." Upon another occasion the chief justice and attorney-general united "in representing the extreme inconvenience and dissatis-"faction which resulted to the suitor, from the admi-"nistration of equity being intrusted to the commander "in-chief of the colony, who is from education, incom-"petent to perform the important duties imposed upon "and exacted from him."

## THE SUPREME COURT.

In this court are united (by an act of the island, No. 87,) the authority of the court of King's Bench and Grand Sessions, (formerly established by an act No. 30.) and the jurisdiction of the court of Common Pleas, and court of Complaint, (revived by an act, No. 62.) The Supreme Court of judicature, by virtue of this consolidating act, is composed of a chief justice and four as-

GRENADA.

SUPREME COURT.

sistant judges; is held six times in the year, and is said to have all the jurisdiction of the courts of King's Bench, Common Pleas and Exchequer in England. It does not however exercise the equitable jurisdiction of the court of Exchequer in England; and fines cannot be levied or recoveries suffered, under its jurisdiction as a court of Common Pleas; but a deed acknowledged before a judge of the court of Common Pleas in England or Ireland or the colonies, will have, under No. 25, Smith's Laws, the same operation as a fine or recovery; as will also under the marshal's sale, by cl. 101, of No. 62, the marshal's conveyance of an estate-tail.

There are no holidays in this court, except Sundays.

The court follows the rules and laws of the respective courts in England, with a few rules laid down by the different acts of assembly and by the judges, at various times.

As these rules are framed with an anxious desire to prevent delay, a judgment may be obtained, when the parties or their evidence are in the colony, in four months "at farthest." A commission to take evidence abroad, which is the greatest source of delay, might protract the cause for eighteen months or two years.

*Clause 3 of the court act* directs the mode of serving process on absent defendants, *videlicet* nailing a declaration on the Court-house door. Persons, who have never been in the island are considered as absent defendants, for such purpose.

A power of arrest is given and regulated by the court act. The debt must amount to 10*l.* except in the case of transient persons, and there must be an affidavit of the debt. Arrests are allowed, in other cases, upon a special order from a judge. "When a party is about to leave "the island, the chief justice has allowed him to be ar-"rested for unliquidated damages." In uncertain demands, the judges in court, or a judge at chambers, are empowered to moderate and settle for what sum bail shall be demanded. There are no exemptions from arrest. By cl. 14, of No. 62, the plaintiff is compelled to proceed with his action in six days, or costs may be

GRENADA

SUPREME COURT.

given, for want of prosecution. The attachment of debts is frequently resorted to. The expense is about 21*l.* 4*s.* 3*d.*

Continuances are restrained by rules of court. Three or four days are occupied by *nisi prius* business; when the court adjourns for a week, and holds what is called a court of special pleading. Paper books are directed to be made up by a rule of court.

Pleadings are filed. Under 89 Smith's Laws, a record need not be made up; but according to the attorney-general it *is* "sometimes; when necessary."

Depositions are used on trials as in the other islands, and without affidavit that the witness is still absent or unable to attend. The chief justice observed, "we follow the "court act, and that does not require it."

The names of the jurors returned by the marshal, are written on tickets and put into a hat, and then a sufficient number drawn out to compose two juries of twelve each. Special juries are known in practice here.

The jury have been allowed in civil cases to adjourn, and even to go to their homes; but "not in the time of "the present chief justice, either in civil or criminal "cases;"—"nor should I allow it," said that gentleman.

"Under No. 89, in certain cases," said the attorney-general, "no judgment is necessary to be entered up." By which is meant, that under a practice long prevailing and at last sanctioned by that act, a party may take out execution upon the *verdict*, without at all entering up judgment; in order as the act avows, "to save expense." But clause 56 of the court act requires the secretary to keep a book of judgments, called a docket-book.

On a judgment by default, execution may issue immediately; on a verdict, not till four days before the next court, that is, not till after an adjourned court of special pleading has been held, at which the defendant has an opportunity of moving (if he chooses) in arrest of judgment. By a rule of court, No. 8, "In all cases where "the defendant shall apply to the court for time to "plead, judgment shall go with the verdict, and execu-"tion may issue at the expiration of four days after the

GRENADA.

SUPREME COURT.

" rising of the court at which the verdict is obtained, " unless the defendant move within four days in arrest " of judgment."

Executions are taken out, lodged and suspended. By cl. 66, they bind from the time they are lodged in the marshal's office, and the marshal is bound to minute the precise time of their delivery.

GOODS, bought at marshal's sale, are payable in money only.

SLAVES are sold, one by one, except that a child or children under the age of twelve years shall be set up with the respective mothers.

Under cl. 100, of No. 62, it is considered that an equity of redemption is saleable at marshal's sale.

LANDS the marshal may sell under the appraised value. The appraisement is only to guide his judgment. Lands and tenements are sold, on the thirtieth day after the levy.

Notices of the time and place of sales are required to be given by publication in the Weekly Gazette of the island; of goods, by cl. 94; of lands, under cl. 95.

Court Act.

BODY.—A bill was under the consideration of the legislature, at the time the Commissioners left the island, which had for its object to compel creditors to make a certain allowance to prisoners in confinement for debts not exceeding 100*l.*

Injunctions are frequent to stay executions; more so than to stay proceedings.

There is a table of fees of the officers of the court, kept in their respective offices. There is also a table of fees of solicitors, as between party and party. Costs are taxed as between party and party; they are taxed by the secretary by an old docket of fees, and the suitor may insist upon a taxation of his bill of costs if he wishes it; but if there are no objections, the taxation does not take place. A judge's certificate is necessary in certain cases to give full costs, as on similar occasions in England.

The attorney-general represented the decisions of this court as uniform and governed by precedent, and was not aware of any improvements that were required. The

GRENADA.

SUPREME COURT.

chief justice said "it would be an improvement if there "were another barrister made a judge of this court. But "I have not found any embarrassment from the assistant "justices not being lawyers." Subsequently the chief justice in conjunction with the attorney-general, observed, "In case of the indisposition or absence of the chief "justice, the court as at present constituted, is left "under the guidance of gentlemen, whose avocations "are remote from the duties they are called upon to "discharge."

Memorandum.

## COMPLAINT COURT.

Actions denominated complaints, are brought in this island under a provision of the court act, for sums not exceeding 10*l.* and where the original cause of action if it have been reduced to 10*l.* did not exceed 30*l.* The court is held before a single judge of the Supreme Court. These trials do not occupy more than one day, and are very speedily decided. Counsel or solicitors are seldom employed. The plaintiff and defendant in such cases, plead in person, and may both, be put upon their oath. It is considered a very useful jurisdiction, and that it would be desirable to increase the amount for which an action of this sort might be brought.

## COURT OF ORDINARY.

The Governor by virtue of his commission is sole judge in the court of ordinary; which is held at the Court-house, whenever there is occasion. He has no assessor. Marriages take place by banns in this island, as well as by license from the Governor. There are no means of obtaining a divorce in this island, or by which a wife may obtain separate maintenance.

The practice is to prove a will though it relates only to real estate.

GRENDA.

COURT OF ORDINARY.

Wills are returned to the parties proving them.

Costs are taxed, and an attachment it is supposed, might issue to enforce payment of them.

## COURT OF ADMIRALTY.

This court, in the opinion of the attorney-general, " derives its authority from the act 7th and 8th William " 3rd. c. 22. The subjects of its jurisdiction are mat- " ters of revenue." It doubtless existed before the 7th and 8th Wm. 3., but that Act enlarged its powers. The jurisdiction is exercised only in the instance Court. There is no prize court. The judge is appointed, by the Governor as vice-admiral. In its decisions and practice it follows partly the law and practice of the court of Exchequer, and partly of the Instance Court in England. For the statute 7 & 8 Wm. 3. c. 22., is supposed by the Crown-officers of this island to enable the Admiralty court *here* to do, whatever may be done in the court of Exchequer at home.

By reason of a recent and less expensive remedy for the recovery of seamens' wages by proceedings before justices, (by an act of 1819) *suits* for this purpose are not frequent. Fees are taxed by the registrar, according to a docket. Until lately, the chief justice was the judge of this court. It is thought to require a professional gentleman upon the bench.

## COURT OF APPEAL AND ERROR.

This court is established (under Nos. 27 and 88 Smith's Laws) for writs of error from the Supreme Court, and that court only. The judges are, the Governor and three members of council, who have not sat as judges in the court below. The act provides for security from the plaintiff in error or appellant. The appeal must be brought within twenty years. The proceedings are not attended with much expense.

## CRIMINAL JURISDICTION OF THE SUPREME COURT

This branch of the Supreme Court is held under the acts, (Nos. 30 and 87 Smith's Laws). Whenever the attorney-general sees occasion, he applies for a court and that a grand jury may be summoned. The act provides that no writ for a grand jury shall issue *of course*, but only by direction of the court. In such case the marshal is commanded to summon thirty persons of the best note, freeholders and inhabitants, to serve as grand jurors; and forty-eight persons to serve as petit jurors. Their attendance is secured by fines of 10*l*. and 5*l*. The proceedings before trial, are precisely as in England. For crimes, free coloured persons are tried in the same manner as whites; and in offences committed by free persons against slaves, prosecutions may be brought (*for cruelty*) under the Guardian Act; "and I think," said the attorney-general, "at *common law*." By the Guardian Act (No. 82), if, ill-treated by a white man, a slave complains to the guardians, and "the offender may be indicted as if the offence were against a free person, but "we do not consider the slave entitled to give evidence." The chief justice concurred, "as to common law, as well "as statute;" and mentioned a recent case of a "prosecution for an offence against a slave in Carriacou, "which was not under the Guardian Act. He thought "it a question too, whether slave evidence might not be "admitted, as there is no act to prevent it; except by "implication. When it is stated that they shall be admitted *against each other*; it seems an exclusion of "their evidence against *whites*."

Informations *ex officio*, are sometimes filed by the attorney-general, and criminal informations are also sometimes granted at the instance of private persons, as in England.

GRENADA.

KING'S BENCH

The number of commitments to gaol in criminal cases, within the last eighteen years, has been *thirteen.*

The names of witnesses are indorsed on the bill by the attorney-general out of court, before it goes to the grand jury; but the witnesses cannot be objected to before the trial, or until a bill is found. Counsel are allowed to address the jury on behalf of prisoners in this court expressly by an act of the island, and the attorney-general considers that in the colonies, where the judges are not lawyers, such an act is particularly proper.

The chief justice presides in this court and sums up, when present; if he is not present, the senior assistant judge. That situation is, at present, filled by a very able and intelligent man.

*Hon. G. G. Munro.*

Indictments and pleas are drawn as in England, but only filed and not made up as a record; except when necessary.

Prosecutors and witnesses are not allowed their expenses and costs.

Nothing is paid to the attorney-general for a *noli prosequi;* but sometimes the private prosecutor compounds with the offender and receives a compensation, and on such agreement the attorney-general enters a *noli prosequi,* and the prosecutor pays him what he thinks proper.

Only *seven* capital convicts have been executed during eighteen years.

We are greatly at a loss says the chief justice, "for "want of a modification of punishment; the court is "placed in a great difficulty by it; there is no medium "punishment; no public labour, &c. &c."

## SLAVE COURT.

By the act 54 Smith's Laws a justice of the peace is empowered to hear charges against slaves in capital cases, and to commit them to prison. The information is not reduced to writing and the slave is never bailed. A court is composed in the usual manner, by the acces-

GRENADA.

SLAVE COURT.

sion of another justice and three freeholders, who must meet and proceed to trial within ten days, or the slave must be released and taken up again. There is no indictment, or written charge or grand jury.

All such felonies committed by slaves as are capital in England, are made capital also, in this island.

Slave evidence is admitted, and slaves are sworn according to their religious belief. The attorney-general said, " I think their evidence is in general correct and to " be depended on." And the same gentleman thought " it might be admitted, when corroborated by circum- " stances or other evidence, in *all* cases." The chief justice agreed with the attorney-general " when slaves " are under the influence of some religious belief, he " thought they should be admitted." For giving false evidence they are liable to be tried before the slave court, and, it is said punished as free persons convicted of perjury. There is no record of proceedings in this court, except a *minute* made by the justices who try the case, and kept by the magistrates themselves. There is no appeal. Sentence of death must be passed upon conviction, and is to be, " *carried into effect forthwith.*" *At his request* it is the *practice* for the justices to lay the trials in all cases before the governor previous to the sentence being executed; but there is no legal obligation upon them to do so. The chief justice thinks the words in the act, " *carried into effect forthwith,*" require only an immediate sentence, but not immediate execution; as that would be inconsistent with the power in the governor to reprieve, or the King's power to pardon.

The terms of the warrant are " to cause immediate " execution by such slave or slaves as the provost-mar- " shal or his lawful deputy shall appoint." The magistrates appoint the place of execution.

Misdemeanors committed by slaves, are tried in the same manner as capital offences.

The attorney-general, after suggesting various improvements, (as " to attend to the instruction of negroes," " to render the Guardian Act more effectual," and to " facilitate manumissions," proceeded,) " I would further

GRENADA.

SLAVE COURT.

"add to these, that I think the slaves should have the "benefit of trial by a jury of twelve white men, in capital "cases at all events, and for misdemeanors, if of conse- "quence. I am pretty certain that a regulation of this "nature will shortly be adopted by the legislature of the "island." The chief justice said, "I should recommend, "that for capital offences, slaves should be tried before "the Supreme Court; in which case it would be de- "sirable that some rule be laid down, for the admission "of the testimony of slaves." To carry this recommendation into effect little change would be necessary, if another opinion of the chief justice should be considered well founded: "I think" said he, "the Supreme Court "has a concurrent jurisdiction with the Slave Court, "under its general powers, as the court of King's Bench "for this government. The King's Bench Act, No. 30, "Smith's Collection, was passed previous to the Slave "Trial Act, No. 54. And there are no words in the "latter act to restrain or take away its jurisdiction. "Should the Slave Trial Act be repealed, the Supreme "Court (according to this view of the case,) would be "the only court in which a slave could be tried, for any "offence."

No. 30, it appears to me was never intended to confer any jurisdiction over slaves; and in framing the act, No. 54, the legislature could not have thought it necessary to restrain or take away a power, never given or exercised at that period in any of the islands. If slaves were before tried at the court of King's Bench and Grand Sessions, the act constituting a slave court must have narrowed their rights. But the chief justice had not seen any record of such trials, or heard of any instance of the kind. His opinion proceeded on not finding any earlier act, than that appointing the slave court. But an earlier act can be pointed out, giving an express authority to the court of King's Bench and Grand Sessions, to try all persons committing a particular offence, of which slaves are always considered most likely to be guilty; (*Arson, burning canes, &c.*) under which term "*all persons*," slaves are held to be included. This *particular* provision as it appears to me conclusively shews, that such court was *not* to be considered as possessing a *general* jurisdiction over slaves, as well as free persons. GRENADA. SLAVE COURT.

## RECAPITULATION AND REMARKS.

The court of Chancery in this island has jurisdiction in cases of manumission by will, to establish freedom, under an act of Assembly. Chancery.

The colonial master in Chancery in this island does not give security for the due performance of the duties of his office.

No appraisement of an estate takes place, previous to a sale under a decree.

Injunctions are granted in an unexceptionable manner, but it is to be feared upon too frequent occasions.

An appeal lies from all orders, interlocutory and final. The respondent on giving security, takes the benefit of the decree below.

Fees are said to be exorbitant and costs will be found excessive in this court.

The mode of serving process of the Supreme Court on absent defendants, is nailing a declaration on the Court-house door. Among absentees are included such persons as have *never* been in the island. SupremeCourt.

Depositions are admitted upon trials in lieu of *vivâ voce* examinations, to a surprising extent, and as it appears to me, with alarming facility.

The jury have formerly been allowed to adjourn and go to their homes; but it is no longer the case, and has not occurred in the time of the present chief justice.

Judgments are not entered up in all cases, but executions are sued out upon verdicts "*to save expense.*"

Injunctions to stay executions have been frequent.

Originals of wills after being proved are delivered to the party proving them, instead of being left with the registrar and deposited in the office, where they might be consulted by, or on behalf of, parties supposed to Ordinary.

GRENADA.

RECAPITULATION.

take an interest under them; as, slaves promised their freedom at their master's death, &c.

There are said to be no means by which a wife can obtain a separate maintenance in this island.

Admiralty. See 59 Geo. 3. c. 58.

Seamens wages are usually recovered before justices of the peace in this island, by which great expense is saved.

King's Bench.

There is no record of the proceedings of the criminal branch of the Supreme Court.

There is no medium punishment.

Slave Court.

The Slave Court is obnoxious to all the same objections, as were before represented to apply to the court for the trial of slaves for capital offences in Barbados and in Tobago,—before the repeal of the slave act of the latter island.

JUDGES.

The chief justice has a salary of 2,500*l.* currency established by an act of the colony, and also fees according to a docket in the possession of the secretary said to be about 700*l.* per annum. The assistant judges have no salary, and from curtesy do not receive fees; except when they transact business in the absence of the chief justice. It is "doubtful whether they have not the "*right.*" They are appointed by the governor and council.

ATTORNEY-GENERAL.

The attorney-general in this island has no salary. He has an account with the legislature, for fees for public business.

BARRISTERS and SOLICITORS.

By a rule of court recently re-modelled, a person keeping *twelve terms* at home, or *six* at home, and attending during the sittings here *two years*, (making twelve courts) may practise as counsel and attorney; the two characters being blended in this island.

PROVOST-MARSHAL GENERAL.

The duties of this important office we found performed in this island by the provost-marshal general in person.

A reduction of the fees of the office was under the consideration of the legislature at the time the Commissioners were in the island. The question presented the usual difficulties, his commission granting to the patentee all the fees, profits, and advantages of the office, in as

GRENADA.

RECAPITULATION.

full and ample a manner to all intents and purposes, as they were enjoyed by his predecessor. The existing docket was established by the governor and council. Great labour and responsiblity attach to the performance of the duties of this office, and the expenses incident to it are very considerable. The average emoluments for three years preceding had not exceeded 1000*l.* annually.

The whole expense of the establishment of the gaol falls on the provost-marshal, and during the two years that the present patentee had held the office he had suffered a loss by the gaol of 600*l.*

The places of confinement are one gaol and three cages in the island, and one cage in Carriacou, one of its dependencies.

The persons confined in the gaol are debtors, criminals, delinquents under the militia act; and slaves taken in execution! It is not sufficiently large, there being no separation of debtors, criminals, and slaves, males or females. It is not clean or commodious, for a filthy reason assigned in the examination.

It is very insecure, and escape practicable at any time; "which" it is justly observed, "is a serious hardship "upon the marshal."

There is no division of men from women; not even a separate apartment; the accused and the convicted are kept together and treated in the same manner. One pound of bread a day, is allowed indiscriminately to all persons, criminals and debtors, and they have nothing else found them. The gaol is not under the superintendance of magistrates, and is not visited by them. The chief justice occasionally visits it. A prisoner who is acquitted is immediately set at large in this colony. "No fee whatever is taken from a criminal prisoner."

Medical attendance is always afforded to prisoners when ill in gaol, at the expense of the colony. A regular medical man is kept for attendance upon the gaol, but there are no separate apartments for the sick.

The records of this office are said to be "in a most

GRENADA.

RECAPITULATION.

" ruinous condition. The reason assigned for it by the " provost-marshal in his return is, that " each officer finds " his own office; the public records are removable, and " are deposited in a fresh place, whenever it suits the of- " ficer to move."

CAGE-KEEPER.—Runaway and disorderly slaves are confined in the cage. "That," it is said, " is not a very " strong hold;" it is frequently broken, (sometimes with the assistance of the friends of those who are confined,) *from without*. Slaves are sent thither for all sorts of misdemeanors, sometimes for confinement, and sometimes to receive corporal punishment. No public punishment had taken place for a year and a half, and for the last two years the magistrates had not sentenced women to the punishment of whipping, in cases where it would have been inflicted on men. The magistrates *confined*, instead of *whipping*, women, and men they put, for half an hour or an hour, in the *pillory*.—The same ill-disposed slaves are " again and again" the tenants of the cage.

There is no employment of slaves, in the cage. The cage-keeper said " it would be an improvement if there " were, but it must be compulsory." It would also be a manifest improvement, " to have a yard for them to " exercise in."

The most serious and well-founded subject of complaint in this island, is the expense of all law proceedings, and particularly in the court of Chancery, A specimen is afforded, by copying a bill of costs, presented to the Commissioners at their request, by one of the parties to a suit.

Many complaints were made, and charges preferred in this island; but principally by Mr. or Doctor Lumsden. Of the charges preferred by Doctor Lumsden, the following only were of general application:

1. " The state of the election-law of the island and " the admission of managers into the House of Assem- " bly."

The Commissioners were of opinion that they could

not enter upon the question of new modelling the election-law; the subject being of a political rather than a judicial nature.

2. "Persons filling judicial situations should not be "members of the legislature; it preventing inquiry into "their official conduct, and affording opportunities of "gratifying on the Bench their personal animosities, "conceived from opposition and conflict in the Assembly."

This might be true; but was also, considered hardly within the scope of the Commissioners' authority. It forms no doubt, morally, an objection to the system, of great weight. I should add, that of its occurrence, no instances were made out by proofs.

3. "Great losses have been occasioned to parties, by "neglect in the secretary's office. Nonsuits have taken "place from records being missing, &c." Upon hearing this charge, the Commissioners solicitously inquired whether such abuse, if it ever existed, was still subsisting? They were told that there were good offices for the preservation of papers belonging to the different courts; that they were properly kept, the papers regularly arranged, and readily consulted. The attorney-general was not aware of any complaints of neglect or misconduct, or of any losses from want of attention of these officers to their duties. The chief justice spoke in the highest terms of the manner in which the registry of deeds, judgments, &c. is conducted. I have never known any instance "of a document wanting, or a non-"suit taking place, or a loss resulting from deeds being "called for, which were not forthcoming. I have my-"self referred to judgments of eighteen years ago." The Commissioners (it is incumbent upon me to state,) procured without difficulty, every record or document for which they had occasion to call.

4. "Juries have been in numerous instances, returned "by favour and at the choice of the secretary, and often "acted upon by violence." There did not appear upon inquiry, any ground for supposing, that juries in this island are improperly selected; and in the presence of

GRENADA.

COMPLAINTS.

an efficient judge, (and such is Mr. Bent,) it is not easy to conceive—a likelihood—of their being *intimidated*, or even *influenced*, in the discharge of their duties. It is otherwise in occasional instances, where trials take place before judges not qualified by professional education for the office they hold. Of this, Doctor Lumsden succeeded in establishing an instance; though not entirely such as he represented it. "An action was brought against "Doctor Lumsden, by a coloured man of the name of "Clozier for calling him a slave, and a verdict and da-"mages obtained in the following manner:

Mr. Lumsden's charge.

"The opinion of the attorney-general, written in "court (in favour of the freedom) was given to the "jury as they were going out. A new trial was granted "on that ground. There were only two judges on the "Bench, neither of them lawyers. One was for it. The "Bench being divided, nothing was done. Mr. Ross was "the judge who tried the cause. Mr. Hoyes was the "judge, who thought that the new trial should be granted "and Mr. M'Mahon the judge who dissented from that "opinion."

The Commissioners *found* an opinion of Mr. Whitfield's (as to its sufficiency in law,) on the back of Clozier's manumission. It appeared too that such document *was* given in evidence, and *taken out of court by the jury* on the trial, which took place on the 10th of November, 1809. A rule for a new trial *was* granted on the 15th. On the 18th the court *were divided* upon the question of a new trial.

The Commissioners requested the attendance of the judges [Mr. Ross and Mr. Hoyes.] On hearing the charge, Mr. Ross said, "some papers were put in to "prove that Clozier was free. On the back of one of "them I observed Mr. Whitfield's opinion on the case. "I said *that* might satisfy the jury, if they doubted the "effect of the deed. Mr. Lumsden objected that it was "not evidence. I told the jury that it certainly was "not evidence. But being on the back I could not "separate it. I believe I told the jury, I could not pre-"vent their attending to it, if they thought proper so to

GRENADA.

COMPLAINTS.

"do. I ought to say, that I do not think Mr. Whitfield "insisted on the opinion he had before given; my meaning was, that being on the back I could not *prevent* "their giving it any attention they thought proper. This "is what I meant to convey. I thought the other papers "produced sufficient proof of the man's freedom without "it. I can't say whether I did or did not tell the jury "this. There is an act of the island that says, that if a "person be reputed free five years, that shall be *primâ* "*facie* evidence of freedom."

Mr. Hoyes said, "I sat on the motion for a new trial "on Clozier and Lumsden; not at the trial. I thought "a new trial should be granted, because the jury might "have allowed themselves to be biassed by Mr. Whit-"field's opinion. I believe the counsel made the point "that Mr. Whitfield mentioned in the speech the opinion "he had given to the jury, and that the judge had suf-"fered the opinion to be *seen* by the jury. There was "not at that time a third judge in the island."

Mr. Whitfield was a man of great talent and experience in his profession, and any opinion given by him before the action, would deservedly have great weight with every class of persons in these islands, where he was unrivalled as an advocate and lawyer. Mr. Lumsden is very incorrect in stating, that the opinion was "writ-"ten in court, and given to the jury as they were going "out?" but undoubtedly the indorsement ought to have been *kept from* the view of the jury, instead of *presented to it.* I would add also, that the services of gentlemen (planters and merchants,) as assistant judges are not only gratuitous, but also laborious and painful; and often performed with great inconvenience to themselves, and at a considerable sacrifice of ease and personal comfort. It may still, be matter of regret, that any other than lawyers, should be *judges.*

Dr. Lumsden said, "I do not know that juries are im-"properly returned *now*, or are influenced or intimidated; "but they will be, as soon as the Commissioners are "gone."

The remaining charges, though numerous, related

GRENADA.

COMPLAINTS.

only to one or other of the various cases, in which Dr. Lumsden was *personally* concerned as plaintiff or defendant, or prosecutor or defendant; and in which he loudly complained of all the governors, presidents, judges, Crown officers, barristers, grand jurors, and petty jurors, for the last thirty years; including chief justice Ottley and a great number of other persons absent and dead. The only question of solid importance, even to Dr. Lumsden individually, is whether the convictions of himself for libel and perjury, were properly obtained, according to due form of law? a point which I shall request permission to examine, at a future time.

No court of quarter sessions is held in this island for the trial of petty offences.

An act has passed since the Commissioners left the island, for relieving free coloured and free black persons from certain disabilities under which they laboured.

Injuries to slaves are examined into and redressed in this island under the Guardian Act, but the protection afforded them under the present administration of that law, cannot be deemed effectual. The colonial master in Chancery observed, in reply to some inquiry of the Commissioners, " It is astonishing the reduced number " of punishments and improved treatment of negroes, " within the last few years, since the abolition act. They " are infinitely better treated; better clothed; and better " fed; but there is room for improvement still. The " Guardian Act is not carried up to its spirit. I know " of *one* conviction of a manager or overseer. Where a " case is referred to the guardians, they do their duty; " but they would make enemies of all the planters, if " they went upon estates."

Defects of jurisdiction.

Slave evidence excluded.

The provost-marshal thought " in some cases the evi" dence of slaves should be admitted, he meant in cri" minal cases; before a jury, and in a court where they " are examinable by counsel; not where there is white " evidence, and not of a single slave. A discharged " soldier of a black regiment," he proceeded, " stole a " sheep of mine: three of my slaves saw him, and took it " from him; but as there was no evidence that could be

GRENADA.

WANT OF REMEDY.

"received in a court, I was unable to prosecute him; "though I knew the man perfectly well."

Injuries to Slaves by third persons, whether punishable by indictment?

It is observable, that the chief justice and Crown officers both of Tobago and Grenada expressed an unqualified opinion, that an OWNER might obtain redress, by indictment as well as by action for an injury done to his slave. It is difficult to reconcile this doctrine with the established principles of colonial jurisprudence. If a slave is considered only as *property*, upon which a *trespass* may be committed, to be the subject of an indictment is what, I apprehend, cannot be predicated of a mere trespass, unaccompanied by a breach of the peace. If a third person can be indicted at common law, for an assault upon a slave, unattended with atrocious and aggravating circumstances, (of which I fear, there is no instance) the *personality* of the slave is virtually acknowledged; and when that is the case, a great advance is immediately made in improving his condition. Considered as a MAN and a subject, a slave will then be properly regarded as entitled to the protection of the general law of the empire, in all those cases for which the municipal law has not provided. To the question, "Have the jus-"tices any, and what, jurisdiction over slaves, except "that which is given them by the legislative acts of the "island?" the attorney-general replied, "I think they "have not." The chief justice said, "I think they have "no jurisdiction for the trial and punishment of slaves, "but by the act; but I think they have the general ju-"risdiction of magistrates, the same as over white per-"sons; a common-law jurisdiction. I look upon slaves "as within the King's allegiance; upon the slave laws as "a customary law, superadded to the law of England. "Being thus only supplemental to the common law, I "think slaves entitled to the protection of the common "law."

Slaves cannot prosecute.

Power of delegates restricted.

By clause 5 of the Guardian Act the power of punishment delegated to managers and overseers, is restricted, in case of proprietors or their attorneys being resident on estates, to *twelve* lashes. Proprietors of estates

GRENADA.

WANT OF REMEDY.

themselves, attorneys, &c. cannot exceed *thirty-nine* lashes.

Excess of punishment indictable.

Guardians have a power of disposing of a slave cruelly treated.

By clause 6, any proprietor, attorney, or manager, inflicting other or greater punishment, than is allowed by the act, shall be indicted, as if the offence were committed against a free person; and in case of inhumanity or mayhem, the guardians are empowered to dispose of the slave, to another master.

Cl. 5. For enormities, two magistrates to appoint the punishment.

Another excellent provision, securing the master and at the same time protecting the slave, is that where the fault is of enormity, the punishment shall be at the discretion of two magistrates; and no further punishment than *they* shall direct is to be inflicted on the slave for that offence, under a penalty of "20*l*." This penalty, however, is surely very inadequate, and by no means proportioned to the offence.

Quantum of food and clothing not ascertained with certainty.

These parts of the act are believed to be carried into effect. Clauses the first and third are those which are disregarded; the former requiring only "*sufficient* "grounds or provisions," and the latter an annual allowance of "*decent* and *sufficient* clothing, *to be ap*-"*proved of by the guardians*," matters which require to be regulated with certainty and by positive law

In injuries to property: slaves cannot sue.

The chief justice said, "It is generally held as a prin-"ciple in slave colonies that slaves cannot acquire pro-"perty except for the benefit of their owners. I know "that my slaves *have* goods, in point of fact." The attorney-general said, "By law they cannot, but only by "indulgence."

No redemption from slavery.

A slave has not in this island any means of enfranchising himself. The attorney-general said, "*That* ought "to be altered, and a slave should be admitted to pur-"chase his manumission, at an appraised value."

Inquests are held.

A coroner's inquest is held upon the body of a slave, in the same cases, as upon free persons. The attorney-general said, "There are a great many of them, and it is "a very proper thing.—There is a docket of fees for "the coroners."

Alefsen's fourth complaint.

A charge was preferred by Charles Robert Alefsen,

"that a coroner's inquest had not been held in a case "where a slave had been flogged to death on the Corinth "estate." Mr. Alefsen added, "that the burial was "without a coffin. The slave, though he had refused to "go into the hospital three days before, was sick; and "though he might deserve a whipping, ought not to "have been flogged when ill. He (Mr. Alefsen) at the "time complained to the attorney of the estate of the "cruelty of his manager."

GRENADA.

WANT OF REMEDY.

The Commissioners learnt, that as soon as Mr. Alefsen's representation was received, the attorney to the property caused an investigation into the circumstances to take place publicly before the magistrates; all the respectable gentlemen of the neighbourhood attended, and the speaker of the Assembly of Tobago, Mr. Irvine, and Mr. Robert Kerr, of Grenada, men of the highest honour and integrity as the Commissioners had reason to know, were stated to have been present with many others. Mr. Sharpe the barrister also, who had become interested in the property and slaves, took a part in it. "The examination was conducted with as much formality as if "it had been in the courts of law." The "question was, "whether the slave had been improperly flogged, and "whether the flogging had occasioned his death? Nothing was known or heard of the burial without a "coffin." "The result was, a deliberate opinion of the "magistrates, that *though it was to be lamented that a* "*slave was flogged when sick, there was no reason to think* "*that the flogging was in any other respect improper, or* "*that it had occasioned, or accelerated his death.*" We received a confirmation of this statement from the magistrates; and Mr. Sharpe said, "I attended the investigation and was satisfied with the result."

Minutes.

The Commissioners considered themselves at liberty to ask "Whether the provisions of the Guardian Act "had been complied with?" The magistrate assured us, that "the *Hospital Book was* consulted, by which it "appeared that the man had been in the hospital two "days before he ran away. He was absent three days. "He was always an ailing negro; and there was no

* Required by clause 10.

GRENADA.

DEFECT OF JURISDICTION.

† Required by cl. 11.

‡ Required by cl. 12.

" reason to suppose when he was brought in, that he " was worse than usual; he did not complain of sick- " ness. He had always had indulgences; and been put " on lighter work because he was a weakly negro."

"The manager WAS examined; the driver WAS ex- " amined;† the hospital woman WAS examined, she was " examined for a long time; the surgeon WAS examined."‡ The overseer said, "I saw the flogging myself; it was " thirteen or fourteen lashes laid on lightly." The manager said, "I have given you every light work, and " yet you ran away. Now, I will flog you." "I thought " at the time the manager was right in giving those " lashes." But on cross-examination, the overseer afterwards admitted, "I should not have thought so, if I " had known the negro was ill."

Of the propriety of the determination the Commissioners could not form a judgment. But the promptitude with which the inquiry was instituted; the spirit in which it seems to have been conducted; and the minuteness and fulness of the investigation, appeared to me to deserve great praise, and "gave us real satisfaction."

Mr. Alefsen it should be observed, is out of possession of the estate; but he is an imprudent and unfortunate man, and great allowances are to be made for him owing to the situation in which he is placed, if the charge (certainly not frivolous) should be considered by any of the parties, a little vexatious!

No public schools.

There are no public institutions in this colony, by which infant or adult slaves are instructed in religious principles and useful knowledge. There are no Sunday schools. There are some schools on estates. And the Wesleyan Methodists also go upon some estates, and afford religious instruction. But the greater number of the slaves in this island, are Roman Catholics.

It is the just remark of a calm and accurate observer, the sober-minded attorney-general of this island, that " every thing should be done to improve the intellect of " the slave population." I agree with him as to the importance of establishments for the education of negroes; a system which will create and improve means of greatly ameliorating their condition; an instrument of incalculable power for doing good with safety!

GRENADA.

DEFECT OF JURISDICTION.

The information acquired by the Commissioners had by this time, fully convinced them, among other matters of subordinate importance; that,—

THE ADMINISTRATION OF JUSTICE IN THESE ISLANDS IS VERY DEFECTIVE, AND REQUIRES GREAT IMPROVEMENTS AND AN EXTENSIVE CHANGE OF SYSTEM!

And further of—

THE ADVANTAGES OF A LEGAL EDUCATION IN ALL JUDGES, APPOINTED TO PRESIDE IN THE SUPERIOR COURTS, WHETHER OF LAW OR EQUITY; SO, of—

THE WANT OF A NEW SET OF RULES OR REVISED COURT ACT, TO REGULATE THE PRACTICE OF THE COURTS, AND PRODUCE A GREATER DEGREE OF UNIFORMITY; also, of—

THE NECESSITY FOR NEW TABLES OF FEES, AND THE APPOINTMENT OF PROPER PERSONS FOR THE TAXATION OF COSTS!

All which various matters, comprised in this my first Report, the result of the joint inquiries of Mr. Maddock and myself, into the administration of justice, in the islands of Barbados, Tobago and Grenada, I very respectfully request, that your Lordship will be pleased to submit to his Majesty's most gracious consideration.

(Signed) FORTUNATUS DWARRIS, (L.S.)

The Right Honourable
The Earl Bathurst, &c. &c. &c.

Dated, *May* 16, 1825.

# SECOND REPORT,

*&c. &c. &c.*

ADDRESSED TO

THE RIGHT HONOURABLE EARL BATHURST,

&c. &c. &c.

## ST VINCENT.

HIS Majesty's Commissioners reached the island of St. Vincent on the 31st day of May, 1823.

The governor made an early communication upon the subject of the judicature of the island, and the improvements it appeared to him capable of receiving.

The printed acts of the Assembly commence in the year 1767, and have been continued to the present time. There are two volumes of these "Laws;" but the chief justice could not "venture to call them complete." In answer to another question, Mr. Wylly observed, that "he supposed all the acts extant, and in force, were in "print."

ST. VINCENT.

LAWS.

The most remarkable of the laws of this island are,—

## VOLUME FIRST.

P. 20. *An Act for the better regulating of Seamen and Sailors, &c.*, which law contains a provision, "that all "warrants from any of his Majesty's justices of the peace, "against any person on board any ship or vessel riding "within any of the harbours, creeks, or inlets of this "island shall be directed to the provost-marshal or his "deputy, or any lawful constable of the peace, who are "hereby empowered to execute the same," &c.

The want of such a clause was sensibly felt at Tobago, and some other islands.

P. 51. "*An Act for the supplying the place of Fines "and Recoveries, &c.*" This act contains the usual provisions, but as it related only to deeds "acknowledged "before a justice of the court of Common Pleas in Eng-"land and Ireland," (as was the case, it will be remembered, with a law at Grenada,) another act p. 99, extends its operation to deeds acknowledged "before any "justice of a court of Common Pleas, or any other court "of a similar nature (by whatever style they be called "or known) in any part of his Majesty's dominions," &c.

P. 86. *An Act against fraudulent and covinous conveyances, and for establishing a public registry in this island.* This act contains the usual provisions.

P. 108. *An Act for establishing the Court of King's Bench and Common Pleas, and the Court of Error, and for the better advancement of justice, &c.*

The Court Act of this island, passed in 1786. Of certain clauses of this act the chief justice, it will be observed, does not speak very respectfully.

P. 390. *An Act establishing the Court of Grand Sessions, &c.*

## VOLUME SECOND.

P. 41. *An Act to explain and amend the Court Act, and to alter the Docket of Fees therein established.*

P. 76. *An Act to alter and amend the Act establishing the Court of Grand Sessions.* This act reduces the number of judges in the Court of Grand Sessions, by omitting "all his Majesty's justices of the peace for these "islands," retaining however, "the members of council."

P. 80. *An Act to amend and explain the Court Act, and declaring the jurisdiction of the Supreme Civil Court.* "To have, use, exercise, and enjoy all the powers and "authorities whatsoever, in all matters, criminal and "civil, relating to the crown or subject, as fully and am- "ply to all intents, constructions, and purposes whatso- "ever, as the courts of King's Bench and Common "Pleas, within the kingdom of England, have, &c."

Cl. 2. *Any two of the justices shall be competent to form and hold a court at all times, and if the other judges be interested, &c. then one; and at all times one shall be competent to hold and form a court for the purposes of adjournment.*

The chief justice, it will be seen, alludes to the provision of cl. 2. in the following terms:—"By the first sec- "tion of the Court Act, any one judge was competent to "hear, try, and determine all actions, suits, and prose- "cutions." But to decide "on demurrers and issues of "the law, the 30th section required three, or at the least, "two justices. And the act of 7th December, 1807, "Vol. II. p. 80, does not seem to have materially "amended the 30th section of the old act."

P. 115. *An Act to alter and amend the Act establishing a Court of Grand Sessions.* Cl. 4 declares it expedient that the provisions of the 19th and 20th clauses of the Court Act should be adopted in prosecutions at the suit of the Crown, and proceeds to enact that witnesses in such prosecutions "*leaving the island, or prevented by* "*sickness or otherwise from attending at the trial, their*

ST. VINCENT.

LAWS.

" *depositions shall be taken and esteemed good evidence,* " *and recorded with the other proceedings, and a copy of* " *that record, attested by the clerk of the Crown, shall be* " *good evidence upon the trial, provided the person making* " *the deposition be absent from the island, or disabled from* " *attending.*"

P. 186. *An Act to alter and amend the Court Act.*

Cl. 1. All judgments, and executions in sterling money, are to be regulated by *the rate of exchange, allowed by the last verdict of a jury for a sterling debt.*

Cl. 2. directs how satisfaction may be entered upon judgments or executions standing open in the marshal's office, but which are proved to have been paid.

Cl. 3. requires persons who are entitled to judgments or executions, obtained prior to 1794, to lodge certificates of the amount due within two years, or forfeit their priorities.

Cl. 5. recites, that *it hath frequently happened that* " *moneys due or belonging to a defendant, have been at-* " *tached in the hands of the debtor; and doubts have been* " *entertained, whether the plaintiff who shall have served* " *the first notice of attachment, or the plaintiff who shall* " *have recovered the first judgment against such defendant,* " *shall be entitled to receive the money; enacts that the* " *person who shall have entered up the first judgment, shall* " *have priority in payment over all other persons, provided* " *that such final judgment shall not have been obtained by* " *bond and warrant of attorney, and entered up after such* " *attachment shall have been laid.*" Upon which Mr. Shepherd remarks:—" This is contrary to the maxim " *vigilantibus non dormientibus leges inserviunt:* it must " be admitted a hard case, when an active creditor, after " incurring the labour and expense of an attachment, finds " a prior judgment creditor entitled to the effects of his " industry." The remark is just: the rule however, it may be observed, is greatly in favour of the merchant in England, of whom the colonial creditor can commonly get the start by means of such attachments: and therefore conducive to credit; on which account, no doubt it was passed.

St. Vincent's Practice.

Cl. 6. By this clause, the security required from the marshal is raised from 2,000*l.* to 5,000*l.* currency. ST. VINCENT. — LAWS.

P. 351. The existing *Slave Act* (1823) repealing all former laws upon the subject.

This act passed in September 1820, and by cl. 83, was *to continue and be in force for five years from its publication.* It will admit no doubt, upon a revision, of material improvements; but as far as relates to the trial of slaves, (of which alone I was capable of judging,) it appeared to me to *work* the best, to be the most effectual provision (having regard to the adaptation of means, and the attainment of the end,) of all the meliorating laws we found in operation in the West Indies.

P. 386. *An Act to regulate Masters of Ships and Seamen.*

Cl. 11. Disputes as to wages or other matters are made triable by justices. If the amount be under 10*l.* the case may be decided by any *one* justice; if above, by *two* justices; *and every other dispute, complaint, assault, or breach of the peace, not extending to felony*, may be disposed of by *three* justices, in all cases where the ship would sail before the regular sitting of the court of Sessions.

P. 408. *Market Act.* Slaves may sell or dispose of any *pork* out of the market; (persons offering for sale *other* meat within two miles are finable.) This is observable *only*, as appearing to recognize *pro tanto*, a right of property or a *jus disponendi*, in the slave. Cl. 2.

VOLUME THE THIRD was commenced, and had proceeded as far as page 20, but contained nothing material or of any other than local interest.

## COURTS OF JUDICATURE.

The Courts established in this island for the administration of civil justice, are the court of Chancery, the court of King's Bench and Common Pleas, and a branch of the Superior Court, the court of Complaints, the court COURTS, ENUMERATION OF.

ST. VINCENT.

COURTS.

of Ordinary, the court of Vice-Admiralty, and the court of Error. There is no court of Exchequer in this island: "A very few words by way of amendment," said the chief justice, "might be sufficient to give to the court of "King's Bench and Common Pleas, all the necessary "powers of a court of Exchequer."

The court of Grand Sessions is the only court of criminal jurisdiction; but by one of the clauses of the Sessions Act, stated sittings of two justices of the peace are required to be held on the first and third Wednesday in every month, at the Court House at Kingstown, to hear and determine matters concerning the public peace.

There is no court of Quarter Sessions; "nor do we "seem to require one," said the chief justice.

## COURT OF CHANCERY.

This court derives its authority from his late Majesty's proclamation in 1763, and the governor's commission and instructions. The governor is sole chancellor.—"I "do not know" was the observation of the chief justice, "whether any special authority is delegated to the chan- "cellor in cases of lunacy."

The court has three masters (and examiners) appointed by the chancellor. The colonial secretary *acts* as register, and the provost-marshal as serjeant at arms.

The court is considered as always open; but, "for "more than two years last past," the chief justice "had "not heard of the filing of any bill, or the making of a "single motion, in this court."

The court is guided, "Mr. Wylly presumed, by the "law and practice of the High Court of Chancery in "England, and by its own rules."—"When the latter "are silent, the practice of England uniformly prevails."

The court is said, to have "a great many rules laid "down for the regulation of its practice." The chief justice referred the Commissioners to a work upon the practice of all the courts, by a gentleman of the colonial bar, Mr. Shepherd.

ST. VINCENT.

CHANCERY.

St. Vincent's Practice, p. 68.

"Of late years," says Mr. Shepherd, "the freedom by "implication, has been much countenanced; and in "conformity with the doctrine laid down in Littleton, "sect. 204, 205, 206, a legacy or gift by a master to a "slave, will imply manumission, otherwise the party in-"tended to be benefited would be incapable of enjoying "it."

For any further information relating to proceedings in this court, the chief justice again referred the Commissioners to Mr. Shepherd's work, "no business having "been transacted in it, since he (the judge) reached the "island." In answer, however, to the concluding question of the Commissioners,—"Whether he could sug-"gest any improvements in this court?" the chief justice replied, at some length:—"I take the liberty to say, "that more than thirty years of very extensive practice "in different colonial courts, may perhaps warrant me "in suggesting that the best improvement, which can "probably be made in the jurisprudence of our trans-"atlantic colonies, would be to supersede the present "puisne judges, to put another lawyer upon the bench "of the supreme court of common law, and give him the "court of Chancery as Vice-Chancellor. I was three "years at the bar at New Brunswick, where there was "a vast deal of business in all the courts, &c. The "governor never sat as chancellor, without having a "judge on each side of him. These judges drew up the "decisions; not one of which was appealed from. At "the Bahama islands, &c. the chief justice is *ex officio*, "president of the council, and in upwards of twenty "years, there was only one appeal," &c.

The governor candidly admitted the want of a lawyer to preside in the court of Chancery.

ST. VINCENT.

KING'S BENCH.

## COURT OF KING'S BENCH AND COMMON PLEAS.

This, the Supreme Court of common law, was established by the Court Act, which passed in 1786, and is said to possess all the combined powers of the courts of King's Bench and Common Pleas in England. It is held in Kingstown, upon the third Thursday in March, April, May, June, July, and August, and is styled the court of King's Bench and Common Pleas. The court meets regularly upon these days, and sits one, two or three days, as business requires; "and the next Thursday, the fourth "of the month, is a paper-day, called here a court of "Special Pleading."

C. Justice. "The pleadings subsequent to the declaration (matters "are often managed without a declaration) being *ore* "*tenus*, we get on with wonderful rapidity."

There is a volume of rules and orders regulating the practice of this court. Courts "that proceed *ore tenus*," continued the chief justice, "cannot require many rules: "our's are few and *sui generis*. Every thing here, is "different from what is seen in Westminster Hall." The collection consists of "thirty-eight rules, commencing the 21st January, 1786, and ending the 17th of "July, 1821. One of these rules is couched in nine "words; several in two, three, four, five, or six lines."

"This court" says Mr. Shepherd, "was established in "1786; with a power of establishing general rules for "the regulation of the practice, *as near as may be, to the* "*court of Common Pleas, in England;* which rules are "dictated by the judges, and are entered in a book by "the secretary, being all that is necessary to give them "validity."

When the plaintiff is absent, a power of attorney from him to some person in the island, duly proved and recorded in the secretary's office, must be produced. Foreign powers of attorney under notarial seal, and recorded, are sufficient. The person acting becomes liable for costs. ST. VINCENT. KING'S BENCH.

Process is served as in other islands by hammer and nail, in the case of absentees who have no attorney upon record.

Appearance by cl. 13 of the Court Act, is directed to be entered *on* the court day of the second court: a practice peculiar, I believe, to this island, and not deserving imitation. "This may be done *ore tenus*," says Mr. Shepherd, "on the day of the trial, of which the secretary "makes a short entry; but in such case the defendant "can only plead the general issue, except for actions for "debt, or for penalties, where payment generally, con-"cluding to the country, may be pleaded."

Judgments are generally obtained the *second* or *third* court. "Nothing but the consent of the attorneys can "possibly keep a suit pending here, longer than five or "six months." C. Justice.

By a rule of this island, no defendant can be arrested for less than *30l.* currency, except when the affidavit states "that he is about to leave the island, and has no "property by which payment of the debt can be secured." By the established practice (however strong the affidavit may be,) no arrest can be made without a judge's order. "I see no rule, however," added the chief justice, "for this practice." In such cases (where a judge's order has been obtained) arrests are allowed for unliquidated damages, as in case of defamation, &c.

"Where pleadings are *ore tenus*, there is no room," said the chief justice "for sham pleading."

'It is not the practice here to make up records.' "No "records are made up either in civil or criminal cases; "every thing remains in paper, as long as the paper can "be preserved from the cock-roaches." Depositions are receivable in evidence, under the same circumstances as in the other islands, but they do not seem to be taken with equal care, and there never is sufficient circumspection. A summons left at the dwelling house, *even of the counsel*, entitles the party to proceed in the absence of his opponent, and have the deposition taken *ex parte*.

ST. VINCENT
KING'S BENCH.

A general *venire* issues, and *thirty-six* persons are summoned; of these two juries (called the *first* and *second* jury) are formed, and those juries are sworn "once for all, for the court, and for the trial of all the "causes on the list. The jury," proceeded the chief justice, "does not retire after the evidence has been "taken, and the counsel heard; but the presiding judge "then sums up the evidence, and states the law to the "jury, after which, they proceed to the next cause, until "ten or a dozen have been got through; when having "both their hands and their heads full, they go out of "court to consider what verdicts they shall give, and the "second jury then go to work, proceeding in the same "manner, until the first jury return. In this way an "immensity of time is saved. We know the value of "time."

About *two hundred* causes are entered in a year, and about *one hundred and twenty* prosecuted to trial.

"We have no interlocutory judgments. Soon after "my arrival," said the chief justice "I made a rule for "their introduction, but it met with so much opposition "that I was under the necessity of rescinding it."

Causes are sometimes tried by special juries; our ordinary juries are very "intelligent."

The party against whom a verdict has been obtained, has time, until the next court, to move an arrest of judgment, or for a new trial. But by the 34th section of the Court Act, in actions that have been tried at the August Court, judgment may be entered up at the court of Special Pleading. To the judgment, an affidavit is annexed that the sum is due, which is lodged with the secretary, who enters the day, minute, and hour of filing it in the Docket Book; and the judgment is binding on lands and slaves, and all property annexed to the freehold from that time. "Until I came here," said the chief justice, "judgments were never signed "or dated."

The form of the writ of execution, and its operation, are the same as in the other islands. "The law on this "head," said the chief justice, "is contained in twenty-

"six very long sections of the Court Act of 1786; "which appear to be wonderfully well contrived to perplex the marshal, and produce new suits."

Goods are bound in this island from the *teste* of the writ, and not from its delivery to the marshal. Executions are taken out and used as securities, as in the other islands, and though returnable into the secretary's office at the end of *thirty days*, are allowed to be levied without suing out a *scire facias*, at any distance of time. Well might the chief justice exclaim:—"Our law of "execution is perhaps, the very worst in the world." By the 45th section of the Court Act, it is enacted that, "*Whereas executions are returnable into the secretary's* "*office at the end of thirty days, yet if it shall hereafter* "*happen that the body or goods of the defendant may be* "*found, the marshal shall and may proceed to the levy, or* "*may take the body in execution, without further writ or* "*order.*"—"And I believe," continued the chief justice, "it has appeared to the Commissioners, in the case of "William Kladen, to be the practice of the marshal's "office to take both the body and property of the defendant in execution, more than twenty years after its return, and this, although the plaintiff had long been "dead."

A gentleman of the name of Rickard, complained to the Commissioners of a decision of the chief justice, which gave priority to two executions, kept in the pocket of the party bringing them forward, till the day of sale of certain property, levied under another execution of him, (the complainant.) By the Court Act it was enacted, that all persons having executions open in the office, should within twelve months swear to the amount due, and lodge such certificate with the marshal, and in case of neglect, the execution should be deemed satisfied. So in a law amending the Court Act, I find it provided, wholesomely as it should seem, that persons who had obtained judgments or executions prior to 1794, should within two years, lodge sworn certificates of the amount due, &c.; and in default, such judgments or execution shall be postponed to all such as are duly certified.

ST. VINCENT.

KING'S BENCH.

St. Vincent's Practice, p. 64.

" These enactments, however," Mr. Shepherd observes, " are scarcely sufficient to prevent the evils intended (to " be guarded against), *as it generally happens* in cases " of levy and sale, that some old and apparently unsatis- " fied execution is brought forward, to the great injury " of the real creditor, and is productive of much trou- " ble and expense in procuring the proper persons to " enter satisfaction, which must be done before the sub- " sequent executions can be paid, unless there are funds " sufficient to pay all; in which case the amount of the " unclaimed executions remains in the hands of the mar- " shal."

Mr. Rickards also mentioned, that in a case in which he was a party, an injunction had been obtained merely for delay. This, however, must be taken as opinion and assertion only, it not have been carried further by proof.

John Bowen " complained to His Majesty's Commis- " sioners of a judgment having been entered up in a cer- " tain action for 114*l.*, and costs and charges 26*l.*, when " the particulars of the plaintiff's demand amounted to " 58*l.* only. He (Bowen) confessed judgment in person " and generally, but he supposed it would not be entered " up for more than the amount of the plaintiff's particu- " lars previously furnished." *Answered by Mr. Ross, Solicitor-General, and counsel for the plaintiff in the cause.* " It was done with Bowen's consent. The understand- " ing was, that judgment should be entered for the whole " balance due to the plaintiff, (which arose from use and " occupation of a house,) including all intermediate, ac- " cruing rents to the time of entering up judgment, but " it was charged in point of fact, a month short. This " was done out of tenderness to Mr. Bowen, instead of " bringing a fresh action, of which he would have had " to pay the costs. He was not much aggrieved, if it " were mistakenly done, for he had paid nothing at all. " The plaintiff had lost the whole debt and costs, and " Bowen had been discharged, as an insolvent."

Forty days are allowed to purchasers of real estate, and fourteen to purchasers of goods and chattels and slaves, to complete their payments; during which time the latter *remain in the custody of the marshal*, at the risk of the purchaser.

Of real property, the marshal executes a conveyance by lease and release, or often by feoffment (without livery), duly acknowledged and recorded in the register's office, either to the purchaser, or to a trustee for the purposes of settlements or barring dower. Personal property is transferred by the marshal's certificate, or by the sale only.

A defendant in actual custody, either on mesne process or in execution, within *six* days after his imprisonment may declare himself *insolvent*, and give an account and schedule of his effects, which is lodged with the marshal, that the goods may be levied on; and then he shall either be allowed 2*s.* a-day, by the detaining creditor, or be discharged from prison, and the debt considered satisfied.

William Kladen complained to the Commissioners, that his creditors having made default in the payment of the 2*s.* for a fortnight, he applied for a *habeas corpus*, and was brought up before the chief justice, but was remanded to prison by the judge.

Answer.—First:—" There was an irregularity of a fa-" tal nature on his part, he had not sworn to the affi-" davit. Secondly, The marshal's return shewed that " his insolvency was fraudulent: instead of being insol-" vent, there remained of his (Kladen's) money in the " marshal's hands 600*l.* and four slaves." By the Act, a person swearing falsely, is deemed guilty of " felony " without benefit of clergy."

The allowance of 2*s.* a-day from the creditor is by the Court Act. By dockets, established by more recent acts of assembly of 1816 and 1817, an allowance is made to the marshal at the following rates:—

| | *s.* | *d.* |
|---|---|---|
| *For runaways, per diem* - - | 2 | 0 |
| *For white persons committed on civil and criminal process, per diem* - - | 4 | 6 |
| *For coloured persons, on criminal process, per diem* - - - - | 3 | 0 |

ST. VINCENT.

KING'S BENCH.

But the docket not stating *by* whom the fees are to be paid, "the usage," said the provost marshal-general, "has been to receive it *from the debtor, where he is able* "*to pay it. In criminal cases it is in the breast of the* "*court and is paid by the public.*"

John Bowen "complained to the Commissioners of "extortion in the provost-marshal, in the charge of "4*s*. 6*d*. a-day from the debtor in gaol. I have been "kept in gaol three months, after an order by the court "for my discharge. My creditors having made default "in the payment of 2*s*. a-day under the act, I applied "to the court, who ordered my discharge, but the mar-"shal detained me for *fees,* including this objectionable "item, and *that* charged for days subsequent to the time, "when as an insolvent, I had been allowed 2*s*. a-day, "and indeed after I had been ordered by the court to be "discharged."

Walter Thomas Keighly :—"The like complaint. I "was in prison under the sentence of the court for an "assault. I applied to the marshal by letter, for the "4*s*. 6*d*.; I received an answer, from which I learnt "that I should be personally charged with it. I had "received two dollars in money before that letter; after "it, I did not venture to take any. There were other pri-"soners who did not take it, from the same apprehension "of having to repay it. Yet, I conceive, *we* are entitled "to it, and clearly not the marshal. The words of the "Sessions Act are,—

"*Provisions for a day for a white person*, 4*s*. 6*d*.

"After Mr. Nanton's letter, I received neither money "nor provisions."

John Tyley Priddle "begged to object to the mar-"shal's charge of 4*s*. 6*d*. a-day against prisoners, for "keeping them in gaol. I was arrested for 67*l*. and "lay twelve months and four days in prison; as soon as "I could (after being four days in gaol) I took the be-"nefit of the insolvent act. The marshal's fees amounted "to 120*l*. and upwards, for which I gave a security, "with interest at six per cent., with two other persons.

"The marshal has arrested one of my securities, who has "been compelled to satisfy the debt."

Answer—By the acting provost-marshal:—

"The fee of 4*s*. 6*d*. per day is by an act of the island, "allowed *to the marshal for* each white prisoner, but "without its being stated how, or by whom, it is to be "paid."

*By the provost-marshal-general himself.*—

"The fee of 4*s*. 6*d*. a-day from each debtor in gaol is "not applied in support of the debtor, but is received "by the marshal, as I conceive, for the safe keeping of "the prisoner; as a compensation for his (the marshal's) "risk."

I conclude that long before the appearance of this Report the legislature of St. Vincent will have felt it necessary to *explain*, if not to *alter* and *amend*, the acts in question, declaring the real intent and meaning of their provisions. In the mean time I find it hard to believe that by "an allowance of 4*s*. 6*d*. a-day for "each white person," could be contemplated the compulsory payment of such sum to the marshal *by a* debtor, for preventing his escape and safely keeping him in custody.

The fees both of the judges and officers of the courts are regulated by tables annexed to the acts.

Every verdict in this island carries costs, "meaning" says Mr. Shepherd, "full costs. The common practice "respecting executors and administrators is here *ex*-"*tended*, as they are generally subject to costs on a ver-"dict passing against them." No costs can be levied without having previously been taxed by the Prothonotary.

A complaint preferred before the Commissioners by C. D. Horne resolved itself into a question, as to the *weight of evidence*, upon which the presiding judge and the unsuccessful party entertained, as is not unusual, widely different opinions.

In answer to the question, "whether he could suggest "any improvement in the administration of justice in this

ST. VINCENT. — KING'S BENCH.

"court?" the chief justice replied: "It would be an "easy matter to suggest various improvements in the "acts which regulate the proceedings of this Court. "Issues intended for trial ought to be committed to "writing, and copies of all issues that have been made "up, whether of fact or of law, ought to be delivered "to the chief justice.

"Another lawyer ought to be put on the bench and "two of the assistant justices might very safely be dis- "pensed with. The fees of the chief justice ought to "be paid into the treasury, and in lieu of them his salary "might be increased.

"Every process ought to be served personally on the "defendant or his known agent, and should never be "nailed up, except during the occasional absence of the "defendant.

"All judgments of the value of 1,000*l.* currency, ought "to be regularly entered up, and the rolls brought into "court, as in Westminster Hall.

"No execution ought to be levied after the expira- "tion of a year, without a scire facias, &c."

## COURT OF COMPLAINTS.

The Complaint Court in this island was established in 1786, by the eleventh section of the Court Act.

Its jurisdiction is limited to actions under the value of 20*l.* currency.

Proceedings in this court are *ore tenus*. The chief justice thinks it a very useful court, but would not advise any increase of the amount for which actions may be maintained in it.

Messrs. Bowen and Rickard were not satisfied with the judge's exposition of the law, as to the right of the plaintiff to be examined in this court, which the chief justice considered as resting in the discretion of the judge, to admit or refuse. Mr. Rickard also complained that debts

ST. VINCENT.

COURT OF COMPLAINTS.

originally exceeding 20*l*., so debts secured by note or bill, had improperly, as he conceived, been allowed to be recovered in this court. The chief justice replied, that "it was every day's practice for the amount above "20*l*. to be given up, in order to sue in the Complaint "Court; and a *good* is not a bill within the exception "in the Act, it is only an acknowledgment of the debt."

*i. e.* good for so much, like I. O. U.

## COURT OF ORDINARY.

"So little business is done in this court," said the chief justice, "that I suppose the governor never goes "out of his own house, for the purpose of holding a "court."

"A will in this island requires the same formalities "in its execution as in England. For," says Mr. Shepherd, "although the legislature of the island of "Grenada, thought it necessary by a declaratory Act, "to confirm the statute of frauds in that colony, *that* act "has always, with the rest of the statute Book to 1763, "(excepting laws having a local or political operation,) "been considered as the law of the island. And the "statute 25 Geo. 2. c. 6., expressly extends the statute "of Charles to all colonies where it has been adopted "by act of Assembly, *or received by usage.*"

Wills are proved by affidavit made before the governor, as ordinary, by one of the subscribing witnesses, &c.

Letters testamentary are issued by the register, and the will is entered in books kept for that purpose, "but "the original is not delivered out to the party, as in "case of deeds."

The duties of executors and administrators are the same as in England, with the exception of the contingent exercise of the *qualified* right over slaves, who, it has been stated, though real property, are made assets for the payment of debts, on a deficiency of personal estate.

ST. VINCENT.

ADMIRALTY.

## COURT OF ADMIRALTY.

The chief justice informs us, " My commission is " dated the 7th day of November last; since which time " no business has been done in this court, and that may " perhaps serve for answer to the remaining questions."

There is no prize court in this island.

The course of proceeding in the Instance Court, is by information, to be filed by the register within ten days after the seizure.

An appeal lies from a judgment of this court, to the High Court of Admiralty in England. It has not been usual to construe the limitation of time, for appealing from the Vice-Admiralty Courts, with a great degree of strictness; nor does the Court of Appeal it is said, tie down the Vice-Admiralty Courts to nice rules of practice.

## COURT OF ERROR AND APPEAL.

We heard great, and I believe well-founded, complaints from various quarters, of the vicious constitution of this court.

" I presume," observed the chief justice, " no judge of " the court *a quo* is to sit in this court; to constitute " which the governor, and at least three members of " Council are necessary."—" The judges of the court " below," says Mr. Shepherd, " if members of Council, " may *give their reasons* for their former judgment, but " not vote."

" The judge, who presides in this court," proceeded the chief justice, " ought, without doubt, to be a lawyer."

# CRIMINAL COURTS.

## GRAND SESSIONS.

This court is constituted by act of Assembly, and is held on the second Tuesday in the months of February, June, and October in every year.

The members of Council are *virtute officii*, judges of this court; a circumstance which we heard lamented. We were ourselves, witnesses of its tendency to occasion unseasonable discussions to the interruption of the proceedings. The court is further composed of the lieutenant-governor, the justices of the court of King's Bench and Common Pleas, and the judge surrogate of the court of Vice-Admiralty. *Three* are a *quorum*, and the chief justice is directed to preside; "but the opinion of the "court upon each case, is to be taken separately, be-"ginning with the youngest member first, and so on up "to the president."

The judges sit by virtue of the act, without any further writ, commission, or authority.

The attendance of witnesses is secured by subpœna; but even in criminal prosecutions in this island, depositions of witnesses may be taken in case of sickness, or intended departure from the colony, before the trial, and are declared to be admissible in evidence, under the same circumstances, as in civil cases.

During the two years preceding the arrival of the Commissioners, only six persons had been tried for offences in this court, of whom but two were convicted.

When a bill has been ignored, or when the prisoner has been acquitted or is discharged by proclamation, and the court shall certify the prosecution to have been frivolous, vexatious, or malicious, the prosecutor is liable to the payment of costs, which are to be taxed by the clerk

Q 2

ST. VINCENT.

GRAND SESSIONS.

of the Crown; and in all cases, when the prisoner is unable to pay his fees, the court may direct them to be paid out of the treasury.

The court has a power, by act of Assembly, to order transportation of offenders to some other part of the world, in their discretion.

The chief justice thought this court should be invested with the powers of a court of Admiralty Sessions; and when enlarged, he would have it, as soon as possible abolished. It appeared to him "badly constituted." In its stead he would have "a supreme court, possessing all "the powers of the court of King's Bench, Common "Pleas, Exchequer, court of Oyer and Terminer and "general gaol delivery;" sitting however much less frequently.

To prove the faulty composition of the present court, instances were given of the chief justice having been more than once over-ruled by the other judges. It was established that the assistant justices do occasionally differ from the chief justice *on points of law*, and as to the *punishment* of convicts in *criminal* cases. One case of a grave and important but at the same time delicate nature, as involving the exercise of the prerogative of mercy, it became unnecessary to investigate, as the opinion of the chief justice, favourable to life, although deeply entertained, was most unfortunately, not fully expressed.

There is no slave court in this island properly so called. Slaves charged with felonious offences are tried at the court of Grand Sessions, in all respects in the same manner as free persons, except that in all such cases, "*the evidence of any slave or slaves shall be taken* "*upon oath, for and against any slave or slaves*," *and except that* "*counsel are to be assigned to slaves, at the expense of the colony*."

Two cases in which the evidence of slaves in opposition to the testimony of white witnesses, was believed and acted upon by colonial juries, are correctly reported by the chief justice. In Baptiste's case, if I remember right, the manager was detected in an equivocal situation with the prisoner's wife.

ST. VINCENT.

GRAND SESSIONS.

SLAVE CASES.

For misdemeanors and offences of an inferior nature, slaves are tried in a summary way before two justices of the peace.

The Grand Sessions, by the act constituting that court is to proceed, "according to the laws and statutes of "Great Britain, so far as they are in force in this island, "and according to their own acts of Assembly; and if "any slave commits any of the crimes mentioned in the "60th section of the Slave Act, or any other crime not "provided for by that act, the commission of which by "white persons, or persons of free condition, would sub-"ject *them* to a prosecution for felony, by the laws of "these islands, or by those of Great Britain in force "here, every such slave, for any such offence, shall on "trial and conviction, suffer death, &c. or such other "punishment as would be inflicted upon any white or "free person, &c."

No court of justice, in the opinion of the chief justice has any jurisdiction here, over the persons of slaves, except such as has been given them by act of Parliament, or act of Assembly.

Slaves are sworn (on the trial of slaves) in every respect as free persons.—"Few slaves I fear," said the chief justice, "have a due sense of the sanctity of an "oath. The incorrect swearing of slaves I suppose to "proceed in general, from want of knowledge. It is "hardly possible to teach a slave to think as a free "man." "The frequent escape of great offenders among "the slaves is a serious evil," said the provost-marshal general. "I ascribe it to the defects of evidence, and "the loose framing of the colonial acts. Slaves have "little regard to truth. There was a black man con-"victed in a case, where great rewards had been offered, "and the proof depended upon a wretchedly ignorant "woman, who could not understand the counsel or be "understood by the court. I think slave evidence "dangerous against blacks as well as against whites, "'till they are better instructed."

Slaves who wilfully and corruptly give false evidence,

ST. VINCENT.

GRAND SESSIONS.

SLAVE CASES.

are to receive such punishment by whipping, as the justices who try the case shall think proper to direct.

"In my opinion," said the chief justice, "every man "whatever may be his complexion, who asserts that he "is free, is to be considered as free, until the contrary "is proved." "And this I believe to be the law of the "different courts in which I preside." "*Partus se*-"*quitur ventrem*," the chief justice believed to be "the "law of all countries in which slavery is authorised by "law;" it forms however *the* important particular in which slavery differs from villeinage.

"Slaves may certainly be sold like cattle, and where "does the blame lie?" asked the chief justice.

"In aggravated cases, prosecutions will clearly lie in "the name of the Crown, for cruel treatment of slaves, "under the provisions of the Slave Act, from cl. 15 to 20, "inclusive." "It is most clear," thought the chief justice "that our slave law must depend '*entirely upon* "'*statute or written laws*.'"

"The office and authority of the coroner are derived "from the common law; and without any doubt," proceeded the chief justice, "the statute 4 Ed. 1. is in force "in this island. It is emphatically, the duty of the "coroner to hold an inquest on the body of any slave "who may seem to have come to an untimely end. The "written law to which soldiers of this garrison are sub-"ject, is, perhaps as rigorous to the full, as the acts of "the Assembly which have been enacted for the govern-"ment of our slaves. There is not one word in any "law, that enjoins the coroner to hold an inquest over "the body of a dead soldier, any more than that of a "dead negro; the common law protects them both."

"The trials of slaves charged in this island with "capital offences, are perfectly fair. A free white man, "who has no money, may plead his own cause, as well "as he can; but the humblest of our slaves, in such "cases is entitled to the assistance of counsel, retained "for him at the expense of the colony."

J. Bowen mentioned a case to the Commissioners,

ST. VINCENT. — GRAND SESSIONS. SLAVE CASES.

"in which the overseer of an estate was indicted for "cruelty to a slave. The proprietor was absent in "England, and had two gentlemen in the island, acting "for him as attorneys. The examinations were taken "in town, before magistrates, of whom, one of these "gentlemen (the attorneys on record) was one. The "other (attorney) was upon the grand jury. The pro- "secutor was a free man of colour. A charge of arson "was preferred against him; he was indicted, and his "case stood first in the court list. The grand jury threw "out both bills, and put an end to the cases."—We mentioned this statement, at the time, to a gentleman holding an official situation in the colony. His reply was, "The case excited universal indignation."—It cannot be a strained inference that the story had some foundation in truth; but I desire to add, that it was otherwise unauthenticated.

COMPLAINTS.

There were no complaints in this island, of a general nature, except from the lawyers of the paucity of suits.

CHIEF JUSTICE.

The chief justice receives his Majesty's warrant under the privy seal of the colony. He holds his office during the King's pleasure, and his residence in the colony. A colonial salary of 2,000*l.* currency per annum is settled on the present chief justice, so long as he shall fill the office, and reside in the island of St. Vincent. "It "would be a desirable thing," it was observed, "that "the act should be amended, so as to enable the chief "justice to leave the colony, in a long vacation, without "incurring a risk of losing his salary." I can only observe, that so reasonable a request must, it appears to me, be secure of a favourable reception.

The chief justice is also entitled, in addition to his salary, to certain fees which are regulated by law.

JUDGES.

"The governor has the appointment of the assistant "justices; and let them," said the chief justice, "be "suspended or displaced at his excellency's pleasure. "But the chief justice is sent out by his Majesty's go- "vernment, and ought *not*, it is submitted, to be placed "in this slavish state of dependency. His commission "ought to be *quamdiu se bene gesserit*: at all events, he

ST. VINCENT.

PARTICULAR OFFICERS.

"ought not to be *so* liable to suspension, except by "order of the King, signified through a secretary of "state. As matters now stand, the chief justice holds "his seat at the mere pleasure of the governor, and is "dependent for his salary upon the Assembly. No "situation can be more humiliating."

ATTORNEY-GENERAL.

The attorney-general of this island is paid by a salary provided by the colony, at present 500*l.* per annum (currency); but this sum is expressed, in the act, to be allowed for conducting "the business of the sessions (in "lieu of the fees, which are paid into the treasury,) and "drawing the acts of the legislature, which it is his duty "to prepare on the requisition of any member."

COUNSEL AND ATTORNEYS.

The same persons act in this island as counsel, attorneys, solicitors, and proctors.

No person is to be admitted to this bar, unless he has been entered at one of the inns of court in England or Ireland, and shall produce a certificate of having kept twelve terms. But this rule has been "occasionally dis-"pensed with."

PROVOST MARSHAL.

The provost-marshal general is here, as in the other islands, the executive officer of all the courts. The chief justice said, "He *claims* a right of acting as marshal in "the court of Admiralty."

For carrying the sentence of the law into execution in criminal cases, the marshal is allowed by the colony 13*l.* 12*s.*; but he stated, that "it had always cost him "70*l.* or 80*l.*" "It is after all," he continued, "exe-"cuted in a miserable manner. The culprit is tied to "a tree, and placed on a rum puncheon, which they pull "from under him."

In the gaol are confined persons of every description: debtors, criminals, runaways, and lunatics. It is quite large enough, and separations might be made very easily. The upper part is quite commodious and airy; the lower part (the cells) very much the contrary, they are dark and damp. "I knew a man," proceeded the marshal, "confined there from September to February, who came "out so altered that I scarcely knew him; so changed "from black to yellow."

ST. VINCENT.

PARTICULAR OFFICERS.

The wall is strong, but there is only a single door, whence it has happened that the turnkey has been often knocked down by a stout fellow; and it is easy, by means of some of the buildings, to get to the top of the wall.

There is no separation of criminals from debtors, or men from women, and no classification according to the nature of the offence, or age of the accused. The judge once directed solitary confinement, but they had no means of carrying it into effect. Prisoners get medical attendance when ill, "immediately that they complain."

Transportation is known as a punishment here: it is "to some other part of the world, in the discretion of the "justices."

The prisoner's fees, on a prosecution at "the Grand "Sessions, as given the marshal by the clerk of the "crown, amount to £18 0*s.* 9*d.* including the judges', "the attorney-general's, the clerk of the crown, and the "marshal's fees. If the man is acquitted, the prosecutor "pays them, in case the court certify the prosecution fri-"volous."

"A slave *can* apply to a magistrate in case of cruelty "or ill-treatment by his master, or his delegate, and "there is a book kept by the sitting magistrates, shew-"ing the result of such applications. The application "is made to the sitting magistrates in town, in prefer-"ence to the magistrates in the country. The book is "kept by the clerk of the crown."

The Commissioners applied for and obtained the magistrates' book. The cases did not appear to be very numerous: of such instances as occurred, the account was very meagre, and, the result not being always given, must be pronounced unsatisfactory.

A specimen of the loose manner in which this volume (intended as a book of reference) was found to be kept, is the following:—

EXTRACT FROM THE MAGISTRATES' BOOK.

"May 10, 1816.—By direction of the governor, to "enquire into the ill-treatment of a negro named Apollo, "of F—— estate.

ST. VINCENT.

PARTICULAR OFFICERS.

"*Doctor* —— who attends the estate, was of opinion "that the punishment was not uncommonly severe, or "more so, than he had known to have been inflicted on "other slaves, for the same offence.

"Mr. R.——, the manager on the estate, gave the "slave a very bad character for insolence and running "away."

No decision appears.

The cage, it was said, is secure, and is kept clean and comfortable.

CAGE-KEEPER.

The slave-gang is very objectionably composed in this island, not only of convicts, but of runaways; and chiefly, according to the marshal, of slaves complained of by their masters, to the "town warden, who has the "powers of a justice of the peace in the town, and can "and does order slaves to be worked in the gang for "*thirty* days."

The cage-keeper, however, only enumerated "run-"aways, disorderly negroes, and such as were *sentenced* "*to it by magistrates* for small thefts."

Public punishments have decreased. Slave offenders are often improved in bodily health, by their confinement in the cage. Two instances had occurred within the year "of their having conducted themselves better, after their "return to their masters."

JUSTICE OF THE PEACE.

In regard to slaves, the magistrate said he considered himself governed entirely by the colonial laws. The commission of the peace is filled "with the most respec-"table persons that can be procured. Proprietors are "for the most part, not resident. It is the principal "class of managers and attorneys who are magistrates."

The police is very effective and good. Offences against the public peace are rare. "Certainly," said the justice of the peace, "slaves can prefer complaints in "case of ill-usage; it is provided for by the Slave Act. "Such complaints are not frequent. I only recollect "*two* in the last *three* years, and they were complaints "preferred by slaves against their owners, who were "coloured people. They sometimes prefer them to the "magistrates. I do not recollect any such being made "to me, but I have heard of them." ST. VINCENT.

PARTICULAR OFFICERS.

The magistrate did not think the reason of there being few complaints was, the fear of being punished for making unfounded charges. Their *practice* in such cases, was he thought, to reprimand, not to punish.

"The statement of the negro is received and taken "down in writing; but not on oath, and the manager "is then summoned, and if it is not refuted, we reprove "the manager, on this statement, though not on oath, "and that in the presence of the slave. Their com-"plaints are always attended to."

The magistrate had not known any instances "of "claims of manumission being brought before justices, "except one case, referred to him by His Majesty's Com-"missioners."

CORONER.

There is one coroner in this island, appointed by the governor.

Inquests are held in the case of slaves, though the law is entirely silent upon the subject. The coroner rightly observed, "I think this step especially required in the "case of slaves."

Information of sudden or violent deaths is received in general, from notes written by the managers or attorneys. They generally give the information for their own protection; if *they* did not, the negroes *would* let the coroner know it. The coroner had received information from the negroes, in the case of a wound inflicted by a mulatto woman upon another mulatto woman. These were both free persons. He did not recollect any of slaves; but he thought he should hear of *murders* from them.

The coroner had held the office seven years, and during that time he had never but once, held an inquest on the body of a slave, killed by the severity of the master or manager; and, in that instance, the charge was not substantiated. It was held at the request of the attorney, to clear the character of the manager. The inquisitions are returned and filed in the office of the clerk of the crown, and the coroner is bound to make his return, *six* days before the sessions.

ST. VINCENT.

DEFECT OF JURISDICTION.

There is no commission, sent out to this island, for holding a court of Admiralty Sessions.

There is no magistracy, board, or council, to discharge the delicate duty of investigating the complaints of slaves, (whether of cruelty, oppression, excess of work, or subtraction or deficiency of food or clothing,) except the attorneys or managers of estates; hence the salutary provisions of the Slave Act are in danger of being rendered ineffectual.

The regulations contained in the "Slave Act of this "island from sect. 15 to 21. inclusive, will afford some "answer," said the chief justice, "to the question, 'Can "a slave claim any redress, &c.?' But what is every "body's business is nobody's."

There ought to be in every colony, an "officer of the "crown appointed to take care that the laws enacted for "the protection of slaves shall be duly enforced; other "wise those laws will continue to be no more than "waste paper." It is proper, however, to add, that the chief justice informed the Commissioners, that he had never heard of cruel treatment of slaves in this island, and he did not think they *were* treated with severity.

In no case can any coloured person in this island be deemed a freeholder, except for the purpose of leasing, or assigning his property. He is entitled, however, when free "*to hold lands* and *slaves*," and have, I apprehend, a freehold interest though not a freehold tenure (to qualify him to vote at elections, &c.)

Slave evidence is not admitted against free persons, in cases where other evidence is unattainable. Upon this defect in the laws, the chief justice remarked, "The "admission of slave evidence against free persons, would "seem to be, sometimes indispensably necessary to public "justice. The first person who was tried before me for "murder, in this island, was a free negro, who had most "probably committed the crime of which he was ac- "cused; but he escaped, because the dying declaration "of the murdered slave could not be admitted in evi "dence against him."

In this case as we were informed, a dollar, the *pre*

St. Vincent.

Defect of jurisdiction.

*tium amoris* had been paid to the deceased by the prisoner, a soldier in a black regiment. After the gratification of his passions, the fellow insisted on the restoration "of the silver;" the girl made an animated resistance, when the soldier stabbed her with his bayonet, and left her bleeding on the ground, a little way in a wood; in which situation she was discovered shortly after, in a dying state. She gave this account (which could not be received at the trial) before she expired. The defect in the laws could not perhaps, be rendered more apparent. With this exception, and the frequent interruptions, and a degree of disorder, occasioned by too great a number of judges,—I feel it incumbent upon me to state, that the slave in St. Vincent (as I was satisfied from personal attendance in court on successive days), has criminal justice administered to him, at the Grand Sessions, with a fairness and impartiality formerly unknown, and in the highest degree creditable to this Island. Indeed the law and the administration are both such, as to confer honour upon the Legislature and the Judge!

# DOMINICA.

HIS Majesty's Commissioners landed at Roseau, the capital of Dominica, on the 29th day of June, 1823. From the governor and other official persons, they experienced during their stay in the island, (which as no complaints were preferred, was not protracted,) the greatest courtesy and attention.

The laws in force in this island are, (besides such as are local and municipal,) the laws of England applicable to their situation of colonists, as they existed at the time of the cession of the island; and acts of parliament passed since, extending to the colonies. But the attorney-general observed, "the rule upon this subject is so vague, "and so little understood in the colonies, that decisions "founded upon it, will be often contradictory."

An edition of the laws, including all acts to October 1818, with an elaborate introduction, advertisement or memoir prefixed, was published by the present chief justice in 1819, and is a very useful work, by which Mr. Gloster has laid the colony under great and lasting obligations.

The most important of these laws are No. 2, *An act establishing a registry*. By clause 2, every deed, affecting lands made in the island of Dominica, shall be executed in the presence of at least two credible witnesses.

"What jurisconsult, out of the colony, knows that " every deed, affecting lands, must, in the island, be " executed in the presence of at least two credible wit- " nesses?"

No. 3, *An Act to oblige creditors of debtors, confined in the common gaol for small debts, to pay a daily sum, as maintenance for such debtors, &c.*

No. 5, *An Act for the more speedy recovery of small debts, and to empower judges of the court of Common Pleas, and justices of the peace of this island, to hear and determine simple contract debts, not exceeding 6l. 12s. currency, or balances of accounts of 6l. 12s. or under, that never exceeded 15l. of like money.*

No. 9, *An Act for the punishing those who shall wilfully and maliciously set fire to canes, coffee, cocoa, &c.*

A summary conviction, and the punishment—death; and in the case of a slave, and *not* of a white or a free man, the *attempt* made capital!—This law is still in force.

No. 10, *An Act to regulate manumissions of slaves.* This act is said to be partly in force, but many of its clauses of the most offensive nature, and extremely unjust in their operation upon free persons of colour, I am happy to add, have been repealed.

No. 14, *An Act, supplying the loss of a former act, for associating the Members of Council with the Governor or Commander-in-chief for the time being, in holding a court of Chancery, and for regulating the proceedings of the said court.* The preamble recites, that *the suitors in his Majesty's court of Chancery might thereinafter find many inconveniences from the court being held by one person only, and sets out the advantage and ease from a different form of holding that court.*

The fees are to continue to be paid to the commander-in-chief.

No. 15, *To vest in his Majesty, his heirs and successors, for certain public uses, two lots of land, with the court-house, offices, and buildings thereon erected, and to oblige the*

DOMINICA.

LAWS.

*secretary and register of deeds and his deputy, and the provost-marshal and his deputy to keep their offices and the records of their offices, respectively, in the stone buildings, erected for that purpose, &c.*

No. 17, cl. 5, *No negro, or descendant of a negro, shall gallop any horse, mare, or mule, in any of the streets of the town; or disobeying this law, if free, shall be fined, if a slave, shall be whipped.*

This clause was objected to, and has been altered. It appears to me that it only required to be *extended*, and that no person of any colour, should be permitted to gallop through the streets of a town.

No. 19, *An Act for the preservation of the game of this island.*

The first game law we had met with;—an English sportsman will be amused with the novel species of game enumerated, as *wild pigeons or ramiers, parrots or ciceroes, doves and grieves, besides partridges or perdrix*;—the eggs or young of which all persons are prohibited from taking from the nest, as well as from sporting, hunting, or shooting in the woods, from the first day of March to the end of July.

To persons guilty of a breach of this law, a different punishment was assigned, accordingly as they belonged to the class of white or free-coloured persons, or were slaves. But its provisions have been varied by a recent act, as far as relates to free-coloured persons, who were before subject to both fine and imprisonment; whites being liable to penalties only. Slaves offending against the act, are of course visited with corporal punishment as in other cases; as *they* could not be fined or imprisoned, without the punishment falling upon their masters

No. 20, A slave act passed in 1788, and for that early period,—before the attention of the government and parliament of the mother country, had been seriously drawn to the indispensable duty of providing more effectual security and protection against the neglect or ill treatment of slaves,—a measure entitled to the appellation of "*humane and liberal.*" "It is well known," says the chief justice, "that the slaves thirty years ago, were "not the slaves of the present day; many were then "of recent importation, savage, stupid, &c. At that "period it was the more meritorious to make them the "objects of the guardianship of the law."

Cl. 12. *And whereas the right of trial by jury in all criminal cases, is consonant to the spirit of the British constitution,* it is provided, *that the marshal shall summon twelve freeholders, merchants or traders, any six of whom being duly sworn, shall constitute a jury, whose unanimous verdict shall determine the fact; provided that such court shall not in any case prescribe modes of execution, or inflict punishments unknown to the laws of England, for similar offences.*

By *cl.* 19, *any white or free person, convicted of the wilful murder of a slave, shall suffer death;*—by *cl.* 20, *any white or free person, convicted of maiming or cruelly torturing slaves shall be imprisoned and fined;*—by *cl.* 21, *any white or free person guilty of striking, or severely beating any slave, the property of another, or of depriving such slave of any property in his possession, shall be fined.*

This act is repealed by No. 79, and again by the slave law passed in 1821, in consequence of the disallowance of No. 79; but I briefly notice its provisions, though no longer in force, because they will bear a favourable comparison with some laws in other islands, of much more recent introduction. I would particularly notice the greater degree of protection afforded to slaves, against injuries from *third* persons by cl. 21.

No. 28, *An Act to make the testimony of slaves admissible in certain cases and under certain restrictions for a limited time and for other purposes.*

The preamble recites that many evil-disposed persons carry on an intercourse with the runaway slaves, and supply them with necessaries, arms and ammunition, being *emboldened in the said wicked practices by the difficulty, (the admission of testimony of slaves not being allowable in any case, as the law now stands) of convicting them of the said offences:—for remedy whereof, it is enacted, that it shall and may be lawful to examine as wit-*

DOMINICA.
LAWS.

*nesses, on their corporal oath, any slave or slaves, other than the slave or slaves of the person accused, before any judge, &c. in any court, &c.* then follow the guards and limitations at that time considered necessary; *provided always nevertheless, that no white person, or free person of colour shall be convicted of any of the offences aforesaid, unless two of the said slaves, at the least, clearly and consistently with each other, depose to the same fact, act, or circumstances, and also unless the said slaves are examined apart, and out of hearing of each other, and unless the same be prosecuted within* TWELVE *months after the commission of the offence aforesaid.*

This act is deserving of particular notice, as "being," the chief justice observes, "the first time the legislature "(of Dominica) relaxed the old rule; and *then*," he adds, "it was for the general advantage, and regarded "the security of society at large; while in a later in-"stance it was conceded for the negro's own security." The act is certainly important, both as it establishes a PRECEDENT and involves a PRINCIPLE.

No. 29. relates to the apprehension of runaways, &c. Cl. 6. contains a wholesome provision that *a committee of the council and assembly be appointed to inspect the gaol and enquire into the treatment of slaves confined there, and see that they receive their daily allowance of wholesome food; with power in the committee to fine the gaoler.*

The gaol was nevertheless in worse condition than any we had yet seen, with the single exception of Tobago.

No. 37. The Court Act of this island, "which," says the chief justice, "comprises the structure of four dis-"tinct courts, with their regulations and forms of pro-"cess."

No. 38. *An act to prevent masters of vessels from carrying debtors or their effects from off the island, and from leaving their seamen on shore;—to oblige persons intending to leave the island to give security, or publish their names in the secretary's office, and to empower justices of the peace to determine disputes between masters and seamen.*

No. 41., amended by No. 43. *An act for the appointment of town wardens to superintend the streets of Roseau;*

"*so as to render it healthy, safe, and comfortable to its* "*inhabitants!*"

No. 49. *To regulate manumissions, and impose a tax thereon, &c.* The tax on the manumission of slaves born in this island is 16*l.* 10*s.* current money, and for this sum the treasurer is required to sign a receipt at the foot of the manumission; and the register is forbidden to record any manumission without such receipt of the treasurer.

Cl. 4. *Persons of colour coming from other islands, to be entitled to the privileges of free or manumitted persons, shall pay a tax of thirty-three shillings, and shall record their manumission, or an authenticated copy thereof, certified under the hand of the secretary of the island where such manumission shall have been recorded.* Proviso, *that a person proved by the oath of two credible witnesses to have passed as a free person for the period of* FIVE *years, on paying the tax, shall be entitled to the rights and privileges, &c.*

Cl. 5. *No slave directed to be freed by any will, &c. shall be deemed free till manumitted by the executor, and the tax paid.*

No. 53. *For the more speedy recovery of small debts, not exceeding 25l. currency; and for confirming and enlarging the jurisdiction and power of the court of complaints in this island.*

By cl. 7 a party dissatisfied may appeal from the judgment of the court of Complaints, and refer the case to a jury at the court of Common Pleas, lodging the amount of the judgment with the secretary, and entering into security to proceed; and in case of the judgment being affirmed, to pay treble costs, unless the judge shall certify that there was probable cause for such appeal.

Cl. 10. At the trial of any complaint the judge may insist on *further proof, production of books, &c.;* and need not *give judgment till satisfied.*

Cl. 11. Judge may call for the aid of another judge.

No. 54. alters the punishment of burning in the hand, &c.

No. 55. Persons buying or receiving goods knowing them to be stolen, or receiving offenders knowingly, shall

DOMINICA. — LAWS.

be deemed accessaries, and on conviction *suffer death as felons!*—a harsh and inhuman law.

No. 58. For extending to this island the 43 Geo. 3., commonly called Lord Ellenborough's act.

No. 61. repeals and alters various former acts; and Cl. 13. provides a punishment for any slave charged with murder, but convicted of manslaughter, *by banishment, and working in the chain-gang, and public whipping, not exceeding thirty-nine lashes.*

No. 72. *An act to establish courts of petty sessions, at stated times, for the trial by jury of runaway slaves, in custody of the provost-marshal for crimes; for regulating their punishments, &c.*

Cl. 1. A petty sessions court shall be held *the first Wednesday in April, June, October, and December,* to consist of FIVE justices and twelve jurors.

Cl. 5. The justices of every court of King's Bench and Grand Sessions of the peace, *after the termination of business before the said last-mentioned court, are authorized to adjourn such court, and to form themselves into a court of petty sessions and gaol delivery of and for the trial, punishment, or release of all and every slave or slaves, person or persons, then confined in gaol, or in custody.*

Cl. 6. The court may *vary and mitigate punishments,* and instead of *banishment* may order *solitary confinement.*

No. 74. *An act reviving an act constituting a court-merchant.*

No. 75. *An act concerning the probates of letters of attorney in this colony.*

No. 78. *An act for regulating the proceedings and duties of coroners in calling juries in this island, and also for authorizing trials for murder, and inquests in certain special cases.*

No. 79. *An act for regulating the government and conduct of slaves, and for their more effectual protection, encouragement, and the general melioration of their condition.* This act was disallowed, and an amended bill passed June 2, 1821.

Cl. 12. *If any master, &c. manager, &c. shall mutilate or dismember any slave, or wantonly or cruelly whip, beat, bruise, cut, wound, or imprison, or keep in confinement, without sufficient support, any slave or slaves, a single justice is authorized upon complaint or* INFORMATION THEREOF, *to summon the offender to appear before him, and all witnesses, &c. and shall take down the examination* OF SUCH OFFENDER *in writing, and also the state, appearance, marks, and condition of the slave, or slaves, and all other circumstances necessary to prove the facts, and return the same to the clerk of the crown, and bind over the* SAID OFFENDER *in any sum not exceeding* 300*l.*, *with two securities, to appear at the next court; and the clerk of the crown shall send the recognizance to the attorney general, who is required to proceed against* SUCH OFFENDER *by indictment; and upon trial of such offender, his examination, if signed by him,* OR THE STATEMENT IN WRITING OF THE MAGISTRATE, *shall be primâ facie evidence of such offender having committed the offences and upon conviction, he shall be punished by fine, imprisonment, or both; and in atrocious cases the court is empowered to order the slave to be sold to another owner.*

Every principle of law and justice seems to me to be violated in this clause. To afford protection to the slave and at the same time to attain that necessary end *without the admission of slave evidence*, a circuitous course is taken,—indirect means are resorted to;—and the most perverse justice, or the most flagrant oppression, under the name of justice, is administered. The accused, invariably denominated *the offender*, is called upon to *prove* his own *innocence*, under the strongest temptation to commit perjury; or rather, it may be said, to prove his own *guilt*, for he is almost compelled to criminate himself; or proving refractory, he is sent to trial with the written representation of the committing magistrate, (perhaps his personal enemy) made *primâ facie* evidence of his guilt! It is clear that the legislature of Dominica has in this instance conceded GREATLY MORE to importunate clamour than it can be prevailed upon to yield to natural justice.

Cl. 13. But though a punishment is denounced against any free person who shall beat, wound, &c. any slave, yet, *as the testimony of such slave is inadmissible for his*

DOMINICA.

LAWS.

*conviction, by which such enactment has proved of little effect, since,* proceeds the recital, *such offence may occur when no white or free person of colour is present, if any person shall beat, wound, &c. any slave or slaves, the property of another person or persons, or deprive such slaves of their property, on complaint being made thereof* BY THE OWNERS, *or their representatives; and the slaves being produced, and the marks of the blows or wounds exhibited, such justice shall summon the accused and examine him upon oath, and on his refusal to be examined, such contumacy shall be construed an admission of the fact, and the justice shall bind him over in a recognizance to appear at the next court, when the oath of such slaves as have been baptized shall be admitted under certain restricttons, that is to say,* TWO *must clearly and consistently agree and depose to the same fact, and the slaves must be examined apart and out of the hearing of each other, and such prosecutions must be commenced within twelve months.*

*Cl.* 14. Is framed to punish third persons *taking property from slaves, or refusing or omitting to pay them for goods sold, or labour performed, or who otherwise trespass against slaves, on complaint made by the owner, without oath.*

The chief justice's observation upon these clauses is as follows: " The concession to the competency of a " slave's testimony must be deemed consonant to both " justice and humanity, and I am not aware of it's in- " troduction into any other West Indian code." The propriety of the measure as far as it goes, is unquestionable, and the merit was I believe at that time, exclusive;—but it is surely very limited, and hardly to be regarded with so much complacency. When slaves are beaten by *others than their owners,* and their *owner makes the complaint,* in such cases *only,* are slaves made competent witnesses, under certain, and those not improper, restrictions. Certainly, redress in case of injuries to slaves, committed either by subordinate agents of the owner's, or by third persons, who are strangers to him, is matter of considerable importance, and will not be undervalued by any persons duly informed upon the subject; yet the provision is surely incomplete, "to secure "the legal protection of the slave peasantry of Do- "minica."

Cl. 16., regulates *the quantum of punishment with the whip allowed on plantations, no more than* FIVE *lashes by any overseer,* TWENTY *by any manager, and* THIRTY-NINE *by an owner; it being necessary for the preservation of discipline and order, that proper punishment should be inflicted to a certain extent.*

Cl. 18, 19, 20, 21, 22., regulate the punishment of offences committed by slaves.

Cl. 34. *All free-born or manumitted persons of colour are competent witnesses, in all cases, civil and criminal.*

No. 82. *An Act for providing a Curate, to promote religious Instruction among the slaves, in the several parishes in this Island.*

No. 87. *An Act for printing and publishing the Laws of this Island.*

---

Of the Manuscript Laws, the most important are:—

19th January, 1820. *For settling the modes of putting judgments and sentences into execution awarded and pronounced by the Criminal Courts of Judicature and of Record in this Colony.*

23rd August, 1820. *For granting a salary to His Majesty's Attorney-General, in Dominica, in lieu of all fees heretofore paid out of the public Treasury.*

22nd August, 1820. *To appoint the Chief Justice to preside in the Court of King's Bench and Grand Sessions of the Peace.*

27th July, 1822. *For making conveyances and assurances of lands and tenements, &c. in this colony, by deed, effectual for the barring of entails, and passing of estates of tenants in tail.*

Such are the principal of the Laws of Dominica, which in the opinion of their editor, (the chief justice,) "will lose little in comparison with the codes of the other "British Colonial Settlements."

## COURTS.

ENUMERATION OF.

The Courts of Civil Jurisdiction, established in this island are,—The court of Chancery; the court of Common Pleas; the court of Complaints; the court of Error; the court of Admiralty; and the Court Merchant. Although Cl. 11, of No. 2. speaks of judges, or BARONS OF THE EXCHEQUER, there is no Exchequer court in Dominica. "The crown," said the chief justice, "can "sue for and recover its debts in all the regular courts "already existing."

The courts of Criminal Jurisdiction, are—The court of King's Bench and Grand Sessions of the Peace, and the court of Petty Sessions for the trial of slaves.

## COURT OF CHANCERY.

The court of Chancery, as at present constituted, was established by an act of the island, No. 14, Laws of Dominica. It is composed, as at Barbados, of the Governor, associated with the members of council; *three* of whom, together with the commander-in-chief, are necessary to form a court. They are then supposed to have the same jurisdiction as the High Court of Chancery, in England, and are governed, in their proceedings, by the practice of the English courts, and manuscript rules of their own. They have one member of council, (and therefore a judge of the court,) a receiver to an estate, nominated by the court, in the case of Warner and Coles. "I "have known a recent case," said the attorney-general, "in which a receiver was appointed by the court, who "had been rejected by the master, and was opposed by "the mortgagees."

By No. 14., no members of council shall sit in any

cause, brought into this court from the courts of King's Bench or Common Pleas, in cases where they were judges of those courts, when the cause was determined therein.

The act provides that the governor shall receive all the fees formerly paid to the chancellor, (when the governor was sole chancellor); and shall grant, sign, and seal all processes issuing out of this court. So by act No. 61, he shall and may sit, alone, as chancellor, in granting all orders or motions of course.

With respect to the jurisdiction of this court, in cases of lunacy, the chief justice said, "I never heard of any "delegation of that trust to the Chancery of Dominica. "The governor has by his commission, authority, if I "recollect right, to give orders and directions for pre-"paring grants for the custody or commitment of luna-"tics; and, therefore, being governor and chancellor, "with direct power under the royal sign manual, I ap-"prehend lunatics to come under his peculiar jurisdic-"tion, independent of the members of the Chancery "court."

The court, as in the other islands, is always open.

There is only one master in Chancery, who is likewise examiner, appointed by the governor, and paid by fees, which for the last fifty years, had not exceeded fifty pounds sterling annually. He does not give any security. The fees and perquisites being so inadequate, a professional gentleman is never induced to accept the situation. The governor has also the nomination of the serjeant-at-arms, such office being held, as we were informed, under the hand and seal at arms, of the governor. The provost-marshal is usually, if not invariably, appointed to the office; partly, I suppose, from his practised dexterity in the discharge of similar duties; but chiefly, I apprehend, from the insufficiency of the perquisites to induce another person of respectability to accept the situation. The chief justice, it will be observed, proposed to abolish the office, as altogether useless.

The court has been employed, "but scantily," with

DOMINICA.
CHANCERY.

the ordinary business of a court of Equity. By his next friend, or by information of the attorney-general, a slave may institute a suit for the recovery of his freedom. "Such," said the attorney-general, "is the acknow-"ledged opinion in this island." "There is, however," the chief justice added, "no act to warrant this juris-"diction." It is not meant, I conceive, to admit as a principle, that a slave may sue, at his own relation; as he cannot be made responsible for costs; so that this concession, apparently liberal, is really insignificant. It is sufficiently hard that a man because he is a slave, shall not be allowed to sue in his own name, or in *formâ pauperis*, but must be driven to an almost impossible remedy; *viz.* to file his bill or information by his next friend, who is able to pay the costs of the suit, and who will be deemed answerable for them.

In 1822, several slaves, attached to the Souffriere Estate, conceiving they had claims upon the proprietors of that property, for the freedom of themselves and families, moved to be brought up, by *habeas corpus*, with the cause of their detention in slavery; but on the ground, that they had only an equitable claim to freedom, and had not been deprived of their liberty against law, the court refused the rule. The slaves then filed their bill of complaint by next friend, and prayed, on an affidavit, (by the next friend,) that, as they, the complainants, were not worth 5*l.* they might be allowed to prosecute their suit, by next friend, *in formâ pauperis*. To this it was said, that "none but persons suing in their "own name, and in their own right can be admitted to "sue *in formâ pauperis*;" and again—"the affidavit must "be made by the party himself," and the prayer was denied.

The parties, next, instead of continuing their suit by next friend, and giving security for costs, (the mode pointed out by the attorney-general,) withdrew their bill, and filed an information by His Majesty's solicitor-general, *at their own relation*. The defendants demurred that the complainants and relators, being slaves, were under such a personal disability, as precluded their suing

DOMINICA.

CHANCERY.

*in manner, sort and form &c.* and the court held the demurrer good.

Where a suit is heard upon bill and answer only, and the parties reside in the island, a decree is commonly obtained within four months after the filing of the bill.

The regular sittings of the court are on the *first* and *third* Tuesday of every month, at the Court House.

Rules and Orders.

In all cases of demurrer, pleas, and final decrees, printed cases, or written paper-books must be delivered to the different members of the court, *one* week before the argument is to be heard.

Fees and costs, here as in the other colonies, are EXORBITANT, and the chief justice observed, "*positively* "*render the court almost inaccessible.*" There is no table of fees, except for the officers of the court. Bills are not delivered to the party, but to the adverse solicitor, and are rarely taxed.

Appeals lie to His Majesty in council, on the usual terms, of the appellant giving bond in 500*l.* with two sureties, conditioned to prosecute the appeal within a year and a day, which bond is lodged in Chancery. The chief justice conceived there was no restriction from appealing from *all* interlocutory orders, as well as final decrees. The court below decides on "the appealability of the matter." The effect of an appeal is, it was said, to put a complete stop to all proceedings in the colonial Chancery. The attorney-general excepted the master's office, where according to him accounts are allowed to be taken, the successful party giving security, for the expenses so occasioned, in case the decree should be reversed. But in a recent case this exception was not admitted.

On the subject of executors, (their powers and duties,) the attorney-general made the following observations: "By the 5th Geo. 2. chap. 74. lands and real es- "tates in the colonies being made assets for the satis- "faction of debts, and executors having the power "of aliening the assets for the payment of debts, it "has been generally considered in this island, that "executors are vested with the power of disposing "of real as well as personal estate for the satisfac- "tion of debts. There have been doubts, however,

DOMINICA.

CHANCERY.

"entertained on the subject; though I have never "heard of the question having been decided in any of "our courts. It is a point that it would be very desira- "able should be settled by authority of law, particu- "larly, in a country, where property is subject to such "casualties, and where real and personal estate are so "necessarily connected, as almost to prevent, without "the greatest injury, a separation of the one from the "other. I do not conceive that it is so generally under- "stood, that administrators are vested with the power; "the grant of administration under which they are au- "thorised to act, giving them administration only of the "goods and chattels, rights and credits of the intestate." I cannot conceive that executors, as such, have any power over real estate, and heard with amazement, of their being considered by lawyers, as vested with the power of disposing of lands and houses for the payment of debts. And, though slaves are considered, in almost all the islands, as chattels for the payment of debts, executors, I apprehend, have no right to take them into possession.

The chief justice considers—"the best improvement "which could be made in this court to be,—

1st. "To make the governor *sole* chancellor, and to "give him an assessor, or legal and equitable man, with "a suitable salary.

2d. "To have the fees of all concerned, reduced to "a moderate standard, to encourage suitors to seek re- "lief, and particularly the poor and oppressed legatees, "and others claiming under wills and testaments; so, "to make the master's commission on sales or final de- "crees more moderate. And lastly to abolish the ser- "jeant-at-arms, as a useless officer."

The answer of the attorney-general, to the same question of the Commissioners, is too manly, sensible, just and candid, to be either omitted or retrenched.

"The present constitution of this court (the governor "associated with the members of council) is wholly in- "adequate in my apprehension, to the due and proper "administration of the law. The governor who is "mostly of the military or naval profession, cannot be "expected to be possessed either of the habits or the "knowledge to qualify him for the office of chancellor. "And the members of council, being mostly men of ex-"tensive connexions and influence in the colony, and "not bred to the legal profession, are also, in general, "very little qualified to sit in this court, and I conceive, "it would be much more advantageous to the suitors, "and greater satisfaction would be given, if the governor "were to sit ALONE.

"There have been frequent occasions, where the mem-"bers have been summoned to form a court, who either "from sickness or other cause, have not been able to "attend, and the party, applying for the court, has, "thus, been put to a fruitless expense of from 15*l.* to "20*l.* currency. This I have known to have happened "more than twice, in succession, so that a party *having* "*a motion to make* may be put to a fruitless expense of "from 50*l.* to 60*l.* or 100*l.* before he can be heard; be-"cause the members are not able to attend; whereas the "Governor sitting alone would have the power of hold-"ing a court whenever there might be business to be "done.

"But, THE GREAT DESIDERATUM—that which would "bring gladness and joy, which alone could afford se-"curity and confidence to the colonists—would be the "appointment of a lawyer, of tried knowledge and "ability, to fill the important situation of Chancellor. "I consider this measure as likely to enhance the value "of property, at least 15 *per cent.*"

## COURT OF COMMON PLEAS.

The constitution and practice of this court resemble, but with considerable improvements, those of the Supreme Civil Court in other islands. The establishment of the court is larger, consisting of a chief justice and FOUR other judges, with the usual officers.

The court is held in Roseau, on the first Monday in March, April, May, June, and July. Each court

DOMINICA.

COMMON PLEAS.

may be continued or adjourned by the justices, or the majority of them at their discretion, but the adjournment cannot extend beyond the time appointed for the next sitting of the court.—" Except only, that at the " close of the July term, the court shall be adjourned " to some day, not less than *fifteen*, or more than *thirty* " days, after the commencement of that term."

Three judges are competent to hold a court, and the majority of those present, to adjourn it. And now by Cl. 2. of No. 44, it shall be lawful for *one* or more justices to adjourn the said court.

Slaves are deemed chattels, in this island; but are recoverable, in EJECTMENT, in this court, together with lands, " under similar title." We have seen, that in other islands, where slaves are made real property, they may be sued for and recovered by action personal.

" Estates-tail, reversions, or remainders," said the chief justice, " are docked by an acknowledgment be- " fore a judge, and dower barred by an examination " of feme coverts, also before a judge; a cheap and con- " cise way of effecting the same purposes, much supe- " rior to the expensive and tedious modes of fines and re- " coveries in England."

The dues of the crown are recoverable in this court. It is considered that the Crown may attach debts, like any other plaintiff.

No. 37. admits *all* plaintiffs to that privilege.

Rules and orders have been framed, from time to time, to guide the practice of this court, and are now, in manuscript, in the secretary's office.

The commencement of an action in this court is by summons or capias. By cl. 5. of the Court Act, it is provided that no service, by nailing up a writ of summons on the door of the court-house, shall be good and effectual against any defendant, who hath never resided, and hath no land or slaves in this island. So by cl. 7, no writ of summons, capias, &c. shall issue, at the suit of an absentee unless the same be authorised by a letter of attorney, duly executed and authenticated, and recorded, or lodged to be recorded, in the office of the register, &c., from the person, or one of the persons, at whose suit such process shall issue. Foreign powers of attorney, if authenticated, according to the forms of authentication used in such foreign country, with a translation attested and sworn to, and recorded, or lodged to be recorded, are sufficient. In cases where a plaintiff proceeds by capias, an affidavit to hold to bail must be made before a judge, stating the amount of the debt and cause of action. The act does not authorize an arrest for a less sum than 15*l.* currency; unless it be a part of the affidavit that the defendant is about to leave the island, and hath no property therein, and then the secretary shall endorse on such writ, "Take bail for the "sum of ——*l.* current money, being double the sum "sworn to."

For the benefit of persons arrested and confined in gaol, for want of security, it is provided, that in default of the plaintiff's proceeding in *nine* days, after arrest of a debtor, by filing his action (declaration), the debtor shall be discharged, and the plaintiff pay the costs. So under the Petty Debt Act, persons confined sixty days for 50*l.* costs inclusive, except crown and colonial debts, are to receive from the creditor 1*s.* 6*d.* currency daily, as maintenance.

The pleadings and practice obtaining in this island appear, from the answers we received, to follow with tolerable exactness those of the courts of England.

The proceedings on attachments entirely resemble those in the other islands, except that *eighty* days are given for the payment of the sum awarded to the plaintiff; or if the debt arise on a contract in writing, and the day of payment is beyond the eighty days, the debt shall be ordered to be paid *in eighty days after the same shall become due*, and not sooner.

All causes are numbered, and directed by the court act to be heard as they stand, being ripe for trial. "Actions," we were told by the attorney-general, "are "often brought merely to get priority in the list." This law of priority is in force in all the islands, with the exception of Antigua, and is thought by the chief justice to

DOMINICA.

COMMON PLEAS.

be mischievous; being, he observes, the "reverse of the "bankrupt law in England, which pays, *pari passu*, all "the creditors of the unfortunate trader. It might per- "haps also," he proceeds, "be desirable in these islands "to have a fair division of an insolvent's estate. At pre- "sent, the first judgment and execution creditor seizes "all the real and personal estate of the debtor, by "means of the marshal or sheriff, and nothing is left for "other claimants." But the subject matter of the bank- rupt laws is the peculiar case of *traders*. In other cases, would not the effect of such alteration of the law, as the chief justice recommends, be to make mortgages of lands, (and perhaps of goods) exacted in every instance, as the only available securities? With respect to the bankrupt laws the chief justice admitted "it would be nearly im- "possible to apply the actual bankrupt laws of England, "or indeed any modification of them, without first re- "pealing all the colonial acts which grant priorities to "the first creditors on the record. No man but one "constantly in these islands, can conceive the looseness "with which mercantile business is done in this part of "the world. A bill or note is seldom thought of after "signature; the holder may apply twenty times before "he is paid; simple contract debts or specialty the same. "If acts of bankruptcy followed such negligence or de- "lays as in England upon failure of payments, there is "scarcely a day in which there would not be a call for a "commission; and oh! what confusion, litigation, and "expense! However, it is considerate to think of bank- "rupt laws for us, who are broken in fortune."

"The court," we were told, "discountenances all arti- "fices to procure delay. The plaintiff, when his action "is ready for trial on the court list, is generally called "upon to give reasons for postponement: and defend- "ants, if harassed by the action remaining on the roll, "may move for striking it off." An absent defendant, suffering judgment by default, may have redress under cl. 39. of the court act, by which the court is empowered to stay proceedings, by order, till the claim is adjusted; or, if that cannot be effected, to direct the question to be

DOMINICA.

COMMON PLEAS.

tried by feigned issue. When a defendant makes default at the trial, "*he is called out three times;*" judgment is then entered against him; and the jury who would have tried the action, assess the damages *instanter*. No notice of writ of enquiry is served, or issues; but the jury who are in the box decide upon the *quantum* of damages. Depositions of witnesses about to depart the island, or sick, or incapable of attending the trial, and taken in the manner prescribed by the act, are admitted, as in the other islands; but by cl. 28. if such witness shall recover, return, or be in the island ten days before trial, the adverse party giving eight days' notice thereof, the deposition shall not be used, unless the witness, having been subpœnaed, shall not attend. The chief justice said, that he *had* required in some cases, an affidavit, when a deposition was tendered at the trial, of the party being still sick, absent from the island, or unable to attend.

In debts of large amount, and when the claims have arisen upon complicated accounts, the attorney-general had known evils result from the mode of proof directed by the act of the 5 G. 2. c. 7. The chief justice, whose experience in the administration of justice in different islands had been remarkably extensive, was induced at my particular request, to give an explicit answer upon this subject. "If "only evidence of deeds or other papers were legalized, "it would be well; for that is only the proof of a name "to solemn instruments of writing, wherein both parties "speak. But to prove simple contract debts, as it is "daily allowed to do, is what I cannot approve. It is "difficult to conceive to what expenses it has driven the "debtors who fly into Chancery for injunction, disclo-"sure, discovery, and relief. The city seal may, and "often has, sanctioned gross perjury, or confirmed abo-"minable errors. I have seen demands of 15,000*l.* and "20,000*l.* sterling, cut down to 5000*l.* and 10,000*l.* before "a Master in Chancery, and his report confirmed and "decreed. If they had remained at common law the "defendant was cheated and irreparably ruined. The "great security of the British litigant is the power of "seeing, hearing, and above all, cross-examining the "witness (mercantile or other) against him: all this is "lost, and you get more what the artful attorney may "compose, than what the witness really knows. Never, "too, did act perplex attorneys as this does! Not one "city-seal proceeding in four is agreeable to the statute. "They make *parties* swear, instead of clerks or disin-"terested witnesses: no bills of parcels or elucidating "documents are sent out, but often a mere copy from "the plaintiff's ledger.

"We have been obliged to alter and amend the act by "our practice. The act says, the action shall be first "brought for the debt or claim, and then you are to get "your proofs. Now, did that prevail, every English "creditor who thus attacked an involved debtor, would "lose his debt, (the defendant being insolvent,) because "the bringing one action is the tocsin for another; and "while the English plaintiff is rummaging for city-seal "proofs in London, verdicts, judgments, and executions "would give the colonial creditors their full advantage "of priority of payment. To avoid this, no lawyer now "brings the suit until his proofs are here in his office."

As a record of the proceedings, the secretary transcribes them briefly into a large book kept in his office.

Free persons of colour are always admitted in evidence, but a slave is incompetent, and is never produced in the court as a witness. The chief justice, however, declares, "I never yet knew a slave tried for perjury, in giving "evidence against a slave, which our law admits:" and he thus accounts for it;—"Much allowance is properly "made by our practice for their habitudes, and want of "knowledge of the nature and obligation of an oath."

A witness, requiring in open court payment of his travelling charges and expenses, the amount thereof shall be adjusted and settled by the judges, and paid *before* he shall be required to give his testimony. Members of the House of Assembly are exempted from serving on common juries; but they, except the Speaker, may be summoned, and shall be liable to serve on grand and special juries.

No execution shall issue upon any judgment which

has or shall have lain dormant for the space of a year and a day unless a *scire facias* shall issue thereupon, except where the plaintiff has been staid by injunction or writ of error.

Cl. 48. gives the form of the writ of execution; and several succeeding clauses, down to cl. 81., regulate the proceedings under it. The effect is, that all rights and titles of defendants to lands, tenements, or slaves are saleable by the provost-marshal.

There is no person expressly appointed for the taxation of costs in this court. Costs are said by the chief justice, to be in the discretion of the court.

The judges, secretary, and marshal are required by the court act to have dockets of their fees fixed up in the secretary's office, and the taking more or other than the docket fees is made punishable by indictment, as extortion. "*And the chief justice and all other justices of the "said court, and the secretary for the time being, are "hereby respectively directed not to tax or allow any other "or greater fees than the docket fees.*" I am gratified to perceive by the last answer of the chief justice, that the task of improving the administration of justice in this court has been undertaken by a professional gentleman of so great talent and promise as Mr. Henry Glanville.

## COMPLAINT COURT.

A court of Complaints, similarly constituted to those in the other islands, is established in Dominica, for the recovery of debts to the amount of 25*l.* which the chief justice considers "quite high enough." Some difference of opinion prevailed, as to debts, not exceeding 6*l.* 12*s.* 8*d.*, which are recoverable under the Petty Debt Act, and the attorney-general conceived in no other way: the chief justice considered *this* court as possessing a concurrent jurisdiction.

DOMINICA.

ORDINARY.

## COURT OF ORDINARY.

In the court of Ordinary the governor sits alone and unassisted, in all cases.

There is not any taxing officer in this court.

All original wills and testaments, after probate, are lodged in the secretary's office, and are never suffered to be taken away; copies, duly authenticated, being always delivered.

" Reform it altogether," recommended the attorney-general.

## COURT OF VICE-ADMIRALTY.

The court of Admiralty has all the jurisdiction of the Instance Court in England: it is besides authorised, by acts of Parliament, to try seizures, or penalties, incurred by breach of the laws of trade, navigation, and revenue.

The chief justice is sole judge. His authority is from the governor, under his seal at arms to be "*his* deputy " and surrogate in the court of Vice-Admiralty in this " island."

There is no standing commission for holding Admiralty Sessions, and offenders are sent to Barbados or Antigua for trial. As " pirates are roaming about the " seas," the chief justice recommends, that " the usual " royal commission for holding Admiralty Sessions may " be lodged in this island."

## COURT MERCHANT.

This court is revived and regulated by No. 74, Laws of Dominica, passed in 1817. By cl. 13. of the expired act for constituting a court merchant, it is made a court of record; by cl. 14. the process and proceedings are to be comformable to the practice and proceedings of the court of Common Pleas.

## COURT OF APPEAL AND ERROR.

The governor and *five* of the council form this court, which receives appeals from the Common Pleas, as does the Common Pleas, from the Complaint Court. The justices of the Common Pleas are expressly prohibited from sitting in this court. There is no limitation of time for bringing appeals from the common-law court to the court of Error. The chief justice considers the regulated *amount* for which "appeals may be brought, both "from the Common Pleas to the court of Error and "from thence to the King in Council, as much too "high!" that "the privilege of appealing to the highest authority, in cases, which, though trifling in value, "may involve very important rights, should not be too "strictly limited." Some other very just remarks and sprightly illustrations occur, in the course of the answer: "There, the rays of the sun are not so powerful, or the Cayenne pepper so strong, &c." The attorney-general said, "it would be still more important to "have professional men to sit as judges, in *this* court. "In *all* I think it very desirable."

DOMINICA.

# CRIMINAL COURTS.

## COURT OF GRAND SESSIONS.

The judges of this court are the lieutenant-governor, (not being commander-in-chief,) the members of council, the speaker, and all the justices of peace, who are members of the House of Assembly! The chief justice, however, presides in this court, and the other judges very seldom interfere.

The court assembles twice annually.

Any three justices of the court (being members of council), may, at any time take bail, as it is done by the court of King's Bench, in England, in term time, or by the justices thereof, in vacation.

During the absence, at any time, of the chief justice, the bench frequently refers any legal point, either arising or brought before them, to the attorney-general.

No record is made up as in England, but the proceedings are entered in a book; not including however the pleadings.

Prosecutor's expenses are not paid, "nor defend-"ant's that I have ever known," said the attorney-general.

The evidence of slaves is not admitted on the trial of free persons, except in the cases pointed out by the Colonial Act. "They can give evidence against ma-"nagers and overseers," said the attorney-general, "not "against owners. In 1818 or 1819, I indicted a ma-"nager for ill-treatment of a slave, by putting mixed "dirt and ordure in his mouth, and examined half a "dozen witnesses at least, who were slaves. It was a

DOMINICA.

GRAND SESSIONS.

" remedy against *mal d'estomac*, and on that account " defendant was acquitted; I thought improperly."

The chief justice considers the sentence of this court as final; — has never known a writ of error applied for;—and is not " aware to what tribunal it could be " referred."

The same gentleman gives it as his opinion, that " justice is fairly administered, as the court is consti- " tuted."

## SLAVE CASES IN GRAND AND PETTY SESSIONS.

The court of Grand Session sits as a Slave Court *twice* a-year. And there is also a court of Petty Sessions, composed of *five* justice of the peace, which court sits *four* times a-year, and takes cognizance before a jury (of *six*) of all crimes or offences, either *by* or *to* slaves. With respect to jurisdiction in such matters, the acts of the island, the attorney-general believed, fully provide for every possible case; " but where acts " of the island are silent, yet if any ill-treatment of slaves " or offences, either by or to slaves, were to occur, I " should think," said that gentleman, " I could proceed " at the common law." In confirmation of this opinion, the crown officer observed, that cl. 12. and 19, of No. 79, making the murder of a slave by a white man or of a white by a slave, punishable with death, " *or* " *such other punishment as the court may adjudge*," he should, in both instances, indict in one court at least, on the common law. So the provost-marshal said: " Cer- " tainly slaves, who are ill used, can complain to a ma- " gistrate, and it is the duty of the magistrate to take " cognizance of their complaints, generally."

The proceedings in these cases are said to be the same as in prosecutions against white offenders, except that slave evidence is admitted. Slaves are never bailed in

DOMINICA.

SLAVE CASES.

capital cases; "no person, if they were admitted to "bail, would, in a wild and mountainous country, like "this, in a serious case, answer for their appearance."

The marshal returns to the attorney-general a few days before the holding of the court of sessions, a list of all slaves confined for trial, with the warrant of commitment.

The attorney-general upon this prepares a charge, "*in the nature of an information.*"

There is no grand jury.

Slaves take the usual oath, the same that is administered to white persons. They are generally asked, whether they have been baptized; if not, the magistrate cautions them, and explains the nature of an oath; and the attorney-general does the same, addressing them in the negro dialect. The same gentleman was sorry to say he had not found slave evidence in general correct. This he attributed wholly to the want of moral and religious instruction; not, by any means, to the want of capacity.

The chief justice had found some slaves correct, and to be depended upon; but the number of slaves deviating from truth in giving testimony, far exceeded the former class. There have been no convictions for perjury in these cases; but the chief justice has heard of a slave "being whipped, by the court's order, for perjury." The attorney-general said, that, "where they "had been detected in the grossest perjury, he had "known them quietly suffered to depart. In one case "he, (the attorney-general,) sent up a bill against a free-"woman of colour, in a very bad instance; but the "grand jury threw it out."

This the chief justice ascribes to the degree of indulgence and considerate allowance made for their want of cultivation and unfortunate situation in society.

The attorney-general thinks the admissibility of slave testimony might be extended. The chief justice thought the legislature of Dominica had gone as far as they ought to do in policy, at present, "until there is an evident "change in the morals and religious feelings of that class "of the population."

Both the gentlemen had known counsel employed for slaves by their owners; but counsel do not in general attend these courts.

All the proceedings in these courts are filed of record in the secretary's office.

There is no appeal; but the governor is by law apprized, within twenty-four hours, of the proceedings, and acts as he thinks fit, (subject of course to his instructions); sentence of death, in the absence of such notification, is without effect. The execution of a slave takes place with the same solemnities, as in the case of a white person.

The presumption of law, in opposition to the former practice, is said to be, now *in favorem libertatis.* The party objecting to the competency of a witness, that he is a slave, is called upon to give evidence, to make out a *primâ facie* case of his slavery. This is to be rebutted, by proving his recorded deed of manumission, or calling two witnesses who will speak to his having been born free, or passed as a free person for *five* years. "A re- "putation of freedom or constructive emancipation, our "courts are in the habit," said the chief justice, "of re- "ceiving and allowing liberally." To the question "Whether the power of the master over the slave was "considered absolute in this island?" the chief justice exclaimed, "This query nearly astonishes me; but I "thank my God I can easily answer it. A slave is as "much within the King's peace as any other subject, "&c. &c." The attorney-general said, "No; he has "no such power. He has only the power of inflicting "such punishment as the law allows. And I am happy "to say that a law for the improvement of the condition "of the slaves is under consideration." The chief justice said, "there must be a necessary subordination and "obedience from slave to master. It is incident to his "unfortunate political situation in West Indian society; "but abuse of this authority will subject the master to a "prosecution."

DOMINICA.

SLAVE CASES.

The master may delegate his authority to his attorney, who will then have the same powers. "But the power "of the manager and overseer," proceeded the attorney-general, "is restrained by the laws of the island. By "general opinion, custom, and practice universally, if "not by law,—slaves may and can and do, acquire pro-"perty, and deal with it and dispose of it as their own. "There is an act" continued the attorney-general "now "before the legislature, (and it will probably pass,) esta-"blishing such a right in slaves." The chief justice said "he had known many slaves purchase their own freedom "with their acquisitions," and mentioned a particular instance then occurring. "Industry and prudence have "afforded many the means of being enfranchised, and "they have been so; but it is not yet legally obligatory "upon the masters to acquiesce in it. I hope to see the "day arrive." "It is intended to be done shortly," said the attorney-general. There are instances in this island, of slaves purchasing slaves.

Inquests are always held, when death by violence or accident "is notified." They are "held generally," said the attorney-general. But the Crown officer "remembered "one instance in which it was omitted, and on that com-"ing to his knowledge he indicted the mistress. It was "done from ignorance: but he wished to put all the "planters, especially the French, upon their guard."

There was a school for all colours just established, and which had met with every encouragement.

"I have nothing further," observed the chief justice, "to say as to the trial of slaves for capital offences. I "think it fair, and the few executions on record speak "volumes. There are improvements certainly, to be "made in the slave laws, and I trust they will meet with "early attention."

COMPLAINTS—NONE.

No complaints of any kind, were preferred before the Commissioners in this island.

JUDGES.

The chief justice is appointed from England. He receives (besides an allowance from home) a colonial salary of 1,500*l.* currency per annum, and certain fees, re-

DOMINICA.

PARTICULAR OFFICERS.

gulated by docket, amounting to about 300*l.* or 400*l.* currency per annum. All the judges hold their office during pleasure.

ATTORNEY-GENERAL.

The attorney-general is appointed from home, but has a salary of 300*l.* currency per annum provided by the colony. "The bill that gives a salary of 300*l.* per "annum was passed for three years, as an experiment." Before that act the attorney-general's *bill* was submitted to the committee of public accounts annually, and subjected to deduction at their discretion. and was sometimes not passed for two or three years. The salary of 300*l.* currency is stated by the attorney-general to be in lieu of all fees, for conducting prosecutions in the several courts of criminal justice. "But since I have had the honour "of holding the appointment," said that officer, "I have "been repeatedly applied to by the governor for opi-"nions and advice, and to draw proclamations and a "variety of other business, which necessarily interferes "with my private engagements, and for which no fees "are allowed.'

COUNSEL and ATTORNEYS.

Counsel and solicitors are "consolidated," and the qualifications required, are having been admitted to the bar in England or Ireland, or served the necessary number of terms to entitle the candidate to be so admitted; or having been sworn an attorney in England; or having practised *five* years in the colonies, or served a counsel and attorney, for five years.

On admittance in the court of Common Pleas, any gentleman is entitled to practise any branch of the profession in all the courts of law, and as proctor in the court of Admiralty:—to practise as solicitor in Chancery, he must be admitted in that court. In equity, twenty johs are allowed, in taxation of costs, for a retaining fee. But, with a person capable of paying, *fifty* and in important cases a *hundred pounds sterling* is usually charged: but this is understood to cover what is not got in taxed costs.

From five to ten johs are received as a retaining fee in the courts of law.

The return of the provost-marshal in this island does

DOMINICA.

PARTICULAR OFFICERS.

PROVOST MARSHAL.

not go further back than April 1816, the period at which the examinant took the office. "No gaol-book," he observed, "being left in the office by my predecessor, it "is impossible for me to give any return, prior to that "period."

From the year 1816, only one person has been executed,—a white soldier of the ninth regiment, for the murder of a slave named Casimir, belonging to Joseph Court, Esq.

There is only one gaol, and no house of correction in this island. In the gaol, debtors and all persons charged with offences are confined.

The gaol is sufficiently large, regarding the average number of slaves at present confined there; but it is admitted by the provost-marshal to be incommodious; "sufficiently airy in the upper rooms, but by no means "so, in the lower rooms;" "insecure" and such as to make it "impossible for the marshal to ensure, not only "the security," but the "safety of the prisoners con-"fined therein." The whole building was in a very "dilapidated state, and the gaoler's apartments so far "situate from the gaol itself, that it was impossible for "him to hear any noise in the gaol during the night."

The condition of the gaol, will best be collected from the following relation of what occurred to myself, on my visiting it, for the purpose of a personal inspection of the degree of accommodation it afforded. I found the outer door open, and an inner door off its hinges, and broken; and entered without any obstruction into the yard, when I ascended a crazy staircase, and found myself in the debtors' apartment, the roof of which was greatly decayed, and in several places admitted the rain. A debtor whom I saw there, a gentleman, and a major in the army, informed me that the reason he did not walk *out*, precisely in the same manner that I had entered was, because he had given his *parole* that he would not. He however, forcibly represented his serious, and I thought well-founded, apprehension that, in the probable event of a hurricane happening in a few weeks, (it being the commencement of the hurricane season,) the building and its

DOMINICA.

PARTICULAR OFFICERS.

tenants would be all swept away together. I had, afterwards an interview with the governor upon the subject, and Lord Huntingdon promised to do every thing in his power to effect the removal of the debtor to a more secure place.

The gaoler "has particular orders to apprize a medical man of the illness of any slaves, immediately it "occurs, and to provide any comforts they require: the "expenses are defrayed by the owner of the slave or by "the colony." "Debtors, if ill, procure their own medical attendants." As the best preservative of health, on the humane suggestion of the Earl of Huntingdon, the gaoler usually employs prisoners in the garden, for an hour or two, in the cool of the morning and evening.

To debtors in prison no allowance is made.

Free persons committed for crimes or offences receive *3s.* currency per day; slaves, *2s.* 1½*d.*:—the former in money, the latter in provisions.

Prisoners acquitted are set at large immediately, without the payment of any fees. Slaves are only flogged by the public officer in cases where that punishment makes part of their sentence, pronounced by magistrates or courts of justice.

CAGE-KEEPER.

The cage is the place of confinement for slaves, who are sent there by order of the magistrates or town wardens;—"that is," says the cage-keeper, "disorderly persons; slaves saucy to their masters, &c."—"runaways, "or thieves, are sent to the gaol."

It is large enough for three men and three women; and the present cage-keeper, though he had been in office nearly three years, had never had charge of above half that number.

It is the duty of the cage-keeper to whip slaves, or see them whipped, though slaves are not punished in the cage; but, when sentenced to be flogged, are sent to the gaol. He flogs them with a cat, upon the shoulders. Women are flogged as well as men, to the extent of thirty-nine lashes, and upon the shoulders. The cage-keeper receives a dollar for each slave flogged. The cow-skin and cart-whip, as instruments of punishment,

DOMINICA.

WRONGS WITHOUT REDRESS.

are done away with. It is in the character of clerk of the market, not as cage-keeper, that this officer acted in inflicting these punishments, and he had flogged about *fifteen* slaves in nearly *three* years. "The flogging some-" times draws blood. Punishments are fewer than they " used to be. Slaves do not mind a private whipping, " but they feel a disgrace from a public punishment in " the market. The clerk of the market don't," he insisted, " favour any; he is on oath to flog all alike; he " hits the women just as hard as the men."

Slaves are never committed to the cage in this island for a longer time than twenty-four hours.

N. B. *The commissioners required the cat to be produced: it was a military cat-o'-nine-tails.*

JUSTICE OF THE PEACE.

" Slaves," said the magistrate we interrogated, " are " examined before justices, and either committed to take " their trial at the petty sessions, or if it is provided to " that effect by statutes, disposed of by the justice himself, " and the whipping the magistrate orders, is inflicted in " the market square.

" A day or two ago," said the magistrate, " a slave " preferred a complaint to me against a free man, who " owed him for three days' work. I issued a warrant " upon this complaint against the employer, for the mo" ney as due and owing to the slave's master. If it were " a charge for taking any thing from the slave's own hut " or garden, I should do the same. I should consider " it as his master's property, left by custom always with " him."

A committee of the legislature (the magistrate believed the committee of public works) is appointed, *inter alia*, to visit and inspect the gaol; but this instruction is not duly attended to by them; and the task is not performed by the magistrates, because it is made the duty of the committee.

The tax of 16*l.* 10*s.* is all that is now payable on manumission in this island.

There is no law giving a preference to debts incurred for plantation supplies; and the attorney-general says great inconvenience is felt from the want of it.

DOMINICA.

WRONGS WITHOUT REDRESS.

I before stated (p. 245.) my strong repugnance to the law (Cl. 12. No. 79.) empowering magistrates to compel persons against whom offences were surmised, to purge themselves on oath, or be sent to trial with the justice's report made *primâ facie* evidence of their guilt. My opinion upon this subject may be influenced by the circumstance of my having been able to trace, at least the origin, —perhaps the result,—of certain capital prosecutions in these islands to the basest motives of personal hostility,—revenge, fear, and hatred. But I am bound to state, when speaking in due course, of the *administration* of this law, that the evils most frequently experienced are of a totally different description. The persons usually appointed to act as magistrates are not either indifferent or independent men. A slave, placed under the superintendance of an attorney who has large concerns and extensive influence, should he conceive himself aggrieved, will complain with slender hope of redress to "the nearest magistrate," when that magistrate is the manager and immediate servant of the accused. Can the magistrate be expected, as required by the act, to "SUMMON" his employer; and, if it become necessary, in obedience to the law, "*to commit him to the common gaol of the island?*"—it is idle to expect it. The wrongs of the slave are, therefore, of necessity, imperfectly redressed.

With this observation I very respectfully conclude my present Report, the result of the joint enquiries of Mr. Maddock and myself into the administration of justice in the Islands of St. Vincent and Dominica.

(Signed) FORTUNATUS DWARRIS, (L. S.)

The Right Honourable
The Earl Bathurst, &c. &c. &c.

Dated *March* 6, 1826.

# THIRD REPORT,

*&c. &c. &c.*

ADDRESSED TO

THE RIGHT HONOURABLE EARL BATHURST,

&c. &c. &c.

MY LORD,

BEFORE I proceed to examine the laws, judicature, and practice of the islands of Antigua, Montserrat, Nevis, St. Christopher, and the Virgin Islands, (the latter, as administered at their capital, Tortola,) which will form the subject of this, my third, and concluding Report, I shall request your Lordship's permission to supply, very briefly, some deficiencies in my former Report upon the island of Dominica. In reporting upon that island, I omitted to mention, that his Majesty's Commissioners were personally present, during the sitting of the court of Common Pleas, at the trial of several jury actions, as, also, on one day devoted to hearing motions; and that the proceedings were conducted with great regularity and propriety. In one case, a coloured man obtained a verdict against a white, where there was conflicting testimony; but the evidence very strongly preponderated upon the side for which the verdict was found, and the judge summed up in favour of the successful party.

Preliminary Remarks.

Minutes, July 7, 8, & 9, 1823.

Before we left the island, a deputation from the coloured inhabitants of Dominica waited upon the Com-

July 11, 1823

ANTIGUA.

LAWS.

missioners, with a memorial, stating their grievances, and reciting the disabilities under which they continue to labour.

In consequence of one of the questions of the Commissioners referring to the establishment of schools, or other institutions for the religious instruction of slaves, we were referred, for information on that subject, to the

July 23, 1823. Wesleyan minister, Mr. Catts. That gentleman gave a very favourable account of this island, (Dominica,) and represented the "prospect through all the remaining "islands, as bright and cheering to a degree never before "witnessed in this part of the world. From all the "planters, except those of the Roman Catholic per- "suasion, the ministers of religion were now meeting "the greatest encouragement and support, and the negro "character was rapidly undergoing a most salutary "change. The French slaves however were in a most "debased state, ignorant, and brutal; those belonging "to English masters were a little more cultivated; all "were baptized; a few married; many were taught, "and much was hoped from the new school just esta- "blished, where children of all kinds and colours at- "tended. The slaves were yet far from being in a state "fit for freedom, and such a measure would be injurious "to them; but they were in a course of mental and "moral improvement, and with a few exceptions, as will "always be the case, there was a kindly feeling towards "them, on the part of their owners."

No complaints, as has been stated, were preferred before the Commissioners, in the island of Dominica. A case, however, I find was mentioned to Mr. Maddock out of the office, in which a point arose, as to the jurisdiction of the Complaint Court to decide controversies, where the sum in dispute does not exceed 6*l.* 12*s.*; debts to that amount being recoverable by an Act of the island, in a summary way, before a justice of the peace. The Commissioners, it will be seen, framed a question, so as to bring the subject under consideration.

## ANTIGUA.

His Majesty's Commissioners landed at St. John's, the capital of Antigua, on the 24th day of July, 1823. The complaints preferred, during their stay of nearly three months in this island, were very numerous, and indicated, in at least one of the parties into which the island was unfortunately divided, a very strong dissatisfaction with the existing institutions, and judicial habits of the country. In addition to the prejudices with which they had generally to contend, there were some peculiar and local circumstances which rendered the uncompromising discharge of their duty at this period, most painful and difficult to the Commissioners; such were—the violent personal animosities prevailing at the bar and invading even the bench; the jealousies of the contending parties; the secret hostility to the commission, (which was supposed not to have extended to Antigua;) the influence of some, and the fears of others. Proceeding however, steadily, in the performance of the duties with which they were charged, his Majesty's Commissioners entered upon the perusal of the laws of the island and inquired into the constitution and practice of the courts; affording meanwhile to all classes of persons the same facilities of making representations, in any case connected with the administration of justice.

There is a complete edition of the laws of this island, up to the 13th of June, 1817, in three volumes, quarto.

VOLUME THE FIRST, to page 46, contains what are termed the LAWS OF THE LEEWARD ISLANDS; after these, follow the LAWS OF ANTIGUA.

The most remarkable of the former, are,—

No. 28. This Act establishes the general councils, and general assemblies, formerly held for the Leeward Islands; securing, at the same time to the particular islands, their peculiar laws and local jurisdictions. It is provided, that *five representatives shall be elected from each island,*

T 2

ANTIGUA. — LAWS.

*to make general laws. The absence of the representatives of any one island, is not to exempt, or excuse, such island from obedience to the general acts, provided a majority of the whole number was present at the passing of such law.*

No. 31. *For preventing tedious and chargeable law suits,&c.* The preamble recites, *that through the partiality of some, and ignorance of others, contradictory judgments have been often given, in cases founded on the same rules and principles of law and reason, for the redressing of which mischiefs it is enacted and declared, "that the common law of England, as far as it stands unaltered by "any written law of the island, confirmed by yonr Majesty, or some of your royal predecessors in council, or "by some Act or Acts of Parliament of the kingdom of "England, extending to these islands, is in force in each of "these your Majesty's Leeward Charibbee Islands, and "is the certain rule whereby the rights and properties of "your Majesty's good subjects, inhabiting hese islands, "are, and ought to be, determined; and that all customs or "pretended customs, or usages, contradictory thereunto, "are illegal, null and void."*

*No. 36. An Act more effectually to provide for the support, and to extend certain regulations for the protection of slaves; to promote and encourage their increase, and generally to meliorate their condition,* (1798.)

This is the Act so often alluded to as THE GENERAL AMELIORATION ACT OF THE LEEWARD ISLANDS; a law too familiar to render it necessary to swell this Report with any abstract or analysis, of its provisions.

## LAWS OF ANTIGUA.

No. 5. *An Act for establishing a Register's office, and the fees.* No time is limited in this Act for recording deeds; a singular omission! but it contains a curious enactment, (since repealed,) that *no deed, made by any other person than the Register himself, or his clerk, should be any ways binding.*

ANTIGUA. LAWS.

No. 39. *For the establishing and confirming of the inhabitants of this island in their title to their lands.*

Proprietors and possessors of lands, *enjoying them five years quietly, shall be deemed to have a good title.* The Act contains the usual exceptions in the cases of persons under disabilities, as married women, infants, &c.

Cl. 5 and 6, recite and amend the Registry Act, (No. 5,) by limiting a time, (twenty days;) after which, deeds not recorded shall be void.

No. 83. cl. 9 and 10, provide that, *an executor or administrator may inventory negroes, but not take them into his custody; to the intent that if there shall not be sufficient goods, &c. to pay the debts of the deceased, the said negroes shall be considered assets for that purpose.*

No. 97. An Act for regulating trespasses, contains, *inter alia*, this humane and excellent provision: "*All* "*pound-keepers shall feed and water every beast im-* "*pounded for forty-eight hours, under a penalty of dou-* "*ble the value of each beast, dying for want.*"

No. 129. This Act has an amusing preamble, conceived however, in a laudably devout and grateful spirit: *Whereas Providence has blessed us, in all parts of this island, with ground very proper for ponds, &c. the Act provides for* "*making, cleaning, and repairing such* "*ponds;*" appoints commissioners, &c.

No. 137. Under this Act, disputes respecting seamen's wages, where the amount does not exceed 10*l.* shall be determined by *one* justice; where the sum in dispute exceeds 10*l.* by *three* justices, &c. It is also provided by this Act, that *warrants issued against persons on board ship are to be directed to the marshal or constable, who are empowered to execute the same, any law or usage to the contrary notwithstanding.*

No. 150. An Act for constituting a court of Chancery, recites great corruption and delays, and other inconveniences, resulting from the court being held by one person, and appoints the court to consist of the commander-in-chief and five counsellors, and proceeds with the

ANTIGUA.

LAWS.

following extraordinary provision: "*And all proceedings, which shall hereafter be had, before any person or persons whatsoever, as chancellor or chancellors of this island, contrary to this Act, shall be null and void;*" but by No. 188. *post.* so much of this Act as presumed or affected to restrain the King from appointing a person to preside in the court of Chancery in this island, is repealed.

No. 158. An Act for constituting a court merchant.

No. 176. A barbarous old slave law; partly, it is to be feared, still in force.

No. 212, is an Act of which the provisions are rather miscellaneous, and must have been originally framed, without due regard to that article of the instructions, which directs, that no two different matters should be comprised in the same bill.

No. 270. *An Act to supply the several defects in the laws of this island, concerning conveyances, &c.*

Deeds containing words which pass the fee-simple, provided they are recorded, as the laws of Antigua require, shall bar interests as effectually as fine and recovery; if the party transmitting the right be of full age. In Scotland the acknowledgment shall be before a lord of session, or sheriff; in any other place belonging to Great Britain, before a judge of the court of Common Pleas. Such deeds shall not be evidence, till registered at Antigua.

No. 438. *For the prevention of fraud and perjury.* This Act adopts the provisions of the statute of frauds; but by

Cl. 3, *Devises of lands, slaves, &c. shall be in writing, and signed, in the presence of* ONE *white witness, by the devisor, or by a third person under the devisor's express direction, or be wholly written by the devisor.*

Cl. 4, provided that *the wills of persons of colour may be attested by persons of colour, &c. &c.*

No. 472. *An Act for the more equal distribution of estates, sold by virtue of executions.*

Moneys raised by the marshal, under writs of execution, shall be applied towards satisfying, in equal shares with the first, all writs of execution, lodged in thirty-nine days after the first; surplus moneys remaining with, or coming to the marshal, after satisfaction of the first class of executions, shall be applied towards discharging equally the first writ, not lodged in time for the first class, and all writs lodged in thirty-eight days after the first of the second class, &c. &c.

No. 475. An Act for establishing courts of Common Pleas, Error, King's Bench, and Grand Sessions, and for the better regulating and settling due methods for the administration of justice.

This Act has been framed with unusual care, and contains some excellent provisions.

Cl. 1 and 2. The first court to be held in April.

Cl. 3, regulates the *service of process, &c.* Nail service is recognized, and without the qualification found in the Dominica Act; but the Attorney-general remarks upon this subject;—"Nailing up the writ, at one of the gates "of the Court-house, is a sufficient service under the "Court Act; but it has been ruled in the courts at home, "and is the understanding of the bar here, that judg-"ments founded upon such a service, would not be valid, "against a person who had never been in the island."

Cl. 18. No person is to be exempt or privileged from arrest, unless he has a freehold of *ten acres of land, in actual possession,* &c. When any one of several defendants is not a freeholder, all must give special bail.

Cl. 21 and 22. The provisions, with regard to bail, are very good; as, that costs shall be allowed only on one action on the bail bond, &c.

Cl. 24. By this clause a plaintiff is to declare against a defendant in custody, not in *nine* days, as is appointed by the Dominica Court Act, but in *six* days, or the defendant will be discharged. But the plaintiff is not required to proceed against those defendants who are in custody, if there be others who are not; while at Dominica a plaintiff, in such case, declares against those in prison *de bene esse.*

Cl. 26. gives a power of attaching debts due to the defendant; a useful power, found also in the Dominica Court Act, cl. 80.

Cl. 31. This clause requires *four days notice of all motions to be made to the court, unless it shall appear to the court that such notice could not conveniently be given within the time aforesaid.*

It is the constant policy, (perhaps it may be found the governing principle,) of the laws of England, founded in reason and constitutional jealousy, to leave as little as possible to the discretion of the judges. On such ground this clause may appear objectionable.

Cl. 33. On a judgment obtained on a breach of covenant, the judgment will stand as a security against future breaches.

Cl. 149. By this clause, produce of the island is made a legal tender in payment of debts, except where the contract provides specifically for payment in gold or silver money. The tender is to be made at the towns enumerated in the Act; the notice, appraisement, power in a magistrate to name an umpire, and all the proceedings necessary to be had, are stated in the following clause.

No. 522. This Act repeals clauses 40 and 41, of No. 176; and enacts, that any white or free person, charged with murdering or maiming a slave, shall be proceeded against *as he would be for murdering or maiming a free person, and on conviction shall suffer death, or such punishment as the law of England inflicts, &c.*

No. 527. The preamble to this Act recites, that in the old slave trials the magistrates were judges of the fact as well as of the *law*, and establishes the mode of trial by two justices and six inhabitants, &c.

No. 531. An Act, adopting the 14th Geo. 2. c. 6. Under this Act, the stealing the carcase of any sheep, or other cattle, *by any person or persons*, is made felony without benefit of clergy.

No. 537. The preamble of this Act recites the *convenience of judges of either court being able, on their circuits, to take the examinations of femes covertes, &c,;* and provides, that deeds, intended to pass estates, under Act No. 32, of the Leeward Islands, *acknowledged before a justice of the court of King's Bench, or baron of the Exchequer of England or Ireland, shall be as valid, and the examination of the parties as effectual, as if the transaction were before the justices of the Common Pleas in England or Ireland.*

No. 557. *To amend the Act constituting the court of Chancery.* If a member of council, though not named in the proceedings as a party, be agent to a party, or interested in the suit, the captain-general, or temporary governor (in his absence), and two members of council, shall be a competent court, in the same manner as is directed by sec. 3, of No. 150, where a member of council is directly a party.

So where the commander-in-chief is absent from the island, and the *locum tenens* shall be interested in any suit, the next senior resident member of council, and two other members not interested, shall be a sufficient number to sit.

No. 621. *An Act for the speedier obtaining partition of lands and slaves in coparcenary, joint tenancy, and tenancy in common. Whereas proceedings, or writs of partition, are dilatory, chargeable, and often ineffectual, an action of partition is given in the court of Common Pleas,* and the proceedings regulated.

No. 623. By cl. 156, of the Court Act, the *members of council composing the court of Error are required to be* FIVE, *but such as are judges in the court of Common Pleas, or barons of the Exchequer, are deprived of a deliberative voice, from which great inconveniency has been found to result;* therefore enacts, that *any three members of council, the president being one, or in case of the illness of the president, any other three, not being judges, shall be competent to sit as a court of Error.*

No. 626. This Act continues the Court Act, and the several Acts amending it. By cl. 2, *Whereas much inconveniency, and some intricacy and difficulties have often attended the execution of parts of the Court Act, declaring that there might be a legal tender of commodities, where there was no specific contract to the contrary;* enacts, that

ANTIGUA.

LAWS.

*no cotton, ginger, or other produce, except sugar and rum, shall be legal tender for any debt, &c. &c.*

No. 636. *An Act for the further protection of the slaves within the island of Antigua, "from cruel or excessive "punishment; and for amending certain provisions in "No. 36, Laws of the Leeward Islands." Whereas there is no law at present in force in this island (Antigua), for limiting or restraining the arbitrary punishments of slaves, except the general provisions contained in an Act of the Leeward Islands (the Melioration Act), and for punishing such person or persons as shall be convicted of cruelty or maltreatment, &c.* enacts, that *no slave shall receive more than six lashes, unless some person having authority (owner. or his representative, jail-keeper, &c. &c.) be present; and no owner, &c. shall punish any slave with more than thirty-nine lashes at one time, and for one offence, nor on the same day, nor within fourteen days, nor until delinquent shall have fully recovered from the effect of any former punishment, under the penalty of* 100*l. for every offence.*

*And whereas, by the Act of the Leeward Islands, owners and directors of slaves, &c. are directed and required to make sundry returns, and take certain oaths; and whereas, there being no provision for summoning or giving notice to the said persons, of the particular days and times, to make the said returns, and take the said oaths, and such having been found to be likely to be productive of great inconvenience, and no such summonses having ever been issued, no returns made and no oaths taken, &c. and no prosecutions ever instituted for neglecting to take the said oaths; and whereas, it is too much to be feared, that requiring persons to make returns and declarations on oath, as to performance of any duty required by law, might be productive of perjury, and therefore the law has very rarely exacted such, in any country; in lieu, appoints magistrates and vestries in each parish a council for the protection of slaves.*

Cl. 3. makes further provisions as to *coroner's inquests on slaves, &c.*

No. 659. An Act, adopting Lord Ellenborough's Act,

and making the construction of law which has obtained in England, a part of the enactment.

No. 664. *An Act to alter and amend an Act for the better government of slaves and free negroes, &c.* (No. 130.) No slave committed to the marshal as a runaway, shall be sold until six months after notice by advertisement in the public papers.

Cl. 3. If any person claiming to be free shall be committed as a runaway, the provost-marshal shall, within six days, give notice of such claim to the chief justice, or his *locum tenens*, who shall order the claimant before him and another justice of the Court. *If, on hearing, claimant shall appear legally free, or in equity and conscience to be considered so, or so from long reputation, they shall, by their warrant, discharge him out of custody, otherwise remand him; if discharged, his jail fees to be discharged by the public.*

## MANUSCRIPT ACTS.

No. 709. *An Act for repealing the former Acts for the same purpose, and for establishing a more regular and solemn judicature for the trial of slaves accused of felony without benefit of clergy, or other capital crimes.* The preamble recites, that it is expedient that the trial in such cases, should be assimilated to those of whites; and the Act provides, that the court of Grand Sessions shall form a court of record, on the last Friday in January, and the last Friday in July, for the trial of slaves, and shall try them, like whites, with a power of adjournment and the usual machinery of a criminal court. Prosecutions are appointed to be conducted by the attorney or solicitor-general, or king's counsel, and counsel to be assigned to the accused, on application of the slave or his proprietor, or *his* attorney. The evidence of slaves is to be admitted for and against slaves, but what seems anomalous and objectionable, without oath.

ANTIGUA.

LAWS.

A regular indictment and every other legal formality is required.

The court is declared ancillary to the court of King's Bench and Grand Sessions of Antigua. After sentence of death passed, due notice is required to be given from the president or the court, to the governor, within thirty-six hours

No. 724. To compel the creditor to support his debtor while in jail.

## COURTS.

ENUMERATION OF.

The Courts of Civil Jurisdiction in this island, are the court of Chancery; court of Error; court of Common Pleas; and court Merchant, for the benefit of transient persons. The courts of Criminal Jurisdiction, are the court of King's Bench and Grand Sessions for Antigua; and the courts of King's Bench and Grand Sessions for the trial of criminal slaves.

## COURT OF CHANCERY.

This court is constituted in the same manner, as the court of Chancery at Barbados and Dominica. It is held whenever applied for, as business occurs.

There are two masters in this court, who are required, by a recent regulation, to give bond with two sureties, in the sum of 10,000*l.* for the faithful discharge of the duties of their office.

This court, it is said, "exercises jurisdiction, in cases of "manumission, by deed or will, as the Court of Chancery "would do, as to other interests under deed or will "in England, where relief could not be obtained at law. "Unless so circumstanced, manumissions are triable "by writs of *habeas corpus*, and where any one claims "to be free when committed as a runaway slave, such "claims of freedom are to be inquired into, agreeably to "the 3d clause of the Act, No. 664."

ANTIGUA.

CHANCERY.

Receivers are chosen by the Master, subject to the approval of the court, and give security according to the value of the property; but, usually, it is said, to the amount of 20,000*l.* Antigua currency. A receiver ought to pass his accounts, annually before a Master; but this duty the chief justice and the attorney-general agree in stating is not always punctually performed.

Members of council, who in this island it has been seen, are the judges of the court of Chancery, are sometimes appointed receivers to estates. The attorney-general said, "They are, and I think it objectionable; "they are in the habit of voting upon it, and I think that "is not right."

A decree upon bill and answer only, where it is the object of the complainant to have the suit brought to a very speedy decision, can be obtained within four months after the filing of the bill. Where the parties proceed to the examination of witnesses, commonly in *five* or *six* months.

An estate is always appraised previously to a sale, (under a decree;) "but it is not necessary," said the attorney-general, "that the biddings should go up to "the appraised value. The biddings would be opened "under the same circumstances as they would be, on "motion, in the courts of equity in the mother coun-"try."

By the 41st clause of the Amelioration Act of the Leeward Islands, debts contracted for food and clothing for slaves are made a prior lien on slaves, except as against debts to the King; and it has always been considered, according to the attorney-general, "that per-"sons making advances for the necessary expenses of "management of an estate, have an equitable lien upon "such estate, with priority to the claims of persons be-"neficially interested in it. I am not aware," adds the attorney-general, "that any inconvenience has been found "to result from the existence of these liens."

"The court," said the chief justice, "not being com-"posed of professional gentlemen, its decisions are not "uniformly regulated by legal principles. A conscientious

ANTIGUA.

CHANCERY.

"discharge of duty, according to the received impression "of equity, always regulates its judgments. Unless the "court be *otherwise constituted*, I can suggest nothing for "its improvement."

## COURT OF EXCHEQUER.

Four Barons of the Exchequer have always been appointed by the governor; but there is no law of the island which regulates the constitution or proceedings of a court of Exchequer. "A court of this description," said the attorney-general, would seem, by a reference "to the records in the Secretary's office, to have been "occasionally formed for the purpose of aiding the pro-"cess of the court of Exchequer in England, against "defaulters in the Post-office department."

No court of Exchequer, however, has been held, during the experience of the present chief justice, from the commencement of his practice at the bar of this island, a period of twenty-three years.

## COURT OF COMMON PLEAS.

This court is composed in the same manner, in Antigua, as in the other islands, and is held by appointment of Act, No. 475, on the first Tuesdays in the months of April, May, June, July and August.

There is little or no arrear of business. The court always sits on the appointed days, and adjourns from time to time, as often as may be necessary to get through the business before it. The court has never any difficulty in getting through the business before it, with the aid of its adjournments. There is a vacation of seven months; and no particular inconvenience, according to the attorney-general, has been found to result from it.

The court has no particular rules of practice, except such as are embodied in the Court Act.

ANTIGUA.

COMMON PLEAS.

Judgment is usually obtained in this court in rather more than two months time; and except where the testimony of non-resident witnesses is required, it is not in the power of a defendant to create a delay of more than four months.

There is, "generally speaking, much less of rigid "adherence to form, in the proceedings of this court, "than is observed in the court of Common Pleas in "England."

A record of all the proceedings of this court is kept in the Secretary's office, but it is not made up with great formality, and is in general loosely kept.

By a recent law, the creditor is compelled to allow his debtor, in prison, 1*s.* *per diem*, if the debtor, on his oath, proves that he is incompetent to support himself.

"Costs," said the chief justice, "are not commonly "made a subject of contention in this court, because they "are by no means oppressive."

"The judges," said the attorney-general, "being, ge- "nerally speaking, private gentlemen, uninstructed in "the law, it cannot be reasonably expected that their "decisions should be characterized by any great degree "of uniformity. But I think I may safely venture to "affirm, that their judgments are, upon the whole, as "upright and consistent, as they would be under the "same circumstances in any community."

## COURT OF COMPLAINTS.

Actions are brought in this court for debts not exceeding 10*l.* currency. It is considered as a branch of the Common Pleas, and is constituted by the same Act, No. 475.

## COURT OF ORDINARY.

This court derives its authority from the King's commission to the Governor, who is the sole judge. The ordinary has the power of collating to benefices, granting licences for marriages, probates of wills, and letters of administration. "Neither the Acts of this island "nor the Royal Instructions," said the attorney-general, "make any mention of an appeal from his decisions, but "an Order in Council might, I should think, under particular circumstances, be obtained, for allowing an appeal to the King in Council."

There is no table of fees in this court.

## COURT OF ADMIRALTY.

This court (of Vice Admiralty) is held by virtue of a commission from the lords of the Admiralty, or, in default of such commission, by appointment of the governor.

In the last two years there had not been more than six causes tried in this court.

There is a docket of the judge's and register's fees, established about seven years since, it is said, by Commissioners in England.

Seamen seldom proceed in this court for the recovery of their wages, such suits being expensive.

There is no special commission for the trial of offences committed upon the high seas.

## COURT OF ERROR.

The judges who have decided in the court below, are peremptorily excluded from sitting and giving judgment in the court of Error; but they may attend and assign their reasons for the judgment they gave.

This court decides by a majority, and there is no time limited for bringing a writ of Error.

Appeals are not frequent, and the expenses in the island are said to be very inconsiderable.

# CRIMINAL COURTS.

## COURT OF KING'S BENCH AND GRAND SESSIONS FOR ANTIGUA.

The judges of this court are the Lieutenant Governor of the Island, all the members of council, the judges of the court of Common Pleas, the barons of the Exchequer, and all the justices of the peace of the island. The chief justice considers that the court is thus "over-"loaded with a plurality of judges, and that the greater "part of the business which comes before it, might more "properly be brought before a court of Quarter Sessions, "if such were established; at which a chairman and "justices of the peace will compose the court." The chief justice further "thinks it absolutely necessary that "a professional gentleman should preside on all occa-"sions to discharge the duty properly." The commission of the chief justice does not extend to the Criminal courts; he takes precedence there "*next to the members "of council.*"

This court is held twice a-year.

ANTIGUA.

KING'S BENCH.

It has never been the practice in this island for the attorney-general to file informations *ex officio*.

The President of the court sums up the "evidence, "and other judges also occasionally offer their senti-"ments to the jury, upon particular cases." Points of law arising in the course of their proceeding, are determined by the opinion of the majority of the judges.

Capital punishments, it is said, are seldom inflicted. They are sometimes commuted for working in the criminal gang, employed to repair and cleanse the streets of St. John's.

A party against whom a bill has been found, though he should be acquitted afterwards, pays the costs of the court; but if the bill is thrown out, he is discharged free of expense.

## COURT OF KING'S BENCH AND GRAND SESSIONS FOR THE TRIAL OF CRIMINAL SLAVES.

SLAVE COURT.

This court has been recently established by an Act of the island, for the trial of slaves charged with capital offences. It is framed upon the same principle as the court of King's Bench and Grand Sessions for Antigua, and consequently gives to slaves the same form of trial in every respect in capital cases, as white and free-coloured people are entitled to.

This court is also held twice a-year, at the Courthouse.

There are some old enactments, "not very creditable "to the colony," said the attorney-general; and there are others, which he did not at the moment recollect, "making offences capital in slaves, which would not be "so if committed by white or free-coloured people." But these, it is agreed, are disregarded in practice, and considered a dead letter. Attempts to poison, obeah, &c. are made capital by No. 611, cl. 2 and 3, but there are no words which expressly take away the benefit of clergy.

ANTIGUA.

SLAVE COURT.

The information given against slaves by white or free persons of colour is upon oath, but not the information of slave against slave; no oath being administered to a slave on any occasion.

Slaves are bailable in all cases in which a free person would be entitled to be admitted to bail, and under the same rules. Any slave confined on a charge of felony, from which benefit of clergy is taken away, is entitled to be brought up on writ of *habeas corpus*, and may be remanded or discharged, with or without bail.

There is a regular indictment in this court, and it is sent before a grand jury.

The court may assign counsel to the prisoner, upon application from the slave or his proprietor or the representative of such proprietor, under the authority of the MS. Act.

Slave evidence is admitted in this court; "but what is "very singular," said the attorney-general, "the law "does not allow of its being given upon oath." The same gentleman observed, "the character of the evi- "dence of slaves must depend most essentially, as well "upon their natural capacity, as upon the degree of re- "ligious instruction which they have received, and the "extent to which they have profited by it. I have, on "some occasions, known a very clear and consistent tes- "timony delivered by slaves of a more cultivated mind, "while in others, I have found it almost impossible to "comprehend their meaning." The chief justice said, "in my experience, as it regards the slave population, "I consider, generally speaking, that their prevailing "vice is a disregard to truth; and on many occasions, "in giving evidence, I have known them exhibit a very "imperfect idea as to *time*, although, in other respects, "apparently intelligent."

Slaves giving false evidence in court, would, we were informed, be ordered a public whipping or confinement, at the discretion of the court, without any trial. The detection and punishment of such offences are not frequent.

ANTIGUA.

SLAVE COURT.

If the admissibility of their evidence were extended "beyond slave against slave, it must be under very judicious restrictions," thought the chief justice.

The attorney-general was of opinion, that "where "death is charged to have ensued from an unlawful punishment of flogging, and there is a strong and violent "presumption of the truth of the charge, and the party "accused cannot make it appear to the satisfaction of the "coroner or magistrates, who investigate the matter, "that the punishment was inflicted in the presence of "some other free person; in such a case, under a combination of these suspicious circumstances, slaves ought "to be received by magistracy and upon the trial, as "competent witnesses, under proper restrictions; such "as their having been baptized, and understanding the "nature and obligation of an oath; giving a clear and "connected testimony, and being generally free from any "kind of objection, which would go to disqualify a witness in the courts of the mother country. I am not," the attorney-general added, "altogether prepared to "offer an opinion as to its being advisable to admit their "testimony in any other case."

Per Attorney-General.

After sentence is passed in this court, it must be communicated to the governor in thirty-six hours. The president of the court generally puts the governor in possession of the circumstances of the case, after which the commander-in-chief, it is said, always communicates it to the officers of the Crown, previously to allowing the sentence to be carried into execution.

Misdemeanors at common law committed by slaves, as well as offences under the laws of the island below the degree of felony without benefit of clergy, are cognizable by the magistrates. The presumption of law has formerly been against the freedom of a negro; but now, where he has been reputed free any length of time, he will not be required to adduce any positive proof of his freedom, and this is provided for by Act of the island, No. 664, cl. 5. A negro complaining to the governor, or law officer of the Crown, of being illegally held in slavery, is always

ANTIGUA.

SLAVE COURT.

brought before the judges of the court of Common Pleas, by writ of habeas corpus, and discharged, upon his establishing a strong equitable claim to freedom.

A master is not considered, in this island, as having an absolute power over his slave. He has the right of punishing, but that right is placed under particular restrictions. By No. 36, laws of the Leeward Islands, regulating the authority of masters over their slaves, any owner or director maltreating a slave is liable to a prosecution in the court of King's Bench and Grand Sessions for Antigua, and may be fined or imprisoned, or both, at the discretion of the court, and is also subject to have such slave taken out of his possession and sold.

Strictly speaking, slaves are not considered as having a right to acquire any property, except for the benefit of their owners, "save stock, fruit, vegetables, and some "few other trifling articles."

For the general instruction of slaves, several Sunday schools are formed in different parts of the island, and religious establishments abound in every quarter.

The slave laws of this island, the attorney-general thought, (though generally better than those of other West India colonies,) are still capable of much improvement.

The chief justice thought "much had been done for "improving the condition of the slave population, within "the last twenty-five years; and what is further to be "done, for the melioration of their condition, was a sub-"ject upon which a Committee of the two Houses was "then zealously engaged."

The respect, in which the proceedings on the trial of criminal slaves in this island, appear to me less completely satisfactory than those I have before noticed with approbation, in the island of St. Vincent, is (not to mention the circumstance of the trial in the latter island, taking place at the same time, or sessions, with those of all other offenders,) that,—

First, in St. Vincent, a lawyer, the chief justice, presides, which is not the case in Antigua. See Second Report.

Secondly, The evidence of slaves, which is admitted

ANTIGUA.

SLAVE COURT.

in the same cases, and nearly to the same extent, in both islands, in St.Vincent, is given *upon oath;* while at Antigua, slaves are not sworn.

---

Attendance at.

The Commissioners regularly attended all these different courts, at the period of their respective sittings. The proceedings of the bar were not a little intemperate and irregular; but the conduct of the bench, (at least upon these occasions,) was decorous and dignified. The assistant judges in this island, belong to a different class of persons from those sometimes appointed to the situation in the smaller islands, and discharge the duties very respectably.

Arguments upon points of law were of course, very embarrassing to the court; but were in general, rightly decided. The juries seemed remarkably intelligent and well-disposed. There was a great deal of business. The court of Common Pleas, which we attended on the 19th of August, was sitting in consequence of a *second* adjournment. Causes, which had been more than FOUR terms in the paper, were struck out of the list. Upon the whole, justice *was* in most instances, rudely administered; but it was repeatedly stated, that similar cases had in former instances, been differently decided; and this remark was suffered to pass without contradiction.

Minutes.

Sept. 30. The Commissioners attended the court of Grand Sessions. They first breakfasted with the attorney-general, with the bench and bar, and afterwards went, according to established custom, in procession to the Court-house. The senior member of council presided. The chief justice sat on his right hand, and took notes. The causes were unimportant. By a local Act, the being found with sugar in his possession is made evidence of a party having bought it from a slave, (who must have stolen it,) unless the accused rebut the presumption by sufficient proof of having bought it from a free person. In a prosecution, founded upon this Act, it appeared, upon the *ex parte* evidence before the grand jury, that the prisoner did buy it from a free person, and the jury naturally, and properly, hesitated to find against the fact proved before them, and thought the presumption would only exist in the absence of any proof of the fact. Being pressed by the attorney-general, they did find the bill; but the petty jury acquitted the prisoner, upon the point, and were censured by the court for so doing. ANTIGUA. SLAVE COURT.

The Commissioners were this day present in the court of Error. A technical difficulty occurred, arising wholly from the irregularity of the proceedings in the court below. The Governor, who presided, said, "Now here "is a point of law, and I am sure I don't know how we "are to decide it." The other judges were equally at a loss. It was got over by an amendment with the consent of parties. There was great disorder and confusion. Minutes. Oct. 8, 1823.

The principal complaints in this island had reference to the irregularity and expense attending proceedings in the court of Chancery, though several other grievances, of no trivial nature, were forcibly urged upon the attention of the Commissioners. COMPLAINTS. Irregularity and expense in Chancery.

A person, of the name of Henry Donovan, preferred a complaint, respecting some proceedings in the court of Chancery. The Commissioners thought a demurrer ought to have been allowed in this case, (which was not,) and, consequently, that the decree on appeal would be reversed; but, as they were of opinion that his (the complainant's) claim would not ultimately prevail, it did not appear that *his* interests were materially affected by the course, which improperly perhaps, had been pursued. Mr. Donovan observed, that "great costs had been un-"necessarily incurred in the suit in Chancery;" (these it appeared had been all paid out of the property.) Mr. Donovan further pressed "the illustration which this "case afforded, of the impropriety of members of the "court, (judges deciding upon the case,) being appointed "receivers, and contended that it presented a flagrant "instance of precipitation, partiality, and jobbing." The Commissioners promised to call for the taxed bill of costs. Donovan's case. Minutes, Aug. 11, 1823.

Mr. Lee, a very respectable barrister, of high reputation as a man of honour and integrity, "to shew that Sept. 17, 1823.

ANTIGUA.

COMPLAINTS.

"proceedings in the court of Chancery were governed by "favour, influence, connection, and party feeling, referred "to the Registrar's book, in the case of *Taylor and "others, representatives of Valentine Morris, against "the assignees of Balma and Francis Willock, admi-"nistrator of Alexander Willock.* Balmas were se-"cond mortgagees. In a suit by their assignees against "the mortgagee in possession (Willock), he was reported "to be overpaid, and to be 10,000*l.* in debt, and up-"wards. On the 13th of February, 1812, Mr. Lee "moved that this report be confirmed; and the same day "that the estate be delivered up to the second mort-"gagee, which was refused. Before this, on the 12th, "(the day before,) the bill Taylor and others, &c., "had been filed; and on the *same* day, the 13th, the "*subpœna* was served, and (without notice) a motion for "a receiver made; the equity of the second bill being, "that the assignees of Balma were fully paid out of the "proceeds of another estate, of which they were in "possession, (which might have been introduced in the "answer to the former bill.) Mr. Kirby, the attorney "to the estate, was one of the judges; his father-in-law "was another; and two of his intimate friends, with "the Governor, formed the rest of the court. The "Master reported Mr. Kirby to be the receiver; Kirby "always consigning to the house of Turner in Lon-"don, and Turner being the son-in-law of the master. "Kirby voted for the appointment of a receiver.

"6th March, 1817. On an affidavit, that the bill filed "on the 12th of February 1812, was without the au-"thority of the deponents, who were made parties "thereto, and that they had sold all their right and in-"terest therein, it was moved by Mr. Lee, that their "names be struck out and the bill dismissed; the other "party Taylor, being dead, and so the suit abated, and "the rest having been made parties without their con-"sent, and the original bill filed without authority. "This motion was refused. Kirby, who filed the bill, "had an old power of attorney from Taylor only. The "object was to prevent Mr. Willock having so large a

" sum of money (10,000*l.* and upwards,) to pay. The " court of Chancery is always resorted to upon such oc- " casions, *to save the party in power from being forced to* " *pay;* and where the creditor is absent, there is great " delay occasioned; Kirby continued receiver to his " death, when he was indebted, according to the report " of the Master, 8,493*l.* He died insolvent; but his se- " curity is able to pay."

ANTIGUA.

COMPLAINTS.

Mr. Lee explained the mode resorted to, (by " throw- " ing it into Chancery") to " delay the payment of a just " debt to a creditor in England. A demand may always " be staved off, by obtaining an injunction; for though " the attorney with a power, may put in an appearance, " he cannot put in an answer; and for want of answer, " the injunction goes, &c. &c. Six months are given for " time to answer; then, if exceptions are taken and al- " lowed, there may be six months more."

Mr. Lee said, " he brought this case under the notice " of the Commissioners, avowedly and expressly, *to ex-* " *pose the iniquity of the court of Chancery*, composed " of the council and the governor, (the governor coming " last, and being a mere cipher.) Every decision was " anticipated. It was known which way the interest of " each member lay, and his vote could be with certainty " calculated accordingly."

Minutes, Aug. 29, 1823.

A black woman, of the name of Mary Morris, " wished " to complain of the conduct of the executor of her late " master, Captain Morris. She had three children by " Captain Morris: to these children, by his will, Captain " Morris left the use or hire of fourteen slaves, to sup- " port and educate them till they came of age. The " executor said it was necesssary to sell two of the slaves " to pay the testator's debts; but he also sold the other " twelve, and promised to place the money out at inter- " est, for the benefit of the children. He had since that " time paid some small matters on account of the chil- " dren, but the amount was trifling, and he now refused " to do any thing; and in answer to the application, " told 'her to go to Wilberforce.' She had called upon

ANTIGUA.

COMPLAINTS.

Sept. 3, 1823.

" a lawyer, who told her she had a remedy in the court of " Chancery, but she must pay 100*l*. She had not the " means of paying any thing."

Mr. Buntin, the executor of Captain Morris, attended before the Commissioners "to answer the charge pre-" ferred by the black woman, calling herself Mary Mor-" ris. He admitted the sale of all the slaves, as repre-" sented, but said it was done for the benefit of the estate, " with the best advice of the friends of the family. They " were principally seafaring people, who were likely " to be drowned or to run away. The money produced " by the sale, he, at that time, considered he could not " do better than lay out on his own estate, and pay in-" terest for the money; but now he could pay little or " nothing. He had certainly told the woman to go to " Wilberforce; because he and she, and all the West " Indians were reduced to this state of inability to pay, " by *his means and misrepresentations*." On examination, Mr. Buntin admitted, that "Captain Morris had " been dead ten years, and he, as executor, had never " accounted for what he had received. He believed there " was a balance coming to the children, certainly; but " his books were not made up. He could not tell what " it would be; he had always paid the interest, and " more than the interest, for the maintenance and educa-" tion of the children. He still continued to pay some-" thing, as he was able, for their support, though a " lesser sum. He did the best he could; if he had two " dollars, he gave them *one*. His estate had been worth " 25,000*l*., and he could not now get 12,000*l*. for it: " in the present state of things, it mattered not what " was due to them, or to any one else, for there were " no means of paying." On being pressed, whether, if he could not pay, he would promise to state his accounts, and shew what was due? He answered, "Nobody had a right to call for the accounts; there " was another property in the island, which he had " held as executor and manager for eighteen years, and " he had never accounted for that." In reply to an intimation from the Commissioners, he said, "he was "aware he might be sued in Chancery, and might have "to pay costs." ANTIGUA. COMPLAINTS.

Mr. Buntin again called at the public room, and in some trifling respect varied his statement, but could not be brought to promise to account. Minutes, Sept. 4.

Mr. Osborn, a spirited and enterprising member of the colonial bar, preferred a complaint, relating to certain proceedings had in the court of Chancery, on a motion made by the attorney-general, (the present chief justice,) to DISBAR him, (Mr. Osborn.) After much discussion, and on the suggestion of the Commissioners, it was arranged, that this charge, and another relating to the prosecution of the collector, should be left with the Commissioners, to use in any way they pleased, and to be considered only as illustrative of the constitution and practice of the courts in the island of Antigua. Sept. 2, 1823.

Two professional gentlemen, Mr. Lee and Mr. Scotland, attended before the Commissioners, and deposed to the facts of Mr. Osborn's case. Both, in general terms, represented "the present administration of the "law in this island, as objectionable in very many re- "spects; as ignorant, prejudiced, partial, and conducted "with such undue regard to particular interests, as to "be almost corrupt. Interest and connection in a small "society, without the control of public opinion, a free "press, judges unconnected with the island and its inha- "bitants, and an enlightened bar that could venture to "act independently, bore down every thing before them. "The court of Chancery, where the greatest interests "were at stake, was most exceptionable." Sept. 5, 1823.

In the course of his statement of his complaint, Mr. Osborn introduced the following narrative, making no part of his charge, but mentioned by way of illustration:—

"I defended the collector, and another indicted for "extortion. Eleven of the twelve judges on the bench "had signed a paper, declaring the fee taken by the de- "fendants, (and which was the charge against them in

ANTIGUA.

COMPLAINTS.

" that case,) oppressive and illegal, &c. I was about to " address the court, certainly intending to ask, whether " they could sit as judges upon this occasion? when one " of them asked, 'If I meant to challenge the judges? " for if I did, they would commit me.' I said, 'I was " aware that I could not do *that*; but I only meant to " put it to their own delicacy and feeling of propriety, " how they could sit as judges, when they had already " expressed an opinion?' They continued on the bench, " and the trial went on. My case required me, for the " benefit of my client, to act with spirit and firmness, and " to make some shew of independence.

" After the trial was over, before I reached the door " of the Court-house, and in the presence of the judges, " a person of the name of Otto, to whom I had given " offence upon some former proceeding in court, came " behind me and struck me violently, and then ran away. " One of the judges came down from the bench, and " encouraged him; and when he run away, he said, " 'run, Otto, run'; and then returned and took his seat " again upon the bench. Mr. Otto escaped, and was re- " ceived into the house of the chief justice. To pro- " tect Mr. Otto from my vengeance, fifteen special con- " stables, persons residing in his immediate neighbour- " hood, were sworn in. This is the case to which Mr. " Shiell refers in his affidavit before the court of Chan- " cery, when he addresses, to a court of justice, discus- " sions on the propriety of violating the law. 'Depo- " nent says, that on reaching home, he consulted and " advised with a friend, on the line of conduct the depo- " nent should adopt, who was decidedly of opinion that " deponent should not send a message to Mr. Osborn, " in consequence of the pusillanimity which Mr. Osborn " had betrayed, in an affair which he had some time be- " fore had with Mr. Otto.' Mr. Shiell's affidavit of June " 20th, 1821."

The observations contained in some of the cases which have last been reported, (the complaints of Mr. Lee and Mr. Osborn, for example,) being the representations of professional gentlemen, might obviously be the fruit (though quite unconsciously to themselves,) of disappointed hope, or frustrated ambition. But subsequently, three respectable merchants of St. John's, who sat upon the jury that tried a person of the name of Grant, (whose case will be mentioned hereafter,) attended, and afforded the explanations required of them in that case. After the business was concluded, one of the gentlemen addressed the Commissioners, "in the name, and on the behalf "of the merchants of the colony." He stated, "the general wish for a reform in the judicature of the colony, "and particularly in the court of Chancery, and the satisfaction afforded by a prospect of having a sole chancellor, a lawyer, unconnected with the island, to sit in "that court. For himself, individually, he (the speaker,) "had, he said, several suits to bring, which he was deterred from instituting, by the circumstance of the defendants, in each case, having several powerful friends "upon the bench, who could not help shewing favour to "their connections. He therefore implored the Commissioners to recommend such beneficial changes."

ANTIGUA.

COMPLAINTS.

Minutes, Sept. 10, 1823.

Mr. Lee, the barrister, complained to the Commissioners that, "the judges of the court of Error, before "which the case of the collector was about to be brought, "were members of the council, who, in their legislative "capacity, had voted that the expense of the prosecution "in that identical case, (including the fees of counsel for "arguing the writ of error), should be paid out of the "treasury; in their resolution, prejudging the case, upon "which they now claim to sit judicially. He had applied, without success, for an extract from the journals, to shew what members of council were present, "and voted for such resolution." The Commissioners thought the members of council were not legally disqualified to sit as judges in the court by their having taken part in those proceedings, though there might be indelicacy in their doing so; and that as the journals were not *printed*, it might be doubtful, whether it was matter of right to inspect and take copies of them, unless

Sept. 17, 1823.

ANTIGUA.

COMPLAINTS.

Sept. 12, 1823.

the council can be considered as composing, like the House of Lords, in England, a court of record.

Mr. J. C. Gibbs laid a long and important case before the Commissioners; *in re Burton and others.* He also mentioned the case of Burke and Underwood, in which an injunction had been granted to stay an action at law, brought by a merchant under the Amelioration Act, for supplies furnished to an estate. Mr. Gibbs said, "the "throwing that case into Chancery, had shewn the mer- "chant how easily the preference given him under the "Act, might be evaded; and the consequence was, that "since that time, for the space of a year and a half, and "at the period when it was most wanted, such assistance "was now withheld from plantations, and a most bene- "ficial act entirely defeated."

The facts stated in the complaint of Mr. Gibbs, *in re Burton and others*, were, if true, the most extraordinary and unjustifiable of any brought under the notice of the Commissioners, in their circuit through the islands. We were precluded from entering into the merits, as we intended, by the circumstance of the case being then *sub judice;* an appeal having been (specially) allowed to his Majesty in council. But though for this reason, we did not inquire into the grounds of the complaint, and I can consequently offer no opinion upon the case, I should not consider myself warranted in wholly suppressing THE CHARGE; part of the statement which affected himself, having been answered by the attorney-general, and the remainder throwing great light upon the general question of the due administration of justice.

Oct. 7, 1823. J. C. Gibb's Complaint *in re* Burton.

"Rowland Burton, the testator, died in the year 1814, "appointing, by will, the Honourable Thomas Nor- "bury Kirby, the Honourable James Athill, and the "Honourable Paul Horsford, Esquires, trustees and "executors, &c.

"The testator gave and devised the surplus produce "of his real estate, '*in rateable proportions,*' *to such* "*persons as might be of affinity and near kindred to him;* "*but in no degree beyond that of a second cousin, and in*

ANTIGUA.

COMPLAINTS. STATEMENT.

" *immediate paternal descent from his grandfather, who* " *was called Colonel John Burton, &c.*

"Mr. J. Halloran, in right of his wife, who was re- " lated to the testator in the degree and mode pre- " scribed by his will, wishing to interpose a claim, called " upon Mr. Burke, knowing him to be the most upright " and experienced practitioner at the bar, for the pur- " pose of employing him. That gentleman, with uni- " form integrity of conduct, declined to act, on the " ground that he had been already retained, in the same " case, by Mr. Harris, 'which would render it, he said, " 'impossible for him to undertake *his* (Mr. Halloran's) " 'cause, satisfied that he could not do justice to both;' " and, 'according to the will, thinking Mr. Halloran " 'should engage some other professional gentleman to " '*oppose* him.' Mr. Halloran was recommended to " Mr. W. Musgrave. The question put to that gentle- " man, was, 'whether or not Mr. Harris had employed " 'him?' it being thought, that Mr. Harris had retained " every lawyer in the colony. Mr. Musgrave declaring " himself to be 'perfectly disengaged in the suit,' re- " ceived a fee of 50*l.* sterling, to enforce the claim of " Mr. Halloran exclusively, and to oppose the claim of " all others that might be set up, on any but the strictest " legal foundation.

"On the arrival of Mr. Rowland Ashe Burton, the " brother of Mrs. Halloran, who stood in the precise " degree of affinity with his sister, to the testator; appli- " cation was made to Mr. W. Musgrave, to include, in " the same bill, the claim of the said R. A. Burton; but " which Mr. W. Musgrave refused to do, stating, that it " ought to be done in a distinct bill, for which, he should " expect 50*l.* sterling, more. This seemed so odd, that " it was thought best to employ another member of the " profession, in that separate behalf. All the claims " might have been included in one bill, but this would " not suit the rapacity of the lawyers; who, blind to all " other interests, save their own, rendered it necessary " that, as the claims were each of a different nature, se- " parate bills should be filed.

ANTIGUA.

COMPLAINTS.

" Before the cause came on to be heard, it was rumoured " that Mr. Musgrave, (who always avoided conference " with Mr. Halloran, and was never clear and intelligi- " ble, when obliged to speak upon the subject) had not " acted true to his trust, as he had received fees from " Mr. Harris, to the serious injury of the prospects of " Mr. Halloran, his client, and that he was employed " also by the said Harris, as counsel for other unentitled " claimants. But not until the bills, setting forth the " right of those other claimants, were filed, could this " report be received as correct, when Mr. Musgrave's " perfidy was established, beyond the possibility of doubt. " But where was relief to be obtained? One of the " illegal claimants, represented by Mr. Musgrave, was " the creditor to an alarming extent of the chancellor!

" The solemn tribunal met; but it would be a mere " mockery of justice to say, that they met for the purpose " of hearing arguments: none were offered; no conten- " tions set up; and indeed it was pretty well known, out " of doors, what the decision would be; it had been can- " vassed often, over the bottle, by the different members " of the court, and it was evident to every one, they now " met for no other purpose than to have the credit in " form, of passing a decree; perhaps as in other instances, " written for them. The Master's report was read. A " motion was made for confirming it. Mr. W. Musgrave " then, in open defiance of every legal and moral con- " sideration, stood up in behalf of Mr. Harris, and mov- " ed, that in a cause, in which Harris was complainant, " and the Trustees of Burton were defendants, the " Master's report, which admitted his right to a share of " the property in question, be confirmed; and in a cause, " in which J. Roberts was complainant, against the same " defendants, the like motion; and in a cause, in which " Louisa Liott was complainant, against the same de- " fendants, the like motion, and this to the manifest in- " jury of Mrs. Halloran, his first client. Mr. Gibbs " being in court, instructed the counsel employed for " Mr. R. A. Burton, to oppose these latter claims; but " HE, too, had become the advocate of Elizabeth Watson,

Gibbs *in re* Burton.

ANTIGUA.

COMPLAINTS.

"and was acting in a double capacity. Thus were the "weak overpowered by the strong; and against their "positive instructions, and the wishes of the testator, a "decree, made in favour of seven, instead of three, "claimants, and no remedy left, until a petitition by "Miss Hannah Burton, to His Majesty in council, though "out of time, was, under the peculiar circumstances of "the case, granted, and an appeal allowed.

"A pretence was then set up, to defeat the appeal in "England, that the property had been divided, by con-"sent of parties. The then representatives of Miss H. "Burton and Mr. R. A. Burton, distinctly negatived "that assertion. Mr. Collins, agent to the former, says, "'I was sent for to the Master's office, where the law-"yers were assembled, when I was asked, 'how we were "to proceed in Judge Burton's business?' The ques-"tion appeared to me, strange, the course before us "being obvious; my reply was, 'the cause must go on "regularly; my instructions are, to resist the claims "of Mr. Harris, Dr. Roberts, Mr. Liott, and Miss Wat-"son, and to allow those of Mrs. Halloran and her bro-"ther, Mr. Rowland Ashe Burton; and such were my "instructions to Mr. Lee; the court must make such a "decree as in its wisdom it thinks fit.' I was then asked, "'if the claims of the parties, whom I was instructed "to oppose, should be allowed, was it my intention to "appeal?' To this I replied, 'I had no funds at my "disposal, to enable me to do so, and *I must therefore*, "abide by the decision of the court.' '

So Mr. Donaldson, executor of Mr. R. A. Burton, states, "I certainly never consented to admit of more "than three claims under the will of the said Rowland "Burton; *viz.* Miss Hannah Burton, Mrs. John Hallo-"ran (late Abigail Burton) and my testator, the said "Rowland Ashe Burton; and further, I, at several "times, in conversation with the counsel for the said "Rowland Ashe Burton, declared to him, that I would, "in the event of there being more claims admitted by the "court here, than these I have just mentioned, appeal "from any such sentence; and this I expressed to him

ANTIGUA.

COMPLAINTS.

"more than once, as my determination; which I certainly should have carried into effect, if the representatives of the said Rowland Ashe Burton had so enabled me, by affording the security requisite for that purpose; but without which I could not think of taking so high a responsibility upon myself."

The evidence of Mr. Lee also shews, that "the decision of the court was submitted to, not consented to. I beg leave to state, unequivocally, that Mr. Collins's statement is correct, in every thing; neither did I, as counsel for Miss Burton, enter into any compromise whatever; indeed, the papers sent home will clearly prove the contrary; for if there had been a compromise, no doubt but the parties so materially interested would have taken care to have had such a record of it, as would have precluded any doubt upon the subject. Mr. Collins and myself were under the necessity (in consequence of Miss Burton's poverty and inability to prosecute an appeal, as we then conceived,) *of taking what we could get.*"

The complaint then speaks of Mr. W. Musgrave's enormous bill of costs, 1,400*l.* and his brother, Mr. Richard Musgrave's costs, amounting to 2,400*l.* sterling, which induced that gentleman to boast, "*that he had proved himself nearest of kin to Mr. Burton.*" Also that the trustees had made free to help themselves to 6,000*l.* sterling, one of them, Kirby, being chancellor of the island when he died; and his estate in debt to one of the illegal claimants in this case, in no less a sum than 10,000*l.*

The charges are summed up in the last and shortest of the papers presented to the Commissioners, which will be found in the Appendix, No. 6. It is in itself wordy and violent; but the charges are of a nature which necessarily require to be disproved, by establishing facts, and not by questioning the composition, or by declaiming in answer in the same taste. Disgraceful proceedings are beyond all question imputed; can these be fairly met

ANTIGUA.

COMPLAINTS.

and categorically answered? I sincerely hope they may; but, as yet, the opportunity for such advantage has not been prosecuted to its fullest extent.

Into the merits of a decision, then under the review of His Majesty in council, the Commissioners could not enter; but it was a debt of justice to Mr. W. Musgrave, then filling the high and responsible situation of His Majesty's attorney-general for this government, to acquaint him with the nature of the charges brought against him, seriously affecting his professional reputation, if not his official character. These were—

1st. The having received a retaining fee from Mr. Halloran, to assert his rights, and then taking fees to support the claims of other persons, whose rights were adverse.

2dly. The having insisted on filing distinct bills, in all the cases; as also the amount of his costs.

3dly. The having, with a view to assist the respondents in combating the appeal allowed by His Majesty in council, irregularly, and without any proceedings before the court, produced and persuaded the court of Chancery to adopt without inquiry, a document, prepared by himself, declaring the affidavit of Mr. Collins, in which that gentleman denied having given his consent to the decree of the court, unfounded in fact, and Mr. Collins, consequently, guilty of perjury.

Mr. Musgrave, as might be expected, lost no time in affording the required explanation. "The conduct of "the executors in retaining the interest, he justly ob- "served, it was no part of his business to defend. He "acted *against* them; and nothing but the dread of the "heavy expense which would attend an appeal, (and "the inability of the parties to bear it,) would have in- "duced his clients to consent as they did to the decree." The decree, therefore, seems to be given up as indefensible. But the attorney-general proceeds, in his own vindication: "I was especially retained by Mr. Harris, "in conjunction with the late Mr. Burke, for himself, "Dr. Roberts, and Mrs. Liott. Mr. Halloran, with a "full knowledge of my being so previously retained by

ANTIGUA.

COMPLAINTS.

"Mr. Harris, thought proper to employ me to assert "his claim to a share of the property. At this time, "there was no idea of any point of law, in favour of "*him*, to the exclusion of any of the other parties; as "Miss Burton had taken it into her head that the de-"vise was void for uncertainty, and that an intestacy "would be decreed, in which event she would take the "whole as heir at law. She afterwards abandoned this "idea, and directions were sent out to her attorney "here, to have the bill so framed, as to admit of her "shutting out all persons who could not trace their de-"scent exclusively through males. Upon hearing of "this, Mr. Halloran for the first time, conceived the idea "of resisting Mr. Harris's claim; and seeing the awk-"ward situation in which I was thus unexpectedly "thrown by his change of purpose, I instantly made "known to Mr. Harris the impossibility of my advocat-"ing his interests in the cause, and suggested the pro-"priety of his engaging some other counsel for Dr. Ro-"berts, Mrs. Liott, and himself. This suggestion was "adopted, and the solicitor-general, (Mr. Richard Mus-"grave,) received a large fee in consequence. This un-"expected turn in the views of particular parties, had "the effect of placing Mr. Anthony Wyke also in an "awkward predicament, (who was concerned for Mr. "R. A. Burton and Miss Watson.) I advised Mr. Har-"ris to send home a case for the opinion of several "eminent lawyers; and those of Sir Arthur Piggott, "Sir James Mackintosh, and Mr. Wetherell, were taken "upon the will. These being exhibited here, had the "effect of inducing Mr. Halloran, and the attorney of "Miss Burton, to waive all further opposition to the "claims of the other complainants."

It will, doubtless, be perceived, that Mr. Musgrave and Mr. Gibbs are distinctly at issue, upon the fact of Mr. Musgrave's prior retainer by Mr. Halloran. In such cases of conflicting statements, the Commissioners had, obviously, no means of ascertaining the truth. I shall leave the disputed point, with the single observation; that I do not think it apparent why if Mr. Musgrave's services were first engaged by Mr. Harris, for himself and the two other parties, he should afterwards, on their interests being discovered to clash with those of Mr. Halloran, declare the impossibility of advocating the claims of these, his first clients, and abandon them, to cleave to Mr. Halloran; a person, who, he says, retained him last, and with a full knowledge of his having been previously engaged by Mr. Harris.

Mr. Musgrave added, "not a murmur was breathed "by Mr. Halloran, on the subject of my being also con-"cerned for Mr. Harris. It was evident, from my name "appearing openly, upon the face of all the proceedings, "that it never could have once entered my mind, that I "was doing any thing objectionable, in acting for more "than one party. You will observe, in the case of Bur-"nett *v.* Honeywood, Ambler's Reports, 708, that, under "a will of a similar nature, there were no less than four "hundred and fifty-six claimants, within the two years; "and had the counsel have refused to act for more than "one, what might have become of the claims of many?" I shall leave the sufficiency of this answer entirely to your Lordship's judgment.

To the charge of having insisted upon the filing distinct bills, nothing was said; but the proceeding was very much reprobated by Mr. Maddock, who was most conversant with Chancery practice. As to costs, it was observed, "the costs were certainly very heavy; but this "was owing to the number of suits which were instituted, "one after another, for the purposes of examining wit-"nesses, *de bene esse.* For myself, I can assure you, on "the honour of a gentleman, that my bill of costs were "not only taxed by the Master Extraordinary, but had "been previously examined and certified by the Master." Unfortunately, the Master and Master Extraordinary are both parties implicated in the charge of having shared largely in the plunder of this property.

Lastly, Mr. Musgrave positively affirms, that the decree was made "with the full consent of all parties." It, perhaps, was so understood by one side; while the other, from inability to appeal, *submitted to what they did not*

ANTIGUA.

COMPLAINTS.

*consent to;* and how was the alleged consent obtained? The private meeting of the lawyers, at the Master's office, and the question put to the agent; "If the decision is "against you, will you appeal?" I do regard, I confess, with strong dislike and suspicion.

Into the allegations respecting the conduct of the Master and Registrar in Chancery the Commissioners did not enter, as the acts of those officers appear to have been brought under the notice, and to have received the sanction of the Colonial courts; and all those proceedings would, we supposed, form part of the subject-matter of appeal. Several questions, however, will be found in the examinations suggested by this case, particularly such as were prompted by the difficulties Mr. Gibbs experienced, in procuring the accounts which had been passed in the Master's office; the vouchers being claimed by the executor as his private papers, and delivered up to him by the Master, at the critical juncture of their being required for the purposes of the appeal. This led us to inquire, in all the islands, into the mode of disposing of papers, relating to accounts which have been passed in the Master's office? "Whether accounts are "annexed to the report, by way of schedule, &c. &c.;" and the answers we received, furnish some information, which may be useful, for future purposes of improvement, when the attention of the Chancellor shall be directed to the abuses in the Master's office; a subject of vast importance.

Mr. Gibbs left his case of complaint in the hands of the Commissioners, to be used at their discretion.

Minutes, Sept. 17, 1823.

Several persons applied to the Commissioners, in cases where they supposed legacies to be left them, or manumissions to be directed by will; but had no means as they stated, of ascertaining the fact, where the will was not registered. From their representations, it appeared that, "because the stat. 5 Geo. 2. c. 7., makes slaves assets for "the payment of debts, executors always take possession "of them, and usually of houses and lands also, and dispose of them, at their pleasure, or use them for their "own benefit." The object of the complainants in al-

ANTIGUA.

COMPLAINTS. Minutes, Sept. 26, 1823.

most every instance, being to obtain our opinion upon the construction of a will, we evaded answering the applications; while, from the information they afforded, we thought it right to listen to their statements.

A Mr. Bailey preferred a complaint against the Solicitor-general, "respecting fees." He "had retained "Mr. Richard Musgrave, in a certain Chancery suit, on "his behalf: that gentleman had declined proceeding in "the case, when pressed to file the bill; but had never-"theless, refused to return any part of the 100*l.* currency, "(or 50*l.* sterling,) paid him, in the first instance; as a "retaining fee, for prosecuting the suit." The Commissioners advised the complainant to prefer a petition to the court of Chancery, at its next sitting, stating these facts to the court, on affidavit; when the nature and amount of the fee, and the purposes for which it was paid and received, being brought under the consideration of the court, the Commissioners would have an opportunity of learning in what light the subject was viewed in the colonies. This was not done; and the reason alleged was, that no counsel would act in the matter.

A coloured man called with a case under a will, of the kind so frequent, so lamentable in themselves, and so distressing to us who could not relieve them. This complainant appeared to have a clear right, (as did Bailey, who called before,) but from want of the means to retain counsel to institute a suit to compel the executor to account, he could not enforce it. These cases, as we proceeded in our inquiries and were more resorted to by the lower orders, occurred every day, aad were of the most revolting nature. One complaint, the Commissioners received at this period, was expressed in the following terms:—"No trust property, here, is sacred; no father "can ever die, with the pleasing assurance, that his es-"tate will be enjoyed by his children." Where there exists such a frightful want of common honesty, some strongly coercive measure must be resorted to. Executors must be compelled to account, at short intervals; and on default, not only be made liable *de bonis propriis* but the prospect of enforced restitution, must

ANTIGUA.

COMPLAINTS.
Minutes, Sept. 6, 1823.

not be left so remote or contingent, as to occasion it to be run against the chances of life, in a dangerous climate.

A Mr. Grant thought proper to prefer a complaint of great length, respecting some proceedings in a case in which HE was indicted, "for cruelly maltreating a "woman slave." The then attorney-general, but present chief justice, was pointedly accused of "attending in the "jury room, and helping the jury to a verdict;" and the magistracy generally, charged with "petty tyranny and "oppression; and it was objected particularly, that the "committing magistrates, one of whom had intruded "upon the property, interfered improperly, and taken a "personal interest in the matter, afterwards sat and "voted upon the trial."

It was also made the subject of complaint, that the chief justice, (the then attorney-general,) upon another occasion, "when HE (Grant) had, in the discharge of his "duty as a juror, not having his mind satisfied upon the "subject, hesitated to find a verdict according to the di- "rections of the judge, addressed the provost-marshal, "and ordered that officer 'not to summon Grant upon "'juries again.' Also, that intimidation, reflections, "and imputations, are used by the court, and the Crown "lawyers, to influence juries, and bear down the opposite "counsel. So that magistrates on the bench make the "most daring attacks on the forms of British jurispru- "dence, and excuse themselves, by *saying they are not* "*lawyers*. The presiding member of council, upon the "occasion alluded to, threatened to commit complainant, "because he would not agree with the other eleven "jurors, and afterwards said he was no lawyer;"—"and "complained, generally, of the errors and partiality of "the bench."

Sept. 6, 1823.

The chief judge "attended before the Commissioners, "to answer certain parts of Grant's complaint, affecting "him (the judge.")  These being read, the chief justice denied the facts. Grant called several witnesses to support the charge, but failed of proving the expressions imputed. It appeared that the jury applied to the court for assistance. The court sent up the attorney-general

ANTIGUA.

COMPLAINTS.

to assist them in framing a special verdict. The attorney-general threatened to move the court to commit Grant, and moved, or said he would move, that he should not be a juror again. In the end, something did appear to have been said, which had perhaps have been better omitted; there having been infinite provocation on the one side, and, it is to be feared at last, a little human passion on the other. A barrister we examined, stated, "The jury came down; a warm conversation ensued between the court and jury; I do not recollect exactly the expressions used by the president. My impression was, that the proceeding was very irregular and improper."

The same day, Colonel Brown, the magistrate, produced an authority under the Amelioration Act, "for going upon the estate to investigate the case, and for removing the slave therefrom." And it appeared, that the committing magistrates did NOT, in this case, sit and vote as judges.

A black free man, of the name of William Darrell, complained that his wife, a free woman, had been levied upon for taxes, (due from her former mistress,) and when he (Darrell) applied at the gaol for her discharge, *he* was beaten and ill-treated; and complaining afterwards to a magistrate upon the subject, he could get no redress. The Commissioners directed their secretary to write to the magistrate, and request that he would furnish them with the grounds of his decision. Minutes, Aug. 15, 1823.

The gaoler and turnkey proved, that the woman, claimed by Darrell as his wife, was discharged in ten minutes, on the mistake being discovered.

Mr. Shiell, the magistrate, attended before the Commissioners, and explained, that the complaint brought before him was for an assault and battery: which charge he dismissed, because the complainant was proved by an indifferent person, to have conducted himself riotously in the gaol.

Darrell, this day, brought a witness with him, who was not examined before the magistrate, to prove intemperate and violent conduct towards him, by the turn- Aug. 18, 1823.

ANTIGUA.

COMPLAINTS.

key, in the gaol. There appeared to have been great warmth and irritation on both sides; but in Darrell this was considered more excusable, and the case was dismissed with a reprimand to the turnkey, for the harshness of his behaviour.

A Mr. Kelly wished to complain "of the treatment he "had received from the solicitor-general acting as a ma- "gistrate. He (Kelly) had been charged with a com- "mon assault, under a personal quarrel with an officer "in the army, when the legal adviser of that officer, the "attorney-general, by his interference with the attorney "of the estate, on which the complainant lived as ma- "nager, procured his dismissal from the situation, (by "which he lived); and afterwards his brother, the soli- "citor-general, acting as a justice of the peace, bound "him (Kelly) over to appear and take his trial at the "Grand Sessions, in unusual and excessive bail. He "did appear, was tried, and was acquitted."

Mr. Kelly was told, that though the bail required from him might appear excessive and unusual, still his own representation hardly seemed to shew a case, in which the Commissioners could interfere with any good effect. Mr. Kelly said, his object was chiefly to shew the state of the country; the oppression and oligarchical tyranny, under which it was suffering. He "did not seek relief; "he would leave his case with the Commissioners."

A coloured man, of the name of Donowa, represented, "of a magistrate, or rather of the magistracy, that the "various justices of the peace, to whom he had succes- "sively applied, had all refused to entertain his com- "plaint against a store-keeper of the name of Pitt, for "an assault and battery, committed upon him (com- "plainant) in an auction-room where the sale of goods "was carrying on and where he (Donowa) had given "no provocation and was conducting himself peace- "ably." It appeared that this complaint had regard to a transaction which had taken place a year and a half before, which rendered it somewhat late and stale, as a ground for an action or prosecution. Donowa however, begged "to leave it with the Commissioners, to shew

ANTIGUA.

COMPLAINTS.

" the want of adequate protection under the existing " system, for persons of his unfortunate description."

The magistrates, to whom Donowa had made application, stated their reasons for declining to proceed with the case. " On his own shewing, Donowa was in the " wrong: he had forced himself, improperly, into a pri- " vate room; and it was there, he alleged, the assault " took place, and not in the tent; the auction" (a fact which Mr. Donowa suppressed before the Commissioners) " taking place in a temporary room erected *without*, " and that alone, being public, and no person justified " in entering without permission of the owner, into the " private store. Their reason then (not for declining to " act, but for refusing to go further,) was simply, that " the complainant admitted that the auction was held " *without*, in the temporary room; the merchant, in " whose store the goods were deposited, having suffered " so much before, from depredations committed by per- " sons going professedly, to view the articles before the " sale, that he raised a tent without, and admitted none " but those of whom he had some personal knowledge, " within the store; which he retained as he had a right " to do, as private. In short, Donowa did not make out " a case."

The gist of the question was, whether the *locus in quo* were public or private? If the store was to be considered private, Donowa was confessedly, dealt with in due form and procedure of law (*molliter manus imposuit;*) if public, (as an auction room must be held to be,) Donowa was improperly and unjustifiably expelled the room. But is it not decisive of the case that the auction was not in the store?

PARTICULAR OFFICERS.

JUDGES.

The presiding judge, in every court of this island, is paid by fees. The chief justice has no salary. The fees received by the chief justice, upon an averrge of ten years, do not exceed 200*l.* sterling, per annum. The tenure of office of the judges, is *during pleasure;* they do not seem to be punishable for misconduct, otherwise than by degradation. It is not required that they

ANTIGUA.

PARTICULAR OFFICERS.

ATTORNEY- and SOLICITOR-GENERAL.

KING'S COUNSEL.

BARRISTERS

should be barristers or have gone through any previous course of legal study, as a qualification for the office.

Besides His Majesty's attorney and solicitor-general, several other members of the bar have been admitted to the rank of King's counsel in this island. Persons admitted to the bar in the court of Common Pleas, practise afterwards, as a matter of course, in all the courts. No one is entitled to admission, under the existing rules, who has not been called to the bar in England, or kept a sufficient number of terms at one of the inns of court, to entitle him to admission there. This qualification was formerly unnecessary; several gentlemen, therefore, who are now practising, have not been called to the bar in England.

SOLICITORS and ATTORNEYS.

All barristers, in this island act also, as solicitors and attorneys. It is admitted not to be desirable, that these distinct branches of the profession should be all followed by the same persons; but it is said, that the business of the court is not sufficiently lucrative, or extensive, to allow of separate practice in any one of them.

PROVOST MARSHAL.

The number of commitments to jail, in criminal cases, in this island, presents an average of *three* in each year, for the last *eleven* years; the books for the previous years not being in the marshal's office. The total number of persons executed within the last *eleven* years, is *fourteen;* being, on an average, more than one for each year.

No instance has occurred, in this island, of the jail having been full, for many years; yet, with the exception of the cage, where vagrants are locked up for the night only, the jail is the sole place of confinement in this island.

The jail of Antigua is liable to one very serious objection, (*viz.*) its situation in the centre of the town. It is commodious, and very airy; every apartment having some (one or more) windows to the east, the quarter from which the trade wind generally blows. It is, moreover, always kept in perfect repair, and consists of long buildings, two stories in height, with broad galleries to

ANTIGUA.

PARTICULAR OFFICERS.

the west, which keep off the heat of the sun, and admit of the prisoners taking exercise. In the inclosed yard or area of the prison, is a range of rooms, of one story only, called the dungeons from being of greater strength and security than the other building; and this also, has windows open to the east. In the yard are large cisterns of drinking water, and a well, or it is said, but very improbably in this island, spring of water, for washing clothes; yet, with all these advantages, I am compelled to state, that this place was spoken of, as being at all times, very filthy. There are also a kitchen, oven, and other offices.

Debtors are separated from criminals and occupy the upper story of the jail, where the apartments are large and airy and the doors seldom closed, except at night, so that their friends can visit them during the day. Men and women are invariably divided from each other. Persons committed for serious offences, are confined in the dungeons; those accused of more trifling delinquencies, are kept in the jail. Medical attendance of the highest professional ability, is secured in all cases which require it, and the charge for it borne by the island treasury.

White and free coloured prisoners are allowed 1*s.* each, *per diem.* Slaves are allowed 1*s.* 1½*d.*, being 1½*d.* more than is allowed to free persons; from the consideration of slaves having fewer resources *aliunde.* Some of the prisoners in this jail, employ themselves in working at their trades, as shoemakers and tailors; some in manufacturing coarse straw hats, an employ of easy acquirement, and the article of ready sale. A committee of the legislature is appointed for the superintendence of the jail, and the arrangements do them credit.

The cage is a building near the Court-house, also in a very public situation; consisting of one large inclosed room, and one other, fronting and open to the street, secured only by railing, so as to admit a perfect view of any persons confined there. In it are confined all slaves apprehended by the police, wandering about at the dead of night; these vagrants are kept in the cage for the night only, and the following day are either taken

ANTIGUA.

PARTICULAR OFFICERS.

away by their owners, or carried before a magistrate, to be dealt with according to law.

Slaves are publicly whipped in this island, only by the direction and under the warrant of a magistrate, and with a cat-o'-nine-tails. The public whipper is an officer under the particular appointment of the governor.

"A magistrate," said the provost-marshal, "considers "himself imperatively called upon, beyond almost any "other duty, to pay immediate attention to the redress "or protection of a slave, for which the Amelioration "Act affords him full power and authority."

JUSTICE OF PEACE.

The duties of a justice of the peace in this island, are, according to the very accurate answers of Mr. Lee, "to "hear and investigate crimes and offences of all kinds, "whether committed by whites, free people of colour, or "slaves; to commit the parties in felonies; to bind over "whites and free persons in recognizances to the Grand "Sessions in misdemeanours; and with respect to slaves, "to punish them for offences within the benefit of clergy, "as well as to commit them for trial, in offences which "are excluded from the benefit of clergy. Magistrates "also exercise jurisdiction over slaves, in murder, rape, "and burglary; and act in a variety of cases, according "to the laws of the island."

Information is "invariably received upon oath, except "with regard to slaves, and then never."

The justices are part of the court of Grand Sessions, and are generally punctual in attendance.

The same proceedings take place against slaves, before the justices, as against white or free persons, except the testimony of slaves not being upon oath.

Offences against the public peace are said to be numerous.

A justice of the peace in this island, would certainly entertain a complaint made by a slave of ill treatment by his master; "to refuse, would be a great dereliction "of duty."

In offences, which would be bailable when committed by whites or free persons of colour, slaves are punishable by the magistrates.

ANTIGUA.

PARTICULAR OFFICERS.

"Manumission questions often arise before magistrates "in the course of some investigation, on persons being "produced as witnesses who are objected to as slaves. "In such cases, the party who is objected to, is required "to state or prove, in what manner he claims or is en-"titled to his freedom, whether by deed, will, or birth; "and if proof is produced of the party's having been in "a state of freedom for several years, the magistrate has "considered such proof *primâ facie* evidence of freedom, "and admitted it, unless evidence to the contrary ap-"peared."

CORONER.

There is one coroner in the island of Antigua, who is allowed a salary from the public treasury of the island, of 600*l.* currency. No qualification by estate or personal property, is required in a person who acts as coroner. The coroner in this island, is guided in the performance of his duties by certain local laws. The Amelioration Act provides for and regulates the taking inquests, in cases of slaves.

The coroner obtains information of the cases in which inquests are to be taken, from the proprietor, attorney, or manager, and in some instances, from the constable and police officer; he has never received such information from the negroes. The coroner of Antigua has no reason whatever to think that there have been any cases of death by severity, of which he has not received information. He never, but in one instance, held an inquest upon a slave killed by the severity of an owner, which was the case of a free black woman, named Penny, for killing her female slave; but never for an offence committed by a person acting under the authority of a master.

The coroner confines his summons to "good and sufficient persons to serve;" in almost every case it would be impossible to procure a sufficient number of *freeholders*. In cases of slaves six persons are summoned, "from which a jury of not less than *three*, is required by "the Melioration Act, to be chosen." The coroner in general, "takes as many of the six as attend," and those who do not attend are fined.

ANTIGUA.

PARTICULAR OFFICERS.

It has sometimes been found necessary to adjourn, for other witnesses to attend to be examined; and in such cases the persons of the accused have been given in charge of a constable or police officer.

WRONGS WITHOUT REDRESS.

The Act of the Island, No. 636, admits that the provisions of the Amelioration Act have not been complied with; "no returns made, and no oaths taken;" and substitutes for those ineffectual provisions, the appointment of magistrates and vestries in each parish, to act as councils for the protection of slaves. Except as regards the magistrates, who are in general, men of honour and integrity, for many of whom I conceived from my observation of their conduct, a very high and sincere respect, there is reason to believe that the substituted provisions of No. 636, are equally disregarded with the directions of the former Act. At the same time I would add, that the Commissioners remarked a very decided superiority in the mulatto and negro character in this island. I certainly believe the treatment of slaves to be nowhere so generally humane, and so laudably attentive to their religious instruction and intellectual and moral improvement.

# MONTSERRAT.

MONTSERRAT.

HIS Majesty's Commissioners landed at Montserrat on the 10th day of October, 1823, where they were kindly received by the president and chief justice, and entered immediately upon the perusal of the laws of the island. These are contained in one printed, and two manuscript volumes, in folio. Of these the principal are:—

LAWS.

No. 1. An Act passed in 1668, declaring the *former grant of the duty of four and a half per cent, lost and null, within this island.* The preamble states, that the former grant was destroyed by the French, "and so become "void and null; and the same is hereby declared null "and void accordingly."

No. 3. *An Act for new granting and confirming the duty or custom of four and a half per cent.* It is said, I know not on what authority, that the first grant limited the uses to the service of the islands: "hence the pre-"tence, that the French invasion had destroyed it, in "order to get another passed, which should not contain "any limitations or restrictions."

No. 4. An Act which on like grounds, condemns as forfeit, all the lands in the island; "*the island having "been fully subdued, notwithstanding all resistance pos-*

MONTSERRAT. — LAWS.

"*sible was made by the inhabitants, so that the island is* "*become lost unto his said Majesty King Charles the* "*Second, &c.;*" it is therefore enacted, that *all the proprietors, their heirs, executors, &c., have lost all and every part and parcel of their respective lands, to his said Majesty.*

No. 5. An Act which re-invests the proprietors, but with some exceptions; and in certain instances annexing conditions.

No. 6. *An Act for the raising a maintenance for a preaching minister.* It is said to be the *true intent and meaning of this Act, that the minister, for whom it makes provision, shall not deny the baptizing of any infants, born of any of the inhabitants of the island, without demanding any payment, &c. nor churching women, nor demand more than an appointed value for marrying; neither shall any such minister deny the burying of any of the inhabitants of this island, upon request, &c. without demanding, &c.;* yet it was stated by the coroner, as will be seen in his examination, that in the case of slaves, who are certainly inhabitants of the island, no funeral "service is performed "by the clergyman of the established church."

No. 11. *An Act against opprobrious language;* which, it says, *if not duly prevented, may overshadow the good government and administers of justice in this island, with the staple clouds of reproach and infamy.* The terms prohibited, (the use of which too it may be observed, will make a man a mutineer,) are TORY, ENGLISH, IRISH, or SCOTCH DOG, &c.

Of Acts passed before the war, and which appear to have been revived and continued, are:—

No. 1. *An Act for the observation of the Lord's day.*

No. 2. *An Act, by which it is accorded, and thought fit to be established, that all merchants and dealers, in future, with this island, may have and enjoy, from time to time, the liberty of free trade, reserving to the governor the privilege of twenty-four hours, for his* PARTICULAR *with the inhabitants.* (Qy. *what?*)

No. 7. *An Act for the marshal's attending the governor once in every twenty-four hours, to know his pleasure.*

No. 8. *An Act against going through fields of cane with lighted pipes.* MONTSERRAT. — LAWS.

No. 29. *An Act, allowing marriages to be contracted before justices of the peace:* but a later Act, passed in 1739, No. 120, for preventing clandestine marriages in this island, requires all marriages to be by banns or licence.

No. 33. *An Act for the making restitution for cattle stolen by negroes; and licences for tap houses.*

The owner whose slaves are convicted of thieving, shall pay,

For every cow stolen, 800lbs. of sugar:

For every assi-negro, 400lbs:

For every beast, fit for drawing in the mill, or cart, 1,000lbs.

What an assi-negro is, nowhere appears; but there seems reason to believe, that negro is added, to denote an inferiority in the species; as the penalty for an assi-negro is much lower than that, in the case of a beast fit for drawing in the mill. If this notion be correct, it affords a melancholy proof of the dreadful debasement of the blacks and coloured population at this period; and furnishes a scale, by which to estimate the degree of moral improvement effected since.

No. 36. *An Act to restrain the insolence of slaves, and for preventing them from committing any outrages; as also for the better ordering such slaves.* Of this Act, and three others, his Majesty in council, 31st December, 1696, was graciously pleased to declare his approbation; and the said laws were thereby confirmed, finally enacted, and ratified accordingly. Nos. 35 to 38.

Cl. 1. *Negroes stealing to the value of* 12*s.* (6*s.* sterling,) *shall suffer death; the value not amounting to* 12*d.* *current money, such negro shall only suffer a severe whipping, and have both his ears cut off, for the first time; but for the second offence, shall suffer death, in the form aforesaid.*

Cl. 2. *Negroes stealing provisions, above forty feet from the common path, may be shot.*

Cl. 4. " *For flesh of any sort that shall be found, the*

MONTSERRAT. LAWS.

"*negro in whose house it was taken, unless he or she can*
"*make it plainly appear they came by it honestly, shall*
"*undergo a whipping, and have one of their ears cut off.*"

Cl. 13. *Any slave that shall absent himself three months, and is afterwards taken, shall suffer death.*

This Act is nowhere stated to be repealed: it may perhaps, be considered as superseded by the Melioration Act of the Leeward Islands.

No. 47. *An Act, empowering justices of the peace to decide differences not exceeding* 6*l.*

No. 54. *An Act for quieting possessions, and for the better securing and confirming the titles to lands, in this island.*

Persons seised in fee, and for ten years in peaceable possession, are declared *the lawful and rightful proprietors*, except in excepted cases of femes covert, infants, &c.

No. 76. An Act, for the exempting the several members of the council and assembly, and other persons from arrest, on public days.

No. 86. An Act for holding a court of Grand Sessions.

No. 89. An Act, establishing a court of King's Bench and Common Pleas, and a court of Error, &c.

Cl. 5. Any *two* justices may hear and try all general issues.

Cl. 7. In actions of account, and upon bills, bonds and assumpsits, the plaintiff need not file any declaration. Nail-service is allowed.

Cl. 8. Suits under 10*l.* may be tried without a jury.

Cl. 36. Fees settled; and cl. 37. Officers shall be obliged to hang up, in their offices, a table of the said fees, for public view.

No. 90. A statute of limitations.

No. 121. An Act for the better recovery of debts from judges, &c.

No. 135. Ticket Act.

No. 143. *An Act for the performance of specific agreements;* giving merchants interest, factorage, &c.; and providing that they shall be paid in money.

No. 147. *An Act for prevention of frauds and perjuries.*

No. 151. *An Act for the public registering of all deeds, conveyances, and wills, &c.*

Every leaf of the register book is *required to be signed by the chief justice, or in case of his sickness, by two other justices.*

No. 185. *An Act for constituting a court of Chancery, to be held in and for this island.*

The court is to consist of *the commander-in-chief, and five members of the council.* No member of council, who is a judge of the common-law court, shall sit, *if the cause has been determined first in his court.* This is a confirmed Act.

No. 193. *An Act for the amendment of the law, and advancement of justice.* A statute of jeofails.

No. 222. *An Act to alter, amend, and explain the Act for constituting the court of Chancery.* Where five disinterested members cannot be found, three or four of the council shall make a court.

No. 223. An Act to alter, amend, and explain the Court Act. This Act relates to executions, and the duties of the marshal.

## MANUSCRIPT ACTS.

These were very numerous; the material ones are:—

1800. *An Act to amend the Act for the performance of specific agreements.* On actions brought for goods and merchandizes, expressly sold for gold and silver money, the jury shall find a verdict for gold and silver money, and judgment shall be entered accordingly.

1800. *An Act constituting a Court Merchant for transient traders.*

1819. *An Act for the punishment of obeah.*

1821. *An Act adopting Lord Ellenborough's Act.*

1822. *An Act for the trial of slaves, accused of criminal matters or offences, by jury.*

MONTSERRAT.

LAWS.

1823. *An Act to aid and assist the magistrates; establishing a police and nightly watch, as also a criminal gang, in the island of Montserrat.*

---

COURTS.

I regret that it is not in my power to enumerate the courts of judicature in this island; no answers having been received to the questions addressed by the Commissioners to the chief justice and the resident crown lawyer. It should be observed in explanation, and may, perhaps, be accepted as an apology for the omission, that the chief justice is not a lawyer by profession, but a private gentleman of considerable fortune, and equal liberality, devoting a portion only (however considerable) of his time, to services of public utility. So, the resident crown officer in this island, is not attorney-general; but only one of His Majesty's counsel, without salary or other advantages, derived from the situation. Upon certain points, both these gentlemen *did* afford the Commissioners the information they required; and the president of the council and the chief justice were not only unremitting in their attentions during our stay, but unreserved in their communications of any facts which occurred to them as likely to be useful, and to assist us in our inquiries.

## COURT OF CHANCERY.

A court of Chancery appears to have been constituted by No. 185, of the laws of Monsterrat, and amended by No. 222. By the former Act, the governor or president (Montserrat being a dependency of Antigua, and under the government of the captain-general, though usually administered by the president of the council) and FIVE members of the council, composed a court. By

MONTSERRAT.

No. 222, in case of the governor or president being a party to a suit, the next senior member of council is appointed to preside; and, for want of five disinterested persons to act as judges, three or four members of council are allowed (with the commander-in-chief) to form a court.

Minutes, Oct. 11, 1823.

The president informed us, that the " court of Chan- " cery in this island, had been several times presented " as a nuisance; but that, with the exception of one " sitting this summer, he thought no business had been " transacted in it, for seven or eight years." He added, that " it ought not be held in the island, for it was im- " possible, out of so small a society, to get judges in any " case, unconnected with the parties."

The chief justice said, " there was formerly (about " fifteen or sixteen years ago) great dissatisfaction with " the court of Chancery in this island, and, he believed, " not without reason. He feared there were some un- " righteous decisions; certainly there was no uniformity " in their judgments; and there was thought to be in- " fluence and favour; and whether this were true or not, " it was not desirable to have it suspected."

The King's counsel said, " There has been no sitting " in Chancery since 1815. There was NO suit depending " lately; now there is ONE."

There is a Master in Chancery here.

| | £ | s. | d. |
|---|---|---|---|
| A barrister's fee, for attending before him, is | 3 | 6 | 0 |
| The Master's fee, for *his* attendance, is . | 1 | 10 | 4 |
| Every court of Chancery costs . . . | 20 | 0 | 0 |
| The fee to the Chancellor is . . . | 5 | 8 | 0 |

" And this is paid down immediately," said the King's counsel; adding, " surely it and counsel's fees ought to " be paid out of the estate, before assets are wasted."

The retaining fee of counsel in a suit, (50*l.* sterling,) is the same here, as in Antigua. " You have nothing," proceeded the King's counsel, " with a brief, or rather " no brief, but are paid for arguments and for motions."

KING'S BENCH and COMMON PLEAS.

## COURT OF KING'S BENCH AND COMMON PLEAS.

The Act of the island, No. 89, creates a court of King's Bench and Common Pleas, with an establishment of one chief justice and four assistant judges, "to "try causes according to the laws and usage of Great "Britain, and the laws and usage of the island."

"In the courts of law too," said the worthy old president, after speaking of the court of Chancery, "it "is at all times difficult to get juries at all; and when "there is a matter of any interest, and any feeling ex- "cited, quite impossible to have a matter dispassionately "considered."

Minutes, Oct. 13, 1823.

A person of the name of Sweney, a debtor in the jail of the island, "complained to His Majesty's Commis- "sioners, that though he had property, which, by the "laws of the island, ought to be levied upon *before the* "PERSON, yet that he had been taken in execution by "the marshal." It did not appear that the complainant had pointed out the property to the marshal, either before or since he was taken in execution; and this the Commissioners thought he was bound to do, before he was entitled to complain.

William Bell preferred a similar complaint.

Minutes, Oct. 18, 1823.

Mr. Mac Alpine complained, that "in a certain case, "he had been improperly nonsuited, upon a point "of law." It appeared that the court was divided in opinion, two to one; and the chief justice, who was alone, seemed to be right. Mr. Mac Alpine was advised to bring another action.

## COURT MERCHANT.

A Court Merchant for transient traders, was established so late as the year 1800.

## COURT OF ERROR.

The chief justice mentioned, in illustration of the vexatious proceedings in this court, a case in which he was personally interested, where justice was inexcusably delayed, and nearly frustrated, and great expense occasioned. A sufficient number of members of council to form a court, *would* never be collected; and after five successive and fruitless attempts, at a cost of nearly 20*l.* each experiment, a court was only at last procured, under a threat of exposure; when however justice, though tardily, was administered.

---

There is also a COURT OF VICE-ADMIRALTY; and it seems, under Clause 8, of the Court Act, a COURT OF COMPLAINTS in this island, or, at least, a jurisdiction for the recovery of small debts.

# CRIMINAL COURTS.

## COURT OF GRAND SESSIONS.

This court was established under an Act of the Island, No. 86; which Act however, provides only for *one* jail delivery in the year.

Minutes, Oct. 14, 1823.

A deputation from the free people of colour in this island, waited upon the Commissioners, to make a representation of several cases, in which they conceived " that an " equal measure of justice had not been dealt out to " them, and to the whites." There is no complaint, they said, " of the laws, but of the irregular and par- " tial administration of them, and of their being some- " times entirely set aside and disregarded in our case. " There are no laws that militate against our interests; " we are not excluded from any situation by law, but " we are in practice. As freeholders, we are entitled " to vote at elections; but the House of Assembly passed " a resolution, that our vote should not be taken. A " coloured man was appointed, in England, to a situa- " tion in our custom-house; but when he came out, they " refused to administer the oaths to him: another, was " regularly named for constable; but though every way " qualified, he was rejected, because he was a man of " colour.

" Imprisonment and fine have been inflicted upon free " persons of colour, by a court, or by a bench of magis- " trates, without conviction by a jury, and when the pro- " secutor refused to proceed."

Complaints.

The deputation named " *three* cases, which they had " selected to bring before the Commissioners: that of " Samuel Lee Irish; of Thomas Duberly; and the

MONTSERRAT.

COMPLAINTS.

"case of Allis, the captain of a small vessel, then gone "to Antigua.

"Irish's case was one, they admitted, which took place "in troubled times, immediately after the insurrection "at Barbados, when a military force was first sent to "this island; and the alarm and agitation which pre- "vailed, might occasion, and almost excuse, under the "policital circumstances of the colonies, the exercise of "a vigour beyond the law. The complainants there- "fore, only wished it to be noticed, to mark the devia- "tion from the course fit to be pursued, (as pointed out "by law), and to prevent a recurrence of any unwar- "rantable proceedings of a similar kind." Such was the temperate tone—such the spirit (superior to insult) of candor and moderation, in which the charge was preferred, in this case of Samuel Lee Irish: a case in which no depositions were taken; sufficient bail was refused; and a sentence of imprisonment for thirty days, was passed (for an alleged assault upon an officer in the army), without any regular conviction of the accused. Let the free people of colour in all the islands, continue to display this true elevation of feeling—this peaceable wisdom "from above," and they will not only establish, incontestably, their fitness for the situations from which they are excluded, but must eventually, conciliate the esteem and confidence of their countrymen, whose prejudices they will have insensibly subdued.

Upon inquiry we found, that when the House of Assembly of Montserrat passed certain extraordinary resolutions in violation of the existing law, (to prevent returning officers taking the votes of qualified persons of colour), they admitted it to be contrary to their own statutes; but declared, that it was agreeable to the custom of the island, "that venerable unwritten law."

In Allis's case, the charge was, "that the prosecutor "refusing to act, the court took upon itself to sentence "the defendant to fine and imprisonment, without his "being found guilty by a jury." The complaint was supported by the evidence of the defendant, who stated that

MONTSERRAT.

COMPLAINTS.

the offence of which he was accused, was a misdemeanor, and that it was not a case for a summary conviction.

In Duberley's case, it was represented, that the defendant was "charged with an assault upon a white "man; and a Bench warrant issued for his apprehen-"sion. He was not taken, but shortly afterwards he "delivered himself up, and was bound over to appear "and take his trial." A reward had been offered for his apprehension; and though he surrendered himself, the Committee withheld 40*l.* due to him "from the public "for work done, to pay, as was avowed, the expenses "of the prosecution and the reward offered for his ap-"prehension."

These cases, when mentioned by the Commissioners, were not attempted to be answered; but were referred to panic and the agitation of the public mind at the period of their occurrence, when civil justice was, by common consent, for a short time suspended. The complainants themselves added, that "since the passing of "the Police Act, such cases have not occurred." The president said, "within the two last years, there has "great good resulted from—1st, the Police Act; and "2dly. The unwearied exertions of the Wesleyan Me-"thodist minister, who has established schools, and in-"structed the adult slaves, as well as children. The "slaves in this island are peaceable and well disposed, "but are in a very uninstructed and barbarous state."

Minutes,

General Complaint.

It was further generally complained in this island, that the fees of of all the courts are such as to deter persons from entering them.

SLAVE TRIALS.

A Manuscript Act passed in 1822, provides for the trial of slaves, accused of criminal matters or offences, by jury.

The crown lawyer said, there had been two trials since the Act.

The president said, "In the criminal court a negro "had been lately sentenced to suffer death, for stealing a "goat; but the punishment was commuted for hard la-"bour, in the street gang. Stealing above the value of

" 12*d.* currency, was still," the president believed, " a " capital offence." MONTSERRAT.

SLAVE TRIALS.

O'Garra, a black man, complained to the Commissioners, that he was improperly detained in slavery. He had paid his mistress (his master's widow) 200*l.* for his manumission, which she had never executed. Same day, Daly, a black man, complained that his manumission was improperly withheld. Minutes, Oct. 15, 1823.

The Commissioners investigated the cases of Daly and O'Garra, respectively. In both instances, there was stated to be a deficiency of assets to pay the debts. In the former, complainant's master, who had been dead nineteen years, by his will emancipated the mother and five children, of whom he was one; the mother had been suffered to make a will; the executor made it for her. Since the Registry Acts, the children had been recorded as slaves, but no service had ever been claimed of them, or earnings required. Oct. 16, 1823.

The executor said, that " it was so; they were pitied; " and nothing was exacted of them; but they could not " be manumitted, without the consent of the mortgagees " and creditors." In the latter case (O'Garra's) the property was devised subject to the payment of the debts and legacies. The widow clearly appeared to have no authority to manumit the slaves; and, as she must have known her situation at the time, acted most unjustifiably in receiving the poor slave's money; especially when it is considered, that under the existing law, he could not sue or prosecute her, or even prove the fact of payment by his oath.

PARTICULAR OFFICERS.

PROVOST MARSHAL.

In this island the deputy provost-marshal was unable to state the number of commitments to jail in criminal cases in each year, " as no records are kept in his office." A committee from the council and assembly, is appointed annually, to inspect the public accounts, and the commitments are laid before the committee, and torn up after inspection. From the best information the provost-marshal could obtain, there had been but four capital convicts executed for the last twenty years.

The places of confinement in this island are the jail,

MONTSERRAT.

PARTICULAR OFFICERS.

and a room on the ground floor of the same building, over which a police officer resides. There is no cage; but the room before mentioned is under the charge of the head of police. The jail is "not trust-worthy;" and "is, in every respect, in very bad condition." There is no separation of debtors from criminals, or men from women; but there is a division of free persons from slaves. The number of persons in confinement, however, has seldom exceeded from THREE to FOUR at a time, during the last two years.

The marshal is allowed "by the country, 9*d.* per day "for slaves, and 18*d.* for free people, which he pays a "person for feeding them."

Three slaves tried in 1821, for stealing the custom-house chest, were sentenced to transportation. Convicts are sent "to any of the islands."

The jail is not superintended, or even visited, by magistrates.

A prisoner who is acquitted, is instantly set at large; the fee is charged to the public. The expense of prosecutions of slaves, and of free persons who are acquitted, is borne by the country; but persons found guilty of assaults, pay for the prosecution.

Magistrates sit weekly, to investigate complaints by or against slaves.

There is a criminal gang in this island, which is under the direction of the police office, and is employed in sweeping the streets.

JUSTICE OF THE PEACE.

The senior justice of the peace informed us, that information is always given upon oath in this island, except in cases where a slave complains against a free person. Depositions are not taken, either in felonies or misdemeanors; and recognizances are seldom entered into.

By the Act constituting the court of Sessions, all magistrates are required to attend. The proceedings on the trial of slaves for capital offences, are the same as in the case of a free person.

Justices exercise a summary jurisdiction in civil matters in this island in all cases where the debt does not

MONTSERRAT.

PARTICULAR OFFICERS.

exceed 10*l.* Appeals are allowed, where the sum exceeds 3*l.* currency.

A great many trifling offences against the public peace have been committed in this island; but the present Police Act is said to be useful and effective.

The only case in which the practice of granting search warrants in this island, differs from the proceedings in England, is in the mode of searching negro houses for stolen goods, when no warrant is necessary; but the master, mistress, or overseer of the plantation must be present.

Justices here have jurisdiction in disputes as to seamen's wages.

Slaves are never bailed.

CORONER.

The coroners in this island complained heavily of the reduction of their fees, without any previous intimation; and at the period when their account became payable. "Before this reduction, the coroner's account amounted "annually, to upwards of 150*l.*; at present, it does not "exceed 40*l.* currency: its real value is above seven "guineas. This depreciation is owing to the article in "which the coroner is paid; he receives rum, at the "rate of 3*s.* 6*d.* per gallon, which is marketable at only "1*s.* 3*d.*" It was alleged, that this reduction was made in conformity to the Melioration Act; although, observes the coroner with some spleen, "this Act is in "other respects, unattended to in this island:" he excepts however, that part which relates to "inquests on "slaves."

Inquests on white and free people, are taken as in England; on slaves, in the manner the Melioration Act prescribes.

Information of sudden or violent deaths, is received from the owner, attorney, or manager; never in this island, from the slaves.

The examinant had acted as coroner for TEN years; and had in ONE instance, held an inquest on a slave, killed by severity. "The party, against whom the coro- "ner's jury returned a verdict, was regularly tried and "acquitted, in the court of King's Bench and Common "Pleas."

MONTSERRAT.

PARTICULAR OFFICERS.

Negroes sometimes are buried in coffins, sometimes not. No funeral service it is said, is performed by the clergyman of the established church.

The coroner has frequently attended "without meet-"ing a competent jury; in such cases no inquisition "could be taken, and he has reported the circumstance "to the court of King's Bench."

White and free people are sworn as witnesses before the coroner, but slaves are not. "In respect to taking "depositions in writing, it is sometimes done, when a "free person can give any account of the death of the "deceased; but the coroner has not been permitted to "take the evidence of slaves in writing. I received," continued he, "a note, some years ago, stating that a "negro had died the day before on M—— estate, and "that his death was occasioned by starvation; I issued "my precept to the marshal, to summon a jury; one was "formed, and as none but slaves were witnesses to the "treatment of the deceased, I took their testimony in "writing. From this it appeared, that the deceased had "been improperly neglected. I was anxious that the "matter should undergo further investigation; and I "therefore inclosed the substance of the inquisition, with "the doctor's report, and the testimony of the slaves, and "the note from the person who gave the information, to "the chief justice of the court of King's Bench and "Common Pleas, who laid them before his brother "judges. A majority of the court decided upon sup-"pressing" (*query rejected*) "the testimony of the slaves, "and refused to transmit them to a grand jury; conse-"quently no further inquiry took place. The honour-"able and reverend ———, one of the assistant judges "of the court, strongly reprobated my conduct in taking "the evidence of the slaves."

WRONGS WITHOUT REDRESS.

It will not I am sure, escape your Lordship's attention, in what a surprising manner (as the Report proceeds through the different islands) proofs constantly accumulate of the repeated failures of justice occasioned by the exclusion of slave testimony.

# N E V I S.

Nevis.

His Majesty's Commissioners embarked for the island of Nevis, on the 21st day of October, 1823. In landing from the vessel late at night, Mr. Maddock had the misfortune to break his right arm; and at Nevis in the month following, our secretary Mr. Clement, fell a victim to the fever of the country. The entire duties of the Commission consequently devolved upon Mr. Dwarris, for a considerable period, singly, and without assistance.

Laws.

Besides the general Acts of the Leeward Islands, published by order of the Lords Commissioners of Trade and Plantations, there is an edition of the Laws of Nevis, from 1664 to the middle of 1818, printed by the authority of the council and assembly of this island: but this edition is said to be inaccurate, "the press not "having been properly revised or corrected by regular "authority." The Acts, from May 1818 to the present time, remain in manuscript. By No. 31 of the General Acts of the Leeward Islands, the common law of England unaltered by Act of Parliament or Act of Assembly, is declared the certain rule, by which the rights and properties of the inhabitants of these islands ought to be

NEVIS.

LAWS.

determined. So, all Acts of Parliament applicable to the colony, antecedent to a certain period, are considered operative; "but," says the King's counsel, (whose answers will be found full of information, at once exact and comprehensive,) "THAT *certain period* does not appear to have been settled, by any judicial decision on "record. Possibly, the date may be fixed, soon after "the first settlement of the colony, in 1625, or the early "part of the seventeenth century."

Of these laws of Nevis, the principal are:—

No. 2. An Act for ascertaining lands; as also for affixing slaves, coppers, &c. to the freehold. *Lands, plantations, &c. are ascertained and made firm to the* (then) *present possessors respectively;* and this Act was confirmed February 8th, 1681.

No. 18. *An Act for making the negroes, coppers, mills and stills, of intestates' estates, chattels.*

Cl. 1. recites the provision in No. 2; but enacts, that if any person, having any estate, &c. shall die intestate, in such case slaves, coppers, &c. shall be chattels, and shall be parted, shared and divided as such, to and among deceased's children; with an option to the heir, of retaining them for seven years, maintaining and educating his brothers and sisters during that period, and afterwards paying their appraised value.

Cl. 6. This Act is expressly excepted out of the operation of that part of No. 31 of the Acts of the Leeward Islands, which make slaves, coppers, &c. freehold.

No. 31. *An Act for speedy payment of labourers hire,* gives authority to a justice of the peace to hear and determine such cases.

No. 32. *An Act for the relief of poor prisoners.* A very humane and excellent Act. *Whereas divers poor inhabitants of this island, have been imprisoned for their debts; and forasmuch as the prison fees alone, are sufficient to continue such in that restraint, whose liberties are necessary for the payment of their debts, and maintenance of themselves and family,* enacts that, *all such poor prisoners may, within eight days, by one judge and two of his assistants be put to work, if able, or be employed, &c. to the end the creditor or creditors of the prisoner or prisoners may in time be satisfied their just debts, and the said prisoner more easily enlarged, (the marshal being to take no more fees after the eight days are expired,) one moiety of such poor prisoner's hire to be paid to the creditor, and the other moiety towards the maintenance of such poor prisoner and his family.*

No. 33. *An Act for regulating the Coroner's office;* and appointing the fee for the coroners and chirurgeons that shall be commanded to inspect dead bodies.

Cl. 1. enacts, that the coroner shall execute his office, *pursuant and according to the laws and statutes of England.*

No. 82. *An Act for the good government of negroes, and other slaves, in this island.*

Cl. 2. Any one justice shall have power to issue his warrant and of inflicting corporal punishment for crimes not capital; but for felonies, and other capital crimes, it shall require *two* justices, at least, to hear try and determine the same; *at all which trials the evidence of* TWO *or more slaves shall be taken and deemed good and sufficient.*—Proviso, that the stealing of turkeys, fowls, any poultry or other small stock shall not be punished, in any slave, with the loss of life or limb; but any justice of the peace may cause him to be whipped, &c.

The requiring the evidence of two slaves at the least, is unusual, and therefore deserving notice. The greater part of the Act is conceived in a very mild and indulgent spirit, for the year 1717. By

Cl. 5. The wounding or maiming any white person, is declared felony in a slave; not treason.

No. 100. The Court Act of this island, intituled, *An Act for establishing the courts of King's Bench and Common Pleas, &c. &c.* with such powers as the judges of the two courts at Westminster respectively, have or exercise, *subject, nevertheless, to such jurisdiction, power, &c. as the court of King's Bench, at Westminster, hath usually had over all other courts in his Majesty's dominions, &c.* What this jurisdiction of the court of King's Bench in England

NEVIS. LAWS.

over the courts at Nevis may be, is not defined by the Act, and would, I fear, be unprofitable to inquire.

No. 111. *To amend, explain, and make more effectual the Act above cited, No.* 82.

Cl. 7. No slave shall suffer death, for stealing sheep, goats or hogs under the value of *five* pounds, current money. And a justice is empowered to award payment to be made by the owner of such offender, to the party whose sheep, goats, &c. were stolen, with costs.

No. 135. *An Act for holding a court of Sessions, once every year.*

Cl. 3. The justices of the court of King's Bench and Common Pleas are exempted from sitting in the court of Sessions, which is composed pretty vaguely, of "about "three justices of the peace."

No. 164. *Amending an Act to settle the secretary's fees, by making it necessary to record all deeds, conveyances and wills, and other incumbrances, and to prevent covinous and fraudulent dealings and transactions therein.*

Cl. 10. *All wills shall be registered within the space of three calendar months after the death of every respective devisor or testatrix dying within this island, or within the space of two years after the death, &c. upon the sea, or in any parts beyond the seas.*

No. 175. *An Act for the better securing mortgages, &c.*

Cl. 2. Mortgages are to be registered immediately, if executed in the island; if made in parts beyond seas, within twelve calendar months.

No. 196. *An Act to prevent the malicious burning of canes, buildings, &c.* Offenders upon conviction shall suffer death, without benefit of clergy. *Proviso, that no evidence of any free Indian, free mulatto, or free negro, shall be admitted on the trial of any white person, who shall or may be prosecuted by virtue of this Act.* This law continues in force: consequently no white man can be convicted of the crime of arson, unless his guilt can be clearly established by the testimony of white witnesses only.

Cl. 3. Slaves, who, *travelling in the highways, or other part, or wandering about the towns or plantations, with fire, lighted torches, smoking tobacco, or any other means whatever, shall burn, or attempt to burn, any canes, mansions, &c. &c.* being legally convicted thereof, shall suffer death, and their bodies be burned, or suspended on gibbets, according to the discretion of the judges.

Cl. 4. PROVISO; *in case it shall appear to the justices that the fire proceeded from accident, and without any malicious or mischievous intention, then the said justices shall not condemn to death the offender, but order him to be whipped.*

No. 246. *An Act for punishing with death, all negroes and coloured persons whatsoever, who shall practise what is called confu, or obeah doctor, or who shall take away, or attempt to take away the life, or injure the health, of any person or persons whatsoever.*

I am happy to find that this Act, so disgraceful to Nevis, is said by the King's counsel, to be "generally "reprobated," and that there has been "no instance "even of an accusation of a free person;" the Act extending to *all* negroes or coloured persons (but not to whites) who, *practising or pretending to practise obeah, possessing, keeping, preparing, advising or wilfully administering drugs, &c. in the practice of obeah, or otherwise; or injuring, or attempting to injure, the health or life of any person thereby; or in such practice, or otherwise, are declared felons, and shall suffer death for the same, and may be tried for those offences, before two justices of the peace, in a summary way.*

No. 249. *An Act to enable John Richardson, Esquire, to make sale of a certain parcel of land, with the buildings thereon erected, &c. to trustees therein named, for the use of the public of this island.*

Cl. 1. In trust for the *use, benefit, and advantage of the inhabitants of the said Island of Nevis, for a public hall or court-house, as well for the courts of justice, as for the council and assembly, to meet and sit in, and for other public uses and purposes, &c.* "There are two

NEVIS.

LAWS.

"public offices, for the preservation of papers," said the King's counsel, "the secretary's and the marshal's; and "the rooms are admirably calculated for the purpose, "being two wing's of the Court-house, and entirely of "masonry, except the doors and windows."

No. 268. *An Act for settling and regulating the trial of criminal slaves by jury.*

Cl. 2. Two justices constitute a court.

Cl. 4. Six reputable inhabitants (being whites) compose the jury.

Cl. 7. To all witnesses examined upon such trial, if whites or free people of colour, the oath therein contained, shall be administered.

Cl. 11. Notice of sentence of death shall be given to the commander-in-chief within thirty-six hours.

Cl. 14 and 15. Marshal and public secretary shall attend these trials, under penalties.

No. 270. *An Act for further supplying the want of fines and recoveries, &c.*

No. 271. *An Act to repeal an Act, intituled, an Act to regulate the manumission of slaves.*

No. 282. *An Act for altering and amending the tables or docquets, of fees to be taken by the chief justice, secretary, and marshal.*

No. 284. *An Act for establishing a registry of negro and other slaves, in the island of Nevis.*

No. 288. *An Act further to extend the provisions of a certain Act of the general council and assembly of the Leeward Islands, intituled, "An Act more effectually to "provide for the support, and extend certain regulations "for the protection of slaves; to promote and encourage "their increase, and generally to ameliorate their con-"dition."*

The 26th clause of the Amelioration Act of the Leeward Islands, provided, that no owner should *restrain* or *prohibit* slaves from receiving religious instruction or baptism; the present Act directs, that all owners, &c. shall endeavour to *fit them for baptism*, and, as soon as conveniently may be, *cause them to be baptized.*

Cl. 2. No shop shall be kept open on the sabbath day.

Cl. 3. No mills shall be worked between eight o'clock on Saturday night, and five o'clock on Monday morning.

Cl. 15. of the Melioration Act, after pointing out the mode of prosecuting (at the grand sessions,) and punishing (by fine or imprisonment, or both,) persons cruelly whipping and maltreating slaves, empowers the justices, if they deem it necessary for the further protection of the slave, to order the marshal to sell such slave at public outcry: but

Cl. 4. of the Nevis Act, authorizes the justices to declare such slave *free, and discharged from all manner of servitude;* and directs the fine paid by the owner, to be appropriated to the slave's future maintenance.

Cl. 5. No slave shall receive more than ten lashes, unless the owner, attorney, or manager is present, and in that case no more than *thirty-nine,* under penalties.

Cl. 6. On groundless complaints, the magistrate may give up the informer's name, that the injured party may seek redress at law, &c.

## MANUSCRIPT ACTS.

January 4th, 1820. *An Act for rendering justices of the peace more safe in the execution of their office, and for indemnifying constables and others acting in obedience to their warrants, adopts the provisions of the statute* 24 Geo. 2. c. 44.

January 4th, 1820. An Act resembling Lord Ellenborough's Act.

January 8th, 1820. *An Act to alter and amend an Act for regulating the trial of criminal slaves by jury, &c.*

Cl. 2. Slaves apprehended on a charge of felony, may be released, *on bail* engaging for their appearance to stand their trial on any day within ten days.

Cl. 6. Admits by-standers in case of default of jurors, and challenge for cause.

NEVIS.

LAWS.

Cl. 8. *To all witnesses examined, if whites or free people of colour, or other persons, being slaves, who shall appear to be sensible of the nature and religious obligation of an oath, the same oath shall be administered, as would in similar cases be administered to witnesses in the court of King's Bench and Common Pleas, of this island.*

Dec. 10, 1822. *An Act for the relief of the negro population of the island of Nevis.*

After a melancholy recital in the preamble, of the distressed state of the greater number of the planters of this island, it is enacted, that *any debt or demand, accruing by virtue of any contract or agreement made in writing, or any bill of exchange, drawn by any owner, renter, possessor, &c. or, in his absence, by his attorney, agent, &c. for the purchase of flour, grain of any kind, corn, meal, fish, or any other negro provisions* ONLY, *(such debt or demand, or bill of exchange, being certified, as therein directed), shall be deemed and taken the first lien or charge upon the plantation, and also on the ensuing crops of the same.*

Cl. 2. contains a proviso, that a seller shall not be obliged to receive produce. A committee is appointed to buy 3,000*l.* sterling, worth of negro provisions to be sold to planters, receiving in payment, bills of exchange, certified as pointed out, stating for what purpose they were drawn and that they are to be prior liens. An oath is exacted that the bills are drawn only for slaves' provisions; and if this statement be false, taking the oath is made perjury. So *forgery may be committed of the certificate, &c.*

## COURTS.

ENUMERATION OF.

The courts for the administration of Civil Justice in this island are, the court of Chancery, the court of Ordinary, the court of Error, the court of King's Bench and Common Pleas, and the court of Vice-Admiralty; but the court of King's Bench and Common Pleas, and the court of Error only, are established by the laws of the island.

NEVIS.

COURTS.

The courts for the administration of criminal justice are, the court of King's Bench and Common Pleas, the court of Error (according to the classification of the King's counsel), the court of Sessions, the court of Justices of the Peace, the Slave Court, the courts of Oyer and Terminer and general Gaol Delivery, the court of Vice-Admiralty, and the Commission court for the trial of pirates. The first five are established by laws of the island; the succeeding three are derived mediately (*i. e.* through the captain-general) the last immediately from the King.

## COURT OF CHANCERY.

The court of Chancery, in this island, derives its authority entirely from the King's authority and instructions to the captain-general, there being no local law whatsoever, upon the subject. The captain-general is sole chancellor, and holds a court *pro re natâ*, whenever he may be within his government; but there has been very little chancery business in this island for the last fifty years.

There are about fifty-three rules of practice of this court, not recorded in the registry of the court or contained in any printed or manuscript book accessible to the profession at large.

There is one Master in Chancery, appointed by the captain-general, and he is examiner also. He does not give any security.

Costs in this island are taxed by the Master, who is governed by a docket established upwards of thirty years ago.

Estates are appraised previous to a sale in the Master's office; "perhaps never fetch the appraisement."

No fee is given with the brief, the solicitor being most commonly the counsel, or one of the counsel.

The expense of the holding of a court of Chancery, is £17 7*s.* 8*d.*

NEVIS.

CHANCERY.

The Master's per centage on moneys paid and received by him is two and a half per cent.

The only improvements suggested in this court, are, that "the office of chancellor should be distinct from "that of captain-general, and exercised by a sound law-"yer; the expenses of a suit diminished, and the delay "in proceedings, and in appeals especially, obviated, if "practicable."

## COURT OF KING'S BENCH AND COMMON PLEAS.

In this court are blended the separate jurisdictions of the courts of King's Bench and Common Pleas in England.

The court derives its authority from the Court Act, No. 100.

The first Tuesday in the months of March, April, May, June, July and August, are termed court days; and each meeting of the court is analogous to a term in England.

The court has actually sat for the dispatch of business, on an average of the last seven years, ten days in each year.

There are about seventeen rules of this court, but there is no printed or manuscript book descriptive of them. The Commissioners procured, with difficulty, a *copy of an abstract.*

In ordinary cases, where no means of delay are used by a defendant, if an action be entered ten days before the first Tuesday in any of the court months, except August, judgment may be obtained in forty or forty-one days. But in what time, if the defendant uses every method of delay? inquired the Commissioners. "Where "the object is important and the defendants have the "command of money," said the King's counsel, "it may "be indefinite and is incalculable."

By the practice of the court here, writs to arrest the

body are sued out as preparative to, but never as incipient of, an action, nor after it has commenced.

NEVIS.

KING'S BENCH and COMMON PLEAS.

Service of a declaration may be, according to the practice admitted by the courts, by affixing a copy at the door of the Court-house.

The power of arrest is not given, or restrained, or regulated by any local law; yet in practice, a party, not being a freeholder, may be arrested for any sum under 10*l.* currency, and held to bail without an affidavit; while, for a sum above 10*l.* like money, by rule of court, (No. 10,) an affidavit must first be made by the plaintiff and filed with the secretary; and in this case a freeholder may be arrested.

Writs of *capias ad respondendum* (under which the arrest takes place,) rarely lead to anything, said the Crown officer, but the forfeiture of the bail bond.

The writ of *habeas corpus* is obtained in this island, both at common law and in favour of liberty, by Act of Charles the Second; though the legal extension of it to this island is questionable, and its suspension disregarded.

Attachment of the goods and effects of an absent defendant, is often resorted to. The Act, not mentioning debts due by third persons, words are inserted in the writ which imply it, and they have constantly been acted upon; but the point it is said, would be contested, should the case occur again. The expense is 4*l.* 18*s.*; should the third person resist the attachment, the expense in addition to the amount stated, is 9*l.* currency.

There have been only two prisoners in execution for debt, during the last thirty years. 2*s.* 3*d.* current money is allowed by the public to the marshal, for every prisoner.

No record of the pleadings and issue is made up and kept, but merely minutes of these and of the proceedings, which are afterwards briefly noted in a book, called The Court Book.

Depositions are admitted in the usual cases; there must be three days notice given to the opposite party, before the examination of a witness takes place.

Witnesses are supposed to be entitled to their ex-

NEVIS.

KING'S BENCH.

penses; but the King's counsel was not aware of their having been ever demanded or paid.

The writ of execution is in the usual form and there is nothing peculiar in the practice; but it is an important circumstance, that goods bought at marshal's sales, are paid for *in produce*, by direction of the Court Act; and such produce is not appraised, or taken at a fair valuation:—It is appointed "to be paid and delivered down "at the current prices the commodities shall respectively "bear at that time, in the island." The construction of the Act as to the current price, or rather the practice and usage which has long prevailed, makes it worse than nominal. It has not only given rise to infinite intricacy, difficulty, and dissatisfaction, but has been, and continues to be, productive of serious injury to individuals, and to the credit of the island, and is, the King's counsel conceives, a mistaken and therefore a mischievous policy, even for the planter, whose interests it was intended to protect. Rum is the grand medium of payment and of tenders, to the marshal especially; and the current price of that article, considered to be not the price it may bear in the island for money at the time, but the conventional barter price, usually established between the planter and the merchant, at the commencement or in the course of the crop, and which is sometimes *fifty*, and never less than *twenty*, per cent., above its actual value in the market, for cash.

Even specific agreements for payments in specie, (that is money or cash,) cannot, the King's counsel apprehends, be enforced by any means as the law now stands, or as it is construed; except perhaps, in the court of Chancery; and, in certain very special cases, by virtue of the Acts of the island Nos. 305 and 306.

There is a docket of fees in this court established by law for the judges, secretary and marshal. In taxing attorney's charges and counsel's fees, the judge is governed by precedent; sometimes by discretion.

The judges in this court take down the evidence; but imperfectly, or rather merely for their own satisfaction and guidance. They do not sum up the evidence, or attempt except very rarely, to state the law to the jury.

Free or freed negroes or persons of colour are under no other restriction as to giving evidence in this court, than white persons. The evidence of a slave is altogether inadmissible, in any case affecting a white or free person of any description, by usage but by no direct or positive law; and a negro or coloured person who had ever been in a state of slavery would not, the King's counsel apprehended, be admitted in such a case to give testimony relating to any matter or thing, anterior to the time of his emancipation; but there had been no judicial decisions upon the subject, in this island.

Free persons of colour can sue, and be sued, in this court; are competent as witnesses, with the exception last above mentioned; are admissible, but in practice have never been admitted, as jurors; and are excluded by law, from no situation or office, except in the militia.

The King's counsel said, "If, what are called the entering days and court months, were changed to certain "portions of the four quarters of the year; the time for "sales on levies shortened; the tenders to the marshal, "on such sales, altered to money, or entirely new modelled; the present constitution of the court reformed; "judges appointed from among able and experienced "persons of the legal profession from home, for all the "islands; who might be justices itinerant, and one of "such judges to preside in this court, as in sittings at "*nisi prius*, for London and Middlesex; the administration of justice might become perfectly unimpeachable. "A considerable difficulty however, seemed to present "itself, in the case of exceptions to the opinion or direction of the judges: and in cases of writs of error, "which the same gentleman feared would frustrate every "improvement, unless a court of Appeal or of Error "were provided, differently constituted from that which "is now established by law."

NEVIS.

## COURT FOR THE RECOVERY OF SMALL DEBTS.

There is no court of Complaints in this island; but by the 32d clause of the Court Act, justices of the court of King's Bench and Common Pleas have "power to "hear and determine in court, without a jury, all man-"ner of actions and suits under the value of 10*l.* current "money, or 1,000lbs. of sugar;" and likewise, "all "cases relating to servants' wages, and debts due to ar-"tificers and labourers, not exceeding 2,000lbs. of sugar, "or 15*l.* current money; and in such cases the oaths of "the plaintiffs shall, if the court think fit, be sufficient "evidence to prove the debt or demand." At the time of passing this Act, in 1732, accounts were very commonly kept, and actions brought and judgments given, for so many pounds of sugar, *eo nomine*, which may partly account for the making produce a legal tender to the marshal, at sales upon executions; and the practice which has grown out of it.

It was in the contemplation of the legislature to form a distinct court for those purposes, and also for cases relating to transient persons, with summary jurisdiction, and for extended amount; a measure which, in the opinion of the King's counsel, would be a great relief to creditors, and to the court of King's Bench and Common Pleas, and a general benefit.

## COURT OF ORDINARY.

There is no court of Ordinary in this island, established by law. The captain-general (of St. Christopher, of which Nevis is a dependency,) is sole ordinary in his government, by virtue of the King's commission. He sits when applied to, as in the court of Chancery, but deputes generally, the president of the council to grant letters of administration, (but not to decide on a *caveat*,) probate of wills, and marriage licenses.

Notwithstanding the provisions of the Registry Act, wills are commonly proved *per testes*.

As to establishing ecclesiastical courts in these islands, the king's counsel says it is a point of great difficulty and would require much deliberation.

## COURT OF ADMIRALTY.

The court of Vice-Admiralty derives its ordinary authority and jurisdiction, from the commission (as vice-admiral,) and the instructions to the captain-general; and its powers are the same locally, as those of the High Court of Admiralty in England. The court has also a concurrent jurisdiction with the courts of record, by virtue of certain Acts of Parliament; and by special commission of late disused, cognizances of prize causes during war.

The court sits in Charles Town, in this island, *pro re natâ;* but there has been but one court held, and one cause tried, since the year 1818.

There was formerly a registry of the proceedings of this court; but, for many years last past, the papers have been only filed, with minutes of the proceedings, and the sentence in each cause, in separate bundles. The practice has been rather assimilated to the proceedings in the court of Chancery, (the libel and monition excepted,) by petition and order, instead of Acts of Court; "the practisers having been but little acquainted with "the forms and proceedings of the civil courts at "home."

There is a docket of fees for this court. It is understood that a docket of fees was sent out from the High Court of Admiralty at home some years ago, for all the Vice-Admiralty Courts in these islands: but it has never

NEVIS.

ADMIRALTY.

been officially communicated here, and the king's counsel had not seen a copy.

Costs are taxed by the judge.

## COURT OF ERROR.

In this court the captain-general, or person administering the government, and four or more members of the council are the judges.

Writs of error, in the nature of appeals, are brought from the court of King's Bench and Common Pleas, in civil cases. Appeals lie from the court of Error, as from the court of Chancery, to the King in council, notwithstanding the second clause of the Court Act, which seems to reserve the power of appeal from the court of King's Bench and Common Pleas here, to the court of King's Bench in England.

One instance only can be traced of the entire prosecution of a writ of error to judgment in this island, for the last forty years.

The costs are very considerable; "similar to those in "the court of Chancery," added the examinant.

# CRIMINAL COURTS.

OF SESSIONS.

OF JUSTICES OF THE PEACE.

The criminal jurisdiction of the island is vested in several courts; *viz.* the King's Bench side of the court of King's Bench and Common Pleas; the court of Sessions, holden annually on the first Tuesday, Wednesday, or Thursday in October, composed of three justices of the peace at least, one whereof to be of the quorum; the court of Justices of the Peace, consisting of one, two, or more justices, as occasion may require, and as prescribed by the general commission of the peace; and courts of Oyer and Terminer and General Gaol Delivery, depending upon commissions issued from time to time, upon extraordinary occasions, by the captain-general. These courts are all governed by the laws of the mother country, not being affected in their proceedings or practice by any local Act whatsoever.

These courts are all held in Charles Town in this island.

Prosecutions are frequently carried on at the instance of a private prosecutor, who retains whom he pleases, in the court of King's Bench and Common Pleas and at the court of Sessions; but in all the other courts, and in cases termed "public prosecutions," that is at the public expense and noticed by the superior authorities, the senior King's counsel resident in the island prosecutes, unless the attorney-general or the solicitor-general who reside at St. Christopher, are specially called upon, which usually happens in cases of importance or magnitude.

It has formerly been the practice in this island, for persons to be sworn in court, and to go before the grand jury with a complaint as it was termed, in order to procure *a presentment*, and a prosecution in consequence, at the public cost; but this proceeding has of late been discountenanced, as irregular and improper; and now cases are not laid before the grand jury, but by indictment. The grand jury sometimes make presentments from their own knowledge.

The grand jury is scarcely ever addressed or charged; when that duty is performed, it is by the chief justice or senior presiding judge.

If the grand jury are desirous of advice on points of law, they apply to the court, or to the senior crown-lawyer present.

The inconvenience of protracted trials, and of much embarrassment both to the bench and to the jury, is apt to arise in the opinion of the King's counsel, from the practice of barristers addressing the jury on behalf of prisoners, and offenders have thereby escaped, who, he thinks, merited conviction.

NEVIS.

The presiding judge scarcely ever sums up in any of the courts.

Prosecutors' and witnesses' expenses are not allowed by the court, but are granted upon particular occasions by the House of Assembly, upon petition; by which body, or a committee, the costs are examined and ascertained.

In all the criminal courts there have been for the last FORTY years, only *nine* trials for capital offences; which terminated in seven acquittals and two convictions. The two convictions were for the offence of manslaughter, indeed eight were cases of homicide, and the ninth for an offence against an Act of the island, resembling Lord Ellenborough's Act.

Assaults and other petty misdemeanors are frequently tried in the court of King's Bench and Common Pleas during the court months, which might be more conveniently tried at the court of Sessions.

## SLAVE TRIALS.

By an Act of the island, any one justice of the peace is empowered to hear and determine in a summary way, any complaint against any slave for any *misdemeanor,* or for insolent or abusive language or behaviour, or for any other misconduct deserving punishment, and to adjudge and cause to be inflicted any corporal or other punishment, or both, at his discretion; such punishment if corporal, not to exceed at any one infliction thirty-nine lashes, with a cat-o'-nine-tails.

For the trial of felonies committed by slaves, any magistrate is empowered, after examining into the complaint in the same manner as in the case of a charge against a white person, to bail or commit the accused to prison according to law; who is then to be brought to trial within *ten* days, the magistrate having in the meantime associated with himself two or more other justices to complete a court. The court thus constituted, issues process for summoning as jurors, twelve white persons, (of whom six are afterwards impannelled); it also summonses witnesses and all other necessary persons, and proceeds with the trial in a manner as it is stated, conformable in every respect to the practice of the Crown side of the court of King's Bench and Common Pleas of this island.

The same justice, who first entertained the complaint, must by the Act, sit upon the trial. There is no grand jury, but the indictment is laid before the bench in the first instance.

The evidence of slaves is not admitted upon oath; that is, (as I understand it, but I shall cheerfully correct my mistake if I am wrong), slaves are *not* SWORN *where they do not appear to be duly sensible of the obligation of an oath.* "In these cases which too often occur," said the King's counsel, "it has been the practice of the court "not to permit such witnesses to be sworn; but to warn "them of the immediate consequence to themselves, if "detected in giving false testimony, and not speaking "the truth and the whole truth." After this warning (as I collect the examinant's meaning), they are permitted to proceed in relating their story, without the sanction of an oath, and with their credit greatly impaired; a practice strongly to be reprobated. The opinions of the King's counsel, on the subject of slave evidence, are nevertheless entitled to the most serious attention. "Of all the testimony of which I have ever "read, heard, or met with, that of slaves in general has "ever appeared to me to be the least correct, the least "to be depended upon, and at the same time the most "plausible and the most imposing. From a willing wit-"ness it will flow in an overwhelming, and too often, "treacherous tide; from an unwilling one, it is the most "difficult to be extracted; and they frequently possess "or acquire such an extraordinary and wonderful power "of invention, and even of *representing*, so as that, with-"out an absolute breach of truth, the relation shall still "convey an intentional falsehood; and they will adhere "to it with such rigid consistency and pertinacity, as to

NEVIS.

SLAVE TRIALS.

"elude the penetration and the skill of the most expert "or experienced examiner, and consequently to render "their evidence almost invariably doubtful. All this "cannot possibly be attributed to *defect* of intellect; on "the contrary, I impute it to subtlety, force of habit, "education, and *state* of intellect. Want of intellect "may exist in some few instances; but want of integrity, "with the talents and dispositions which I have just de-"scribed, I take to be the prevailing and efficient cause."

There has never been an instance of a slave tried for giving false testimony, but they would be tried, in such case, for a misdemeanor; and the punishment would be corporal, at the legal discretion of the magistrate.

Notwithstanding the character of slave evidence, given by the King's counsel in the above cited answer, and which that gentleman "feared was too often applicable "to the evidence of many of those who have been re-"lieved from slavery;" the leaning of his mind was, to the *unrestricted admission* of the evidence of slaves in all cases whatsoever, as a general principle, leaving their admissibility or competence in particular cases, as a point of law to the court, and exceptions to their *credibility* to their full operation. At the same time the Crown officer delivered this sentiment with great hesitation, alive to the almost insuperable difficulties that would arise, and to the incalculable mischiefs which might ensue, from the adoption of the principle.

The secretary of the island is required by the Act to attend slave trials as clerk and registrar of the court; and the record of the proceedings, and the papers relating to the trials, are deposited and kept in his office.

Sentence is passed upon conviction, or within three days after; but execution must not be done before six days after passing sentence.

Notice of sentence must be given, as soon as may be, (within 24 hours), to the person in chief command on the island for the time being, and by him *forthwith* to the captain-general.

The general superintending jurisdiction of the court of King's Bench is not taken away by any words of the Act;

NEVIS.

SLAVE TRIALS.

but there has been no instance of an appeal. New trials are frequently granted *on convictions*.

The warrant for the execution is directed to the provost-marshal, or his lawful deputy.

Though the case is not yet provided for by law in this island, the just acquisitions of a slave for himself, are generally held sacred by the owner, and the subject was under the consideration of the legislature.

A slave in this island, has at present no means of legally enfranchising himself, without the concurrence of his owner; but this concession was also intended to be made a point for deliberation, shortly after the Commissioners left the island.

Inquests upon slaves are provided for by the Amelioration Act.

As to trials of slaves for capital offences, the King's counsel thought he might venture to state with confidence, that in essentials, these trials are so nearly assimilated to those of the mother country in like cases, that it would be extremely difficult to suggest an improvement, and he thought the same might be said of trials for misdemeanors. Some defects may be discovered in the Act; but he believes the administration of justice under it to be perfectly unexceptionable, and highly to the "credit of the "colony. The want of a grand jury," proceeded that gentleman, "and there being only seven men, including one "of the judges, instead of four-and-twenty or more, to "pass upon the life of a fellow creature, are certainly "striking anomalies at the first view; yet, when the "present state of things and of society in this part of the "world is duly weighed, and when it is recollected that "every other right and privilege allowed to offenders by "law or by indulgence at home, is strictly attended to "in every stage of the proceedings on these cases, they "will not," the King's counsel presumes, "be considered "wholly irreconcileable to British feelings, or inconsistent with the impartial administration of the law."

"Laws for defining the civil rights of slaves, and for "protection in the enjoyment of them, are certainly," the Crown officer conceives, "among the first *desiderata*."

NEVIS.

SLAVE TRIALS.

Mr. Cottle, formerly president of the island and a very intelligent and amiable man, stated to the Commissioners instances within his own knowledge, of offences committed at times and in situations when, only slaves being present, sufficient evidence to obtain a conviction it was known, could not be procured, and upon this calculation the perpetrators proceeded. Mr. Cottle was decidedly in favour of the admission of slave evidence, "without "any qualification whatever."

---

Complaint.

The deputy provost-marshal preferred a complaint before his Majesty's Commissioners, relating to the imprisonment of one of his bailiffs by a court-martial, for an alleged contempt in arresting an officer on his way to the court. The bailiff himself afterwards, addressed a letter to the Commissioners on the same subject, from the gaol.

The Commissioners declined entering into the case of the marshal and his bailiff, as being a matter over which they did not consider themselves as possessing jurisdiction; or at least as one, in which it was open to the party supposing himself aggrieved, to bring his action for false imprisonment in those ordinary tribunals, which they came out to review, but not to supersede.

---

PARTICULAR OFFICERS.

JUDGES.

With the exception of the chancellor, the ordinary, the members of the council, and the commissioners for the trial of pirates (at the Admiralty Sessions), who are all appointed by the King, all the judges and justices of the several courts are appointed by the captain-general, by patents under the great seal. They have no salaries, and (except the chief justice of the court of King's Bench and Common Pleas whose fees are settled by law, and the judge of Vice-Admiralty) scarcely any fees.

"That the persons appointed to be judges should be "barristers, or have gone through a course of legal "study, is," said the King's counsel, "from necessity,

"not an indispensable, though a most desirable qualifica-
"tion." NEVIS.

ATTORNEY- and SOLICITOR GENERAL.

The attorney and solicitor-general for the government, both reside at St. Christopher.

BARRISTERS and ATTORNEYS

Persons who have been called to the bar in England, and persons "whose competency is made apparent by "certificates, or upon motion in open court," by the usage of the courts, are admitted to practise as counsel and solicitors or attorneys, and as advocates and proctors, in all the courts respectively. In the court of King's Bench and Common Pleas in this island however, counsel are not privileged to practise as attorneys, and do not, there being only four attorneys allowed by the Court Act; but the present four attorneys have been admitted barristers also. There is no rule which prescribes the qualification of persons to practise as attorneys; the court is "satis-"fied of their ability or competency, in like manner as in "the case of barristers."

PROVOST-MARSHAL.

The deputy provost-marshal entered upon the performance of the duties of his office in this island in August, 1817; prior to which date, he has not been able to find any records of commitments in any office. A slave named Tom, was executed for felony, in the month of March, 1822, and is the only capital convict executed since the deputy provost-marshal has been in office.

There are two places of confinement in this island; the jail and the cage.

The jail is "never full," and is "considered healthy;" but the marshal had lately reported it to be in a bad state, and the legislature had in consequence, ordered an inspection of it to be made, by the committee of public buildings.

Debtors are separated from criminals in this jail, and men divided from women; indeed the jail has never been so full in the present marshal's time, as to prevent his making the most convenient arrangements.

The allowance to a prisoner is a quarter of a dollar a day, or food to that value; at the option of the prisoner.

In the cage are confined disorderly persons taken up

NEVIS.

PARTICULAR OFFICERS.

in the night by the constable, and slaves sent there by their owners, as a punishment. The condition of the cage is good, but the space contracted. Slaves are sent there not only to be confined but also flogged, by their master's orders. For crimes, slaves are whipped under the gallows; for misdemeanors, at the cage door. There is no employment of slaves in the cage.

JUSTICE OF THE PEACE.

The duties of a justice of peace in this island, are well described to be—"to take care that justice is pro-"perly administered to all parties, whether free or "slaves; and that the laws are not infringed, &c. The "Melioration, the Manumission, and other Acts, have "attached duties to magistrates for the protection of "slaves; in other respects, magistrates have the same "power to examine informations for crimes, and to com-"mit for trial in cases of slaves, that they possess with "free people."

On slave trials, the owner of the slave generally employs counsel to defend the prisoners. The magistrate has known but one instance where it was omitted, and in that case, although the facts were proved, the jury acquitted. A slave (a prisoner) may challenge, either for cause, or a full jury peremptorily.

The magistrate was not aware of justices having any jurisdiction in civil matters in this island.

The police is stated to be very defective indeed, and notorious offenders against the public peace are said to escape punishment.

Complaints by slaves of cruelty or maltreatment in a master or manager, have been made in this island, and trials have taken place; in some, acquittals have been had; in others, convictions: very lately, when the complaint was made to the examinants, "upon the mere "*ipse dixit* (the unsupported statement) of a slave, the "master was found guilty, and sentenced to thirty days "imprisonment, and 25*l*. fine, besides all expenses at-"tending the protection of the slave."

CORONERS.

"For each inquisition" the coroner receives in this island, "33*s*. sterling, payable in rum, at 3*s*. per gallon, "equal to 1*s*. 6*d*. cash."

NEVIS.

PARTICULAR OFFICERS.

There is no other difference in the manner of taking inquests in the respective cases of free persons and of slaves, than that in the latter case, *three* constitute a jury; in the former it is composed of *twelve*.

The examinant had acted as coroner for twelve years, during which time no case of sudden or violent death had ever come to his knowledge where the coroner had not received information. During the same space of time the coroner had never held an inquest on any slave killed by his owner, or any person acting under the authority of the master; but had held inquests in cases where one slave had killed another in affrays.

Inquests appear to be taken, as nearly as the different circumstances of the country will permit, in the same manner as in England.

WRONGS WITHOUT REDRESS.

Upon the subject of injuries for which the existing law and practice of the island does not afford any certain redress, I shall content myself with citing, without any comment, the following passage from the last answer of the crown officer of this island: "It is considered that a slave has no civil rights whatever, or "rather, that they are merged in those of his owner. A "slave, therefore, cannot, as I apprehend, appear in "any court as a claimant for redress, that is, satisfac-"tion in damages, for any injury whatever; but this "must be sought by his owner, or *his* representative. "In certain cases, however, under particular laws for "the good government, protection, or melioration of the "condition of slaves, it seems tacitly admitted, that a "slave may complain to a magistrate against other per-"sons than his owner, and thereby obtain redrees in a "summary way for some wrongs, both of a public and "private nature; and that he may also by the same "means, procure investigation into alleged grievances "and offences against those laws, and punishment of the "offenders, *be they who they may;* provided the allega-"tion be *sustained by legal proofs; but on failure thereof,* "*he appears to be left defenceless.*"

St. Christopher.

# St. CHRISTOPHER.

Preliminary Remarks.

His Majesty's Commissioners commenced their inquiries into the Administration of Justice in this island, on the 3d day of November, 1823. A communication made to them on the day of their arrival, by some respectable merchants of the town of Basseterre, will form the most appropriate introduction to this Report.

"Costs here," said the first gentleman, "are enormous. "In Chancery, you cannot recover any thing under an "expense of 1,000*l.* No man thinks of venturing *there*, "except for large interests.

"There is no court, or proceeding before magistrates, "in this island of St. Kitts, for the recovery of small "debts; hence, they are frequently given up, and lost "altogether.

"The chief justice in this island is paid in a most hor-"rible way: he has 10*l.* each sitting of the court, for "dinner-money, besides fees. And what must render it "particularly unpleasant to a man of gentlemanly feel-"ings, he gives the dinners, thus paid for by the public, "at his own house, his private dwelling. The court ad-"journs for a fortnight, and thus sits intermediately be-"tween each monthly court, and sometimes with very

" little, or nothing at all, to do; which, of course, by the " censorious, is imputed to the 10*l.* dinner-fee.

" The Grand Sessions are held *four* times a-year; and " this attendance, with the adjourned courts of Common " Pleas and King's Bench every fortnight, is extremely " harassing to those, who, as jurymen, &c. are bound " under heavy penalties, to observe it.

" The attorney-general is, and is universally admitted " to be, a good and honest man, as well as a sound and " able lawyer.

" In a country where you cannot procure professional " men to fill the situation, the chief justice is, in an ex- " traordinary degree, suited and qualified for his office. " He is also however, judge of the court of Admiralty, " and master in Chancery.

" The town is without a police, and the country is " overrun with lawyers; and, owing to the latter cir- " cumstance, and the distress of the times, all the estates " of the island are now in the court of Chancery."

A second gentleman added to this afflicting statement:—

" It is the fees of officers of the court which are most " exorbitant. There is no table of fees by which *they* " choose to be governed, or by which the judge is guided " in taxing their costs. There are two or three old Acts " regulating the fees; but these are obselete, and the fees " certainly too low. There is a later docket established " by the governor and council, taken from a bill, which " I believe, had passed the assembly but not the council, " (it was interrupted by a dissolution, or something of " that sort); but *that*, though recent and suitable, they " are not content with.

" Before the present chief justice's time, if you had a " cause entered, there was no getting it tried under two " years. The delays were such as to render it, in in- " stances within my personal knowledge, matter of in- " terested calculation, whether it were not better for a " party who owed a sum of money, to resist payment and " defend an action, though sure of a verdict against him " ultimately with costs, than to lose the advantage he

ST. CHRISTOPHER.

PRELIMINARY REMARKS.

"could make in business, by keeping the money in his "hands and holding the plaintiff off for two years. Now "the arrear is clearing off rapidly; and the country is "greatly indebted to the present chief justice for his "spirited and successful exertions to dispose of all the "causes in the paper."

Minutes, Nov. 5, 1823.

The chief justice in conversation with the Commissioners, confirmed the statement of our informant "as to "the former vexatious delays in the common law courts, "and the commercial speculations to which they notoriously gave rise. He said he found an arrear of "500 causes. He had now disposed of the whole, and "was able, by means of the adjourned courts every fortnight, to get through the list, and prevent any fresh "accumulation. He had also brought the rules and "orders, which he found a mass of confusion and contradiction, into some shape and coherence."

The attorney-general, upon whose opinions the communication itself as well as other information, had prepared the Commissioners to set the highest value, was also found to report "very favourably of the regularity, "order, and decorum of the courts of this island, at the "present time."

From the governor, the president of the council, the chief justice, the attorney and solicitor-general, the rest of the bench and bar, and the magistracy in general, the Commissioners received, during their stay in this island, the kindest attentions, and, in the prosecution of their object, the fullest co-operation.

---

LAWS.

The state of the Laws in St. Christopher as in the other islands, first engaged our attention.

The governor said he "could not supply the Commissioners with a copy of the laws; he had none for himself; he was obliged to grope in the dark."

A copy of the printed laws to 1779 was afterwards with difficulty, procured; but many of the laws of this island remain in manuscript.

St. Christopher.

Laws.

Of the Laws, the principal, are—

No. 15. *An Act for settling the estates and titles of the inhabitants of this island to their possessions within the same.*

Five years possession before the war in 1689, shall be good right and title.

No. 18. *An Act for all public officers putting security;* i. e. the treasurer, secretary, and marshal, and their respective deputies.

No. 29. *An Act for regulating and appointing the fees of the several officers and courts in this island.*

No. 59. The Court Act of this island, intituled, An Act *for the establishing a court of King's Bench and Common Pleas, and for the better administration of justice in this island of St. Christopher, and for settling certain fees, and repealing a former Act of the said island, &c.* To 1724.
which, in the statute-book, is annexed the following note: "Some objections to this Act being made at home, "it was not confirmed by the Crown; neither was it repealed or rejected, but suffered to lie by probationary, "and is the Act by which the courts in this island are "now governed."

No. 69. *An Act against covinous and fraudulent conveyances, and for a public registry in the island of St. Christopher. This Act was explained and amended by a subsequent Act,* No. 177, *passed in* 1758.

No. 96. *An Act for reducing the fee of 3s. per sheet, taken by the secretary as clerk in Chancery, for the copies of bills and answers in the said court filed in the secretary's office, and for appointing a more reasonable fee in the room thereof.*

This Act contained a suspending clause, but was afterwards confirmed by his Majesty, in council, in 1757.

No. 104. *An Act for preventing clandestine marriages in the island of St. Christopher.* No person shall presume to marry any couple, unless after banns, or with a license.

No. 180. *An Act for punishing with death all negroes and slaves who shall attempt to take away the life of any white man, or free person, by poison.*

ST. CHRISTOPHER.

LAWS.

Cl. 3. *And be it enacted, that such negro, or slave or slaves, their accessaries and abettors, being slaves, shall be tried before any two or more of His Majesty's justices of the peace, who shall, upon conviction, have power by this Act, to condemn, &c. and order execution, &c. by warrant, directed to the provost-marshal, &c.*

No. 194. *An Act for the better regulating the practice of the law in the island of St. Christopher.*

"Whereas it will tend to the manifest advantage of "suitors, and also to the saving of unnecessary expense, "that persons, admitted to the bar of the court of King's "Bench and Common Pleas, in this island, should also "be admitted to practise as attorneys and solicitors in the "said courts."

Cl. 2. Persons admitted to the bar of the said court may, upon taking the oath, be admitted to practise as attorneys, &c.

Cl. 3 and 4. Then for drawing, perusing, and settling a declaration, such barrister, practising as an attorney, shall be restricted to the counsel's fee of 1*l.* 1*s.* And no charge shall be made for drawing a brief.

Cl. 5. No person shall be held to special bail, unless affidavit of the plaintiff's cause of action shall be first made and filed; the sum sworn to shall be indorsed on the writ, and bail taken in no other sum than that sworn to.

No. 217. *An Act for the better securing the estates and interests of orphans; and to oblige executors to give security and to return inventories and appraisements into the Ordinary's office of the island.*

The preamble recites, that "*through the necessity of "sending the youth of this island to Great Britain for "education, very many have considerably suffered in their "estates by the death of their ancestors during their ab-"sence, for want of inventories being returned of the per-"sonal estate their ancestors were possessed of at the time "of their death. And whereas it hath frequently happened, "that not only their ancestors, but the executors of such "ancestors, have died, whereby the estates have fallen "into the hands of executors to such executors, and no in-*

*"ventory having been made, it has been impossible to dis-"cover the testator's estate, and such orphans at their re-"turn to this island, have found their estate very much "wasted and impaired:"—" And whereas it is usual for "merchants to entrust cargoes of merchandize with per-"sons whom they send hither as their factors for the dis-"posal thereof, but the same having received great discou-"ragement likewise by the death of some of the said fac-"tors, who having made their wills, and their executors "not having returned any inventories of their goods, it has "been impossible for their principal in Great Britain to "discover the same, or to recover the value thereof, which "has tended to the great discouragement of trade, and to "the general discredit of this island: for the better en-"forcing the duties of executors, as well as promoting the "credit and reputation of the island, it was enacted that "all and every executor and executors for the future, when "the will of any testator is by him or them exhibited to be "proved, shall answer upon oath, before the ordinary or "deputed ordinary, to the value and circumstances of the "testator's testamentary estate, to the best of his or their "knowledge; and shall at the direction of the ordinary, "not only take the oath of an executor, according to the "laws of England, but give such security as the ordinary "shall direct, to return a just inventory of the testator's "estate, with an appraisement thereof, upon oath within "such time as shall be limited by the ordinary."*

Cl. 2. *"And whereas several orphans' estates have been "let out to lease during minorities, without any security "given for returning or making good the slaves and "personal estate so leased, at the expiration of such lease "or leases, whereby several poor orphans have been un-"done; for the prevention therefore of such neglects and "undue practices for the future, be it enacted, that all "guardians or other persons, empowered to lease out an "orphan's estate, shall take good and sufficient security "for the return of all slaves and personal estate leased with "it; and shall annex to the lease a schedule of all slaves, "&c. and record the same within three months.*

ST. CHRISTOPHER.

LAWS.

"*All leases wanting the ceremonies aforesaid to be utterly void.*"

This is an important Act, and might be advantageously extended to oblige executors to account on oath, within a stated period. As it is, the attorney-general said, "The Act, No. 217, is beneficial; and I think the proposed amendment would be useful." So the chief justice said, "With due precautions it might be beneficially extended. I think it is a beneficial act."

No. 225. *An Act to prevent absconding fugitive debtors suing for their debts by attorneys, or assigning over their effects to defraud their just creditors.*

Cl. 1. No person leaving the island without publishing his name, or taking out a ticket, or giving bond in the secretary's office, shall recover any debts by letter of attorney or assignment, except the attorney or assignees give security to make satisfaction to the creditors of the fugitive debtors; or,

Cl. 2. Assignees may be obliged to appear before a judge, to state on oath that the assignment is for a just debt, and not made to defraud creditors.

No. 261. *An Act for establishing and ratifying certain Acts made by the Governor and Assembly of this island, during the late subjection thereof to the Crown of France.*

The Acts thus continued and confirmed are set out at length. The only important one remaining in force is, *An Act to prevent the cutting off, or depriving any slaves in this island of any of their limbs or members, or otherwise disabling them; which recites, that some persons had of late been guilty of cutting off, or depriving slaves of their ears, which practice is contrary to the principles of humanity, and dishonourable to society,* and is made punishable by a fine of 500*l.*, and six months imprisonment.

No. 280. *An Act for establishing a court of Sessions of the peace, to be held in and for this island.*

The preamble recites, that "the administration of justice in criminal cases in this island, hath met with great "delay and obstruction, from the want of a court of "Sessions for the trial of misdemeanors and breaches of "the peace." And the Act establishes a court of Sessions "to be held twice a-year, which shall have jurisdiction to hear and determine all such matters as are "usually cognizable by the court of Quarter Sessions in "England, to whose rule and practice this court shall "conform itself, as near as may be."

This Act has been amended by a manuscript Act of the 14th June, 1820.

---

The Manuscript Laws begin with No. 315.

No. 329. *An act to enable the courts of justice to sit in this island, and transact business in the usual manner, during alarms, and for enforcing attendance of jurors, &c.*

No. 365. *An act to amend an Act, intituled, an Act for constituting a Court-merchant.*

The limiting the sum recoverable in this court to 100*l.*, is declared inexpedient, and it is made allowable to sue in it in all cases. No demurrer is permitted in this court, or new trial, or arrest of judgment, unless sufficient cause be immediately shewn.

No. 375. An act which repeals the 15th clause of the Court Act, and alters other clauses.

Cl. 2. Sugar and rum shall be a legal tender, at a fair valuation; and in case of any dispute, there shall be an appraisement.

Cl. 3. Lands or goods taken under execution shall be exposed to sale at proper times.

Cl. 4. Debts under 27*l.* shall be payable in money.

No. 393. *An Act to repeal an Act for regulating the manumission of slaves.*

Cl. 2. Persons manumitting disorderly and worthless characters shall be liable to a forfeiture of 150*l.*

Cl. 4. Manumissions made before the passing this Act, in other islands where there was no restriction on manumissions, shall confer freedom on this island, if they are duly registered.

All manumissions shall be registered within sixty days.

No. 395. *An Act for settling and regulating the trial of criminal slaves by jury.*

Cl. 1, 2, 3, 4, are repealed by an Act of October 1823.

Cl. 5. Juries shall be ballotted for, and determined upon, in the same manner as juries at the general and quarter sessions.

Cl. 8. If the slave be found guilty, sentence of death shall be passed within *five* days.

Cl. 9. Warrant of execution shall issue within twenty-four hours.

Cl. 10. When the offence is not capital, the justices shall order corporal punishment.

Cl. 11. Notice of sentence of death shall be given to the first in command within six hours.

No. 399. *An Act for establishing a gang of negroes to be employed in repairing the streets of the town of Basseterre, and all other towns and parishes, and other public works in this island.*

The preamble recites, that "it often happens that slaves "convicted of felonies and sentenced to death, receive a "free pardon, and escape without any punishment, be-"cause, although their offences might require some severe "correction, they are not thought deserving of death, "and there is no adequate punishment for offences under "the degree of capital felonies, therefore enacts, that—

Cl. 1. The governor may annex to his pardon a condition that such slave shall work upon the streets, &c. for the period of his natural life, or for any shorter period; and in such case the proprietor of the slave shall receive 6*d.* per day.

Cl. 2. Slaves taken up for not telling their owners' or masters' names, and all unclaimed slaves in gaol, may be employed in like manner.

Cl. 3. For offences less than felony without benefit of clergy, justices may sentence slaves to hard labour, in amending and keeping in repair the streets, &c.

Cl. 4. Every owner or director of slaves, instead of private punishment, may send his slave to work in the convict gang for such time as he shall think proper. In this case the owner pays the fees to the marshal; in other cases, the public.

No. 401. *An Act to prevent the stealing or destroying of sheep or other cattle.*

Cl. 1. adopts the provisions of statute 4 Geo. 2. c. 6. s. 1.—15 Geo. 2. c. 34.

Cl. 2. "As the prevailing practice of staking out sheep "by cords or chains offers a facility for the stealing and "carrying away the said sheep, which the needy and "profligate know not how to resist, the said penalty of "death shall not attach to any person or persons con-"victed of stealing one or more sheep, unless secured in "a pen or other inclosed building from which they can-"not escape, or under care of an able watchman, spe-"cifically appointed for the purpose."

Cl. 3. This Act shall be printed, and a copy sent to the manager of every plantation, who shall be required within fourteen days, to assemble the slaves, and distinctly make known to them the nature and penalties of the Act; and the manager shall attend on a day appointed, and make oath of having so done, under a penalty.

No. 417. *An Act for improving and rendering more secure the common gaol, and for applying certain fines for that purpose.*

Cl. 1, appoints Commissioners, of whom the chief justice, attorney-general, and solicitor-general, are to be three.

Cl. 2, who shall receive all fines levied or to be levied.

Cl. 3, and apply them to building a gaol-wall round the yard, erecting an easement and pump, and carrying water by pipes into the inner part of the gaol, as may be necessary for the health and cleanliness of the prison, &c.

5th June, 1818. *An Act to enable any one justice of the court of King's Bench and Common Pleas, to continue or adjourn the said court, and to grant judgments upon warrants of attorney.* A power is given accordingly

St. Christopher.

Laws.

to a single judge, "so as any adjournment be not for a "longer time than fourteen days."

5th June, 1818. *An Act providing for the payment of costs to parties on complaints determined before justices of the peace out of sessions: so fees of justices and constables.*

The Act also extends to cases NOT *determined* by the justices out of sessions; for where they have bound the parties in recognizances to appear at the sessions, they have still power to award the costs: *for the recognizance, 9s.; warrants, 9s.; witnesses each, 1s.; to be paid by either of the parties, and in manner and form, as to the justices shall seem fit.*

29th July, 1819. An Act for extending to this island Lord Ellenborough's Act, and for repealing No. 272, *ante.*

14th June, 1820. *An Act for amending an Act for establishing a court of Sessions of the peace to be held in and for this island.*

The preamble recites, that, under the former Act, persons might be in gaol eight months before a court was held, thereby incurring heavy punishment before trial; so establishes quarter sessions.

Cl. 2. The former Act is, in all other respects, to continue in full force.

26th June, 1820. *An Act to alter so much of the Court Act as relates to the admission of barristers.*

Cl. 2. From and after the passing of this Act, no person, save and except a white subject or subjects, who have attained the age of twenty-one, shall be admitted to this bar.

Cl. 3. Any person desirous of being admitted, shall produce a certificate or proof on oath, of his admission to the bar at Westminster, or that he has regularly kept terms at one of the inns of court in London, for the space of three years. This regulation not to affect those, being whites, who are now in offices in St. Christopher.

Cl. 4. Justices, however, may refuse to admit these, upon good cause assigned for their so doing.

3d June, 1821. *An Act to regulate the attendance of jurors.*

8th May, 1823. *An Act to regulate payments in produce.*

Cl. 1. Contracts, payable in produce, shall continue so.

Cl. 2. At the price current, unless there is a stipulated price.

Cl. 3. Where an action is brought, the jury may state and adjust the price of produce, reference being had to the price of produce at the time of the contract. In undefended actions the court shall adjust the price.

Cl. 4. Rum, sugar, or molasses, only, &c.

October, 1823. *An Act to alter and amend an Act, intituled an Act for settling and regulating the trial of criminal slaves.*

"Whereas the regulations respecting the mode in "which the court is to be summoned and constituted "are found to be inconvenient, and attended with dif- "ficulty."

Cl. 1. repeals the 1st, 2d, 3d, 4th, and 13th clauses of the former Act.

Cl. 2. regulates certain particulars; as, the warrant to apprehend, commitments for further examination, or for trial, &c.

Cl. 3. directs the summons to twenty-four jurors and magistrates. The trial shall be within twelve days from the commitment.

Cl. 4. Three justices and twelve jurors shall compose a court.

Cl. 5. Justices not attending shall forfeit 20*l.*; jurors, 5*l.* "Provided nevertheless, that the default of any ma- "gistrate, juror, or witness, in not attending at the "time appointed to try any slaves under this Act, by "which the trial of such slave may be deferred, shall not "prevent the ultimate trial of such slave, but the pro- "ceedings may be had and taken DE NOVO."

ST. CHRISTOPHER.

## COURTS.

ENUMERATION OF.

The Courts established in this island, for the administration of Civil Justice, are the court of Chancery; court of King's Bench and Common Pleas; court of Error; court of Vice-Admiralty; and court of Ordinary; also, an occasional Court-Merchant.

The courts established in this island for the administration of Criminal Justice, are the criminal side of the court of King's Bench and Common Pleas, the court of Quarter Sessions, and the court of Special Sessions. Commissions of Oyer and Terminer also issue under the great seal.

## COURT OF CHANCERY.

The governor in this island is sole chancellor, "as "holding the great seal of the colony," said the attorney-general.

The chancellor exercises the same authority as the chancellor does in the high court of Chancery in England, except in matters of bankruptcy.

The court is said to be guided by the laws, principles, and decisions, which govern the courts of Equity in England.

The court of Chancery does not hold periodical sittings. When a cause is ripe for hearing, or a party wishes to make a motion, other than of course, a petition is presented to the chancellor, who appoints a day for hearing the matter, of which due notice is given to the other party, and when the business is disposed of the sitting ends.

There is a manuscript collection of rules, relative to the practice of this court in particular matters, in the hands of members of the profession, differing in some respects, from the practice in England.

There is only one master in this court, appointed by the chancellor, and the business is said not to be sufficient to occupy the time of ONE.

The master, in this island, does not give any security.

Upon the appointment of the present master, (the chief justice,) he applied to his predecessor for the possession of the papers belonging to the office. The reply to this application was, "that he was not aware that he had any "such papers in his possession." Some few documents connected with pending suits, and necessary for transacting the business before the master, were subsequently handed over.

The business which chiefly occupies the court of Chancery, is that which arises on mortgages, appointments of receivers, &c.

If a husband filed a bill for recovery of property in right of his wife, the attorney-general had no doubt that a settlement on her would be directed, if applied for. The chancellor, not being himself acquainted with the practice of the court in England, might not give such direction, as of course.

There is no fine or tax on manumission in this colony.

The practice in the court of Chancery of this island, has, till lately, been extremely limited, and decrees unfrequent. When a suit is heard upon bill and answer only, and the plaintiffs and defendants reside in the island, a decree may be obtained in six or eight months after the filing of a bill. Where evidence is required which is in the island, the matter may be brought to a decree, generally in from twelve to eighteen months. If defendants are absent, it requires much time to obtain their answers by commission; the time generally allowed in the first instance, for taking the answers of persons in England is six months; but answers are hardly ever returned in that time: they are sometimes delayed to double that time.

When accounts are taken before the master, they are usually annexed to the report by way of schedule. This

ST. CHRISTOPHER. — CHANCERY.

does not refer to the accounts of the receivers of the court, of which the result only is contained in the report, the accounts being entered in the master's book. The original accounts and vouchers of all receivers remain in the master's office. " I am not aware," said the chief justice, " that the master could refuse to deliver up the " original accounts and vouchers belonging to the parties " in the suit, the suit being at an end."

The master is paid by fees, regulated by a docket, established by the authority of the chancellor; "and should " any moneys be received or paid by him, he is thereby al- " lowed a per centage of $2\frac{1}{2}$ per cent."

An appeal lies from an interlocutory order, as well as from final decrees. But the appeal has no effect in staying proceedings of the court here, if security be given for restitution, in the event of the success of the appellant.

Costs it is said, are constantly taxed in this court by the master.

The chief justice " believes the law to be most purely " and conscientiously administered in this court; but re- " quired to suggest any improvement, is bound to say, " that during fifteen years, he has known *ten* several " judges of various pursuits and avocations, presiding in " this court: such presidency too is not always of selec- " tion; in many cases it is accidental: it is confined to " the governor, or it may devolve upon the senior resi- " dent member of His Majesty's council. The possibi- " lity of incompetency for such a momentous situation " must be contemplated from such frequent changes, and " especially from such accidental accession to it. It there- " fore occurs to me, that to the master might be confided, " as to a master of the rolls, all matters of minor or " ordinary importance, (or any other matter with the con- " sent of parties,) who might also issue the necessary " papers, and grant petitions in any cause, whilst all " subjects of moment shall be reserved for the hearing " and decision of one or more individuals, (as the busi- " ness of the island may make expedient,) who should " move from island to island, either at stated periods, or

ST. CHRISTOPHER.

CHANCERY.

" according to the urgency of the business, to preside in " the several courts of Chancery."

" It cannot be doubted," said the attorney-general, " that professional knowledge is requisite for the perfect " administration of justice in the court of Chancery. " The appointment of experienced barristers to the office " of chancellor would be an improvement of the colonial " system, and at the same time a relief to the governors, " in what I have always understood to be considered by " them a very embarrassing part of their duty. One " chancellor might preside in the courts of several islands, " and visit them at stated periods for hearing causes and " dispatch of business, leaving with the governor, who " would continue to hold the seals for other purposes of " government, the issuing of process, and all other mat- " ters requiring the seal, and permitting orders of course " and all other matters preparatory to the hearing, to be " determined as at present, or by some other resident " person to whom it may be thought proper to delegate " that authority; some such arrangement for matters of " course, and preparatory proceedings, seems indispensa- " ble. The expense of requiring parties to send from " one island to another on such occasions, would be in- " tolerable; and to defer that part of the business to the " chancellor's periodical visits, would be inconvenient in " point of delay."

## COURT OF KING'S BENCH AND COMMON PLEAS.

This court derives its authority from an Act of the island, No. 59, and comprehends in general, all such criminal and civil matters as are the subject of the jurisdiction of the court of King's Bench and Common Pleas in England.

Real actions are never brought in this court, except dower *unde nihil habet*: ejectments are frequent. Slaves are recovered by action of DETINUE.

St. Christopher.

King's Bench and Common Pleas.

The court is held in the Court-house, in the town of Basseterre. It meets on the second Tuesday of the month of March, April, May, June, July, and August, and may be, and generally is, continued by adjournments; the time prescribed being insufficient for the dispatch of business. There have been periods when the list of actions was so numerous, that causes could not be brought to trial, till very long after they were ready.

In the present state of the court, the chief justice apprehends that thirty or forty days in the year would dispose of all the business.

The court has no particular holidays; but does not usually sit in Passion-week, or of course on Christmas-day.

There are some rules of practice and pleading framed for this court, differing in some respects from those in the courts of law in England. Those rules were laid down from time to time, by the judges, but were lately revised by the court, and have been printed.

Judgment may be obtained in an action in this court, where the parties and their witnesses are in the island in two months. The means of delay, when the plaintiff wishes to push on a cause, are said to be inconsiderable.

The power of arrest, seems to have come in with the law of England adopted in the colonies. It is not limited to any particular sum in this island; a party liable to the process may be arrested for any sum, but the plaintiff must make an affidavit of the debt.

The owner of fifteen acres of land, or of ten slaves, or of a house, in any of the towns of the island, of the value of 10*l.* current money by the year, is exempted from arrest.

The writ of *habeas corpus* is obtainable in this island. Under the statute, it is granted by the judges; and the attorney-general thinks correctly.

If a person arrested goes to gaol for want of bail, the plaintiff is bound to file his declaration at the next entering-day after the return of the writ, otherwise the defendant will be discharged.

The rule of court makes no exception in case of there being other defendants not in custody or within reach.

A record of the pleadings and issue is made up and kept in the secretary's office.

" We have, strictly speaking, no nisi prius," said the attorney-general; " all our trials may be said to be at " bar. Three days are allotted to the business. On the " two first, jurors attend, and causes are tried; on the " third, the court gives judgment on verdicts; in unde- " fended actions; hears motions for new trials; arrest " of judgment; motions in causes; argument of de- " murrers; pleas in abatement, &c.; which are set down " for those days. After argument, the judges confer on " the matter, and the judgment is given by the chief " justice."

On judgments by default, the debt or damages are immediately assessed by the court. This is in practice, confined to actions of debt, and assumpsit, for liquidated damages. In cases of tort and unliquidated damages, the writ of inquiry is executed before the marshal and one of the judges, as an assessor.

Special juries are known in practice in this island.

Goods bought at marshal's sale are not paid for in produce in this island, except in cases where goods are, by particular agreement of the parties, to be paid for in produce. In such cases, the jury settles the price at which the produce is to be taken, upon evidence laid before them of the particular contract. In undefended causes, the price of the produce is fixed by the court, upon evidence laid before it.

The practice of selling equities of redemption at marshal's sale, under executions at law, has long prevailed in this island, and very many titles to estates depend upon such sales.

" Many executions are taken in the month of Au- " gust (the last month of the year for taking them)," said the attorney-general; " which would not issue, if " the creditors were not apprehensive of a change in the " debtor's circumstances, in the long interval between

ST. CHRISTOPHER.

KING'S BENCH and COMMON PLEAS.

" that month and March. I suppose too, it may lessen " credit."

" The march of justice, in this island, is with such a " steady and rapid step," said the chief justice, " that the " debtor seems to require the interval, from September " to February, during which period no execution can be " awarded and very little produce is in hand, to provide " for engagements. But the system may be injurious to " credit, and mischievous to the debtor in its effects, by " compelling the creditor to enter up judgment during " the court months, inasmuch as he can derive little or " no benefit from doing so, during the other period of " the year."

There is a table of fees in this court, and costs are taxed by the chief justice. Two actions have been brought by counsel, for the recovery of counsel's and solicitor's fees, since the present chief justice has sat upon the bench; and although the court expressed great impatience upon entertaining an action for the recovery of fees of counsel, yet it felt itself bound by the previous uniform practice of the court in that respect.

A slave cannot under any circumstances, give evidence in this court; a free negro is dealt with in all respects as a white witness. " I never knew any sworn otherwise, " than as Christians," said the attorney-general. " I " never knew any free person, upon examination, pro- " fess any other belief than christianity."

Free persons of colour can sue and be sued in this court; they are competent as witnesses; they are not admitted as jurors; they are prevented by law from " practising as barristers of the court; they are excluded, " by the terms of the election law, from voting for, or " being members of, the House of Assembly. They do " not hold offices in any of the courts, or situations under " the government." The crown officer does not know any positive law by which they are disabled from holding these latter offices.

The chief justice said, " after the suggestion that has " been thrown out, as to the court of Chancery, it may be

ST. CHRISTOPHER. — KING'S BENCH and COMMON PLEAS.

"presumed, that a similar arrangement would be beneficial in our courts of common law; nor can it be for one moment, doubted, that the appointment of a man of eminence from the bar of England, as a resident chief justice, would be the best means that could be adopted for commanding decorum and regularity in our proceedings, and a pure administration of justice.

"But I say this, without any admission that our proceedings are not regular and decorous, or that there is impurity in our administration of justice, &c. But leaving out of our consideration the practical results of the existing establishment, the best safeguard for their preservation would be, the appointment which I have suggested. But the nature of the business of our court will require the constant residence of such chief justice. Perhaps his jurisdiction might be extended to the island of Nevis, without great impediment to the business here. But I consider, that to include this island in any larger circuit, would be to confer a partial benefit, and fearfully to aggravate the evils of the present system, by throwing the most difficult and important part of the business upon the assistant judges, who are selected on account of the great respectability of their character, but who have no inducement whatever, so far to neglect their private avocations, as to pursue that course of reading, which can alone qualify them to decide in such cases. It is not on the trial of a cause that the most arduous duty of the chief justice is discharged; it is upon the incidental difficulties of a suit, that the decision of a sound lawyer is required, &c. &c."

The attorney-general said, "the observations which have been made, with respect to the court of Chancery, are in principle, applicable to this court. I feel it necessary, however, to observe, that the talents, assiduity, and unremitted attention of the present chief justice to the duties of that office, have gone very far in counteracting the inconveniences, which arose from the want of professional judges."

ST. CHRISTOPHER.

COMPLAINTS.

## COMPLAINTS, OR SMALL DEBT ACTIONS.

Actions, entered in the court of King's Bench and Common Pleas, for sums under 10*l.*, are denominated complaints.

Such actions are tried by the justices of the court of King's Bench and Common Pleas without a jury, at the monthly sittings of that court.

The trial of those actions does not take up much time; but the determination, according to the present law, is not, the attorney-general thinks, sufficiently speedy.

The usual costs upon such complaints, are;—

| | | | | |
|---|---|---|---|---|
| Upon discontinuance | £4 | 3 | 0 | currency. |
| Upon judgments | 4 | 15 | 6 | |
| Upon execution | 7 | 9 | 6 | |

The attorney-general thinks that the jurisdiction is not sufficiently summary: that "it would be advisable to in-"crease the amount, expedite the trial, and lessen the "costs." *E contra*, the chief justice has great doubt, "if it would be advisable to increase the amount for "which a complaint might be brought;" though he thinks no inconvenience has been experienced from this summary jurisdiction, as it at present exists.

## COURT OF ORDINARY.

This court is held under the authority of the governor's commission: the governor, or in his absence from the government, the temporary commander-in-chief, being the sole judge.

Wills, respecting real and personal property, are proved here, when the testator dies, and the will is in the colony. If a testator die in England, and his will is proved there, an exemplification or probate, is recorded in the office of the registrar in ordinary.

The originals of wills, after they have been proved, are left with the officer until they are transcribed into his book of record: after that, they are taken out by the executor or devisees.

A record is kept of the proceedings of this court.

The costs, in case of a contested will or administration, would be taxed by the registrar.

The attorney-general had never known a case of a contested will; and he did not know any mode of compelling payment of costs. There is a table of fees for proving wills, granting letters of administration, and marriage licences.

There are no means of obtaining a divorce; nor can a wife obtain a separate maintenance in this court.

## COURT OF VICE-ADMIRALTY.

The judge of this court (the chief justice,) derives his authority by commission, under the seal of the high court of Admiralty in England, with power to determine those civil, maritime causes, over which the Instance court exercises jurisdiction. The business of this court, which is not great, consists chiefly of prosecutions of vessels seized under some of the laws of navigation and trade, and does not on an average, amount to more than six or seven prosecutions in a year. Proceedings for the recovery of seamen's wages are instituted, but not frequently; as the expense would be too great for the subject matter.

By statute 46 Geo. 3. c. 54, piracy and other offences committed in places where the admiral has jurisdiction, are directed to be tried in the colonies, according to the laws of England, under commissions to issue as therein mentioned. "No such commission," said the attorney-general, "has been sent to this island, and there is no "jurisdiction for the trial of pirates in this island. In "an instance of a person accused of piracy, which took "place a few years ago, we were under the necessity of "sending the party accused and *witnesses*, to Barbados. "A commission is required here, not only for trial of "piracies, but also of other offences frequently commit- "ted at sea about the coasts of this island, and which "we have no authority to try or punish."

This is not a court of record, but minutes of the proceedings are regularly kept by the registrar.

Costs in this court are taxed by the judge, by a docket framed about the year 1780.

## COURT OF ERROR.

It is considered in this island, that writs of error may be brought from the court of common law to the Governor in Council for any sum, notwithstanding His Majesty's intructions have fixed the amount at *300l.*; the Court Act speaking generally of "any judgment "given by the court of King's Bench and Common "Pleas, for any sum, matter, cause or thing" without reference to the instructions, in clause 35; whereas in the 38th clause, respecting appeals to the King in Council, the amount in that case limited by the instructions, is adverted to.

"I think a court of Appeal in this country, from the "decisions of the court of King's Bench and Common "Pleas, very necessary," said the attorney-general, "but "I consider the court of Error, as now established, of "little utility. The persons who are to revise the de- "terminations of the courts of law should certainly be "qualified by legal knowledge : probably improvements "in other departments may furnish such persons." "I "cannot suggest any other improvement in the adminis- "tration of the law in this court, except its annihila- "tion," said the chief justice, "inasmuch as it offers "no gradation in an appeal from the court of King's "Bench and Common Pleas to the King in Council. "The court should therefore be entirely remodelled, or "it should cease to be the immediate step between the "court of common law and the King in Council."

## ESCHEATS.

There is no Escheat court, or escheator in this island: there is a person holding a commission as Casual Receiver, whose duty it is considered to be to take the direction of property falling to the Crown by escheat, or for default of kindred, and to dispose of it for the advantage of the Crown.

# CRIMINAL COURTS.

## COURT OF KING'S BENCH.

Criminal prosecutions of every description are entertained in this island by the court of King's Bench and Common Pleas.

Offenders are generally prosecuted by the attorney-general, at the suit of the Crown. A prosecution is commonly instituted by laying a bill before the grand jury, sometimes, but very rarely, by criminal information. The indictments are generally drawn by the attorney-general. The fee is paid by the public.

The grand jury are selected from the persons who attend on the general venire, and are generally the most respectable of those jurors. They are charged and addressed by the chief justice.

The grand jury, if desirous of advice, apply to the court, which generally refers to the attorney or solicitor-general, if the judges have any difficulty as to the point inquired of.

Informations before magistrates are in general taken on oath, and depositions signed. The attorney-general has known magistrates issue warrants on informations not on

St. Christopher. — King's Bench.

oath, but they have been always in such cases instructed of the impropriety of such proceedings. The party seldom enters into recognizance to appear and prosecute, or the witnesses to appear and give evidence.

There is nothing in the arrangement or form of trial differing from the manner of proceeding in England, except that in cases of felony the prisoner is allowed counsel, to make a full defence for him, and to speak to matters of fact as well as of law.

Witnesses are seldom allowed their expenses. Persons acquitted are not detained for payment of fees, but the fees in such case are paid by the public.

Many cases of assault and battery are brought before this court, which might be tried at the quarter sessions. An instance of capital punishment has not occurred for very many years; the trial of a prisoner in this court for a capital offence is of very rare occurrence.

## QUARTER SESSIONS.

In this court the senior justice of the peace acts as chairman, when there is no member of council present. The matters usually occupying the court, are indictments for breaches of the peace, nuisances, non-repair of roads, &c. and the election of waywardens and constables. Counsel practise in this court.

The attorney-general has the indictment prepared, and usually conducts the prosecution, but it may be put into the hands of other counsel.

The expenses of prosecutions in this court are generally borne by the public.

A record of the proceedings is kept by the colonial secretary, who in this court, acts as clerk of the peace, and takes the costs.

## SPECIAL SESSIONS FOR TRIAL OF SLAVES.

This court, for the trial of slaves, in cases of felony, is composed of the justices of the peace, and a jury of twelve persons, and is appointed *pro re natâ.*

All such offences as are capital, if committed by white or free persons, are capital when committed by slaves; as treason, murder, rape, robbery, arson, shooting at, cutting, &c. under Lord Ellenborough's Act; sheep-stealing under No. 401; so is setting fire to canes.

By Nos. 2 and 52, (Laws of St. Christopher) slaves were made liable to the punishment of death for maiming, bruising, or wounding a white person; so for absenting themselves six months from their owner's service; but these clauses, though not *repealed,* (the constant opprobrium) have not within the recollection of the attorney-general, been *acted upon.*

The information against a slave is taken on oath, and in writing. In capital cases, slaves are apprehended, examined, and committed for trial.

The magistrate returns the depositions and examinations to the secretary's office, and the matter is notified to the attorney-general, who decides whether there be sufficient grounds for putting the accused on trial, upon perusing the depositions and examinations. If the case is directed to proceed, the magistrate associates with himself two other justices, process is issued for summoning the jury and witnesses, and the offender is tried on a charge delivered against him in writing, in the nature of an indictment.

The attorney-general has not known an instance of a slave committed for a capital offence, admitted to bail; but the chief justice is of opinion, that if an application were made to bail such slave, the same course would be pursued, as in case of other offenders, and that one of the justices of the court of King's Bench and Common Pleas would interfere upon the occasion.

St. Christopher.

Slave Court.

The trial of a slave takes place within twelve days after his apprehension. There is no grand jury upon the trial of slaves. A written charge we have seen, is preferred, in the nature of an indictment, and a record of the proceedings is kept; *vivâ voce* testimony is required on the trial, and slave evidence admitted.

Slaves, who are Christians, take the common oath; those who are not, may be examined without oath.

It is the opinion of both the chief justice and the attorney-general of this island, that slave evidence is in general, correct, and ought to be depended upon.

The chief justice further thought, that the evidence of slaves might be properly and beneficially admitted in all cases, under due precautions, without any restrictions. The attorney-general said, "I think, with the qualifications and restrictions suggested in Lord Bathurst's circular letter on that subject, there would be no impropriety in admitting the testimony of slaves in all courts."

Sometimes the master retains counsel to defend his slave; at others, professional assistance is gratuitously afforded. The attorney-general considers it a very important part of his duty, to take care that slaves are not convicted on insufficient evidence, or of greater offences than the circumstances clearly amount to.

Sentence of death must be communicated to the commander-in-chief, within thirty-six hours. The attorney-general thinks there may be an appeal, in the name of the slave, to the court of King's Bench and Common Pleas: there is, however, no provision made for appeal in the Acts by which criminal slaves are tried.

Every negro in this island, is not considered, by presumption of law, a slave. If a negro appears in a court of justice as a witness, the onus of shewing him to be a slave, and, as such, incompetent, is held in St. Christopher to be on the person who shall object to him, on account of that supposed disability. "Free negroes constantly bring actions in the court," proceeded the attorney-general, "and nobody ever imagined it to be necessary for them to shew, in *limine*, that they are not slaves."

Since the passing of the Amelioration Act of the Leeward Islands, the power of the master, before undefined, (but the chief justice says not supposed to be absolute,) is considered as limited to that degree of controul which must necessarily follow the relation of master and slave; but its most effectual limitation is in the feeling of the court and country, which would not endure an abuse of such power. The term, *cruelly maltreat* in that Act, in the opinion of the attorney-general, was intended to afford the slave protection from every species of ill-treatment, which amounted to cruelty: "it goes so far to "qualify the authority of the master," thought the chief justice, "as to expose him to the penalties of the Act for "any, the slightest infliction of undeserved punishment."

ST. CHRISTOPHER.

SLAVE COURT.

In principle, the property acquired by a slave is considered in this island as his master's; in practice, it is his own.

A slave cannot claim redress by way of damages, to be awarded to him, for an injury done to him by any free person. Slaves cannot claim redress in any court, in respect of injuries done them by other slaves of their owner, or by the slaves of other persons.

Coroner's inquests are taken on the bodies of slaves who die suddenly, or under suspicious circumstances, or without visible disease.

The chief justice said, "The slave laws framed from "time to time, from the earliest period of the existence "of the colonies to the present day, embracing a space "of time which includes a great and happy revolution in "the condition of the slave population, certainly admit "of great improvement. The harsh and sanguinary "enactments, which the state of society a century ago "rendered necessary, or in which the unsubdued feel-"ings of those at that time in authority delighted, are "utterly at variance with the benevolent and humane "treatment which the slaves, (with some few and de-"testable instances of exception,) now experience. The "improvements that I would suggest, are these:—1st, a "general revision of our slave laws, so that they be re-"duced to one simple, uniform, intelligible, and prac-"ticable Act; and, 2dly, the admission of slaves as

ST. CHRISTOPHER.

SLAVE COURT.

"competent witnesses, in all cases where they can be "made to comprehend the obligation into which they "enter upon giving their testimony, to speak the truth. "I do not believe, that the ends of justice can be more "securely attained, than by the present mode of trial of "slaves for capital offences." The attorney-general said, "It does not occur to me, that the mode of trial of "criminal slaves requires any alteration. The slave "laws however, ought to be revised, if it were only for "the purpose of expunging many disgusting enactments, "which, though generally condemned, and never put in "practice, have been unaccountably permitted to re-"main unrepealed. But there is every reason to expect "from such a measure, other and more beneficial results "to the slave population. The sentiments which appear "formerly to have prevailed regarding that class, have "in a great measure, given way to the efforts of humanity, "and the appeals to religion and justice, which have "been made on their behalf; and it cannot be doubted, "that the improved sense, which is now entertained very "generally, of what is due to them as men and fellow "subjects, when brought into practical operation, will "go far to forward the establishment of their just rights, "and the general improvement of their condition. The "communications lately received from Lord Bathurst, "will no doubt soon direct the attention of the respective "branches of the legislature to that important subject; "and I feel every assurance they will enter upon the "matter with an earnest disposition to comply, as far as "they reasonably can, with the wishes of the British "government."

---

The chief justice in the suspension of the sittings of the courts, obligingly offered for the perusal of the Commissioners, his manuscript notes of the recent cases, which were thankfully accepted. From the same quarter, the Commissioners were promptly furnished with a copy of the printed rules and orders of the court of King's Bench and Common Pleas.

The Commissioners attended an examination before magistrates, on a charge of cruelty to slaves, brought against a manager. The senior magistrate laid down as law, that "one unprovoked, or unnecessary blow, "amounted to cruelty." The punishment inflicted in this case was slight, and turned out to be merited, and the magistrates very properly, dismissed the complaint. ST. CHRISTOPHER. — COMPLAINTS. Minutes, Nov. 19, 1823.

The examination took place publicly, in the Court-house. The chief justice was present.

The Commissioners again attended a meeting of magistrates sitting at the Court-house, to investigate another case of complaint of ill-treatment of slaves, from the same estate. Eight women had been threatened with a whipping by the driver, for coming too late to their work in the morning. They alleged on their part, that they arrived in the field, at the time when the bell of a neighbouring estate was ringing. They were not grinding now: (that is, it was not crop-time, when they meet earlier than out of crop:) The bell of their own estate was out of order. The first woman whom the driver threatened to flog, said, "She was no well, and could "not bear to be licked." The driver ordered her to be laid down to receive a few lashes. She and all the other women ran away, and preferred their complaint. They said, "they knew well what swear was : no lie." Nov. 22, 1823.

The driver in answer said, "These women false—bad. "They sometimes come late, and forgive them. They "say—drop sleep—and then excuse them by coming "late." He was asked, what he meant by *late,* out of crop time? He said, he meant they ought to be at their work as soon as they could see to work—the sooner the better—in the cool.

He was asked, at what hour the bell of the Fountain (the neighbouring) estate rang? He said, "at five," but it long, long, ring. "They no come till just sun-"rise, and then no excuse coming late. Do it on pur-"pose to make flog, and then go complain."

The manager added, that, "since the dismissal of the "frivolous complaint on the 19th, without punishing the "false accuser, there had been nothing but tumult, and a

ST. CHRISTOPHER.

COMPLAINTS.

" disposition to riot, on the estate, and that the life of a " manager was now becoming intolerable; since all sub- " ordination was destroyed."

The slaves retorted, that, " when deserve, they content " be flogged, but run away to-day, because no ought be " punished." Being asked why they did not first complain to their master? they said, " Because he gave too " much power to driver, who, hard, cruel man; and, " when complain to massa before, no good, but floggee " for tell."

The magistrates said, that if the punishment had been inflicted, they should have considered it unwarrantable and cruel. As it was prevented, they dismissed the parties, with an admonition to the driver and manager, and a little advice to the slaves, to do their duty and behave peaceably.

The manager then complained, that the slave, who was the complainant on the 19th, now refused to go to work at all; and he completely established the fact by satisfactory evidence. The magistrates said, " he had " the power of punishment, and it was a fit occasion to " exercise it." The manager observed, " he was become " afraid of *speaking to* the slaves, or indeed, almost of " *looking at* them." The justices—" Order her to go to " work, and, if she refuses, punish her."

Minutes, Nov. 25, 1823. The Commissioners attended a court of Special Sessions for the trial of slaves. The slaves were prosecuted and defended with competent skill, on the part of the bar; but the bench consisting of magistrates, though extremely well-disposed, was not equal to the duty of deciding upon points of evidence, or expounding the law to the jury. The Act seems deficient, in not requiring the charge to be in writing; in point of fact it was so, and drawn up as an indictment. Seven or eight of the jury were challenged by one of the prisoners. The evidence was taken down in writing. After conviction, the prisoners had benefit of clergy allowed them; but it was prayed for them by others.

Dec. 2, 1823. The Commissioners attended the investigation of a complaint before the magistrates, representing that the due allowance of food, appointed by the Amelioration Act, had not been regularly furnished to the slaves of Mr. ———'s estate. The decision stated, that there was an arrear of the allowance of food for two days, but arising from the owner's distress and want of means. The penalty denounced by the Act was not inflicted, because so excessively severe, that it was never known to have been put in force. The fees of court, and the loss of three days labour, were however, in themselves, something considerable, and would operate, it was observed to the Commissioners, as no slight punishment.

St. Christopher.

Complaints.

Several complaints were preferred at different times, by legatees against executors, and by suitors respecting the amount of costs, at law and in equity, in this island.

Complaints. Minutes, Nov. 10, 1823.

One, preferred by a Mr. Abbott, was satisfactorily explained by the chief justice. Another, exhibited by Mr. MacMahon, established an error, of serious consequence to the party, in the president of the council, when acting as chancellor, in the absence of the governor; proceeding however, I should add, from ignorance, and not from bad intention.

A complaint was preferred by a black woman, called Catherine Disney, of the freedom of her daughter being improperly withheld. Nov. 26, 1823.

The Governor, in conversation with the Commissioners, stated, that he had himself formerly caused inquiry to be made into Catherine Disney's case, and was satisfied that the claim of freedom for her daughter, was unfounded. Colonel Maxwell also spoke in strong terms, of the miserable state of the island of Anguilla; and said, his secretary should make a communication to the Commissioners upon that subject. It was unnecessary for the Commissioners to visit it. It had no charter; no constitution; no courts; no judges; was without a form of government, or system of law; crimes escaped without punishment; and two or three thousand unregistered slaves were left without protection. Nov. 29, 1823.

The Governor sent the Commissioners some despatches and communications from Anguilla, shewing the wretched Dec. 3, 1823.

ST. CHRISTOPHER.

COMPLAINTS.

condition of that island, without laws, and without a government.

The following are specimens and extracts.

---

*Extract of a letter from His Excellency, Charles W. Maxwell, Captain-general, bearing date Dec. 2, 1823; addressed to the Commissioners of Inquiry, &c.*

" As any unnecessary delay in the conduct of your com- " mission, is no doubt, to be avoided, I beg to acquaint " you, that, from the present state of the colony of An- " guilla, I conceive your presence there, cannot be re- " quired.

" The island not being in possession of a constitution, " there are consequently, no legally established courts; " nor are there any public officers, who can, in a strict " sense, be considered as legally appointed: from these " circumstances, I conclude you will have no field in " which to exercise the functions of your commission, " and that your progress would be unnecessarily retarded " by your visiting the island. I cannot, however, permit " this opportunity to pass, of requesting your most serious " attention to the many evils that daily result to the com- " munity of Anguilla, for the want of a properly consti- " tuted government, and to the fact, that a population, " approaching very nearly to *three thousand souls*, are " held in no restraint by any acknowledged laws, or con- " stitutional authority.

" Crimes of the greatest magnitude, have been com- " mitted with impunity, and all property is held by a " very insecure tenure, for the want of that power to re- " dress, and to afford security, which a constitution can " alone, bestow."

---

*Extract of a letter from Anguilla; dated Sept. 22, 1823.*

" I AM sorry, for the cause of humanity, as well as on " a pecuniary account, for the losses that I am so often "meeting with, in the murder of the slaves under my "authority; and I feel deeply for the character of my "native country, placed under a government, that fails "in all the ends for which mankind entered into social "union, I presume for mutual protection, that the "stronger might not tyrannize over the weaker: but "here, those who feel themselves confident in their "strength of body and family union, are left to justify "their imaginary wrongs in their own way. More worth "is attached to a cane, an ear of corn, a yam, or a "potato, than to the life of a fellow creature. Mr. "Hughes goes on to state the death of two slaves."

---

*Extract of a letter from the present Lieutenant-governor of Anguilla, to the private Secretary of Captain-general Maxwell; dated November* 21, 1822.

"I inclose the copy of the inquests on the body of "the man, Scipio. I think it however, necessary to ob-"serve, that the jury then named, were not sworn, there "being no coroner here, and I could not attend in per-"son. Should his Excellency be inclined to support "coroners here, which I think would be highly neces-"sary, I beg leave to recommend, &c."

By the deposition of a Mr. Carty, it appears that the man Scipio, being detected in a potato ground, had been cruelly beaten, and received wounds of which he died.

---

*Extract of a letter of Lieutenant-governor Richardson, relative to a complaint in the case of the man, Scipio; 31st October,* 1822.

"I immediately caused an inquest to be held on the "body of the said Scipio; but for the want of a jail, I "could not proceed to commit the persons suspected of "this horrid act; neither could I obtain a vessel for the "purpose of sending to St. Kitts for a special commis-"sion of oyer and terminer, to bring the matter to issue

St. Christopher. — Complaints.

"during the hurricane months, which is the only neglect "Mr. Hughes can accuse me of."

---

*Extract of a letter of Mr. W. Hughes; dated 7th December*, 1822.

"I can justly say, that the lands of my late father were "converted into common, and the slaves thereon into "game, by the inhabitants of Anguilla."

---

*Extract of a letter of James Hay, principal Officer of his Majesty's Customs; 4th March*, 1822.

"Justice is laughed to scorn; and burglaries, as-"saults, and even attempts at assassination, are allowed "to go unpunished."

---

*Extract of a letter of the Lieutenant-governor; February* 28, 1822.

"I must regret that the want of a jail is loudly com-"plained of.

"It has hitherto impeded the administration of justice; "and almost, nay, altogether, defied authority.

"There are no public funds to erect a jail."

---

*Extract of a letter from the Lieutenant-governor, dated January* 26*th*, 1823; *in answer to certain Charges preferred against him.*

"Admits he did say, under circumstances he explains, "that upon what he conceived of Mr. J. P.'s disposition, "if the said J. P. should attempt to stop him in the road, "(which could not be for a good purpose,) he would in-"jure him. Your Excellency will be pleased to permit "me to make known to your Excellency, with respect

St. Christopher.

Complaints.

" to my riding with pistols, I have been in the habit of " doing so for these forty years past, and yet continue so " to do; and the more so at present, on account of the " many private insidious enemies which I have in the " island."

---

To the representation of the President and Council, concerning the personal character and conduct of the chief magistrate—" Situated as this island is, without " laws, without courts, and without any means whatever " to enforce order and decorum amongst the people;" the Lieutenant-governor replies, by asking, " how is it " possible that the chief resident magistrate can effect any " measure for securing the peace and tranquillity of the " island, under the existing circumstances, emanating from " the want of a jail, and where orders or directions are po- " sitively disregarded?" He then alludes to "violent out- " rages, assaults, and breaches of the peace that have taken " place in the presence of the magistrates themselves, and " without their interposition; and prays for such essential " regulations, as may put a stop to the present evils, so " highly injurious to this, his Majesty's little island."

---

Particular Officers. Judges.

The judges in St. Christopher are selected, as in the other islands, from the first class of the community. It is not necessary that any of them should be barristers, or should have gone through a course of previous legal study.

Barristers.

It is not required, that persons acting as counsel in the courts of this island, should have been called to the bar in England. But by a law lately passed, it is required that they should have kept twelve terms, at least, at some of the inns of court in London, with the exception of those persons who were then attending the offices of barristers, with the view of being called to the bar. They are not admitted as licentiates in this island.

Solicitors and Attorneys.

The persons admitted to the bar, are by a law of the island, allowed to act also as solicitors and attorneys. Besides the counsel, who act as attorneys and solicitors, the Court Act permits four attorneys to be sworn in the

ST. CHRISTOPHER.

PARTICULAR OFFICERS.

JUSTICE OF PEACE.

court of King's Bench and Common Pleas, who are admitted to take the oaths in that court. No previous clerkship is required of them.

The appointment of a justice of the peace is by the governor in council, and he is removable by the same authority. His fees are, for a warrant, summons, commitment and recognizance, one dollar each; for the summons of a witness, half a dollar.

Justices of the peace have no jurisdiction whatever in civil matters, in this island.

The want of a Police Act is sensibly felt in this island. The justices use all means in their power to preserve the public peace; but offences against it are frequent and violent.

Great inconvenience is felt by gentlemen acting as magistrates, from so many of the laws remaining in MS. The printed copy of the laws comes no lower than 1799.

Justices of the peace have no jurisdiction concerning disputes as to seamen's wages.

Justices of the peace of this island, have not been in the habit of visiting the jail; the senior magistrate is not clear as to their jurisdiction; the marshal being a public officer appointed by the Crown, is perhaps under the control of the court of King's Bench only.

Applications are sometimes made to justices of the peace in cases of injury by one slave against another. Justices of the peace in "this island," said the senior magistrate, "are, and ever have been, accessible to com-"plaints made by slaves of severe and cruel treatment "by their owners, and are prompt to afford them every "protection and remedy in their power, and upon due "grounds would bind the owner over to answer in the "proper court."

The same offences are bailable in slaves as in white and free coloured persons; but slaves cannot join in the recognizance, and therefore bail is seldom offered, except by their owner.

Upon the question, whether a negro is free? the senior magistrate thought twelve or even six months, in a small community like that, a sufficient reputation of freedom.

ST. CHRISTOPHER.

DEPUTY PROVOST MARSHAL

There were six commitments in criminal cases in this island, as we were informed by the provost-marshal, in 1821, and fourteen others in 1822. One man was executed in January 1822, for burglary. The present deputy-marshal it appears, entered into office on the 1st of May, 1821, and could only answer the questions of the Commissioners from that period.

There is one common jail for the whole island; and a cage in each of the towns of Basseterre, Old Road, Sandy Point, and Dieppe Bay.

In the jail are confined persons of every description; but the best rooms are allotted to debtors, and males and females are separated at night. The accused and convicted are kept together, except when the offence imputed or established, is murder. Most of the rooms are commodious and airy; those to the westward, however, are said to be "not quite so comfortable as the others." The prison, we were told, is always in as good a state as the nature of the place and the habits of those generally confined there will admit. A daily allowance of provisions, adequate to his or her sustenance, is issued to each prisoner, except debtors, who are not fed by the marshal unless their circumstances are so reduced as to render them incapable of supporting themselves, and in that case the marshal gets no remuneration for maintaining them.

The cage is intended for the confinement of slaves who are taken up in the several towns by the supervisors and constables, for wandering about after the hour of ten o'clock at night.

SUPERVISOR OF THE CAGE.

The cage in Basseterre was in good condition when the Commissioners were in the island; and the supervisor assured us, is always kept clean. The duties of this officer are, to attend at the cage and receive all slaves taken up at night, or sent there to be confined; to keep good order, to the best of his skill; and, as he added, to inspect other matters. The salary of the supervisor is *50l.* per annum; and he is entitled to *9s.* for each slave committed to the cage, and *9s.* for each slave flogged by him. He is appointed and removable by the local legislature.

ST. CHRISTOPHER.

PARTICULAR OFFICERS.

Slaves are still sent to the cage to be confined and flogged by their master's orders, though the instances but rarely occur.

Punishments are not quite so frequent as formerly. The flogging is inflicted with a cat-o'-nine-tails.

CORONER.

There are *four* coroners in this island, appointed and removable by the governor or his *locum tenens.* The coroner is allowed 5*l.* current money of the island, for every inquest he holds. The coroner is guided in his duty by the rules which govern coroners in England. The only difference in holding inquests on slaves and free persons is, that in the former case the jury may be composed of less than twelve persons, but shall be formed of three at least; in the latter, it must consist of twelve jurors.

The Commissioners examined two of the gentlemen filling the office of coroner for this island, one of whom had acted in the situation for twenty-five years. Neither of these gentlemen had reason to think there had been any instances of death by severity, of which a coroner had not received information. One of them had never held an inquest on a slave said to be killed by his owner, or by any person acting under his authority. The other, (the senior,) had held inquests on two slaves supposed to have died from severity, but nothing of the kind was proved.

Witnesses are always sworn, and their evidence taken down in writing.

All inquisitions are forthwith returned, and filed in the secretary's office of the island.

REGISTRAR OF DEEDS.

Complaints have been made in this island, of the delay which occurs in the Register's office, in transcribing deeds and wills into the books of the registry, and the length of time that deeds are kept there for that purpose. The officers of the different courts keep their records and papers in rooms assigned them in different parts of the Court-house. These rooms are sufficient for the preservation of the papers and records, and are said to be properly kept, and that the papers of modern date may easily be consulted.

St. Christopher.

Defect of jurisdiction. Minutes, Nov. 26, 1823.

A deputation of the coloured inhabitants of the island waited upon the Commissioners with a memorial, stating their grievances.

One of the most frequent subjects of complaint in this island, was the expense and delay attending the recovery of small debts. This defect was mentioned to us on our arrival by the merchants, and afterwards by the senior magistrate; and lastly, a lady of the name of M'Cleod, made a specific complaint upon the subject against her lawyer, producing documents to shew that, where the amount for which she sued was 8*l.* 2*s.* his charge came to 30*l.* though the cause was not proceeded in. Indeed, for discontinuing the action, he charged her 20*l.* 14*s.*

Under this head, therefore, of defect of jurisdiction, I beg to notice—

The want, in this island, of a court of summary jurisdiction, for the cheap and speedy recovery of small debts.

The want of a Police Act, for the preservation of the peace, in the town of Basseterre.

The want of a commission for the trial of piracies, and other offences committed at sea about the coasts of this island.

The want of jurisdiction in justices of the peace to decide differences respecting seamen's wages, so as to prevent expensive suits for trifling claims in the court of Admiralty.

I think it objectionable, that for capital offences slaves should be tried before the ordinary magistrates and not before judges habituated to the administration of the criminal law; and that their cases should not be submitted to a grand jury. At the same time, I am anxious to remark, after closely observing the conduct of the magistrates during their periodical sittings at the Court-house, that I sincerely believe that the complaints of slaves, against whomsoever directed, always meet in this island the readiest attention, and are most impartially and equitably decided.

# TORTOLA.

His Majesty's Commissioners sailed from St. Christopher for the Virgin Islands, on the 9th day of December, 1823, and landed at Tortola, on the day following.

On application for a copy of the laws, we learnt with surprise, that in this island the laws all remain in manuscript, and are, as might be expected, many of them in an imperfect state. Among the manuscript Acts, we noticed:—

1783. *The Court Act.*

Cl. 5. The mode of service of the summons is pointed out, very minutely and with great care.

Cl. 8. But no appearance day is fixed.

Cl. 64. It is provided, that if the body or goods shall be found after the return of the writ (of execution) the marshal may still levy or take, &c.

Cl. 142. Directs that fees shall be settled by the legislature; (governor, council and assembly.)

1783. *A Slave Act*, crude and barbarous.

1784. *A Registry Act.*

At a later period, an amended Registry Act; so—

*An Act to compel executors to deliver an appraisement of the state and effects of the testator, upon oath.*

It was afterwards represented to the Commissioners, that "the Act requiring executors to deliver on oath, an "account of the appraised value of the testator's effects, "was rendered perfectly nugatory from the omission of "the legislature, to attach any penalty to neglect or "disobedience." TORTOLA. LAWS.

## COURTS.

The courts established in the Virgin Islands, for the administration of civil justice, are the court of Chancery, the court of common Pleas, and the court of Error. COURTS.

The courts established in the Virgin Islands, for the administration of criminal justice, are the court of King's Bench and Grand Sessions of the Peace, and for the trial of slaves, a Bench of Magistrates.

## COURT OF CHANCERY.

Courts of Chancery for this island are usually held at St. Christopher. A court is only held at Tortola when the governor visits this part of his government, and then for no precise time, but so long as his Excellency may think proper, from the nature of the business to be done. CHANCERY

There is a manuscript volume of the rules of practice of this court, with some slight variations, with respect to *time*, &c. from the practice of the high court of Chancery in England.

There never was in this island, at the same time, more than one Master in Chancery, until within a month before the arrival of the Commissioners, when a Master in Chancery *extra* was appointed, at the particular solicitation of the Master. There is not in general, more business than can be transacted by one Master. The Masters receive no salaries, but are paid by fees; they give no security.

TORTOLA.

CHANCERY.

The fees on the sale of an estate in the Master's office, are—

| | £ | s. | d. |
|---|---|---|---|
| To the Master, per hour - - - | 1 | 10 | 4 |
| To the attorney, where his presence should be considered absolutely necessary - | 3 | 6 | 0 |

The chief justice, who is also Colonial Master in Chancery, said, "Estates would be sold conformably "to the decree of the court; where it should appear ad- "visable to *allot* in order to bring purchasers, that would "be done. I should," he proceeds "as Master, always "cause an appraisement to be made previous to the sale "of property; where the bidding was far below the ap- "praisement, I should consider *that* sufficient cause to "postpone the sale to some other time."

An appeal to the King in Council has, it is said, the effect of staying the proceedings, and when made from interlocutory orders, may occasion great delay.

Costs are, "frequently," taxed in this court by the Master.

There is a table of fees established in this court by a former Chancellor.

The counsel's retaining fee, by the docket, and which is allowed in taxation, is 16*l.* 10*s.* currency, but the fee usually given is, the Master believed, 50*l.* sterling, and a fee he says, is also expected with the brief; but the King's counsel says, the retaining fee ought to be paid with the brief, and no other is given; but there is a fee for argument.

The fees of this court have always been regulated by the authority of the Chancellor.

"I should recommend," said the King's counsel, "the "appointment of a person in this island to issue subpœnas, "hear motions, and transact all the business of the court, "except that of hearing causes, which should be done by "the chancellor. The expense attending the prosecution "of a suit, as things are now circumstanced, is very "considerable."

## COURT OF COMMON PLEAS.

This court derives its authority from an Act of Assembly, passed in 1783. The court generally sits two, three and four days, in the months of April, May and June, respectively, in the month of July probably a day or two more, and the August court is generally continued for every eight or ten days, until the end of September, and sometimes as late as October.

There are a few rules of practice in this court relative to pleadings, motions, and other proceedings.

Actions are commenced by filing not only a declaration but a copy of an account, bond, note, bill, &c. at the defendant's last place of abode, with an indorsement, naming the plaintiff and defendant, and setting forth the cause of action damages, &c. A person who has never been in the island, cannot be sued, unless he has a power of attorney upon record.

Cou. Act, cl. 4 and 5.

The Court Act gives the power of arrest. A person not a freeholder, may be arrested for any sum of money; but if for a sum under 20*l.* the person arrested may be discharged on his swearing that he is an inhabitant, and that he does not intend to depart from these islands, and entering a common appearance.

Bail must be given for all sums above 20*l.*, but a person possessing ten acres of land, &c. is exempt from arrest.

The pleadings are sometimes framed according to the mode in England; at other times short pleas are entered on the back of the declaration in court, thus:—" I ap-" pear for the defendant and plead *non assumpsit.*"

The writ of execution is the same as in the other islands. Chattels are sold at public outcry in thirty days after levy; lands on the fortieth day after the levy. The Court Act requires that public notice of all sales shall be given by advertisement posted up (there being no *paper* published in these islands) in the Road Town of Tor-

TORTOLA.

COMMON PLEAS.

tola, at the town of Great Harbour, in the island of Joes Van Dykes, and in the valley of Spanish Town. Goods sold at marshal's sale are sometimes payable in produce according to the nature of the contract, but generally in cash; but produce taken in payment of debts is always appraised on oath, unless the price be agreed upon between the parties, and sugar and cotton only, are legal tenders; and little or no difficulty is said to have arisen in this island from the making produce a legal tender; or rather, from receiving it in payment at a fair valuation.

" A levy on an equity of redemption is not warranted " by our executions," said the King's counsel; " and I do " not apprehend that it (an equity of redemption,) could " be sold by the marshal."

There is a docket of fees established for this court.

Costs are taxed by the chief justice. But where the attorneys for the plaintiff and the defendant make no objection to each other's bills, taxation never takes place. The suitor, however, if he is dissatisfied, may compel a taxation, by making a special application for that purpose.

Counsel's fees are paid by the client. Actions have been supported for the recovery of them.

Some of the judges take down the evidence, generally the chief justice.

The chief justice sums up, and where it appears to be necessary states the law to the jury.

Free persons of colour can sue, and be sued in this court; are competent witnessess; are not admitted as jurors; are by law excluded from being members of the House of Assembly; are not subject to any penalties, from which a white person is exempted; and are " sub- " ject to no other disabilities, than such as exclude them " from all public situations and offices."

Court act, cl. 19.

The chief justice thinks the clauses in the Court Act, which relate to the qualification of jurors, require alteration. By Cl. 19 of that Act, I find the persons pointed out to the marshal to be summoned upon juries, are, " *Freeholders, or merchants, or traders, or lessees of*

" *estates.*" Of persons thus qualified, there are not always a sufficient number in attendance; which proceeds in a great measure, from the reduced number of white inhabitants, many of whom being aliens, are objected to on that account, and many being residents in remote parts of the colony, their attendance is often unavoidably prevented.

TORTOLA.

COMMON PLEAS.

## COMPLAINT COURT.

Small debts not exceeding 20*l.*, are denominated complaints, and are recoverable in this court. The costs do not exceed the sum of 1*l.* 16*s.* 3*d.*, up to execution, and they are in general speedily decided.

## COURT OF ORDINARY.

This court derives its authority from His Majesty's commission to the captain-general; who appoints his deputy in this island to grant probates of wills, letters of administration, and marriage licences. All wills executed within the Virgin Islands, are proved here; after wills have been proved and registered, they are returned to the executor.

If application is made to the deputy ordinary for letters of administration, and a *caveat* is entered, the case must be referred to the governor. The crown officer did not believe that an appeal would lie from the governor's decision.

Minutes are kept of the proceedings of this court.

There is no table of fees in this court; "I believe " custom governs with respect thereto," was the observation of the chief justice.

The costs of this court are not taxed. There is no process of excommunication, or other effectual mode of punishing contempts in this court.

An action has lately been supported in this island, brought by the deputy ordinary for a fee.

TORTOLA.

ORDINARY.

There are no means of obtaining a divorce in this island, nor is there any mode by which a wife can obtain a separate maintenance.

## COURT OF VICE-ADMIRALTY.

This court derives its authority from the court of Admiralty in England. It has jurisdiction in matters of prize and revenue. It has one judge, a surrogate; the present surrogate was appointed by the governor. He holds his office during good behaviour, and is removable by the governor. The former judge was appointed from England.

There is not much business done in the Instance Court. There have been a few instances of proceedings for seamen's wages; they are not attended with much expense, and are said to be very summary.

No Admiralty Sessions are held in this island; persons charged with piracy must be carried to Barbados.

There is a docket of fees for the Prize and Instance Court, sent out from the court of Admiralty in England, bearing date 1814. The registrar of the court taxes the costs by this docket.

## COURT OF ERROR.

This court is established by the Court Act. The judges of the court of Common Pleas are excluded by law, from sitting in the court of Error.

The members of this court decide by a majority.

The chief justice thinks, but I do not agree with him, that it would be an improvement, to allow any judge of the court appealed from, who did not sit on the trial, to sit in the court of Error; and further, that three members of council should in all cases, be sufficient to form a court; which would certainly, somewhat palliate the existing evil: but a much more effectual remedy will, I venture to hope, be very shortly provided.

# CRIMINAL COURTS.

## KING'S BENCH AND GRAND SESSIONS.

This court derives its authority from certain clauses of the Court Act. The judges of this court are, the lieutenant-governor, the members of His Majesty's council, the justices of the Common Pleas, and the justices of the Peace.

This court is held twice a-year, on the first Monday in March, and the first Monday in September, at the Court-house.

The King's counsel draws the indictment, and prosecutes offenders in this court. A fee of *4l.* *10s.* currency is paid to the King's counsel for drawing an indictment and conducting the whole business before the petty jury. In cases of assault and battery, the fee is paid by the prosecutor in the first instance. In Arthur Hodge's case, the legislature gave the Solicitor-General of Antigua, a fee of *400l.* currency, " and to the King's " counsel for these islands, *330l.* of like money. Lately, " said the present crown officer, I presented my bill to " the assembly, for drawing indictments for breaches of " the Abolition Act, and also for cases of murder; and " my bill was rejected, on the score of my receiving a salary of *33l.* currency, from the public. This fee is " given me for advice to the governor or president, and " other public officers, in lieu of specific charges for business transacted."

The counsel for the crown would draw an indictment in this island, in a case which had not been previously before a magistrate. I did so myself, said the King's counsel, in the case of a man charged with having ille

TORTOLA.

GRAND SESSIONS.

gally imported five slaves into this island, from St. Croix.

The president of the court always delivers a charge to the grand jury. When the grand jury are desirous of advice upon points of law, they apply to the King's counsel.

If the accused party be found guilty, the prosecutor pays no expenses; if otherwise, he does. Witnesses residing at a distance are allowed their expenses by the court in all cases, if they claim them. A prisoner, after his acquittal, is immediately liberated, without being called upon for payment of any fee.

A trial for a capital offence seldom occurs; "*once in* "*seven years*," said the King's counsel, adding, "capital punishments are very seldom inflicted in this "island. I never knew one, except for murder, during "a residenee of thirty-five years." Fine and imprisonment are most commonly substituted for capital punishment.

## SLAVE COURT.

A slave court is established in this island for the trial of slaves, under an Act intituled "An Act for the Go-"vernment of Slaves." The court is composed of three justices; they have jurisdiction over every species of offence committed by slaves. All offences committed by slaves in this colony, are tried by a bench of magistrates.

The slave courts are held, not at any fixed time, but as often as occasion requires.

Besides the offences considered capital, if committed by whites or free coloured persons, there are others which will subject a slave (exclusively) to capital punishment: such are "absence from his owner's service for three "months in one continued space of time, or for six "months in two years." "The ringleader of slaves "above sixteen years of age, running away in gangs of "ten or more, and remaining out for ten days," is also

TORTOLA.

SLAVE COURT.

liable to be punished capitally, as are slaves for "mu-"tinous or rebellious conduct;" for "procuring arms "and meditating their escape to different countries;" for "any acts committed contrary to the safety of these "islands;" and, in some cases, "for striking a white "person;" though it is for each of these offences, discretionary with the justices, whether the punishment of death shall be inflicted or not.

The information against slaves is always given upon oath, and is taken down in writing. The warrant when issued, generally directs the accused and all others who can give evidence, to be brought before the justice; and if, on examining these persons, the charge appears well grounded, the offender is committed to gaol, (a slave charged with a capital offence never being admitted to bail,) and, in fifteen days after, the trial takes place, if the master is ready, having had forty-eight hours previous notice. The offender is in the mean time, informed of the day appointed for his trial, and is required to give the names of *his* witnesses; when application is made by the magistrate to the owner or manager of the estate to send such persons, supposed to be capable of giving evidence, to attend the trial.

When the court assembles, a charge in the nature of an indictment is drawn up by the clerk of the Crown, and the prisoner is thereupon arraigned, to which he pleads, care being taken to prevent his pleading guilty. The witnesses are then examined by the justices on the part of the prosecution, and afterwards by the prisoner's counsel, on his part. The justices then retire to consider the evidence, and decide accordingly.

The magistrate taking the information generally applies to the King's counsel for advice.

The justice who has entertained the complaint, most commonly sits on the trial.

A written charge is always preferred against a slave for the most common offence; it does not go before a grand jury.

*Vivâ voce* testimony is always required. The slaves who give evidence are sworn in the same manner, that

TORTOLA.

SLAVE COURT.

is to the same oath, administered with the same solemnities, as other witnesses. The Crown officer has seldom found slaves incorrect in giving their testimony. But, he says, they are sometimes led away by revenge. The generality of them do "not want intellect." The chief justice says, their evidence sometimes appears correct, and to be depended on; at other times quite the contrary, which may in some cases proceed from want of intellect, but oftener he thinks from want of integrity. The same gentleman is of opinion, that their evidence cannot be admitted to any greater extent (than for and against each other): "it would be a very dangerous "thing; likely to produce many evils, until a complete "change should take place in the knowledge, morals and "dispositions of that class of people." The Crown officer said, "I do not think that the evidence of slaves "ought to be admitted in any other cases, than those "which occur between themselves. Upwards of twenty-"three years ago, two slaves who had run away from "their master's employ, went over to one of the adja-"cent islands, where they were harboured by a free black "man. A slave now alive gave information to their "owner who had them apprehended; they were brought "to Tortola, and in order to be revenged of the man "who gave the information, they accused him of having "murdered a man some time before. The owner of the "slaves took them to Mr. Forbes, then the King's coun-"sel, who took their examinations in writing. The man "accused was apprehended, imprisoned, and brought to "trial; and such was the difference between their oral "and written testimony, that Mr. Forbes, who took their "examination immediately discovered it. Upon being "closely examined, they confessed that the man was in-"nocent. *He* was immediately set at large; *they* were "tried and sentenced to the pillory, and whipped."

The justices assembled for the trial of slaves for capital offences, assign them counsel. The justices themselves are very particular, notwithstanding, said the King's counsel, in examining and cross-examining the witnesses for and against the prisoner.

There is a record kept of the proceedings in these courts.

The clerk of the crown is the keeper of the records of all proceedings in these courts.

There is no appeal from the decision of this court. It has not been the practice, upon the condemnation of a slave, to communicate the fact to the governor. No copy of the trial of a slave is laid before the governor, or any other person, before the executiion takes place, except in the case of an application for mercy.

A copy of the sentence of the justices ordering the execution of a slave, is delivered to the marshal by the clerk of the crown, which is his warrant for the execution.

The law, said the chief justice, does certainly presume every negro to be a slave, unless the contrary shall be made apparent; that presumption has not however, in any instance, to my knowledge, interfered with the rights of free persons, or persons passing for free persons, who are never molested if they conduct themselves with propriety; and after a very short time, unless the contrary shall appear, they are considered from their reputation of freedom entitled to all the privileges that other free persons enjoy. The same gentleman "would, in most "cases, consider that twelve months time would be suf-"ficient to establish a reputation of freedom." So, if a "negro is known to be a slave, he may pass by good "conduct unmolested, as a free person, there being no "proof to the contrary; until he acquires the reputation "of freedom."

The chief justice considers, that the power of the master over his slaves is not so absolute as to excuse him from punishment, if found guilty of undue severity, cruelty, or inhumanity.

The King's counsel considers it limited to "moderate "correction for improper conduct."

It is observable that the chief justice stated, that offences committed by slaves against managers or overseers of estates requiring public investigation, had lately been very frequent.

TORTOLA.

SLAVE COURT.

Slaves in these islands, said the crown officer, "*do* acquire property for themselves;" "by law they cannot," said the chief justice; "they *do*, however, acquire and are permitted to dispose of property to a considerable amount, &c."

A coroner's inquest is always held in these islands, (under the Melioration Act), in all cases of sudden death, or where it would be requisite to take an inquest on the body of a white or free coloured person.

There are no institutions in this colony, by which infant or adult slaves are educated in religious principles, and useful knowledge. A great number, however, said the chief justice, do receive instruction in the Methodist chapel.

"I would propose," said the crown officer, "a trial by a jury of twelve men, for all capital offences committed by slaves; the present slave law will speedily undergo a complete revision, as a committee from the council and assembly has been appointed for that purpose."

## ESCHEATS.

There is no Escheat court established in these islands. When property has escheated to the crown, "that is worth applying for," said the King's counsel, a petition from the parties to His Majesty, is forwarded to our agent, residing in London; he presents it to the Secretary of State for the colonies, who submits it to His Majesty. The Secretary of State directs the governor to issue a writ of inquiry. The governor sends a writ, directed to certain persons, directing them to issue a precept to the marshal for impanelling a jury, to try the question of escheat or not; they hear the evidence and decide accordingly. The judges report the case to the governor, who acquaints the minister with the result, and His Majesty has been graciously pleased, in one case, to grant the land petitioned for, to the parties petitioning.

TORTOLA.

ESCHEATS.

Cases of intestacy are frequent among the unmarried coloured inhabitants of these islands, and property frequently escheats to the crown for the want of heirs.

Slaves escheating, are not thereby considered as virtually freed.

Slaves escheating are not taken possession of by the casual receiver; they are left with the children or relatives of the deceased.

Where there are illegitimate children unprovided for, all the property left by the parent, is allowed to remain in the possession of the infants' friends, for their sole benefit. No case of this kind has ever been represented at home, by petition or otherwise.

## COMPLAINTS.

Minutes, Dec. 12, 1823.

Two cases were brought under the notice of the Commissioners, by Mr. A. M. Belisario the deputy provost-marshal of this island, in which judgments had been obtained and executions taken out which were clearly irregular, and such as, in our opinion, could not be supported. The cases were *Midoux et al.* v. *George*, and *Bouge et al.* v. *George*, both actions against the receiver to an estate (appointed by the high court of Chancery in England) and the executions, directing a levy of the "rents, issues, profits and produce, which were of Ruth "Lettsom, in the possession and at the disposal of the "said W. George." It appeared that in both cases, merchants, not the consignees of the estate to whom the produce was remitted, had supplied the receiver with provisions, stores, and other necessary articles, for the use of the estate. It seems clear, in the absence of any colonial enactment, that a party, a stranger, furnishing lumber, stores, &c. for the use of a plantation, does not acquire a lien upon the estate for the amount. The Amelioration Act of the Leeward Islands relates only to provisions and clothing, supplied for the use of slaves.

TORTOLA.

COMPLAINTS.

The only question which seemed to admit of a doubt, was, whether a receiver being appointed by the court of Chancery in England, and under circumstances of necessity, (as after destructive hurricanes, &c.), taking up articles for the repair of the buildings and support of the estate, when the occasion was urgent and the distance too great to enable him, or the merchant supplying the goods, to apply to the court for its sanction; the court will not adopt the act of its officer, whose possession is the possession of the court?

The nature of the property,—the casualties to which it is peculiarly subject, the distance of the courts, and the time which must elapse before an application could be heard, during which the buildings might fall down and the estate be rendered unproductive,—seemed in some measure to distinguish such claims from cases decided in England under totally different circumstances. But leaving the competent tribunal to decide, whether these parties could, or could not, obtain payment under these circumstances, out of the estate or the remittances of the estate by application to the court, it is quite unquestionable, that, in this instance, where the parties sought their personal remedy against Mr. George, by action, he and *his* goods only were liable, and execution could not be taken out against the rents, issues, and profits of Mrs. Lettsom's estate.

Minutes, Dec. 13, 1823. A professional gentleman, Dr. Van Buren, applied to the Commissioners to know whether he might not proceed to levy on the same estate, for a debt due to him for medical attendance afforded under the directions of the receiver of the estate appointed by the court of Chancery, in England. This application rested on the same grounds as the complaint of Mr. Belisario.

Same day. A manager of the same estate, of the name of Sherr, "wanted to know, why he could not enforce his demand, "for salary due to him under precisely the same circum-"stances?"

Dec. 15, 1823. Mr. Armstrong complained, that the marshal had refused to levy upon an estate, to which he (Mr. Armstrong) was appointed manager by the receiver. His case was distinguished from the others, by the receiver to this property having been appointed by, and being the officer of, the colonial court of Chancery. TORTOLA. COMPLAINTS.

Another case, of Mr. Belisario, resolved itself into an application for advice.

The first complaint of Mr. William Cox Robertson related to a matter judicially pending, a question upon a bond, conditioned to pay a certain sum with 10*l.* per cent. interest, (legal interest here), and if the annual interest "was not paid to pay 10*l.* per cent. upon that interest;" being reserved in the same instrument, was it not usurious? Minutes, Dec. 12, 1823.

The *second* case was inadmissible for the same reason; indeed it consisted only of exceptions to the Master's report. Dec. 15, 1823.

The *third* impugned the doctrine of the chief justice upon a very doubtful point, the effect of the assignment in bankruptcy, made in England, upon property attached in the colonies. Dec. 18, 1823.

The *fourth* successfully established a mistake in point of law, in a decision of the chief justice; that is to say, a mis-direction of the judge. Dec. 24, 1823.

All the charges preferred by Mr. W. Cox Robertson were conceived in a spirit of undisguised and unrelenting hostility to the present system of laws and government, and cast imputations, very unsparingly, upon all persons concerned in their administration, but more especially upon the chief justice, and his partner in business Mr. Isaacs. "Tortola," the captain-general had before admitted to us in conversation, "had, in Messrs. Crabb "and Isaacs, the same persons, attorneys, merchants, re-"ceivers, masters, judges; but, then, they were the only "respectable persons there, and what was more, the only "persons of substance in whom the merchants at home, "who had moneys lent upon all the estates of the island, "could confide."

The Commissioners received, from various quarters, complaints and statements of delay and expense of proceedings in the court of Chancery, "greatly enhanced by Dec. 17, 1823.

TORTOLA.

COMPLAINTS.

"the necessity of sending up to St. Christopher to make, "even, a common motion." Mr. Armstrong said, that, in some cases, the delay occasioned had been "*of years.*" Mr. W. C. Robertson said, that "the bare commencing "a suit was attended with an expense of 200*l.* sterling. "Counsel's fees, (for it was necessary to retain a lead-"ing counsel at St. Kitt's,) being 75*l.* and 100*l.*; be-"sides the expenses of the vessel there, and the ex-"penses of the Tortola lawyer during his residence at "St. Kitt's."

Minutes, Dec. 18, 1823.

Mr. Armstrong preferred a complaint on behalf of Byce Martin and her children people of colour, (the Commissioners required their personal attendance for obvious reasons; the woman was now brought,) "al-"leging a certain interest in estates in this island; com-"plaining of the mal-administration of the property by "the executors, and of malversation in the colonial "master in Chancery, (the chief justice.") The story which the Commissioners listened to with deep attention, was truly affecting. Mr. Martin was said to have left estates once of the value of 50,000*l.*, now insufficient to pay the debts contracted in the management of those estates. We were assured that these poor children, of a rich parent, would be indebted to private charity for a dinner on Christmas day.

To account in some measure, for so extraordinary a result, it ought to be stated, that the estates (if not incumbered), were left *in Chancery;* which circumstance, together with the fatal hurricane of 1819, and the unparalleled depreciation of property in lands and slaves since that period, may have rendered the estate not only unproductive but even chargeable.

We had not proceeded far in the investigation of this case, before we discovered that it was still *sub judice,* and we were of course bound to presume that it would be properly decided by the ordinary tribunals. We declined interposing in the matter, observing, at the same time, that, "as illustrative of proceedings in the colonial "courts, and where executors were concerned in the

TORTOLA.

COMPLAINTS

"management of property committed to their trust, the "case of the petitioners would merit future consider- "ation, and perhaps might meet particular mention."

Under these circumstances, I shall confine myself to a few observations upon particular points of this case. Whatever might be the opinion of the Commissioners, there was slender hope that any good could now be effected. In this instance, as in most others, the trustee, whose conduct as stated upon oath was most reprehensible, was dead, insolvent. The security taken in his case, though quite nugatory, was agreeable to the established practice of the island; a most objectionable practice on the part of *his* executors, the refusing payment of all simple contract debts till a judgment was obtained against them at an enormous expense to the estate, prevails in every instance in this island, and was strongly reprobated by the Commissioners, as soon as we detected it.

The mal-administration of property by executors, in this as in very many other cases in the West Indies, I believe to be a well-founded complaint, calling loudly for redress. But I am bound to state, that I do not think that the *complexion* of the parties had any influence in this case: the fairest infants left without a father's protection, would I firmly believe, have been equally despoiled.

It is fair and proper to state, that Mr. Elliott Armstrong who preferred the complaint before the Commissioners was an unsuccessful applicant for the management of these properties; but he is also guardian to two of the children, and afforded to all the family friendly assistance in their distress; a circumstance which does him honour, and adds greatly to the credit of his statements.

Mr. Armstrong, after urging again ineffectually, the distressing case of Mr. Martin's children, mentioned, to-day another instance, "where two young ladies were co- "heiresses to a property, producing one hundred hogs- "heads of sugar and unencumbered at the time of their "father's death; but in the executor's hands the estate Minutes, Dec. 19, 1823.

TORTOLA.

COMPLAINTS.

" was found wholly unproductive, and one of the poor " girls was recently gone out to service."

Mr. Armstrong also spoke with impatience of the length of time business sent from this island to the court of Chancery at the seat of government, was detained there; and mentioned a particular instance of very unreasonable delay. Mr. Gordon, the King's counsel, on application to him by the Commissioners, said, " that he was not aware of the case instanced by Mr. " Armstrong;" but added, " I lament exceedingly, that " we are under the necessity of sending to St. Kitt's, in " all matters relating to Chancery suits. It puts parties " to a very considerable expense, to say nothing of the " delay occasioned thereby."

Minutes, Dec. 15, 1823.

Mr. Van Buren complained of delay in the court of Common Law: " The chief justice, sitting alone, had " declined deciding a point of law, in a case in which com- " plainant was a party: 'another court was appointed to " 'be held for the purpose of disposing of reserved points, " 'demurrers, special verdicts, &c.,' but was not, and " *could not* be held, from the impossibility of finding the " requisite number of judges not possessing an interest " in the cause."

Dec. 17, 1823.

The President, (himself a professional man), complained " of the strict proof required in actions brought for " medical attendance. The doctor was usually sum- " moned in great haste, by a slave from the estate. He " repaired thither, carrying a small chest of medicines " with him. He could not at the trial, prove his being " *called in*, for it was by a slave not known perhaps, to " his own people; he could not prove the medicines sup- " plied; for there were usually only slaves in attendance " upon the sick person. If the medical man could once " establish the fact of his attendance, he (the President) " contended that the jury, under the circumstances, ought " to presume medicine furnished, &c. &c."

To find *facts*, as their minds are satisfied either from positive proof or reasonable inference, is the province of the jury. The statement of Mr. Porter was neverthe-

TORTOLA.

COMPLAINTS.

less deserving of attention, as serving to illustrate among other matters, the inconvenience resulting to this class of suitors from the exclusion of slave testimony.

Minutes, Dec. 19, 1823.

In conversation with the President, upon the constitution of the courts, that gentleman stated, that, in this colony, "if a debt exceeded 300*l.* so that a writ of error "could be brought on a judgment of the court of Com- "mon Pleas with a stay of execution, payment might be "considered as put off *sine die;* and this indeed, was al- "ways the case. There was no holding a court of Error "in this island. The judges were always parties or in- "terested, in every question."

Dec. 26, 1823.

The Commissioners had a long interview with Dr. Ross, an intelligent physician of this island, in which that gentleman made a representation of several defects in the law, and the practice of the courts. "As the law at pre- "sent stood,—from the qualification required,—from the "exemptions allowed, and the number of peremptory "challenges admitted, sufficient jurors could not always "be found, and instances had occurred of the court of "Common Pleas being unable to proceed in a trial. He "would next mention the defective constitution of the "court of Error, which was such, that a debt of above "300*l.* in amount, could never be recovered, in this "island. He would then complain of the expenses and "delay of the court of Chancery, occasioned, or at least "greatly aggravated, by the court being usually held at "St. Christopher. A counsel was retained here at an "expense of 50*l.* sterling; it was necessary to retain "another counsel at St. Kitt's, at 50*l.* more; then the "expense of sending over, the hire of the vessel, &c. &c. "were very grievous. The act requiring executors to "deliver, on oath, an account of the appraised value of "the testator's effects, contained no penalty attached to "neglect or disobedience. Here a remedy was greatly "wanted. A practice too prevailing in this island, of "executors never paying any debt in case of contracts "made by the testator, without an action brought to "establish the liability, involved estates in great and he "conceived, unnecessary expense. There were three

TORTOLA.

COMPLAINTS.

"institutions in the Danish colonies, which he (Dr. "Ross) considered very beneficial, and capable of being "introduced into the British plantations with the best "effect: THE UPPER GUARDIAN LAW;—THE PEACE "BROKER'S OR RECONCILING COURT;—and the DEAL-"ING COURT. The latter supplying the want of Bank-"rupt Laws in the colonies."

PARTICULAR OFFICERS. CHIEF JUSTICE.

The chief justice in this colony who is also master in Chancery, is, it has been seen, an opulent merchant and attorney to a great number of the principal estates in the island. His charges in these latter characters were complained of as exorbitant, and apparently were so; but they were the charges of all other merchants in these islands, who run great risks and occasionally suffer heavy losses. I do not think, that with due and candid allowance for situation and circumstances, any serious imputation was fastened upon the individual, and such I know was also the opinion of Mr. Maddock. The fault, in truth, is in the *system;* which is abominable.

Not being bred to the profession, Mr. Crabb has been very excusably sometimes mistaken in the law, but I believe him anxious to do right, and found him attentive to his duties. He was made master in Chancery and judge it should be remembered, not because he was fit for the situation, but because he was—or was supposed to be, fitter than any other person, in that very limited society. As it is, he fills incompatible situations; has his private interest and his public duties placed in direct and constant opposition, and brought almost daily into actual conflict, and in the result, though he may be pure, he cannot be unsuspected.

ATTORNEY- and SOLICITOR-GENERAL.

The attorney and solicitor-general for the government reside at St. Christopher.

KING'S COUNSEL.

One Crown officer and King's counsel resides and practises in this island.

BARRISTERS.

It is not required that persons applying to be admitted as counsel in the courts of this island, should have previously been called to the bar in England, or have kept a specified number of terms in any inn of court. A certi-

TORTOLA.

PARTICULAR OFFICERS.

ficate, signed by the attorney or solicitor-general and one practising barrister, attesting their fitness, will enable them to obtain admission to the bar in the courts of this island.

SOLICITORS and ATTORNEYS.

To act as solicitors or attorneys in this island, it is not necessary that persons should have previously served any clerkship. The branches of the profession which it is found advantageous to keep distinct and separate in the mother country, are here always unhappily united. In this colony, these gentlemen must be admitted as barristers in the common-law courts, before they are allowed to practice as attorneys or solicitors, and after such admission, no other formality is required.

PROVOST MARSHAL.

The number of commitments to jail in this colony was, in 1818, one; in 1819, one; 1820, two; 1821 and 1822, none; all offences not capital, being bailable; and persons when brought before magistrates for such offences, almost uniformly enter into recognizances for their appearance at the sessions. Capital offences rarely occur; at the September sessions this year, however, two persons were charged with murder; one, an African apprentice, was found guilty of manslaughter; the other was a free black man, charged with the murder of a slave, but the grand jury threw out the bill; one capital convict was executed in 1819.

Provost-Marshal's Examination.

The enumeration of persons under confinement in the jail, at the time we were in the island, besides one debtor and several criminals, contained, "Joe, slave to heirs of "Ann Neilson, for taxes;" and "Caroline, a slave, put "in by her master;" persons not accused of any crimes or violations of the law, but singular and unfortunate in their location, and to whom I am afraid the benefit of a jail delivery would not be considered to extend.

The jail contains six rooms, about twenty feet square respectively, but only four of those apartments are deemed secure; the two western rooms are, of course, entirely deprived of the sea breeze; the rooms on the third floor, are airy and habitable. Prior to 1819, the jail was enclosed with a good fence, but that was blown away in the hurricane, and has not yet been replaced; at this time,

TORTOLA.

PARTICULAR OFFICERS.

(December 1823) this prison required new shingling, and several other repairs.

There is always a separation of debtors from criminals in this jail. The division of men from women is said to be "very much attended to, but frequently with great inconvenience;" "there are many alterations required "in the jail," added the provost-marshal, "but the state "of the public funds has been so depressed of late, that "the means have been wanting."

Persons charged with minor offences, are kept separate from such as are accused of capital crimes; and the accused and convicted, in such cases, are not kept together.

The allowance to prisoners, in this island, is, to whites and free coloured persons, 1*s*. 6*d*. a day; to slaves, 9*d*. a day.

Transportation is known as a punishment here, and slaves are generally sent to Puerto Rico.

A slave in this island can apply to a magistrate for redress or protection with success, provided he produces other evidence of the facts, confirming his statement. A slave is now flogged with a cat-o'-nine tails, and over the shoulders.

JUSTICE OF THE PEACE.

Informations, in this island, are always upon oath. Justices of the peace have a summary jurisdiction in a few cases, under the Police Act. In case of slaves disturbing the peace of the town on Sundays and festivals, the magistrate gets a fee of two dollars for hearing the complaint. The police of these islands is said to be very good.

Justices have no jurisdiction in civil matters, in this island.

Justices of the peace have no jurisdiction in disputes relating to seamen's wages.

Magistrates, in this island, will and do proceed upon the complaint of slaves of ill-treatment by their owners, under the Amelioration Act.

"I recollect a case," said the examinant, "which oc-"curred many years ago, where information was lodged "with a justice of the peace, that a mulatto woman was "confined in chains on one of the plantations in this

TORTOLA.

PARTICULAR OFFICERS.

"island. The justice took another magistrate with him, "and they went to the place where the woman was con-"fined, and released her from her confinement."

Applications are sometimes made to justices of the peace, in cases of thefts, &c. committed by one slave against another; "a case occurred, only a few months "ago, where one slave robbed another of a young heifer. "The person who had been robbed applied to the gen-"tleman who had the care of the property to which he "belonged, whereupon the offender was apprehended "and committed to prison, and afterwards tried and "whipped. The slave, who lost his heifer, received 6*l.* "from the owner of the thief, as a compensation for his "loss."

Manumission questions are never agitated before magistrates. In cases of suits, for recovery of freedom in this island, two magistrates it is said, under their hands and seals, assign a patron to prosecute the cause.

The Slave Act of the Virgin Islands directs, that free black or coloured persons should apply to a magistrate, and make choice of a patron or protector, but is altogether silent with respect to the mode to be pursued in determining a claim of freedom. The late chief justice Robertson with the concurrence of the assistant justices, in the first case that was decided in this island, adopted a mode which was directed to stand as a precedent in future, and which has since been adhered to.

"The party, who was a female, appeared before two "magistrates, stated that she was free, and claimed the "right of nominating a patron to obtain her removal "from the possession of the person who unjustly kept her "in a state of slavery. The magistrates could not of "course take upon themselves to determine the right, "but made the appointment of a patron under their "hands and seals, to take the necessary measures for as-"certaining whether the claim was well founded or not; "which appointment, with the assent of the person ap-"pointed, was annexed to a petition to the chief justice,

TORTOLA.

PARTICULAR OFFICERS.

"court of Common Pleas to try the right, and to be al- "lowed to sue in *formâ pauperis*, and that her person "might be protected until the determination of her "cause. On which petition, it was ordered, that the "patron be appointed guardian accordingly, with leave "to prosecute in *formâ pauperis*, unless she should pre- "vail and recover such damages from the defendant as "would entitle her to costs, in which case she was to be "accountable; an order was then made, that the woman "be taken and remain under the care of the provost- "marshal, subject to any future order of the court, un- "less the party claiming in the first instance, would, "within four days, give security by himself and two suf- "ficient sureties, to produce the party whenever re- "quired by the court, or by a judge at chambers, to "have her always in court when any business regarding "her should be agitated, and in nowise to treat or suffer "her to be treated with any unusual restraint or seve- "rity, but, on the contrary, to treat her in a becoming "and proper manner; or in case the person claiming the "right to ownership should fail to give such security, "then the guardian to be at liberty to hold her on the "same terms; the bond in such case, to be taken to the "defendant. The bond in either case, to remain with "the records. After which an action of trespass was "entered, and a copy of the declaration with a summons "annexed thereto, served on the defendant."

CORONERS.

The coroner of this island cannot but think that severity may have been the cause of death to slaves, in some instances of which he had no means of obtainining information.

The same officer had never held an inquest on any slave killed by the owner or person acting under his authority; but he had, where acts of severity of such persons had led to the cause of death.

WRONGS WITHOUT REDRESS.

The court of Chancery for the Virgin Islands being frequently held at St. Christopher, the appointment of a competent person in this island to issue subpœnas, hear motions, and transact the ordinary business of the court, is, even under the present defective system, a great DESIDERATUM.

TORTOLA.

WRONGS WITHOUT REDRESS.

The master in Chancery in this island, does not at present give any security for the proper discharge of the duties of his office.

Owing principally, to the reduced number of the white inhabitants of this island, but partly also, it is said, to the state of the law as to the qualification and exemption of jurors, a sufficient number of persons duly qualified to serve upon juries for the trial of causes, in the common law courts of this island, is not always "to be "depended on."

The presence of *three* judges being required to decide reserved points of law, the requisite number for that purpose cannot always be procured; and a special court (as it is called) is often for that reason, not held, for a very considerable time.

A wife has no means of obtaining a separate maintenance in these courts.

There is no commission sent out to the Virgin Islands for the holding of Admiralty Sessions, for the trial of maritime offences.

There is no act of the island giving to justices of the peace a power of deciding summarily, disputes relating to seamen's wages.

Five members of council, disinterested and indifferent persons. not judges of the court A QUO, can never be assembled in this island, to compose a court of Error; and where a writ of Error is sued out in the Virgin Islands, it is considered as postponing *sine die*, the payment of any debt exceeding *300l.*

In the Criminal Court; all the members of the council, all the judges of the court of Common Pleas, and all the justices of the peace named in the commission, compose the court of Grand Sessions. But though the judges are thus greatly more numerous, and it must be owned somewhat less qualified, than in the courts of the mother country, yet all the masterly arrangements, the form and order of the trial, are said to be the same as in the criminal courts in England.

But what would be thought in England, of a counsel for a prosecution opening a case of murder, (in which

TORTOLA.

WRONGS WITHOUT REDRESS.

ArthurHodge's Trial, p. 30.

Id. p. 37.

Id. p. 49.

Id. p. 54.

Id. p. 43.

execution must follow conviction,) who should state, without interruption from the bench; "I now address "you by the direction of a providence, holy and divine, "in the cause of humanity, supported by justice and "virtue, endeavouring to bring to condign punishment, "a wretch guilty of the blackest crimes." "Turn, hu-"manity, turn, from the melancholy dreadful spectacle, "for it is one thou canst not bear to contemplate! turn "from that fatal spot—that modern Golgotha, *(pointing* "*to the prisoner's estate, in full view of the speaker,)* for "every breeze that passes it is loaded with the groans of "dying Africans, and every echo from yonder mountain "reverberates nothing but *murder!*—turn and view the "monster, who has perpetrated these barbarous deeds, "and execrate his cruelties, whilst justice, awakening "from her slumber, shall decide his fate. This man of "blood, charged under oath with the crime, not of one, "but *many* murders."

Again, (accounting for the prisoner's not having been earlier apprehended and brought to trial:) "You well "know, gentlemen, that only on the evidence of *free* "*persons*, can a free person be convicted: *policy* has de-"creed that slaves shall only be permitted to testify "against their fellow slaves, and not against free persons "in any case whatsoever; were it otherwise, I would "here introduce a number of sable wretches as wit-"nesses, bearing the ostensible external marks of the "prisoner's cruely; whose very appearance would make "humanity shudder, and whose tales of woe would "cause every nerve within you to vibrate with mental "agony."

When such observations were patiently listened to, it can excite little surprise, that Arthur Hodge, wretch as he was, and was well known to be, ("these, gentlemen, "are observations only," said the King's counsel, in one part of his speech, "the truth of which are deduci-"ble from the reputation of the prisoner;") and the accused, under this load of infamy, alleging for his defence,—"I acknowledge myself guilty, in regard of many "of my slaves, but I call God to witness my innocence,

TORTOLA.

WRONGS WITHOUT REDRESS.

"in respect to the murder of Prosper * I am sensible "the country thirsts for my blood, and I am ready to "sacrifice it:"—it cannot be matter of wonder, nor except upon the sternest and most unbending principles of justice, of regret, that Arthur Hodge should have been convicted, condemned, and executed, upon evidence slight, doubtful, and suspected.

*For which he was on trial.

Technically speaking, I would observe that there were two counts in the indictment, one upon the common law, the other upon the Amelioration Act.

In the slave courts, I must complain, that slaves accused of capital offences in this island, are not tried by a jury, but by a bench of magistrates.

---

Close of the Inquiry.

The Commissioners having, thus, visited the different islands named in their commission, attended their courts, acquainted themselves with their laws, and acquired, by examinations of official persons and intercourse with the principal inhabitants and most intelligent members of each society, all the information in their power to obtain, closed their labours under the first commission of inquiry, at the Virgin Islands, in January, 1824.

Results and General Conclusions.

# RESULTS

AND

# GENERAL CONCLUSIONS.

HAVING now, in obedience to your Lordship's instructions, related the proceedings under the Commission, stating facts, and introducing observations, as they occurred in our progress through the islands, I have at length arrived at that period when it will be proper to submit to your Lordship for the information of His Majesty, those results and general conclusions, which it would have been premature, and not a little startling to have earlier disclosed, without a clear detail of the various reasons upon which our opinions have proceeded

The Reports which I have from time to time had the honour of presenting to your Lordship, and to which I have annexed the examinations of the chief persons administering the laws, and the returns of the public officers, must have gradually served, as I humbly con ceive, to render the necessity for an extensive change in the judicial system of these colonies, sufficiently apparent. From these it is to be collected, that as far as relates to the LAWS, there is throughout the islands, a total want of any fixed principles of colonial jurisprudence. RESULTS AND GENERAL CONCLUSIONS. LAWS.

The subject first engaging the attention of the Commissioners in every island, was, as has been already stated, the received law of that colony.

This was a point which could hardly be expected to present much intricacy, or to lead to great difference of opinion. But unfortunately, the principle, upon which certain laws of the mother country are operative and held binding in her colonies, far from being clear and precise, as is desirable in presenting rules of action which all men are required to obey, is involved in considerable obscurity, and often found very difficult of application.

The answer generally received, in the case of free persons, was,

1st.—"We acknowledge the common law of England;" but always qualified by, "so far as it is applicable to the circumstance of the colony."

Not so however, in the case of slaves; for in Barbados and Tobago all jurisdiction over slaves is supposed "to be derived from legislative Acts of the island;" accordingly it was doubted in the latter island,* whether slaves were entitled to benefit of clergy? First Report.

*It is expressly given them since, by Act of Assembly.

In Grenada the chief justice thought the magistrates "had a common law jurisdiction, though not for the trial of slaves; that slaves were under the protection of the common law," the attorney-general apparently dissenting. Id.

At Antigua the chief justice and the attorney-general were found to differ in opinion upon this point. Second Report.

In St. Christopher the judge and the crown officer were agreed, that "the justices have no jurisdiction over slaves except what is expressly given them by Colonial Acts." Id.

RESULTS AND GENERAL CONCLUSIONS.

LAWS.

Second Report. In Nevis the King's counsel drew the following distinction—"as *slaves*, the magistrate has no jurisdiction "over them, except such as is given by Acts of the "island; but as *moral agents*, that is human beings, he "has the same, as in the case of other persons."

Id. In Tortola it was said, "only *such* jurisdiction as is "given by legislative Acts of the Virgin Islands."

Id. The chief justice of St. Vincent was of opinion, "that "slaves were entitled to the benefit both of the common "and statute law, except so far as it has been *taken from* "*them* by written laws; and that it has been so accu-"rately laid down how far the laws of Great Britain are "to be extended to the colonies, as not now to admit of a "doubt."

Id. The attorney-general of Dominica on the contrary, said, "the rule upon this subject is so vague, and so "little understood in the colonies, that decisions founded "upon it will be often contradictory."

By a law of the Leeward Islands, No. 31, the common law of England, "unaltered by any colonial Act, "confirmed by His Majesty in Council, or by Act of "Parliament," is declared to be in force in all the Leeward and Caribbee Islands, and to be "the certain rule "for His Majesty's good subjects."

Secondly, it was said, we are bound by Acts of Parliament, passed before the "settlement of the colony," and "applicable to its condition;" that is to say, by the statutes of England passed antecedently, (making, as will be perceived by the subjoined table, a difference, in some cases, of two centuries;")

| | | | |
|---|---|---|---|
| First Report. | In Barbados - | to 1627, | *but not "by the penal laws, "generally," said the solicitor-general.* |
| | In Tobago - | to 1814. | |
| | In Grenada - | to 1763. | |
| | In St. Vincent - | to 1763. | |
| | In Dominica - | to 1763. | |
| Second Report. | In Antigua - | to 1632. | *but not "by the penal laws, "at least in the case of "slaves," thought the attorney-general.* |
| | In Monserrat - | to 1632. | |
| | In Nevis - | to 1625. | |
| | In St. Christopher | to 1713. | |
| | In Tortola | to 1774. | |

RESULTS AND GENERAL CONCLUSIONS.

LAWS.

Second Report.

The crown officer of Nevis, said, "we are bound by "all Acts of Parliament of the mother country, antecedent to a certain period, but *what* that 'certain period' is, does not appear to have been settled by any "judicial decision on record here."

First Report.

In Barbados from the loose wording of the colonial Acts, (upon which they consider it to depend,) it is extremely doubtful whether the taking with intent to steal, any other personal property than horses, cattle and sheep, so that it be effected without force or terror, can be the subject of larceny. In Antigua, the attorney-general thought the condition of slaves at the time of the establishment of the colony, "so totally different "from what it now is, that there could be no one "reason for the adoption of the penal (and *à fortiori* "of the capital,) statutes of the mother country towards "them;" and he always allowed them the benefit of this doubt. Second Report.

Id.

The chief justice of St. Vincent observed, "an Act of "Assembly was passed in the Bahamas in the year "1799, to declare *how much of the laws of England ought* "*to be in force there.* It has been found a most useful "law."

It does appear to me, and I submit it respectfully for your Lordship's consideration, that it might be advantageous, that in the Windward as well as in the Leeward Islands, the common law of England should be declared to be the "certain rule for all description of persons, "being subjects of His Majesty;" and to obviate all doubts real or pretended, upon this head, it might be recited and set forth explicitly in such declaratory law, that all African, or Creole slaves admitted within the King's allegiance, are, and shall at all times, be taken and held to be, entitled to the protection, and subject to the penalties, of the common law; and to this, the slave code carefully compiled, would properly be "*supplemental.*" It might also be serviceable, and would at least, conduce to uniformity, both of practice and construction, to have one certain and fixed period for all

RESULTS AND GENERAL CONCLUSIONS.

LAWS.

the islands, for the term of reception and adoption of Acts of Parliament of Great Britain, (not obviously unsuitable to their condition of colonists); and it would seem advisable to extend to these distant possessions, and to all classes and denominations of persons resident therein, the benefit of the English statute law, to the latest possible period.

All the islands require to have their laws carefully revised, with a view first to their retrenchment, and then to their consolidation and amendment. The improvement however, of which the laws are capable, forms too wide a field of inquiry for the present occasion.

The islands of Barbados, Tobago, St. Vincent, Montserrat, St. Christopher, and the Virgin Islands, stand most pressingly in need of a publication or republication of their respective Acts of Assembly, in a corrected edition, prepared by competent persons, and printed by authority, with a clause in the Act for printing them, providing for the reception of the printed volumes in evidence. In Barbados there were two hundred and forty-seven laws in manuscript in 1822, and the judges who were *ex officio* bound to know them however inaccessible, were not lawyers.

First Report.

SLAVE LAW.

The law of slavery, as it exists at present in all the islands, is partly oral; partly written; though sometimes affirmed to be the one; sometimes pronounced to be exclusively the other. The chief justice of Grenada, we have seen, calls it a "customary law, superadded to the "law of England; supplemental to the common law." The chief justice of St. Vincent says, "it depends en-"tirely upon written Acts." Yet the same gentleman, shortly afterwards, quoted the maxim of *partus sequitur ventrem* as obtaining in all countries where slavery was recognized by law; a rule certainly not established in our islands by any positive law, but depending upon unwritten custom.

*It is found in the Code Noir, Art.* 13.

The remedial laws of the different islands passed by the local legislatures, as I firmly believe and will not shrink from repeating, in a spirit of conciliation and with

RESULTS AND GENERAL CONCLUSIONS.

SLAVE LAWS.

the purest intentions, were however, for the most part, framed upon the spur of the occasion, with little skill and without much concert, and are, as might be expected, rash, crude and discordant. In practice too they have, it was generally admitted, been found to be futile and impracticable.

First Report.

In my first Report I ventured to state my humble opinion, that it might be possible at some future period, with the full concurrence of the local legislatures, to establish a general code (Code Noir,) proceeding upon fixed principles, for all our colonies. This I presumed to think, "if such a plan were to meet his Majesty's ap-" probation and be conducted under the auspices of his "government, would be most advantageously framed, "not out of fresh materials, but by new applications of "old remedies; by selecting the best provisions of the "separate laws of the different islands, and combining "them with skill and attention, with an infusion of the "Spanish cedulas." Since that passage was written, the Trinidad and Demerara Orders in Council have been promulgated. To adapt those Orders in Council to the situation of other colonies, may require many careful variations; but modified, as they are capable of being, with judgment, prudence, and temper, to meet the exigencies of different islands, and embrace the gradations of negro improvement in their advancement towards civilization and freedom, I consider those regulations as admirably calculated to *initiate* and form the basis of such a system of laws as I have described. Still, it must never be forgotten in an intemperate zeal for improvement, that "the blemishes requiring to be removed, are "coeval almost, with the first settlement of the islands." Whilst the institutions designed to succeed them, though "wise and liberal in their nature, and congenial wi h "the enlightened spirit of the age," to be productive of moral good, must also be "adapted to the peculiar cir-"cumstances of the people."

It is obvious that consolidated and amended Slave Bills to attain these objects, should be passed in all the islands, respectively.

RESULTS AND GENERAL CONCLUSIONS.

SLAVE LAWS. First Report.

I have already had the honour of reporting to your Lordship the deliberate opinion of the Commissioners that the administration of justice in these islands, is very defective, and requires great ameliorations, and an extensive change of system.

Id. passim. CHANCERY.

I have also before intimated an opinion, that in those islands where the governor is sole chancellor, the commander-in-chief ought to be disencumbered of an office, which want of technical knowledge must disqualify him to fill, and which only serves to excite animosities, and detract from his dignity and utility as governor.

First Report.

I have given the forcible representation of the chief justice, and attorney-general of Grenada, "who begged "leave to represent the extreme inconvenience and dis- "satisfaction which result to the suitor, from the adminis- "tration of equity being entrusted to the commander-in- "chief of the colony, who is, from education, incom- "petent to perform the important duty imposed upon, "and exacted from him." Also, the opinions of other judges and crown officers, particularly of the gentlemen filling those situations in the islands of Dominica and St. Christopher. To those observations I would only add, that the objections to which this constitution of the court, (the governor acting as sole chancellor) is always liable, are of course not removed, upon the accidental accession of a president of the council to the situation; but on the contrary, become still stronger and more embarrassing.

Second Report.

In those islands where the court of Chancery is composed of all the members of council, as well as the governor, the governor being only *primus inter pares*, and the votes being taken in regular order beginning with the junior counsellor; the administration of justice, as it is less dignified, is also more *uncertain*, and is in general distrusted and hated, in a degree commensurate with its power of doing mischief in the colony. Of the equity judges, besides their frequent connection with the parties, I have before found it my duty to state, that though highly honourable men, their want of a legal education exposes them to continual errors, occasions a want of confidence

First Report.

in their decisions, and is the cause of great expense, uncertainty, vexation, and sometimes delay. At Montserrat, the court of Chancery, thus constituted, had been twice presented by the grand jury of the country as a nuisance. At Dominica, it was said to be "wholly inadequate to "the due and proper administration of the laws, and "that it would be more advantageous to the suitors, if "the governor were to sit alone."

RESULTS AND GENERAL CONCLUSIONS.

SLAVE LAWS.

Third Report.

Second Report.

At Antigua, I must solicit attention to the petition and remonstrance of the merchants; and the same, to the statements of parties to suits at St. Christopher, where however, the governor is sole chancellor.

Third Report.

Id.

The costs of proceedings in the court of Chancery although no stamps are used in these islands are, as I before stated, oppressive and ruinous, and require an entire revision, and the appointment of an independent taxing officer.

First Report.

Id.

Masters in Chancery in these islands, though they receive and pay moneys, do not always give security for the due discharge of the duties of their office. The per centage in general allowed them, is two and a half per cent. on all moneys received and paid.

This they construe to mean, two and a half per cent. on moneys received, and two and a half per cent. on the same moneys paid. In Tobago, the master, upon sales in his office, receives the enormous fee of six per cent.

Id.

Receivers to estates are not always made to account regularly for the proceeds, &c. of a plantation; and what is a more serious evil, they commonly give no other than their own personal security (without sureties,) against mal-administration. The consequence is, that when they die insolvent having wasted the effects, (a very common case,) there is no remedy over.

See Third Report,—Armstrong's complaint in case of Martin's children,—Tortola. Second Report,—C. Justice and Attorney-General's answers,—Antigua.

In the case of executors, there is in all the islands, a most deplorable defect in the administration of justice. The complaints of widows and orphans (white and coloured,) in almost all the islands, excited our deep commiseration, and we were persuaded that their distress and that of others in equity cases, arises principally from the want of a due administration of the powers of a court

See case of widow Morris at Antigua.—Third Report.

RESULTS AND GENERAL CONCLUSIONS.

SLAVE LAWS. Second Report.

of equity. "I recommend," said the chief justice of Dominica, "to have the fees of all concerned reduced to "a moderate standard, to encourage suitors to seek re-"lief, particularly poor and oppressed legatees and "others claiming under wills and testaments; positively, "as the thing now stands, the court is almost inacces-"sible." It is possible that a remedy might in part be found, in a more explicit declaration of the law upon the subject; which there is reason to fear, has been often perverted to the most scandalous purposes. "Because "the stat. 5 Geo. 2. c. 7., makes slaves assets for the "payment of debts, executors," we were told, "always "take possession of them, and commonly of houses and "lands also; and dispose of them at their pleasure or "use them for their own benefit." But the evil would be most effectually cured, if the powers unquestionably residing in a court of equity, were to be called duly into action. In this instance too, as in several others, improvements might very probably, be adopted from the Danish, French, or Spanish islands; particularly some plans might be devised to compel executors to account;—to protect the interests of absent persons;—and to supply, in the few cases in which it is felt, the want of a system of bankrupt laws in our colonies.

Complaints in Antigua. Third Report.

Danish Colonies.

In the Danish colonies are three institutions meriting attention; the Dealing Court; the Reconciling Court; and the appointment of Upper Guardians.

French Colonial Institutions.

In the French islands His Most Christian Majesty's procureur-general is, by virtue of his office, protector of slaves; and I cannot but consider for a variety of reasons, the offices of crown lawyer and official protector of slaves, as beneficially united. By the same code, the separation of families of slaves on sales judicial or voluntary, when the parents are married and the children under the age of puberty, is effectually guarded against; and what I grieve to say, gives their colonial jurisprudence a decided superiority over that of the old English islands, slave evidence is admitted in all cases and against all persons, except the master.

Spanish Colonial Institutions.

In the Spanish system are found several public situations filled by officers, who, if their duties were properly discharged, might be rendered eminently useful; such are the taxador; the judicial referee, liquidator and partidor; the defender of the absent, and the father-general of minors.

RESULTS AND GENERAL CONCLUSIONS.

SPANISH COLONIAL INSTITUTIONS.

The following account of the Danish institutions, was obligingly furnished me by Mr. Berg, an advocate, at the island of St. Thomas, on the 1st of January, 1824.

DANISH COLONIAL INSTITUTIONS.

## UPPER GUARDIANS.

Upper Guardians.

The next of kin of the male sex is the natural guardian, and he is required to undertake the management of infants' estates.

To audit *his* accounts two officers are appointed by the magistrates, for each district; who must be of advanced age, discreet persons, respectable in rank, and wealthy in circumstances. These have power to call for the natural guardians' accounts, as often as they please. But accounts or statements in writing, are generally required once in every year, in the month of March.

The upper guardians again, pass *their* accounts before the magistrates; and this is done in a certain required form; as thus:—

| Assets. | Incumbrances. | Disbursements. | Receipts | Application of Moneys intended to be rendered productive. | Security. | Interest. | Balance. |
|---|---|---|---|---|---|---|---|
| | | | | | | | |

Results and General Conclusions.

Danish Colonial Institutions.

The upper guardians have power to lend money of infants' estates on mortgage, so as the sum placed out, does not exceed two-thirds of the appraised value of the estate.

For deficiencies arising from misapplication of the funds, the infants, &c. have a lien on the estate of the natural, and as we understood of the upper guardian, and priority to all other debts; and if the guardian's estate should not be sufficient to satisfy the deficiency, on conviction of his having wasted the effects, the natural guardian shall be sentenced to hard labour, till the amount is paid.

## DEALING COURT.

Dealing Court.

When a death takes place, it is the duty of every householder to report it to the Dealing Court. The Dealing Court then calls on the natural guardian where there are infants, to act for the benefit of the wards; or, if it cannot find the natural guardian, calls on the government to appoint a guardian; or if a will is found, it calls upon the executors to enter upon their office. In the latter case, or where there is a natural guardian, or there are no minors, or where the heir is of age and *present* in the colony, this court interferes no further.

Its province is in cases of intestacy, or where there are absent heirs. Then it is the duty of this court to have an inventory taken; to realize the property by sale at vendue, and pay the debts, and deliver over the surplus to the upper guardians. Notice is given, by advertisement in the gazettes of the island and of the mother country, for all persons who have claims, to prefer them within an allotted time, (three months are allowed for creditors in these islands, a year and a day for those in Europe, &c.); the creditors on the spot are summoned before the court, and the natural guardian is also present, to examine their demands, and see if he can object to them. Debtors to the estate are in like manner, summoned before the court, to see whether they ac-

RESULTS AND GENERAL CONCLUSIONS.

DANISH COLONIAL INSTITUTIONS.

DEALING COURT.

knowledge the debt, and are willing to pay; if not, the case is referred to a court to recover the amount, and the proceedings are the same as in other cases; passing through the Reconciling Court to the Trial Court. The dealing master does not receive payment where the debt is acknowledged; he has no authority to take moneys, and his receipt would not be a discharge; but, as he regulates priorities, and directs the mode of administering the effects, a knowledge of the law is very essential in this situation; and in Denmark the dealing master is generally a judge of one of the other courts. The dealing master is appointed by the king. He is paid fees; and, as there is no docket for the colonies, these are arbitrary; they are paid according to the number of words and length of the proceedings; hence the process becomes voluminous, as the judge is paid for prolixity.

There is only one dealing master. Abuses have, as will always be the case, crept in. The charges are too high; the process has become expensive.

As natural guardians are to account to the upper guardians, so the Dealing Court at the expiration of the time, pays over the balance in hand to the upper guardians. Executors are under the same inspection as the Dealing Court while that court continues to act. Afterwards, they account to the government through an officer appointed for the purpose; which is, also, a judicial appointment. Executors report quarterly the state of their accounts and dealings, according to a scheme with which they are furnished; and must state, how long they have been acting; what prevents their final settlement of affairs; &c. &c.

*See the form annexed.*

## FORM.

*(Translation.)*

Statement of the Dealing after the decease, N. &c. administered by the underwritten Executors.

| | |
|---|---|
| Date of the decease? | |
| When the dealing was delivered over to the Dealing court? | |
| When proclamation was issued; for what time; when and where recorded; and when the same will expire? | |
| If there have been vendues held; to what amount; when the payment becomes due; and by whom to be collected; if no vendues held, the reason why? | |
| Whether a list of the books, accounts, papers, &c. has been made out; and if the debtors have been summoned to liquidate their accounts? | |
| Amount of the assets; what part of the same is collected; also amounts of the debts due by the dealing of every denomination? | |
| Moneys collected, and how disposed of? | |
| Whether there are plantations under the administration of the executors; with increase and decrease of negroes and cattle; and how the produce has been disposed of? | |
| Whether the heirs are desirous of having the dealing remaining unclosed, after all collections have been made? | |
| The reason of the dealing being delayed after the expiration of the proclamation, and if the same is occasioned by lawsuits pending in court; the nature of the said suits; the parties concerned; the progress of the suits? | |
| Names of the heirs, with the ages of the minors when the dealing took place? | |
| Names of the guardians? | |

RESULTS AND GENERAL CONCLUSIONS.

DANISH COLONIAL INSTITUTIONS.

DEALING COURT.

*Jurisdiction in Bankruptcy.*

An officer of the government superintends and inspects the books, both of the Dealing Court, and of executors. He is a lawyer, selected always with that view.

This court has also a jurisdiction in cases of bankruptcy. It endeavours to secure an equal division of an insolvent's effects amongst his creditors.

---

In our colonies, where executions take priority according to their entry, it was repeatedly said, but the charge did not of course from its nature admit of proof, that large bribes are frequently given to the secretary or clerk, who keeps an execution locked up in his office, till another creditor puts *his* execution in suit, then says, "see, I have a prior one," which he produces.

Nevertheless, I am not satisfied of the expediency of introducing our artificial and complex system of bankrupt laws into these islands, though a more equal distribution of an insolvent's effects does appear desirable. At present, the maxim, "*vigilantibus et non dormientibus* "*inservit lex*," is, as the attorney-general of Tobago quaintly observes, "*in viridi observantia*;" but there is reason to fear, that this state of the law often leads to fraudulent preferences, and sometimes to an undue advantage given to the colonial creditor. The question however, is of too serious importance to be decided hastily; but, with your Lordship's permission, will be properly reserved for the future and joint consideration of all the Commissioners.

## PEACE BROKERS, OR RECONCILING, COURT.

This court is a court of the first instance preliminary to all proceedings in the Supreme Court, and has jurisdiction in all civil cases, except actions on bills of ex-

RESULTS AND GENERAL CONCLUSIONS.

PEACE BROKER'S, &c. COURT.

change, &c. where the time of payment has been already under the consideration of the parties, and these, it is thought, should be punctually paid, without terms of any kind given in this court. The plaintiff having preferred a complaint in this court, is a condition precedent to his recovering in the Trial court, and cases brought there, without the intervention of this court, are thrown out without a hearing. Two judges from this court are chosen by the *community*, out of six persons named by the governor. If the parties are not reconciled, there is no expense; if they are, there is a trifling fee payable to the judges, but which they do not themselves receive but give the servants of the court. They have no salaries.

The proceedings are these: the plaintiff prefers a complaint; the defendant has notice; both are required to attend. Personal appearance is never dispensed with, except in cases of dangerous sickness, &c. and when, in very urgent cases appearance by attorney is allowed, the attorney must have a general power without any reservation, to reconcile the difference. If the defendant makes default, he will have to pay all the costs both of this court and the trial, and that, although he should eventually succeed in the action, and also a small fine to the public, for the contempt.

When they appear the parties are heard at length, and state what they please of their affairs, and *without prejudice;* for the sitting is private and the judges sworn to secrecy; and it is understood the parties are not to be bound by what is offered or admitted there, if they are not reconciled.

The judges usually press the plaintiff to give the same time for payment, as it would take him to enforce it by suit or action.

When the parties are agreed, the judge gives a certificate of the reconcilement: which has all the effect of a final judgment, without appeal; and at the expiration of the time, according to the terms of the judgment, the sheriff levies upon it, as on an ordinary execution.

If the parties cannot settle terms, the judge makes a

RESULTS AND GENERAL CONCLUSIONS.

note that an attempt to reconcile was made and proved fruitless, and it was therefore referred to the court for trial.

PEACE BROKER'S, &c. COURT.

Crimes cannot be brought under the notice of this court, or misdemeanors where the offence is palpably of a public nature; but where the injury is chiefly to an individual, it may: as, *ex. gr.* a battery may be reconciled; an attempt to murder cannot; penalties may, and where a share goes to the King, that share is often remitted to encourage reconcilements; but it is never allowed in charges brought against public officers: *if their* conduct is impeached, there can be no composition.

There are special cases, in which one of the judges is at liberty to try to reconcile, without waiting to form a court; as between mariners and transient persons, &c.

No lawyer or lawyer's clerk is on any account to be allowed to shew his face, while reconcilements are attempting.

Second Report.

To return to our own islands: the attorney-general of Dominica thus concluded his observations upon the court of Chancery in that colony:—"But the great *de-*" *sideratum*, that which would bring gladness and joy, " which alone could afford security and confidence to " the colonists, would be the appointment of a lawyer of " tried knowledge and ability, to fill the important situ-" ation of Chancellor. I consider," he proceeded, "that " this measure would enhance the value of property at " least *fifteen per cent.*"

COMMON LAW COURTS.

In the common-law courts of these colonies the chief justices very often, and the assistant judges always, consist of persons who are not lawyers; and the consequences, as might be imagined, are frequent misconceptions of the law, constant liability to error, total want of confidence in their decisions, and universal discontent.

In Barbados, St. Christopher, Montserrat, Nevis, and the Virgin Islands, the chief justices are not lawyers, though sometimes very intelligent and able men; and there is no where, a second lawyer upon the bench.

The administration of civil justice, in those courts where the chief justice *is* a lawyer, was not often found

RESULTS AND GENERAL CONCLUSIONS.

COMMON LAW COURTS.

objectionable. But even in those colonies, where the chief justice *is* required to have received a regular legal education, his association with colleagues who are not lawyers, served only, in the opinion of Mr. Maddock, to lessen the chief justice's responsibility, while the assistant judges were apt, by their interference (with the chief justice), to diminish the utility of his exertions, and the dignity of his office. My own opinion of the meritorious services of independent gentlemen as assistant judges, is recorded in my First Report, *page* 98, ending with, "it "may still be matter of regret, that any other than "lawyers should be judges." A rule of this nature, while it excluded such persons as not having been educated to the law can never be qualified to fill the situation of judges, would remit a large and respectable class of merchants and planters, to discharge the really useful duties of town and country magistrates, now too often in obscure hands. It would have the further advantage of securing the supply of a greater number of competent persons to act in the capacity of grand, and of special, jurors.

First Report.

A revisal of the practice of the different courts would be desirable; and at a future time, when I propose the division of the islands into circuits, I shall dutifully submit that a Code of Practice shall be framed, suitable for all the islands of one district. In the preparation of this code all the Court Acts of the islands concerned must be carefully consulted; what is useful in them retained, what is obsolete or impracticable rejected, and such alterations made, as an attentive consideration of the subject shall discover to be necessary.

As *e. g.* some regulations to prevent the cruel separation of families, on judicial sales, &c. See First Report.

New tables of fees for all the courts; a careful resettlement of the costs to be allowed upon taxation, and the appointment of proper persons to discharge that important duty, are measures we have always considered indispensable.

It is very desirable if it can be effected in these islands, that the different branches of the profession should be kept distinct.

COMPLAINT COURT.

The Complaint Court exercises a summary jurisdiction

RESULTS AND GENERAL CONCLUSIONS.

COMMON LAW COURTS.

in respect of demands under a specific amount, and should it be new modelled, might admit of an extension of the plan and several useful improvements, with a view chiefly, to expedite the trial and diminish the expenses.

CRIMINAL COURTS. Second Report.

In the Criminal Courts the law is administered in most of the colonies, with little solemnity, by a bench of magistrates who are not lawyers. "I consider this court," said the chief justice of Antigua, "as overloaded with a "plurality of judges. It is absolutely requisite that a "professional gentleman should preside to discharge the "duties properly, and most particularly so in cases of "life and death."

The chief justice sometimes, though by no means frequently, presides in the superior Criminal Court. The attorney-general is the person who most commonly prescribes the law, as well as prosecutes the offender at the grand sessions.

ADMIRALTY. See Third Report.

I cannot add any thing to the observations contained in my First Report relating to the Court of Admiralty, except that commissions for the trial of pirates ought, in my humble opinion, to be sent out to all the islands. At present, not only prisoners but also witnesses, are frequently and I fear illegally, shipped off to those islands which have such a commission. Eventually these cases may be disposed of on the circuits.

ERROR. Third Report.

The Court of Error, or Appeal and Error, appointed to review the decisions of a lawyer judge (in those islands in which the chief justice is a barrister,) is composed of a military or naval governor and three or five planters, who, it may be seen by referring to the reports upon the islands of Montserrat and Tortola, when delay will serve a friend, can never make a quorum. Besides, their jurisdiction is ill defined, or not properly understood. It is *more* than a court of error. I have before stated, that the sum for which an appeal lies from the Court of First Instance to the Court of Appeal or Error in the colony, appears to me to have been fixed too high, at 300*l*. It is so fixed by the instructions, while a different amount is sometimes prescribed by the local laws: an unbecom-

First Report.

RESULTS AND GENERAL CONCLUSIONS

JAILS.

JAIL SYSTEM.

I feel that it can scarcely be necessary after the strong representations in my former Reports, to draw your Lordship's attention to the miserable condition of the jails in all the islands, and to the utter abjectness and wretchedness of the jail system in general. In these dungeons are confined and very often promiscuously, debtors; all persons charged with offences, slaves, as well as others; convicts; prisoners of war; lunatics; delinquents under the Militia Act, and slaves taken in execution. That slaves taken in execution for their master's debts, and not in custody for their own delinquencies, should for any period of time, be immured in prison, even were the jails of a different description and not sometimes such that, "if a prisoner is confined in "them, he must be put in irons for security," is not the least melancholy part of this appalling subject of contemplation. It is one of the allegations contained in a petition presented by the merchants of St. Vincent to the legislature of that island; "That many negroes "levied upon to satisfy executions, are through the in-"ability of their owners to obtain security for their pro-"duction at the end of forty days, confined in jail until "the day of sale, when probably, they are remanded "back to jail from the failure of purchasers, to await "another sale; that during such unmerited confinement "they despond, and contract diseases, which reduce their "value at the day of sale very considerably." And to their infinite honour, the merchants humbly pray, that the legislature will be pleased to "ameliorate the condi-"tion of negroes levied on and imprisoned without crime, "from the inability of their owners to procure security "for their production at the day of sale."

Tobago. First Report.

I can add nothing to these representations; but before I quit this subject I wish to advert to the alleged reason, why the duty of visiting and superintending the jail has been very commonly neglected.

The reason is said to be, that the magistrates are not clear as to their jurisdiction. The provost-marshal it is observed is a public officer, appointed by the Crown, and, perhaps, under the control of the court of King's Bench, *only*.

RESULTS AND GENERAL CONCLUSIONS.

SLAVE COURTS. First Report.

In what respects the Slave Courts:—Slaves, I beg to state, are tried differently in different colonies, while I have before recorded my opinion, that they should in all criminal cases be subject to the same mode of trial as in the case of free persons. They labour now under prodigious disadvantages. A slave is under a personal disability, and cannot sue in any court of law or equity, not even in respect of injuries done to him by other slaves. A slave cannot prosecute in the criminal courts; a slave cannot enter into a recognizance, and can therefore, only be *bailed* by free persons, when *they* can be found so far disposed to assist him, which the master commonly is, and no one else. Slave evidence is not admitted against freemen, white or blacks; even against wrong-doers. In those courts and cases, where slave evidence *is* admitted, it very often is not upon oath, and as opposed to the unsuspected testimony of sworn witnesses, is consequently, and to a certain extent, disregarded.

If the property of a slave is taken from him, *he* cannot personally seek redress. His master it is said, may bring trespass; this however, is very insufficient; for he also *may not*, and if he does and none but slaves are present at the infliction of the injury, as is likely to be the case, there can be no satisfactory proof of the fact. The owner suing, or prosecuting for his slave, must establish his case by competent evidence, and cannot prove the fact by the testimony of persons under legal disabilities.

Again, if a property in goods, the *jus disponendi*, shall, as recommended by the resolutions of Parliament of 1823, be secured to, and legally vested in, the slave, who is to sue where his *peculium* is invaded? Not the slave; he cannot be heard, unless the case is expressly provided for, as in the Tobago Act; and to that law there are serious objections, as it will at all times, furnish a pretence for quitting a property. The master cannot claim to recover, because the goods are no longer even by intendment, *his* property. The slave, I conceive, should be allowed to sue in such cases, not in person but by his *prochein amy*, that is to say, by the natural or the official,

Results and General Conclusions.

Slave Evidence.

protector of slaves, the master or the crown officer; and in such civil cases only (that is to say, against wrong-doers,) and in *all* criminal cases, slave testimony should in my humble opinion be admissible, or the slave is left defenceless. Eventually I have no doubt of the cheerful admission of slave testimony in all cases; but I would begin with *torts* only, and extend the allowance to contracts as the slave advanced in cultivation and the attainment of civil rights. "Laws for defining the civil rights "of slaves, and for protection in the enjoyment of them," said the King's counsel at Nevis, "I conceive among the "first *desiderata*." From all we saw in all the islands it was the firm conviction of his Majesty's Commissioners, that the foundation of every improvement, both as regards the white and black population of these colonies, must be laid in an improved administration of justice, and in the admission of slave evidence.

Second Report.

The only solid objection which occurs to slave testimony, on a careful consideration of the subject, is the danger of excessive perjury committed in favour of the master, or agent of the property.

The history of slave countries in all ages, abounds with examples, confirming the strong natural probability that ignorant, or profligate slaves would be constantly suborned to establish facts essential to their master's interests.

In the present uninstructed state of the negro slaves in the West Indies, I should certainly, regard with considerable apprehension, the admissibility of slaves to support contracts entered into by their owners. Yet I am not insensible to the apparent absurdity, and I well know the practical inconvenience, of excluding them even in such cases. "A medical practitioner," said a complainant in one of the islands to the Commissioners, "cannot at the trial, prove his being *called in*, for it was "by a slave, not known perhaps to his own people. He "cannot prove the medicines supplied, for there are "usually, only slaves present in attendance upon the "sick person, &c."

Tortola. Third Report.

RESULTS AND GENERAL CONCLUSIONS.

SLAVE EVIDENCE.

But whatever rule may be adopted in civil suits, his Majesty's Commissioners have no hesitation in saying, that in criminal cases, we think slave evidence ought always to be admitted. We have seen great failures of justice result from its exclusion. Even, assuming the general character of slave evidence to be of the insidious and perilous nature represented by some of its opponents, (though it is remarkable, that the majority of the judges and crown officers speak of it as "correct, and to be depended on,") still we think, the dangers apprehended from its admission, are not only exaggerated, but as will appear on inquiry, absolutely without foundation. For first, it should be remembered, that such evidence if receivable, would be subject to the test of cross-examination, by acute and practised advocates; secondly, it would be stated and commented upon by a learned and careful judge; thirdly, it would be submitted to a suspicious and sagacious jury, whose prejudices if they entertained any, are not likely to be in favour of the evidence. Under these circumstances, it is difficult to conceive the fabricated tale or concerted charge, that would not be speedily detected. Indeed, in the only instance that was mentioned to the Commissioners, of a conspiracy to prefer a false charge affecting the life of another, in which the slaves were instigated by vindictive motives, so clumsy was the fabrication, so inartificial the contrivance, that it was instantly detected on comparing the testimony given at the trial, with the written depositions taken before the magistrates. Still it would be highly proper, that such uncertain testimony should be received with the greatest caution; none but persons, certified by their religious teachers to have a due sense of the obligation of an oath, should be admitted as witnesses; the credit of their testimony should be open to observation, and its weight upon all occasions, be nicely sifted; it might even be safe in extreme cases, not to act upon such testimony, unless it were supported by other proofs, positive or circumstantial; and experienced persons are disposed to attach more importance to the confirmation of circumstances, than to the accumulation of

See the case of the sheep stolen in the presence of slaves only, at Grenada,—First Report. The woman stabbed at St. Vincent;—Second Report. And cases at Montserrat;—Third Report.

Tortola. Third Report.

RESULTS AND GENERAL CONCLUSIONS.

SLAVE EVIDENCE.

testimony. At all events, I should certainly recommend that no execution should take place in any capital case, when the conviction proceeded entirely upon slave evidence, without a careful review of the case before the governor in council, (and I suppose the chancellor to be a member of the council,) assisted by the attorney-general, having before them the notes of the judge who tried the prosecution, and requiring a certificate under his hand, that *he* approved the finding of the jury.

Before I quit the subject, it will be useful to examine briefly, the alleged grounds for rejecting slave evidence.

Grounds for rejecting, examined.

If the motive for excluding a slave's testimony be the one sometimes assigned, viz. "*his want of religious principles, and a due sense of the obligation of an oath;*" THAT disqualification it should be observed, does not attach to him *quâ* slave; the fact being established, constitutes an unfitness, which will exclude any description of person whatsoever. Let the competency of *a slave* be once generally acknowledged, the objection arising from his want of religious belief in particular cases, or individual instances, will still be properly left in its full force.

Second Report.

If however, the ground of a slave's exclusion be, as is sometimes represented, his "*disregard to truth and habitual misrepresentation,*" then consistently, he should not be allowed to give evidence at all; he should not be admitted *against slaves.* The lives of blacks and the property of whites, are surely never left in so precarious a situation, at the mercy of men "prone to false accusation," "addicted to lying," "unrestrained by the solemnity of oaths!" In such case the sentiment ought to be, "I think slave evidence dangerous at present, against blacks, as well as against whites," according to the manly answer of the provost-marshal, at St. Vincent. Seriously, if such evidence is not to be believed (though technically speaking, the objection only goes to the credit,) it should never be admitted at all; for slaves should be protected against false charges as carefully as free men, and blacks as anxiously as whites.

Again, if the alleged unfitness be "*ignorance of a brutal nature, a total want of intellectual culture,*" then

RESULTS AND GENERAL CONCLUSIONS.

SLAVE EVIDENCE.

an emancipated slave can never be made a competent witness *eo instanti* that he is enfranchised; for though freed, it will never be contended that he becomes at once enlightened, and immediately conusant of all his moral, social, civil, and religious duties. How too, it may be asked, if the being wholly uninstructed were indeed the principle of objection, can the representations of captured Africans and soldiers of black regiments, the most debased and benighted of their species, as soon as they are put on shore, apprenticed or enrolled, become, though the men are confessedly ignorant, good and unexceptionable evidence?

Second Report.

Lastly, if it be rational and proper on any grounds whatsoever, to exclude slave testimony, on what sound principle can the same slaves who would be rejected in courts of law, be admissible (and they always are admitted) on courts martial, both general and regimental?

The result is, that the reasons usually assigned for the exclusion of slave testimony, are manifestly insufficient.

To the extent therefore before mentioned, and subject to the qualifications I have stated, I beg respectfully but earnestly, to recommend the introduction of slave evidence, in trials in Courts of Justice.

Slave Punishments.

Floggings, at the Cage door, at the Bay, &c.

With the domestic authority of the master, as allowed and regulated by law, I have neither warrant nor inclination to interfere. Of punishments supposed to be judicial, the case is different. As regards the latter, I consider it incontestable that slaves should be publicly whipped only at the discretion, and under the warrant of a magistrate; and that the punishment should be inflicted with a proper instrument (a cat-o'-nine-tails;) and upon the shoulders, where the marks in case the flogging was unduly severe would be conspicuous.

Free people of colour.

The policy and justice of admitting the free people of colour (whose numbers are continually increasing,) to an extension of civil privileges, and indeed the title of some among them to a participation in all political rights, is very clear to a dispassionate observer in this country. But so strong are the prejudices existing in the West Indies, founded chiefly on the physical peculiarities of

RESULTS AND GENERAL CONCLUSIONS.

FREE PEOPLE OF COLOUR. Third Report.

the African race, and so impossible is it to alter the habits and feelings of a people, by merely changing their laws, that upon this subject, I am quite at a loss what to recommend. A complaint preferred to the Commissioners and which will be found in the Report upon the island of Montserrat, affords an illustration of the inutility of attempting to effect, by the mere volition of the legislature, advantages, which can only be attained in the course of time and from the predominance of moral feelings, when the dawn of improvement which has arisen in the West Indies since the abolition of the slave trade, shall be succeeded as I have no doubt it will, by a settled day of wise and equal laws, impartially and discreetly administered. In the mean time, that the truly respectable, the well educated, well principled, and well conducted, among the coloured inhabitants of these islands, should be left precisely on the same footing in respect of civil disabilities, with the newly emancipated slave, is a condition of society, which without any violent shock to ancient prepossessions might, I venture to think, admit of some alleviation.

Tortola. Coroner's answers.

There are islands, where from the thinness of the white population it is already felt to be desirable to admit free persons of colour upon coroner's juries. There is in other islands, a manifest indisposition in the white inhabitants to be frequently summoned at the sittings of the courts; and indeed the only objection to the institution or revival of quarter sessions in colonies where it was felt to be greatly wanted for the trial of petty offences, was the inconvenience apprehended by persons engaged in commercial or agricultural pursuits, from being so frequently called upon to attend as jurors. In these inferior courts, in the first instance, free persons of colour possessing a certain qualification in property, and never having themselves been in the condition of slavery might, it does appear to me, and I state it with submission, be not only unobjectionably but with very great advantage, admitted to act as jurymen. In process of time I further expect that the white inhabitants will gladly avail themselves of their assistance on all petty juries,

RESULTS AND GENERAL CONCLUSIONS.

FREE PEOPLE OF COLOUR.

reserving to themselves as possessing the greatest property and consideration in the country, the exclusive privilege of acting upon grand and special juries. For the rest, time, improved feelings in the one class, and continued good conduct in the other, will gradually produce a salutary influence, and be much more efficacious in the result, than any forced changes in favour of a particular class. As a matter of natural right if it were insisted on, these persons undoubtedly ought to compose half the jury when coloured people are on trial, or have *their* interests at stake, but were this measure suddenly attempted, I firmly believe under existing feelings, that no white person would sit with them in the same jury box. The terms in which their very friends in the colonies advocate their cause, betray the deep-rooted feelings of repugnance and disgust, which too certainly exist. "I emulate," says a ridiculous pamphlet now before me, "to behold all liege men, from the prime "lord of the land, to the most abject, wretched, indi-"gent, fœtid Ethiopian, in possession of their inherent "immunities." In conclusion, I can only repeat my earnest recommendation to this deserving class, to continue the same unimpeachable demeanour they have hitherto preserved, and my conviction that they will in such case, not only establish incontestably their fitness for the situations from which they are excluded, but eventually conciliate the esteem and confidence of their countrymen, whose prejudices they will have insensibly subdued.

See *ante*, Report on Montserrat.

ESCHEATS.

First Report.

Of Escheats, and principally with regard to slaves forfeited to the Crown from intestacy, or want of heirs, &c., I have nothing to add to what I before, with sufficient distinctness, took the liberty of submitting to your Lordship in my First Report. The humane regulation of the Spanish law, which concedes *one-sixth* of the property of the ancestor by way of alimentary allowance to the family, I have already noticed with the commendation it deserves. Correction of the evil in this particular instance, must proceed entirely from the grace and bounty of His Majesty. The significant question of the

RESULTS AND GENERAL CONCLUSIONS.

ESCHEATS.

First Report.
Second Report.

Commissioners, "What is usually done with slaves escheating to the Crown; are they taken possession of by "any servant of the Crown; are they set to any, and "what work, and by what authority, and for whose advantage?" was not, I beg to observe, proposed by the Commissioners, without motive, or in the absence of information.

Real Property.

It should be stated, to account for the silence of successive reports upon this subject, that the rules relative to real property in the colonies, are very simple. It is seldom any question arises except as to property in slaves, which by the local statutes, are sometimes, made real property. There are no tithes. The registry of wills of real and personal estate, the registry of all deeds affecting lands, the Acts appointing *five* years for limitation of claims, &c. &c. all render titles to lands very clear and unembarrassed.

Schemes considered.

I will now briefly state the mode in which, in my judgment, the evils at present existing in the administration of justice in these colonies, may be most effectually removed, and the remedies both general and partial, which with great submission, and subject to your Lordship's approbation, I respectfully and very cautiously propose to apply.

The propriety of consolidating the governments, as well as the Courts of Judicature, of these islands, though deserving of deep consideration, is properly a political question, and does not form any part of the proposition I now proceed to develope and discuss. But first, I must, with your Lordship's permission, dispose very shortly of another well intended, but quite impracticable plan.

Plan of Supreme Courts at Barbados and Antigua only, considered.

It would not be possible to administer satisfactorily, the laws of one island in another; still less could *four* distinct systems of jurisprudence be dispensed by the same judges, at one and the same time. All these various colonies, settled or ceded at widely distant periods, and conducted still under separate governments, must not be supposed to have by any means, an identity in their laws, and it has been abundantly shewn, that they

Results and General Conclusions.

Scheme of Improvement.

have a great diversity in their practice. The laws of the different islands have certainly, a general resemblance, owing to their common origin from the laws of England. But they have also an infinite variety of distinctions, occasioned by their having been passed by legislatures separate from, and independent of, each other; as at present constituted too, the judicatures of these islands, and the jurisdiction of their respective courts, to say nothing of their proceedings and practice, vary widely. In Barbados the court of Chancery is differently composed from the same court in Tobago, Grenada, and St. Vincent. The Supreme Civil Court is also dissimilar in its constitution and practice in many important particulars, in all the islands; as, for example, with regard to its holidays; the time for a defendant's appearance; the law as to arrests; the doctrine of continuances; the appointment of juries, sales under executions, &c. &c. To mention one striking instance, the islands of St. Christopher and Tortola, are under the same government; but in one, the attorney-general said, "It is the practice to sell equities of redemption at "marshal's sale, under executions at law, in this island; "it has long prevailed, and very many titles to estates "depend on such sales." "A levy on an equity of re-"demption," said the crown officer of the other, "is "not warranted by our execution, and I do not appre-"hend that it would be sold by the marshal." It would be superfluous to dwell at greater length upon the futility of a scheme, for prosecuting at Barbados, causes of action arising in Tobago, Grenada, and St. Vincent; yet should the islands be divided into districts, as I mean hereafter to propose, a greater degree of uniformity in the legal proceedings of all the islands of one district will doubtless, be desirable, and the practice might in such case, be beneficially revised, and an improved Court Act or Code of Practice framed, with a view to introduce one identical and fixed practice in all the principal courts, in the islands of one circuit.

First Report, *passim.*

I am not disposed to interfere, to any great extent, with the courts already existing for the administration

RESULTS AND GENERAL CONCLUSIONS.

SCHEME OF IMPROVEMENT.

of justice in the colonies. The subject indeed presents very serious difficulties. The King, no doubt, possesses, as a branch of his prerogative, the right of erecting courts of judicature. This power is delegated by his Majesty's commission to every governor, and the King could not delegate to others, an authority he did not himself possess. The Commission confers, "full power "and authority, with the advice and consent of our "said council, to erect, constitute, and establish, such "and so many courts of judicature and public justice, "within our said island, under your government, &c., "as you and they shall think fit and necessary." But though new courts may thus, I apprehend, be at any time created, by the authority and at the pleasure of the Crown, still it may be very doubtful, where courts have been established by confirmed Acts of Assembly, or have existed for a great length of time under Acts left to their operation, have obtained a known and stated jurisdiction, and possess certain established modes of proceeding, whether the Crown can in such cases with propriety, abolish such courts, and abrogate their rules of practice? In Nevis, (to select an instance,) *five* courts out of *nine* are established by the laws of the island; *one* only derived immediately from the King, and three mediately from the governor. If new courts were created, and the old ones not abolished, such a step would only occasion conflicting jurisdictions. In the event then, of new courts being appointed, the old ones it may be assumed must in some way or other, be got rid of, and if the King could not, as I have already intimated a doubt, direct the extinction of such courts established by confirmed Acts of Assembly, could it not, there are persons who will be ready to ask, be effected by Act of Parliament? This leads to a question delicate to raise, and involving a problem of which I am most unwilling to undertake the solution.

My views then, I respectfully submit, are shortly these:

The King can create new courts; but he, perhaps,

RESULTS AND GENERAL CONCLUSIONS.

SCHEME OF IMPROVEMENT.

cannot abolish old ones, established by confirmed Acts of Assembly.

To do the one without the other, would only be to create a confusion of jurisdiction.

Supposing that the British Parliament *can* repeal, rescind, or annul the laws creating such existing courts, although they may have received the royal confirmation, still I conceive, that it is desirable to avoid extremities, while another course is open. I propose then, with great deference, to retain (but not in their present state,) all the judicial establishments, (except the assistant judges, and perhaps, the Admiralty judge,) and only to call upon the colonial assemblies to alter their local laws, so as to modify, in some degree, the constitution and practice of their existing institutions. For this act, of little more than mere courtesy on their parts, it seems likely that they will receive some substantial advantages; and that they would cheerfully contribute their aid to such an object, and cordially co-operate with His Majesty's government to secure an improved administration of justice *at no increased expense to themselves*, is an opinion I am able, after extended inquiries in all the islands, to express with the greatest confidence.

It is the more important I beg to observe, to effect any changes that may be necessary by Act of Assembly, and to have the assistance of the local legislatures in any measures to be adopted, because the greater part of the rules of practice are embodied in the Court Acts, and these must be retained, and cannot, I am of opinion be materially altered, so founded are they in the actual state of the country, its laws, usages, feelings and habits; so interwoven with the relations and peculiar interests of its society. In these observations I allude particularly to the law and practice, as to priorities, executions, sales, and mortgages. Even the fees of the judges and officers of the courts are sometimes esta blished by a docket contained in the Court Act; as for example, in Tortola. Yet, I would observe, that where a court has been established by a Court Act, it is often, as may be perceived with regard to the Court of Error,

Second Report.

Results and General Conclusions.

Scheme of Improvement.

in all the islands, regulated by the royal instructions; and I would certainly have a power vested in the judges of framing rules of court; such rules, however, to be approved and confirmed at home. For the reasons thus submitted to your Lordship, I would recommend the creation of new courts only where there exists some defect of jurisdiction, and would endeavour to persuade the colonial assemblies to revise and amend the local laws establishing their courts, and regulating their proceedings. To these points (the constitution of their courts, and the regulation of their practice,) my present observations will be understood to be strictly confined. It will obviously be necessary to apply to Parliament, to make provision for the judges, &c. &c.

I have already recommended the consolidation of the five courts of Common Pleas, at Barbados, and I now beg leave to suggest that the common law courts in all the islands, in all cases where it can be effected by enlarging some courts already existing without abolishing others, be formed into one combined and extended court, on the plan of the Supreme Court at Grenada. In this Court possessing besides a King's Bench and Common Pleas authority, an Exchequer jurisdiction, revenue cases might be tried at a reduced expense and in a much more satisfactory manner, with the aid of a jury, where thought proper, and upon the *vivâ voce* examination of witnesses. In those islands where there is no Court of Exchequer such cases are now cognizable in the Court of Vice-Admiralty only, and are conducted according to the course of the civil law, at a prodigious expense, on written interrogatories. The Admiralty jurisdiction, I before suggested, might be given to the chancellor. The trial of piracy and maritime offences, to the King's Bench side of the Supreme Court.

A court for the trial of claims of enfranchisement and questions connected with manumissions, proceeding upon liberal and equitable principles, and recognizing the civil as well as the common law doctrines of constructive freedom, (which otherwise, I can never consider binding upon our judges,) but unattended with the heavy expense

RESULTS AND GENERAL CONCLUSIONS.

SCHEME OF IMPROVEMENT.

of ordinary proceedings in the court of Chancery, is almost the only new court I should entertain, (and that not very strongly,) a notion of creating. I am chiefly influenced in this opinion, by the case of Pauline Agatha *v.* J. Bourdieu, (Second Report,) to which I solicit your Lordship's attention, as illustrative of the difficulties attending the present proceedings. A quarter sessions might I think, in most of the islands, be revived, or instituted, with advantage; and particularly in Barbados, St. Vincent, Antigua, and St. Christopher, where there are many small offences to be tried.

Second Report, p. 250.

I do not think it necessary to extinguish many judicial offices, productive of emolument to their present holders; the puisne judges not receiving any pecuniary advantages from the situation. It will not, therefore, be necessary to provide, except to a very limited extent, compensation for losses incurred by persons at present holding such situations.

It now appears necessary to state, that the Commissioners, as they advanced through the islands, became perfectly satisfied of the practicability and fitness of establishing a circuit of judges, in two or more districts.

These facts and observations premised, His Majesty's Commissioners respectfully submit, that the colonies named in the first commission of inquiry should for the purpose of the administration of justice, be divided into two circuits; Barbados, Tobago, Grenada, and St. Vincent to form one circuit; and Dominica, Antigua, Montserrat, Nevis, St. Christopher, and the Virgin Islands, the other circuit. On each of these circuits, we recommend, that there should be two superior judges; one an equity judge, and the other a common law judge, and one attorney-general, for the district; all appointed from England. Besides these two chief judges, we are of opinion that there should be a puisne resident judge, a barrister of some years standing, and a crown officer (called a solicitor-general,) in each island. The equity judge to preside in the courts of Equity, and act as Or-

RESULTS AND GENERAL CONCLUSIONS.

SCHEME OF IMPROVEMENT.

dinary, and perhaps, as Admiralty judge. The *advantage* of such an arrangement would be the saving the large salary paid in time of war to an Admiralty judge, (*viz.* 3,000*l.* sterling per annum;) the *objection* to which it is liable, that prohibitions to that court are sometimes applied for in the court of Chancery.—The appointment of the master in Chancery and the regulation of his office, including the amount of his fees and the per centage on the sale of estates and the paying and receiving moneys, which at present require great alteration, must be confided to the equity judge. Under the existing system, unprofessional and often improper persons, are thrust into the situation; and in proportion to the ignorance and unfitness of the master, is the delay and maladministration in his office. The common law judge we intend to preside in all the courts of common law, and in the Supreme Criminal Court. Both these judges are designed to go the circuit at stated periods, and the common law judge to sit, first at nisi prius for the trial of causes and afterwards in banc, assisted by the local judge, and with a power of calling in the equity judge, in case of difference of opinion; (but then the appeal home must be direct and immediate;) and this is intended to take place at those sittings of the colonial courts, which resemble our terms. The chief acting as chancellor, (for it may be thought advisable to leave the custody of the seals, and, perhaps, the fees of the office, with the governor and to make the equity judge vice-chancellor, and vice-ordinary, or, perhaps, only chief baron,) should be at liberty to visit any of the islands, and to hold a court at other times, as he may find necessary to the dispatch of business. The third judge and the solicitor-general in each island, should permanently reside there, and in the absence of the chief judges, the resident judge might transact all ordinary business and decide on all proceedings, preliminary to the hearing of a suit or trial of a cause; or if it were thought proper, with the governor might be left the issuing of process and all other matters requiring the seal, and, with the assistance of the resident judge as his assessor, the forwarding all orders of course, and mere preparatory proceedings. The resident judge will also, have to preside in the Complaint Court, (a court for the recovery of small debts,) and in the Escheat Court, (where there is one,) as well as to perform various extrajudicial duties, such as the taking the acknowledgment of deeds, private examinations of married women to acts barring dower, &c. &c.; transactions which take place when the courts are not sitting.

Petty larcenies and trifling misdemeanours whether committed by free persons or slaves, should be inquired into at the quarter sessions before magistrates and a jury, as in England; but the island judge, when his other duties will permit him and on all public prosecutions, ought to preside and to be regular chairman. For crimes affecting their lives, slaves ought to be tried like other men at the grand sessions or Supreme Criminal Court, as is now the case at the island of St. Vincent. Questions as to freedom in cases of manumission, ought also to be decided by the resident judge, otherwise a person entitled to immediate freedom may remain for months in slavery; and in order to let in the civil as well as common law constructions in favour of liberty, as it appears to me in a new court, created for the purpose, and possessing a defined jurisdiction and prescribed powers and duties, with an appeal to the district judges on the circuit, upon a certificate by the attorney-general that there are good grounds of appeal. In these cases, and in all prosecutions at the quarter sessions for severity or neglect or ill-treatment of slaves, the resident judge should be required to report the proceedings, with his decision, and the reasons for the same, to the judges on the circuit. So, in all questions of complaints *against* slaves before the ordinary magistrates, there should always be a conviction in writing, which together with all the proceedings in the case should be returned into court at the grand sessions, when the district judges attend.

The resident Crown officer (the solicitor-general) should be the official protector of slaves, whose duty it

RESULTS AND GENERAL CONCLUSIONS.

SCHEME OF IMPROVEMENT.

would be to take care that the laws passed for the advantage of that class of persons were duly carried into execution. The same Crown officer should be bound to act for all parties claiming their liberty, in every case, where in the exercise of a sound discretion, and subject to the judgment of the district attorney-general, he considered them as having any claim to freedom, legal or equitable; but it should be distinctly expressed, that no case should be rejected, without having been submitted to the district attorney-general, and the results recorded in their joint opinions, first transmitted to England.

It would moreover be absolutely necessary, as will be seen by a reference to the case of Pauline Agatha and others, (Second Report, page 250,) that some careful provisions as to costs should be framed to govern such cases. Complaints by slaves against their owners or their representatives, of severity or ill treatment or subtraction of food or clothing, would properly be made to this officer, who ought personally to visit the plantations and investigate the case. Where the accusation proved not only frivolous, but entirely unfounded, and instigated by malicious motives, the protector ought to have the power of inflicting some moderate punishment, at least some mode should be adopted of making the loss of time and labour consumed in the inquiry fall, not upon the master, but upon the false accuser. Where the offence was serious, it would be the Crown officer's business to see the offender prosecuted at the next court. Where the fault was trifling, and of a nature properly visited with a fixed pecuniary penalty, the protector would send the case before the magistrates at the nearest town. The solicitor-general would himself however, be the prosecutor at the Quarter Sessions, in all cases of alleged ill treatment instituted there, while any cases of magnitude, and attended with circumstances of atrocity or cruelty which rarely happen, should be conducted by the district attorney-general, at the circuit court.

The solicitor-general or resident Crown officer may also I think, with advantage, and with great relief to the Government at home, be constituted in each island (an

RESULTS AND GENERAL CONCLUSIONS.

SCHEME OF IMPROVEMENT.

extraordinary remedy, doubtless, but such as the nature and magnitude of the evil seem imperiously to require,) the official defender of the absent, and guardian-general of minors, to whom all claims of property by persons in England supposing themselves entitled under wills or intestacy; all complaints against executors, and those heart-rending appeals of widows and orphans, so frequent and distressing, may in the first instance, be referred; and it may be made a useful part of his duty, on the receipt of certain stated and moderate fees to report upon the facts and the law applicable to such cases; as it may afterwards devolve upon the district attorney-general to found further proceedings upon them. I am aware, that the abuse of the powers confided to persons filling similar offices in Trinidad, has served to render these titles unpopular. But the fault is not in the situation, nor should any unfavourable impression be admitted against the use, from the abuse. In the Danish islands I was assured that the result was favourable; the good preponderating greatly over the evil.

The three judges, the Equity Judge and Common Law Judge together with the Resident Judge, might in each island form in common law cases a court of Error, (a court as at present constituted worse than useless,) with a privilege to the party, in cases where the property or right in question is sufficient to warrant it, of subsequent appeal home. But appeals from the decision of the Equity Judge must, we apprehend, continue as at present, to the Privy Council. I think however, that an appeal should be allowed for costs *per se*, as though the rule forbidding it may be well founded in England, *they* constitute the most frequent and excessive grievance in the colonies.

*& eo nomine.*

Indeed the whole subject of appeals deserves attentive consideration; the present course of proceeding being dilatory and expensive.

We think the circuit might be regularly made twice in each year, and that all the business of each circuit would not ordinarily exceed a fortnight in each island, except in Barbados, and perhaps in Antigua. In each of these

RESULTS AND GENERAL CONCLUSIONS. — SCHEME OF IMPROVEMENT.

islands, we consider, that the business might perhaps occupy nearly three months in a year, not taken consecutively, but distributed according to circumstances.

---

*Idea of the Time required for the Business of a Circuit.*

First Report, p. 30.

| | | |
|---|---|---|
| The court of Chancery in Barbados sits we were informed once in four weeks. The sitting seldom lasts more than one day. The court generally adjourns for three or four months during the hurricane season. The sittings therefore in a year, computing three months adjournment, would be . . . | | 9 days. |
| The governor, as Ordinary, sits in a year, we were informed, about . . . | 14 | |
| The court of Admiralty sits as occasion requires; in the year, about . . | 9 | |
| Making together in the year | 32 | days. |
| At Tobago, the chancellor at present sits twice a month . . . . | 24 | |
| and on other days upon application for a special court. | | |
| In Grenada, on an average, from twenty to thirty days in a year . . . | 30 | |
| In St. Vincent there had been no business for the two years preceding 1823, but say . | 24 | |
| | 110 | days. |

| | | |
|---|---|---|
| The greatest number of days occupied by the sitting of all the courts of Common Pleas at Barbados in the year, if there were no holidays, would be sixty-three days . . . | 63 | days. |
| but now, whenever the first court day is a holiday, there is no court. And less time will suffice when there is only one court, and that one better regulated; add to these the sittings of the court of Grand Sessions twice a year, eight days . . . . | 8 | |

RESULTS AND GENERAL CONCLUSIONS.

SCHEME OF IMPROVEMENT.

which would be reduced to five or six, if petty larcenies and misdemeanors were tried at the Quarter Sessions. The court of Exchequer, appointed to sit every month, but where the judges do not meet, unless there is business, might occupy in nine months nine days 9 days.

First Report, p. 49.

making, at the largest computation, for the law courts at Barbados, eighty days . . 80

First Report, p. 143.

In Tobago, there are five terms or courts of Common Pleas in the year, and the court seldom sits more than three days, making fifteen days . . . . . 15

but it has sat sometimes five days, so add to these five . . . . . 5

There is at present, only one jail delivery in the year; there should be two, requiring six days 6

106 days.

and it is observable, that the attorney-general of the island says, "it would be a great improvement holding the criminal court at the same time as the civil; it will save considerable expense in the summoning of juries."

The Supreme Court at Grenada, sits six times a-year, which may be supposed to occupy twenty-four days . . . . 24

The Court of King's Bench and Common Pleas at St. Vincent, sits from ten to twenty-four days in a year, and has six paper days; on an average perhaps twenty-three days. 23

The grand sessions, three times a-year, may be nine days . . . . . 9

Altogether making . . . 162 days.

Courts of Error, not included in this calculation . . . . . 8

170 days.

We calculate upon the whole, that about seven

RESULTS AND GENERAL CONCLUSIONS.

SCHEME OF IMPROVEMENT.

months would thus be unremittingly employed, either in actual business, or in what is more than equivalent to the severest labour, in sailing from island to island, not always before the wind. After this there would be an absolute necessity from mere physical and mental exhaustion, independently of the climate and seasons, which however will be found to furnish some additional motives, for a three months vacation.

In fixing the periods of the circuits, regard must alike, be had to the convenience of the colonists and to the health and safety of the judges. In all the old English islands it has been usual to have the sitting of the courts contemporaneous with the cutting of the crops, no doubt from the freer circulation of capital and credit at that time. The courts are every where closed in July or August, and never opened again till the month of January. The policy of this arrangement has been questioned; but the majority of the colonists appear averse to a change of which the effect may be doubtful, and it is a recommendation of the scheme of district judges that it does not seem to require any alteration in this respect.

After the middle of July, the navigation between the islands is attended with some difficulty, and it is important that the summer circuit should be concluded before that time. The time appointed for the circuits, must be the beginning of the months of January and June, or perhaps, the end of December and May.

It was supposed, that in case of this plan being adopted a proper vessel with suitable accommodation, would be provided by His Majesty's Government, and, it seemed the general opinion that a steam vessel would be found to answer the purpose. The want of fuel I should think would render such a mode expensive, but the voyages would be short.

All the judges, and the attorneys and solicitors general, must be rendered independent of the colonies, and should receive salaries only and no fees, except for the private professional practice of the two latter, and except also such fees as might be received by the solicitor general in his character of guardian general of minors, and defender of the absent; which fees should be fixed at home, and on no account be allowed to be exceeded, under pain of dismissal from office.

To guard effectually against that local influence which is at least suspected to have prevailed so largely in these islands, no person possessing any property in plantations or slaves (except menial slaves for domestic purposes,) or being managers or overseers of estates, or attorneys for absent proprietors, or engaged in trade or agriculture in the colonies, should be qualified to hold the situation of judge or crown officer, within the district in which such property or interest exists.

The expense of the several judicial appointments furnishes the only serious objection to the plan we have the honour of proposing; but if the present fund each colony appropriates for payment of its chief justice and attorney-general, should, together with all fees now payable to the judges, be placed in one common stock, these will materially contribute to the payment of the salaries of the judges and the crown officers. Each island too, might reasonably be required to provide a furnished house for the reception and accommodation of the judges on the circuit. Still it must not be concealed, that the liberal assistance of the parent country will undoubtedly be required, to secure the full accomplishment of this great measure of improvement.

The judges, if this proposition were carried into effect, would require handsome salaries and retiring pensions, as the duties of the office would be laborious and irksome, and attended often with danger, and always with many disagreeable circumstances. In diminution of the expense, besides the fees and emoluments of every kind at present received by the judges, and attorneys-general, which we recommend to be thrown into an aggregate fund and applied towards defraying the expenses of the circuit, and the salary of an admiralty judge, in war time, which we think might be saved, other local resources may perhaps, be rendered available The situation

RESULTS AND GENERAL CONCLUSIONS.

SCHEME OF IMPROVEMENT.

of custos rotulorum for instance, in lieu of the colonial registrar, might we think be filled to advantage by the resident judge. Besides the emoluments of the situation, to be applied in aid of the expenses of an improved system, the putting the registry of wills, deeds, and other important instruments, under the care of a grave and intelligent functionary, must obviously be productive of beneficicl effects.

His Majesty's Commissioners were both fully convinced, that if such a plan as that now proposed, but matured and improved under your Lordship's eye, shall be ultimately adopted, it will be the greatest blessing the parent state ever bestowed upon her colonies, and will be duly appreciated by them.

Much may have been overlooked in the view thus taken of the subject, and many material points omitted in the statement I have now the honour of submitting to your Lordship. I am far from being insensible to the hazard and difficulty of the most moderate and cautious change, and here the alterations suggested, though far from violent, are certainly extensive. But though much may require to be done, to carry the plan into complete effect, still I have reason to believe, that it may all be accomplished without opposition from any quarter, and with the clearest prospect of decided advantage to every interest; justifying the master, protecting the slave, securing the creditor, relieving the debtor, easing the governor, and giving satisfaction to the public.

---

OFFICIAL EXPLANATIONS

It only remains to solicit your Lordship's indulgence, whilst to this, my concluding Report, I add a very few words of official explanation. I feel myself bound, both in truth and in manliness, to correct any errors or misstatements into which I may have involuntarily fallen in my former Reports, and to explain any passages left open to misconception.

OFFICIAL EXPLANATIONS.

In my First Report, p. 14, I was guilty of an error, in quoting the words "wilfully, maliciously, wantonly, "and without provocation, kill and murder a slave," as forming any part of the existing law of Barbados; the words observed upon having been omitted in a subsequent law, passed in 1817, which law remains in manuscript, "*Idem est non esse et non apparere.*"

I was mistaken as to the *letter* only, in stating in my first Report, that in some of the islands, laws were passed, restraining the delegated power of the manager or overseer, to the infliction of ten lashes. In Grenada it is provided, that the manager or overseer, &c. shall not exceed twelve lashes, while in St. Vincent a manager may not give more than twenty. This explanation will at the same time, serve to shew that I was substantially correct; it being quite sufficient for my argument upon that occasion, that the authority of these subordinate agents had been endeavoured to be restrained; whether they were, in fact, limited to ten lashes, or to twelve, or to twenty.

In my first Report, p. 102, I spoke of the usual retaining fee of counsel, as being 100*l.* sterling; I should have added,—in cases of importance.

In my first Report, I reserved to myself the future consideration of certain complaints preferred against individuals in the island of Grenada; and the inquiry, whether Dr. Lumsden had been properly convicted of libel and perjury?

In the first reservation, I alluded to a charge exhibited againt the chief justice; in which in my own view of the case, I cannot entirely acquit the judge of a degree of intemperance, and of having acted mistakenly as regards the extent of his power of commitment for a contempt; but as, since the Commissioners left the island, the complainant in that case has chosen (as it was quite competent to him to do) to carry his case before a jury of his country in an action for damages, I do not feel myself bound unless expressly required, to make any further observations upon the subject.

OFFICIAL EXPLANATIONS.

With respect to Dr. Lumsden, so perplexed is the case; so conflicting the testimony; so clear the guilt, if not of intentional perjury in himself, of deliberate subornation of perjury of a poor coloured man, his dependent; that though the impression of my own mind is, undisguisedly, that the formal objections are good, and that the conviction for perjury was irregularly, and therefore, improperly obtained; yet looking at all the cases (and there are several,) at the *substance* and *merits* of the whole proceedings, I think that I cannot safely recommend any interference with the verdict or its consequences. At the same time, I could wish to see Dr. Lumsden, now in advanced age, descend to the grave unmolested; and I should hope to hear, of *his* abstaining from giving future provocations.

Motion in the House of Lords, April 1826.

I come now, my Lord, to errors not acknowledged, but imputed; to charges not preferred *before* me, but *against* me; and those of too grave a nature to pass entirely unnoticed; especially when no longer confined to tavern meetings, but addressed by persons of high rank and deserved estimation, to the most august assembly in the kingdom. I am deeply sensible, my Lord, of the candor, moderation and gentlemanly spirit of the observations made upon the occasion to which I allude, and acknowledge, to their fullest extent, the claims of the noble Lord to similar observances of respect and decorum, in any reply by me to his remarks. Nevertheless, when a Peer of the realm in his place in Parliament, arraigns a public functionary (although in the most courteous terms) of interested motives, partial views, inconsistency and misrepresentation, and accuses him by implication, of a shameful indifference to the sufferings of a large and interesting portion of mankind, and makes such, the Commissioner's alleged offence, the ground of a specific motion, for excluding all persons similarly circumstanced from official situations in the colonies, I feel that no man could be silent under such imputations, except one who was conscious in some degree of having deserved them: I find myself compelled

OFFICIAL EXPLANATIONS.

to address to your Lordship, (to whom I am in the first instance responsible for my official conduct) a few temperate remarks, in vindication of my character thus inconsiderately, and I must say, unjustly assailed.

In the first place, my Lord, I do not shrink from avowing, and I must be allowed to observe I never attempted to conceal, my having inherited a property in the West Indies; in an island, however, which I did not visit under the commission. It might be added, that upon that estate, far from being opposed to any sober views and sound principles of rational and progressive improvement, I have voluntarily adopted most of the regulations, applicable to a private property, recommended by the resolutions of Parliament. But I am unwilling to dwell at any length upon topics relating exclusively to myself, and my private concerns. It is sufficient to say, that I had never seen my property in the colonies; had been educated in England, where I had at least enjoyed opportunities of imbibing just and liberal notions of laws, manners, and government, and certainly entered upon the inquiry with no prepossession in favour of the doctrines or practice of slavery. TRUTH, I affirm it openly and I am liable to contradiction if my bearing in the islands was inconsistent with my professions, was the object of my search. FACTS, I most studiously (whether in the office, or out of the office, in the routine of business, or in excursions through every colony) employed myself in collecting; not caring in the pursuit to gratify *either* party, but willing to do justice to *each;* with the strongest probability of displeasing *both.* To have passed unnoticed such laws as we found in existence in Barbados, would, in my view of the subject, have been inexcusable; and noticing them with due severity, it would have been extreme injustice not to have also stated, that the condition of the negroes was nevertheless, not what, on abstract principles and without reference to the state of manners, would be expected from such laws; that the practical evil is not so great as might reasonably be apprehended; that indeed both the master and slave are often, alike ignorant of

OFFICIAL EXPLANATIONS.

the existence of those savage laws, and act, in their relation to each other, wholly without regard to them. And this just and equal dealing, this fair and candid view of *both* sides of a question, is called, by my reprovers, inconsistency! But, my Lord, my real offence is obvious;—I reprobate cruel laws; I expose their vile administration; I spare no individual, who can be *proved* delinquent; but I do not find the slave starved, wretched, and habitually ill treated: this is my delinquency, and this, of course, is owing to the "strength of my "prepossessions." Admitting for an instant my potential bias, which the result in the opinion of all dispassionate persons has completely disproved, are my accusers perfectly unprejudiced judges of my correctness? are *they* not, though most honourable men, biassed and influenced in the extreme? From partizans, as my judges, I respectfully appeal to persons, who, if they have no *interests*, have also no *opinions* to support; who have taken no part in these discussions; who have been, themselves, eye witnesses, and, at the same time, are disinterested; to the governors, the generals, the admirals, and above all, the bishops, the regular clergy and even the dissenting ministers. Let these, my Lord, (all of them fit arbiters, who have enjoyed the necessary opportunities of personal observation, without the alleged bias of private interest,) decide upon the accuracy of my representations. As to going out of my way to give a general view of the condition of negro slavery, I can safely assure your Lordship, that I anxiously wished, and repeatedly tried, to hold a course clear of that obnoxious subject; but I constantly found it impracticable to lose sight of the political condition of a class of persons, constituting four-fifths of those, who were subject to the laws, or affected by their administration.

In the end, my Lord, allow me to say, I have discharged the delicate and arduous duties entrusted to me in a manner to satisfy my own conscience, and I venture to hope, if I may state it without presumption, so as not to disappoint my employers.

OFFICIAL EXPLANATIONS.

All which various matters, in this my Third Report contained, the result of the joint inquiries of Mr. Maddock, and myself, into the administration of justice in the Islands of Antigua, Montserrat, Nevis, St. Christopher, and the Virgin Islands, together with the general conclusions deduced from our inquiries in all the islands, I very respectfully request, that your Lordship will be pleased to submit to His Majesty's most gracious consideration.

(Signed) FORTUNATUS DWARRIS. (L. S.)

To the Right Honourable
The Earl Bathurst, &c. &c. &c.

Dated October 5th, 1826.

*FINIS.*

PRINTED BY J. AND T. CLARKE, ST. JOHN-SQUARE, LONDON.

For EU product safety concerns, contact us at Calle de José Abascal, 56–1°, 28003 Madrid, Spain or eugpsr@cambridge.org.

www.ingramcontent.com/pod-product-compliance
Ingram Content Group UK Ltd.
Pitfield, Milton Keynes, MK11 3LW, UK
UKHW040226290926
15471UKWH00001B/10
* 9 7 8 1 1 0 8 0 2 4 2 9 7 *